**THE
NEW AND REVISED
GUINNESS
WHO'S WHO
of
Soap
OPERAS**

THE
NEW AND REVISED
GUINNESS
WHO's WHO

of

Soap

OPERAS

Anthony Hayward

GUINNESS PUBLISHING

Project Editor: Tina Persaud
Cover Design: Pat Gibbon
Design: Anthony Hayward
Picture Research: Dora T. Goldberg

First published 1991
Second Edition 1995

Published in Great Britain by Guinness Publishing Ltd, 33 London Road, Enfield, Middlesex

Printed and bound in Great Britain by The Bath Press, Bath

A catalogue record for this book is available from the British Library.

ISBN 0-85112-676-6

CONTENTS

READER'S NOTES

This book features eight major soaps currently being screened nationally on British television. They are listed alphabetically, as are the current characters within each soap. Each character biography is followed by a biography of the actor or actress who plays the role. Notes on characters from the past are listed alphabetically in bold type within boxes. Dates relating to storylines refer to the first screenings of episodes: *High Road* stories are at different stages in the various parts of Britain, and episodes of *Home and Away* and *Neighbours* are seen here months after being broadcast in Australia.

PICTURE ACKNOWLEDGEMENTS

The publisher would like to thank the following for their help in supplying pictures for this book: British Sky Broadcasting; Channel Four Television; Famous; Kathryn de Belle at Granada Television; Idols; ITV Network Centre; Rex Features; Kim Millar at Scottish Television; Syndication International; Yorkshire Television.

Answers to puzzlers on the back cover are:

1985
Nadia
La Luz

INTRODUCTION

The power of television has never shown itself more strongly than in the so-called soap opera, which was born between soap-powder commercials on American radio in the 1930s. The advent of radio provided advertisers with new opportunities and they were quick to take advantage of those offered by the daily dramas whose main audience was women. The term 'soap opera' was applied to these programmes because large companies such as Procter & Gamble – which later even entered television production and made their own soaps – were the main sponsors of the serials, which followed the everyday lives of their characters, usually in domestic situations.

Actress Irna Phillips wrote *Painted Dreams*, widely considered to be the first soap opera, for the Chicago radio station WGN. It failed to find sponsors, but Irna later wrote *Today's Children* and worked on six different soaps at once. In 1937, she created *The Guiding Light*, which transferred to television 15 years later and is still broadcast today. The first American soap opera to be broadcast nationwide was *Betty and Bob*, produced by Frank and Anne Hummert, and it established the format of mixing several storylines in each episode.

In Britain, the first radio soap was *Front Line Family*, which began in 1942 and featured the Robinson family coping with war and rationing. The serial was also heard in America and Canada on the BBC's North American Service and, when peace came, it was renamed *The Robinsons*. Veteran actress Dulcie Gray played the daughter-in-law in the serial, but its popularity was modest and, in 1948, the programme was axed. In January of that year, BBC radio came up with a new soap, *Mrs Dale's Diary*, centred around doctor's wife Mary Dale and her family. Ellis Powell, in the title role, epitomized middle-class values. She was replaced by Jessie Matthews in 1963, a year after the serial changed its name to *The Dales*. It finally finished in April 1969, after 21 years.

By then, Britain's most famous – and longest running – radio soap opera was well into its stride. *The Archers* was first heard on 1 January 1951. It was launched as 'a farming Dick Barton', the radio serial about a special agent, and featured Dan and Doris Archer and their close-knit family in rural Britain. Four years later, on ITV's opening night, 22 September 1955, *The Archers* poured water on the new commercial television channel's fireworks by broadcasting a drama-filled episode in which Grace Archer was killed in a stable fire as she tried desperately to rescue a horse. It was an early example of how serials could use high drama to manipulate audiences. *Waggoners Walk*, which took over from *The Dales* on BBC Radio 2 in April 1969, was set in Hampstead and tackled social issues, but it was axed in 1980, after 11 years. *The Archers* is still running today, but other radio serials in Britain and America disappeared and television became the dominant medium after 1955.

The first soap opera to be seen nationally on American television was *Faraway Hill*, the short-lived story of a woman adjusting to life in the countryside. *These Are My Children*, the first daytime serial broadcast daily – created by radio soap pioneer Irna Phillips – was also short-lived, starting and finishing in 1949. America's first successful television soap was *Search for Tomorrow*, which ran from 1951 until 1986, and centred around Joanne Gardner Barron and several generations of the Barron family. Another long-running television serial from the same creator, Roy Winsor, was *Love of Life*, featuring sisters Vanessa and Meg Dale. *The Guiding Light* transferred to American television from radio in 1952 and has become the world's longest-running serial, although its original spiritual values gradually disappeared. *The Brighter Day*, another Irna Phillips creation, also switched from radio to television in 1954, and featured a widowed minister, his five children and his congregation. Other successful American soaps have included *The Storm Within* (renamed *The Secret Storm*), *As the World Turns* – another Irna Phillips creation and the first soap to run for 30 minutes, starting in 1956 and still going strong – and *The Edge of Night*.

British television's first serial, *The Grove Family* – named after the BBC's Lime Grove studios – followed the lives of a lower-middle-class family. It was written by father-and-son team Roland and Michael Pertwee, and ran from April 1954 until June 1957, shortly after the Pertwees had left and were replaced by new writers. The BBC abandoned ideas of producing another serial and it was left to ITV to come up with one that captured the imagination of a nation and runs to this day. *Coronation Street*, launched on 9 December 1960, did for television what such stage plays as John Osborne's *Look Back in Anger* and the films *Room at the Top* and *Saturday Night and Sunday Morning* had already done to reflect working-class life. The programme, a contemporary drama set among ordinary people in the north of England, was part of a cultural revolution in the media.

Four years later, ITV launched another serial, *Crossroads*, set in a Midlands motel and following the lives of its owner, Meg Richardson, her family, staff and guests. But the response from critics, who condemned its writing and acting, signalled that in Britain *Coronation Street* had set a standard for serials that contrasted with the American experience, where the term 'soap' was often used in a derogatory way.

The BBC believed it should respond to the success of *Coronation Street*, but serials such as *Compact*, *United!* and *The Newcomers* failed to establish long runs. ITV continued its dominance in soaps by launching *Emmerdale Farm* – a television version of *The Archers*, later renamed *Emmerdale* – in 1972 and *Take the High Road* (now *High Road*) eight years later. Channel Four got in on the act by running the Liverpool soap *Brookside* from its first night, in 1982, and the BBC finally found a winning formula with the launch of *EastEnders*, which brought the everyday lives of Londoners to British screens.

By then, American soaps had infiltrated British television. *Dallas* and *Dynasty* brought gloss, glamour and sheer escapism to viewers and even spawned two spin-offs, *Knots Landing* and *The Colbys*. The sordid antics of Larry Hagman as evil J. R. Ewing and Joan Collins as Alexis Colby Carrington kept British viewers glued to their screens for a while, but they always switched back to the more humdrum lives of characters in British soaps, to whom they could relate – until Australian teen culture arrived.

Australian soaps such as *The Sullivans*, *The Young Doctors*, *Prisoner* (retitled *Prisoner: Cell Block H* when sold overseas to avoid confusion with Patrick McGoohan's cult series *The Prisoner*) and *A Country Practice* had all been shown on ITV in Britain, but they were screened on different days, at different times, in different regions. With the arrival of *Neighbours* in 1986, an Australian serial was seen nationwide at the same time everywhere for the first time. It also gave the BBC another success, especially by showing each episode twice a day. When the morning and lunchtime screenings were switched to lunchtime and teatime, the ploy succeeded in almost doubling the programme's audience. In response, ITV bought *Neighbours'* Australian rival, *Home and Away*, and began screening it in 1989. These programmes immediately appealed to young audiences and featured mostly inexperienced actors, some of whom went on to capitalize on their fame by trying their hand at pop singing. Jason Donovan and Kylie Minogue formed the first wave of new soap superstars. With a young, but not quite so young, audience in mind, Sky One bought the glossy American soap *Melrose Place* from hit producer Aaron Spelling in 1993 and watched its ratings soar as the storylines became steamier.

However, not all soaps have been successful and Granada Television, which makes *Coronation Street*, was forced to shut up shop with *Albion Market* exactly a year after its launch in August 1985. Another soap that had the plug pulled after only a year was the BBC's *Eldorado*, set on the Costa del Sol and launched in a blaze of publicity. The realistic Spanish settings were not enough to keep viewers glued to their screens and the soap ended in July 1993.

I am indebted to many people who have helped during my research for this book. In particular, I would like to thank Diane Musker and Alison York at Mersey Television (for *Brookside*), Shanti K Bhatia of Shanti Bhatia Publicity, Emily Ogden at Yorkshire Television and John Barraclough of the *Emmerdale Magazine* (for *Emmerdale*), Kim Millar at Scottish Television, Bill Hill of the *High Road Magazine* and, especially, *High Road* script editor Michael Elder (for *High Road*), Amanda Wood of New Media Group (for *Home and Away*), Janet Guest at British Sky Broadcasting (for *Melrose Place*), and Katrina Ray and Liz Harvey at Grundy Television in Australia (for *Neighbours*). I am also indebted to many theatrical agents in Britain, America and Australia who provided information on actors and actresses. Thanks also to the casting directory *Spotlight*, the British actors' union Equity and the Screen Actors Guild of America, as well as the staff of the British Film Institute library and the British Newspaper Library. Special thanks, and love, to Deborah.

Anthony Hayward

Back row: Leo Johnson (Leeon Sawyer), Mick Johnson (Louis Emerick), Gemma Johnson (Naomi Kamanga), Marianne Dwyer (Jodie Hanson), David Crosbie (John Burgess), Barry Grant (Paul Usher), Terry Sullivan (Brian Regan), Mike Dixon (Paul Byatt), DD Dixon (Irene Marot), Jacqui Dixon (Alexandra Fletcher), Ron Dixon (Vince Earl). Second row: Thomas Farnham (Kieran Warham), Patricia Farnham (Gabrielle Glaister), Max Farnham (Steven Pinder), Margaret Clemence (Nicola Stephenson), Penny Crosbie (Mary Tamm), Bev McLoughlin (Sarah White), Katie Rogers (Diane Burke). Front, standing: Jackie Corkhill (Sue Jenkins), Julia Brogan (Gladys Ambrose), Sinbad (Michael Starke), Rachel Jordache (Tiffany Chapman), Mandy Jordache (Sandra Maitland), Beth Jordache (Anna Friel). Front, squatting: Jimmy Corkhill (Dean Sullivan).

Brookside, set on a private housing estate in Liverpool, was the idea of Phil Redmond, who had written the children's serial *Grange Hill*, a drama set in a London comprehensive school. He formed his own company, Mersey Television, so that he could keep control over the production of his idea. The working title was *Meadowcroft*, which changed when Phil bought a housing estate called Brookside Close in the West Derby area of Liverpool. Eagle-eyed viewers might have spotted the programme's characters occasionally watching a fictional serial called *Meadowcroft* while sitting at home.

The aims of the newly launched Channel Four to broadcast challenging, innovative television fitted in with Phil Redmond's goals. *Brookside* was unique in that it was recorded in real houses, using lightweight, hand-held cameras, and gritty realism and presentation of social issues, such as unemployment, pioneered the way for a new form of soap opera. But frequent bad language in its early months resulted in viewers turning their sets off in their droves. The bad language disappeared and the programme settled down to find a loyal following, quickly becoming Channel Four's most popular programme. Its inaugural broadcast was on the channel's first night, 2 November 1982. In July 1990, the number of weekly episodes broadcast increased from two to three, still with an omnibus on Saturdays. There have been two spin-off miniseries, *Damon & Debbie* (featuring tragic runaway lovers Damon Grant and Debbie McGrath) and *South* (following Tracy Corkhill and boyfriend Jamie Henderson on a trip to London).

CARL BANKS

Elder son of Eddie and Rosie Banks, Carl Banks made two early mistakes in life. He married too young and, unknown to his parents, walked out on the army. Soon after his parents moved to Brookside Close, in March 1994, he slept with Margaret Clemence, who was ignorant that he was married. But wife Sarah and baby daughter Rebecca arrived in the Close in an attempt to mend their marriage and two policemen took him away on a charge of desertion. He was then thrown out of the army.

Carl returned to live with Sarah at his parents' house in the summer of 1994, although he was doing so mainly to please his parents after father Eddie tried to persuade him to sort out his marriage. He was soon seeing other women, including Jacqui Dixon, but she dumped him when she realized he was simply using her for sex. Carl made more of an effort to settle down after Sarah threatened that he would lose his daughter if he did not change his ways.

Sarah returned to her parents' in Reading and Carl's father cajoled him into finding a job so that he could keep up maintenance payments. When Sinbad strained his back, he took on Carl as an apprentice. Carl flirted with an older woman in one house, only to discover later that she had been robbing it. Sarah returned but, as the couple began to live separate lives, Carl was shocked to discover she was having an affair with his best friend, Mike Dixon.

After Barry Grant made Carl assistant manager of the La Luz nightclub in 1995, he was left in joint charge with Jimmy Corkhill while Barry went to Florida. Jimmy used Carl to deliver packages of drugs to his clients unwittingly, but Carl rumbled his ploy and was soon up to his own tricks, buying cut-price imported lager from a shady dealer called Donnelly and selling it behind the bar. When Carl realized it must be illegal, Jimmy tried to scare off Donnelly and petrol-bombed his yard, causing a fire. Carl tried to save a firefighter from one of the buildings but ended up in hospital himself, unconscious with burns and a broken leg.

☆ ☆ ☆

Stephen Donald, who trained at Bretton Hall College, had already appeared on television in Josie Lawrence's series *Josie*, *The Law Lord* and *Screaming*, before joining *Brookside*.

On stage he acted in *Road* in both the York Festival and at the Covent Garden Drama Centre, and such plays as *The Royal Pardon*, *Miller and Me* and *Not Now Darling*. He was also in various plays at the Bretton Festival over several years, including *Brimstone and Treacle* and *Dr Faustus*, and played Troy in *Tracy and the Troy Boy* at Oldham Coliseum, Adrian Boswell in the stage production of the TV series *Bread* in both Bournemouth and the West End, and Mickey in *Blood Brothers*, also in the West End.

EDDIE BANKS

Staunch unionist Eddie Banks and his family bought 9 Brookside Close in March 1994 from the Harrison family. Eddie's prized possession was his Harley-Davidson motorbike, which he bought after selling a speedboat he had won in the television darts quiz show *Bullseye*.

He met his traffic warden wife, Rosie, when they were both in the Territorial Army, and the couple had two sons, Carl and Lee. Both caused them problems. Carl was an army deserter whose marriage was on the rocks. Lee had spent the previous two years in a young offenders' institution following a joyriding accident that left a girl in a wheelchair. This had led to the girl's family swearing vengeance on the Bankses, although Eddie and the girl's father finally called a truce after Lee was kidnapped and dumped in the Close in a wheelchair, with the word 'joyrider' written across his forehead.

Factory worker Eddie found himself in another fight at work, against new personnel manager Marianne Dwyer – Mick Johnson's fiancée – when the company, Litrotech, was looking for job cuts. His own shock at son Carl crossing a picket line to work there was tempered when Carl found a secret file revealing that the firm's bosses had bugged the union leader's phone to keep one step ahead of the dispute. Eddie and

his colleague Joey decided to play Litrotech at their own game by feeding the company wrong information, which led to Marianne's sacking.

☆ ☆ ☆

Paul Broughton (b. Liverpool) worked in a variety of jobs, ranging from bingo caller to golf caddie, before enrolling at his local drama college as a mature student. He graduated in 1989 with distinction and has been in demand in television and theatre ever since.

On TV, he appeared in former *Brookside* writer Jimmy McGovern's award-winning drugs drama *Needle* (as Pete), *The Bill*, *Between the Lines*, *Terraces*, *Minder*, *Peak Practice*, *Casualty* and *Cadfael*, before joining *Brookside*.

Paul's stage plays include *A View from the Bridge*, *The Nativity* (as God), *Legends*, *Victory Celebrations*, *Sarcophagus*, *Rock 'n' Roll*, *'Tis Pity She's a Whore*, *The Plough and the Stars*, *As You Like It*, *True West*, *The Government Inspector*, *School for Scandal* and *Self Catering*, as well as *On the Ledge* for the National Theatre. He was also in the BBC radio production *The British Bulldog*. An amateur boxer, Paul also enjoys golf, football, cricket and horse-riding.

LEE BANKS

When the Banks family moved to Brookside Close, residents were puzzled as to why they received hate mail, threatening phone calls and a brick through the window. The cause was Eddie and Rosie's younger son, Lee, who had spent the previous two years in a young offenders' institution after being convicted of joyriding – which left a girl in a wheelchair for life.

It had also led Eddie and Rosie to split up for six months and, after getting back together, they planned a new start in Brookside Close to get away from the stress. But the girl's family, the Kershaws, tracked them down and were determined to get their revenge. As well as the hate mail, a brick was thrown through their window while Rosie was hosting a lingerie party.

Then, Lee was kidnapped on his way to Brookside Comprehensive, put in a van and dumped in the Close, having been put in a wheelchair with the word 'joyrider' written across his forehead. The neighbours looked on aghast as Eddie and Rosie whisked him indoors. Eddie, Rosie and her sister Mo, accompanied by Mick Johnson, went to have it out with the Kershaws. As the two fathers agreed a truce, Mick was injured in the jostling.

Lee and his friend Garry Salter then led Rachel Jordache into shoplifting. Lee and Rachel tried to escape the police charges by running away to London. They returned to Liverpool only after Rachel was almost led into prostitution.

☆ ☆ ☆

Matthew Lewney (b. 29 August 1979) joined *Brookside* in 1994 at the age of 14, after acting in several school plays and appearing as an extra on television. He was also studying for his LAMDA acting examinations at the time.

ROSIE BANKS

Traffic warden Rosie Banks met husband Eddie when they were both in the Territorial Army. The couple had two troublesome sons, Carl and Lee, and split up for six months after the stress caused by an accident in which Lee went joyriding and left a girl confined to a wheelchair for life. In an attempt to leave their troubles behind them and start anew, Rosie and Eddie moved to Brookside Close. With the family were son Carl's wife, Sarah, and baby, Rebecca.

A threat to Rosie's marriage came when she accompanied her sister, Mo McGee, to a singles bar. The barman, Kevin, agreed to go out with Mo in the hope of seeing more of Rosie. Eventually, he made his feelings known to her, but Rosie said she was married and had no intention of cheating on her husband.

Rosie had more of a shock on finding, in 1995, that she was pregnant. Because she was over 40, Eddie was concerned for Rosie's health, but she was adamant that she would have the baby.

☆ ☆ ☆

Susan Twist (b. Liverpool) was working as a temp. in the perfume department of Littlewoods when she heard that she had landed the role of Rosie Banks in *Brookside*. She had, in fact, previously appeared in three episodes of the serial as a character called Jean. Her other television appearances include *God Speed Co-operation*, *Only Fools and Turkeys* and *Vill's New Frock*.

The actress, who left drama school in 1978 and lives in Manchester, has appeared on stage as the surgeon in a national tour of *Having a Ball*, Frankie in *Frankie and Johnny* at the Comedy Theatre in the West End, Elizabeth in *Taking Steps* at the English Theatre, Frankfurt, Rosalind in *As You Like It* at the Oxford Playhouse and Rita in *Educating Rita* at the Theatre Royal, Windsor.

She has also acted in repertory seasons in Exeter, Ipswich, Liverpool, Dundee, Leeds, Cheltenham, Bolton and Liverpool, in roles ranging from Lisette in *On the Razzle* to Constanze Mozart in *Amadeus*.

SARAH BANKS

Sarah Banks was still a teenager when she wed husband Carl and had their daughter, Rebecca. Carl joined the army but deserted and, after being arrested, moved in with his parents, Eddie and Rosie, with Sarah and the baby.

But Carl was soon seeing other women and only resolved to settle down after Sarah threatened that he would lose his daughter. Carl's mother did not help the situation by trying to take Rebecca away from Sarah, who then left to live with her parents in Reading.

However, she returned in January 1995 after things failed to work out but acknowledged that the marriage was over. She began seeing Mike Dixon. Eddie spotted them kissing, but let the couple tell Carl themselves what was happening. However, Sarah and Carl found themselves drawn together again after Carl's brush with death in the fire at Donnelly's yard.

☆ ☆ ☆

Andrea Marshall (b. 25 September 1971) trained at Liverpool Theatre School and the Merseyside School of Dance and Drama before making her first television appearance in a British Telecom commercial, in 1988. She has since appeared on screen in *Bread* (opposite Linda McCartney, who was making a guest appearance), the drama *Mr Blue* and the BBC children's show *On the Waterfront*, in which she appeared in a comedy sketch.

The actress also has experience in cabaret. She worked at Butlins, Pontins and Haven venues, entertained British troops on a tour of Northern Ireland, performed at an annual ball for an American oil company in Bahrain, supported comedians such as Ken Dodd and Tom O'Connor on stage and appeared in a 1992 summer season in Blackpool.

In her spare time, Andrea enjoys listening to music, going to the theatre and cinema, reading, travelling and playing the piano and guitar.

JULIA BROGAN

Doreen Corkhill's interfering mother, Julia Brogan, resented the fact that her daughter had married a Corkhill. But, even when Doreen left Billy, Julia continued to interfere in the family's lives, seeing her grandchildren, Tracy and Rod, and worked in the local grocer's and hairdresser's, generally making her presence felt.

Love came into her life with the arrival of Ron Dixon's father, Cyril. She persuaded him that they should marry but he failed to turn up at their engagement party. He was revealed to be a bigamist three times over and died of a massive heart attack at the end of 1991.

For a while, Julia worked in Ron Dixon's shop, the Trading Post. He falsely accused her of putting her hand in the till when his son, Mike, started stealing money. Ron apologized for what Julia saw as 'defecation' of character.

Julia later found friendship with Patricia Farnham's father, David Crosbie, taking him as her ballroom dancing partner, but he was married to Jean.

☆ ☆ ☆

Gladys Ambrose (b. Everton, Liverpool, 28 December 1930) took singing, dancing and voice projection lessons at the Madam Edith Clarke School in Liverpool and, in 1949, made her professional debut as a chorus dancer in the revue *Joie de Vivre*, at the Theatre Royal, Castleford. She graduated to starring roles and

---

Alan Rothwell (b. Oldham, 9 February 1937), David Barlow in *Coronation Street* during the sixties, played NICHOLAS BLACK, Heather Haversham's second husband, who turned out to be a drug addict. He was also Jimmy Grange in *The Archers* and a magistrate in *Emmerdale*.

Jennifer Calvert (b. Ontario, Canada, 7 December 1963) was Jonathan Gordon-Davies's Canadian girlfriend CHERYL BOYANOWSKY in *Brookside* before starring in the children's TV series *Spatz*, the three-part series *Come Home Charlie and Face Them* and *Westbeach*.

David Yip (b. David Nicholas Yip in Liverpool, 4 June 1951), best known on TV as Det Sgt Johnny Ho, star of *The Chinese Detective*, was doctor MICHAEL CHOI. He also appeared in the films *Indiana Jones and the Temple of Doom*, *Empire of the Sun* and *A View to a Kill*. He is married to actress Lynn Farleigh.

Robert Pugh played JOHN CLARKE, the gunman who held Pat, Sandra and Kate hostage in the siege of 1985. Robert, who is also a writer, began his TV career in *Danger UXB* and, after his *Brookside* role, played ambulance driver Ponting in the first two series of *Casualty*. He has also appeared on television in *TECX* and the drama serial *Thicker Than Water*.

Doreen Sloane (b. Birkenhead, 24 February 1934) played ANNABELLE COLLINS from episode one. She had already played a nurse in *Coronation Street* and Louise in *Emmerdale*, and was in the films *Chariots of Fire* and *Yanks*. Doreen died of cancer in 1990.

Katrin Cartlidge was the first actress to play LUCY COLLINS when the serial began. After being replaced by Maggie Saunders, Katrin briefly returned to the role. During her time away, she acted in Steven Berkoff's stage version of *Salome* at the National Theatre. Later, she starred in the film *Naked*.

Jim Wiggins (b. Birkenhead, 13 March 1922) was PAUL COLLINS, who was the redundant middle-manager forced to leave his large house on the Wirral. Paul found it difficult to come to terms with the fact that his son Gordon was gay but eventually stood by him. Jim was a civil servant and a teacher before turning professional as an actor in 1973. On TV, he has also appeared in *Fallen Hero*, *Angels*, *Emmerdale* (as Mr Bakewell), *The Professionals* and *The Gentle Touch*.

John McArdle (b. Liverpool, 16 August 1949) played BILLY CORKHILL, who divorced wife Doreen and later married Sheila Grant. John had already appeared twice in *Coronation Street*, once as Det. Con. Meadows, when he joined *Brookside*. After leaving the serial, John starred in *Underbelly*, as prison godfather Jack Preston, and appeared in *Gallowglass* and *Spender*.

became a favourite in pantomime as both principal girl and principal boy. While playing the Wicked Queen in the original British stage tour of *Snow White*, she met Dutch-born Johnny Votel (Johannes Duiveman), who was performing as an acrobat in a speciality act at the Wood Green Empire, London. The two married in 1954, Gladys learned the trapeze and the pair perfected their act at an acrobatic training school in Holland.

After her husband fell 5 m (16 ft) during a training session, they gave up 'high flying' and moved on to foot juggling and a comedy knockabout acrobatic routine, touring the Continent and the Middle East for many years. After Johnny retired in 1977, Gladys concentrated on her singing, working in pantomime, summer seasons, cabaret, revue, musicals and variety across the country. She formed her own company, Rose Productions, staging shows along with her daughters, Janette and Wendy, who performed a double act as the Votel Sisters.

Gladys made her television debut in a play called *Match of the Day,* in which Bill Dean – who later played Harry Cross in *Brookside* – was her husband. She followed it with another TV play, *Bag of Yeast*, with Bill Dean as her brother and Peter Kerrigan – grandfather of Justine Kerrigan, who played her granddaughter Tracy Corkhill in *Brookside* – as her husband.

She also played both Eddie Yeats's landlady and Mrs Hindle in *Coronation Street*, Mrs Barrett in *The Brothers McGregor* and a noisy shopper in *Bread*. In 1985, she joined *Brookside* as Julia Brogan. Gladys's 30th anniversary in showbusiness was celebrated in 1989 by BBC Radio Merseyside in a programme titled *They Call Her Their Lillie Marlene.*

JACKIE CORKHILL

Long-suffering wife of Jimmy, Jackie Corkhill met the lovable rogue in 1971 when he spotted her wearing tight white jeans in a pub. On their second date, he bought her the New Seekers single 'Never Ending Song of Love' and the couple eventually married.

They had a son, Jimmy Jr, and a daughter, Lindsey, but the marriage failed and Jimmy Jr caught his faher in bed with Jackie's sister, Val. Jimmy then took up with Sheila Grant's best friend, Kathy Roach, but she eventually saw him for what he was and ditched him.

Jackie was willing to be wooed back, especially when she started working in Ron Dixon's shop, the Trading Post. She resisted Ron's advances and, despite Jimmy Jr's opposition, returned to

JIMMY CORKHILL

Brother of twice-married Billy Corkhill, Jimmy Corkhill has always been on just the wrong side of the law. As youngsters, Jimmy and Billy worshipped their elder brother Frankie, and it was a terrible blow when he was murdered in a gang fight. Billy married and had two children, Tracy and Rod, and built a new life. Jimmy also married, and he and wife Jackie had two children, daughter Lindsey and son Jimmy Jr, but he was determined eventually to get revenge on his brother's murderer, Joey Godden.

When Godden was released from jail and Jimmy spotted him drinking in a local pub, he planned to teach him a lesson and forced an unwilling Billy to help. Jimmy was badly beaten up and, later, his cousin Don was murdered during a fight in the pub with Godden.

Billy, who had just married Sheila, feared for their own safety – and that of her young daughter Claire – so they moved south, to stay with her sister in Basingstoke. Jimmy, who quickly made Billy's home his own, had split up with wife Jackie by this time and had an on-off relationship with Kathy Roach, Sheila Grant's best friend. He was hoping that Kathy might finally agree to live with him, but she realized that he was a leopard who would not change his spots. Instead, Jimmy resumed his 'business enterprises' with no-good window-cleaner Sinbad, with whom he shared a flat for a while.

Some sort of happiness appeared to come into Jimmy's life when Jackie took him back, although son Jimmy Jr did not approve. This time, Jackie stood by him, as he went down the road to hell. Landing himself a job in Barry Grant's nightclub, La Luz, he became involved in drugs deals and was soon an addict himself. Jimmy obtained drugs from Brookside Parade hairdresser Brian Kennedy and, when Kennedy was busted by the police, Jimmy rushed off to hide his own illegal substances and calmed his nerves by taking more. In a panic, Jimmy took

her estranged husband. Since then, she has stood by him through thick and thin – mostly thin. When he admitted to having a drugs problem, she insisted he go for counselling.

Sue Jenkins (b. Susan Elizabeth Jenkins in Liverpool) acted in *Z-Cars* at the age of 17 and trained at the Elliott-Clarke Theatre School in Liverpool, before becoming an assistant stage manager at Chesterfield Civic Theatre. Later, she appeared in 20 episodes of the schools drama series *How We Used to Live*, as well as *Wood and Walters* and *The Beiderbecke Affair*, before finding fame as barmaid Gloria Todd in *Coronation Street*. She left after four years and played Julie Ryan in *Coasting*, then took the role of Jackie Corkhill in *Brookside*. During a break from the serial, Sue acted missing showgirl Mollie Mozelle in an episode of *In Suspicious Circumstances*.

Her stage roles include that of Doreen in *Having a Ball*, written specially for her by Alan Bleasdale. On radio, she played Isabella in a production of *Wuthering Heights* starring Derek Jacobi, Celia in *Middlemarch* and Generra in *Villette*, and has read *Morning Story*.

Sue lives in Cheshire with her husband, actor David Fleeshman – who played nasty Charlie Aindow in *Emmerdale* – and three children, Emily Victoria, Richard Jonathan and Rosie Annabelle. Sue met David while she was playing Pinocchio on tour and the two appeared together in *Brookside* when she was serving behind the counter in Dixon's Trading Post and he walked in, playing David Hurst, and asked how to find the Harrisons, who owed him money. In her spare time, Sue enjoys waterskiing, reading, writing and swimming.

> **Kate Fitzgerald (b. Liverpool) acted shopaholic DOREEN CORKHILL, Billy's first wife. Kate previously appeared on the West End stage as Linda in Willy Russell's musical *Blood Brothers* and has since starred in a national tour of the hit Willy Russell one-woman play *Shirley Valentine*. She has also appeared on TV in *Casualty* and *The Bill*, as well as Willy Russell's *Daughters of Albion*. Kate is the sister of actress Angela Walsh, who played Carol Salter in *Brookside*.**

to the wheel of his car and committed his ultimate crime – causing the death of Ron Dixon's teenage son Tony after Frank and Lyn Rogers' wedding reception. Stoned out of his mind, Jimmy was driving on the wrong side of the road and careered into a car driven by Frank with Tony in the passenger seat. Jimmy went on the run, then turned Good Samaritan by trying to raise money for the boy, who was in a coma. But Tony died and, stricken with grief, Jimmy moved back in with Jackie, who had him back only on condition that he kept off the drugs.

Living with the secret that he was responsible for Tony's death became too much for Jimmy, and he confessed his guilt to Jackie. He wanted to tell the police, but she felt he should get help to beat his drugs problem. But he stole money from the appeal fund he had set up for Tony Dixon so that he could continue to feed his drugs habit. When Jimmy heard that the police were going to charge him only with failing to report an accident, he started injecting heroin.

Continuing on a downward spiral, he shared used needles and became frightened that he might have contracted the HIV virus. To fund his drugs fix, he started breaking into houses in Brookside Close and ended up cutting his hand while smashing a window. He went for a blood test and had to wait two months for the results to show whether he had HIV. In May 1994, he was sentenced to nine months in prison for the Close burglaries. When he came out, he was soon back in his old ways, dealing in drugs while working at La Luz.

☆ ☆ ☆

Dean Sullivan (b. Liverpool, 7 June 1955) graduated from Lancaster University with a B Ed (Hons) and taught in primary schools on Merseyside for six years before becoming an actor. He also taught in a night school, giving drama workshops for adults. He made his professional acting debut at the Pitlochry Festival Theatre in 1984, performing in *On the Razzle*, *Cowardy Custard*, *Wild Oats* and *Gangs*.

As a member of the Neptune Theatre Company, Liverpool, Dean played Tommy in Willy Russell's *Breezeblock Park*, Tony in *West Side Story*, Oberon in *A Midsummer Night's Dream*, Jimmy in *Look Back in Anger*, Horst in *Bent* and Jack Worthing in *The Importance of Being Earnest*. He starred as Freddie Hertzog in Phil Redmond's stage play *Soaplights* at the Liverpool Playhouse, Scullery in the Northern première of Jim Cartwright's *Road* at the Octagon Theatre, Bolton, and Joseph in *The Northern Mystery Plays* at the Crucible Theatre, Sheffield. In pantomime, he performed alongside Dana in *Snow White* at the Liverpool Empire, and Helen Shapiro in *Babes in the Wood* at the Harlequin Theatre, Redhill.

After living in South London, where he combined his acting with work as a supply teacher, Dean moved back to Liverpool in 1988 and formed The Liverpool Theatre Company, for which he has directed *The Importance of Being Earnest*, Victoria Wood's *Talent*, *Ghost Story* and *Hay Fever*. He continued work as a supply teacher and starred as Sam Jackson in the BBC Radio Merseyside soap opera *The Merseysiders*.

On television, as well as playing roguish Jimmy Corkhill in *Brookside*, Dean presented *All I Want for Christmas* on Channel Four. He also runs a Liverpool-based company called The Murder Game, which organizes 'murder weekends'. In 1995, a book called *The Jimmy Corkhill Story* was published, charting the life of Dean's *Brookside* character.

DAVID CROSBIE

Pompous David Crosbie – nicknamed 'Bing' – and his wife, Jean, arrived in the Close in January 1993. At first, they lived with their daughter and son-in-law, Patricia and Max Farnham. Four months later, they bought the bungalow, no. 6, following the drawn-out sale of their Spanish apartment.

It came as a shock to Patricia when she learned of her father's affair, 20 years earlier, with the family nanny, Sandra. Jean had forgiven, if not forgotten, but new attentions were thrust on David when Julia Brogan persuaded him to be her dance partner.

As a bit of a busybody, David was enthusiastic about regenerating the Brookside Residents'

Association and holding committee meetings at the bungalow. It gave him a sense of power and he engineered the moves to pressurize the Bankses into explaining the disturbances at their house – a result of reprisals for their son Lee being convicted for joyriding and leaving a girl in a wheelchair for life – and to make Simon Howe's religious cult leave no. 5.

Despite his own past sexual misdemeanours, David was quick to condemn others. When he learned of son-in-law Max Farnham's night of passion with ex-wife Susannah, he told Patricia, who walked out on Max and divorced him, only for the couple to remarry two weeks after the decree absolute came through.

David also pilloried Beth Jordache when he spotted her kissing a gay university lecturer. But his sense of shock, as well as his morals, was outraged when wife Jean confessed, on their ruby wedding anniversary in June 1994, to having had a relationship with another woman years earlier. David moved out of the marital bed, into the spare room at the Farnhams' house and lived a separate life until the birth of Max and Patricia's second child, Alice, brought him and Jean back together.

In December 1994, David cured his impotence by sleeping with Audrey Manners and, riddled with guilt, spent Christmas trying to avoid her. It was a shock when Jean allowed Audrey to stay with them over Christmas and he was relieved to see her move out, before she was hired by Jean as her assistant in Deborah's florist's. Audrey and her estranged husband, George, whom everyone assumed to be dead, were victims of the virus that hit the Close in March 1995, when both died. Worse came for David when Jean was lying on her deathbed as a result of the virus and, feeling guilty, he confessed his affair to her. She recovered and was not quick to let him forget his sins.

☆ ☆ ☆

John Burgess trained at RADA and, after two years' National Service, acted in repertory theatre in Tunbridge Wells, Leatherhead, Felixstowe and Redcar during the fifties and sixties, and performed Shakespeare on tour with the Elizabethan Theatre Company.

He then emigrated to Canada, where he gained a BA in English and drama and a B Ed in theatre studies from Queen's University, Kingston, Ontario, as a mature student. Returning to Britain in 1973, John picked up his acting career and has since taken about 20 roles with the Royal Shakespeare Company, including Duke Frederick in *As You Like It*, Egeus in *A Midsummer Night's Dream*, the Bishop of Carlisle and John of Gaunt in *Richard II* and the Duke of Venice in *Othello*. His other stage roles have included Morell in *Candida*, Graham in *Time and Time Again*, Philip in *Move Over, Mrs Markham*, Antonio in *The Tempest*, Aegeus in *Medea* and Polonius in *Hamlet*.

John appeared in the films *Give My Regards to Broad Street*, *Sakharov* and *Rosencrantz and Guildenstern Are Dead*, and on television in all 26 episodes of the live daytime soap *Together*, *Murphy's Mob*, *To Have and to Hold*, *The Bill*, *First Among Equals*, *Big Deal*, *Christabel*, *Laura and Disorder*, *EastEnders* (as Mr Ludlow, adoptive father of Kathy Beale's illegitimate daughter Donna), *Hale and Pace*, *The Ruth Rendell Mysteries* (in five different stories, as Dr Crocker), *Casualty*, *Chancer*, *Grange Hill*, *Agatha Christie's Poirot*, *Lovejoy*, *Josie*, *Sam Saturday* and *The House of Elliot*.

JEAN CROSBIE

After moving to Brookside Close with husband David, Jean Crosbie filled her days by working at Deborah's florist's at Brookside Parade. She had spent much of her life putting up with David's womanizing ways and revealed to her shocked daughter, Patricia Farnham, that he had had an affair with her nanny 20 years earlier.

Jean was not without her sexual secrets, though, and on her ruby wedding anniversary, in June 1994, she told David of her relationship with another woman – her best friend Jane – and showed him love letters to prove it. This horrified her husband, who had only recently disapproved of neighbour Beth Jordache's romance with a gay university lecturer.

As a result, David moved in with Patricia and her husband Max, and the couple lived separate

Mary Tamm (b. Dewsbury, West Yorkshire, 22 March 1950) acted PENNY CROSBIE, widow of cheating M.P. Clive, who committed suicide after newspaper revelations that he had been involved with a call girl. Mary had previously played Stan and Hilda Ogden's daughter-in-law Pauline in *Coronation Street* and Romana in 26 episodes of *Doctor Who*, as well as Jon Voight's wife Sigi in the film version of *The Odessa File*.

Betty Alberge (b. Manchester, 27 January 1922), who was cornershop owner Florrie Lindley in the first episode of *Coronation Street*, in 1960, and stayed for four-and-a-half years, played EDNA CROSS, wife of Harry, until the character's death. She also acted in early ITV series such as *The Verdict Is Yours* and *Knight Errant*, and later appeared in *The Ken Dodd Show* and *Crown Court*. Betty died on 18 May 1991.

Bill Dean (b. Liverpool, 3 September 1921) was grumpy pensioner HARRY CROSS. Bill had previously acted in *Coronation Street*, played gas board official Abraham Scarsdale in *Emmerdale* – crossing swords with Amos Brearly – and committee member Jack in the comedy series *Oh No It's Selwyn Froggitt*, as well as appearing in the films *Kes*, *Family Life*, *Night Watch* (alongside Elizabeth Taylor), *'Let Him Have It'* and *Scum*. Since leaving *Brookside* in 1990, he has appeared in videos for the Liverpool rock group The Farm and on TV – as a priest – in *Clarissa* and in a BBC 'ScreenPlay', *Skallagrigg*.

David Banks (b. Hull, East Yorkshire, 24 September 1951) was solicitor GRAEME CURTIS, who was infatuated with secretary Sue Sullivan, falsely convicted of her murder and killed himself in jail. David was previously best known as leader of the Cybermen in many *Doctor Who* adventures and wrote a book, *Doctor Who – The Cybermen*.

Danny McCall acted OWEN DANIELS, who married Sammy Rogers. Danny has since starred in the London musical *A Slice of Saturday Night* and been a presenter of *Saturday Disney* on television.

Gilly Coman, best known as Aveline in *Bread*, played DENISE, who took a fancy to Frank Rogers. She had previously played Linda in *Emmerdale*.

lives. David was away from home so much that Jean thought he must be having another affair, but he was actually attending an over-55s afternoon social club.

The Crosbies were reunited with the birth of Max and Patricia Farnham's baby, in August 1994. Because Alice had Down's syndrome and the birth was difficult, Jean and David often looked after the couple's son, Thomas. At the same time, Jean found outside interests by joining the All Ladies' Brookside Darts Team and formed an over-55s club at La Luz, the nightclub owned by Oscar Dean and Barry Grant.

When DD Dixon left the Close, Jean ran her florist's shop and took on Audrey Manners as her assistant, without realizing that she had slept with David. Audrey had introduced herself as a widow, so it was a surprise when her husband, George, turned up. They had split up years earlier, but George now wanted her back, claiming that he had finally made something of his life. Jean tried to encourage their reunion, but Audrey was reluctant.

Both Audrey and George died as a result of the virus that hit the Close in March 1995. Jean herself was at death's door after contracting the virus and it was while she appeared to be living her final moments that husband David admitted to being unfaithful with Audrey Manners. But Jean recovered and eventually forgave him.

Marcia Ashton was a soap star as Lily in *Compact*, the sixties serial set in the offices of a women's magazine, 30 years before taking the role of Jean Crosbie in *Brookside*. Her other television appearances include *On the Buses*, *Father Dear Father*, *Upstairs, Downstairs*, *The Brothers*, *The Misfits*, *In Sickness and in Health*, *Pulaski*, *Mathspy*, *The Bill*, *Rumpole of the Bailey* and *Bernard and the Genie*.

On stage, Marcia has played the Duchess of York in a national tour of *Crown Matrimonial*, Lily Clamcraft in *Alfie*, in the West End and on Broadway, Titania in *A Midsummer Night's Dream*, Miss Marple in *A Murder Has Been Announced* on tour, Sister Ecclesia in *Valmouth* and Matron in *Goodbye, Mr Chips*, both at the Chichester Festival Theatre, as well as appearing in the revue *Hullo Bulloo* and national tours of *Barefoot in the Park*, *Seven Brides for Seven Brothers* and *Pygmalion*.

JACQUI DIXON

Arriving in the Close as a 15-year-old keep-fit fanatic, tough and independent Jacqueline Dixon was a school swimming champion whose ambition was to make the British squad as a competitive swimmer. She was dedicated and spent a lot of time training.

But Jacqui fell foul of her parents and the law when she tried to help brother Mike to get his own back on another A level student who spiked his drink at a party. Mike had previously caught him trying to tempt Jacqui with drugs and punched the youth.

At a New Year's Eve party, the lad spiked Mike's drink with drugs. Seeking to do the same to him, Mike enlisted Jacqui's help in buying drugs from the youth. Mike waited outside the school for Jacqui to emerge with the drugs. However, plain-clothed policemen parked outside the school were watching and, as Jacqui showed Mike the drugs, they pounced and arrested the brother and sister. They were fortunate in getting away with a caution. The incident led to Jacqui's parents banning her from going out. When she went to her best friend's birthday party, under the pretence of going swimming, they found out and father Ron lost his temper and slapped her across the face.

Ron disapproved of her boyfriend Darren Murphy, part of a group who had been vandalizing Brookside Parade. Jacqui was with them when they broke into Manor Park Primary School and Darren used a lighter to start a fire that razed the building to the ground. As the group ran off, Jacqui was left trapped in the inferno. Fortunately, Barry Grant was passing by and stormed in to rescue Jacqui.

Jacqui's opinion of her father diminished still further when he left her mother for tarty Bev McLoughlin. It was after Ron moved in with Bev that Jacqui's younger brother, Tony, went into a coma after being involved in a car crash. Jacqui and her mother planned to take Tony to Lourdes on a pilgrimage in a last-ditch attempt to cure him, but he died in February 1994.

After leaving school, Jacqui worked at the petrol station opposite Brookside Parade, before becoming a lifeguard at the local leisure centre's swimming pool and moving into a flat with Katie Rogers above Brookside Parade.

Alexandra Fletcher, who is a year younger than her screen character, appeared on television in the children's programme *Why Don't You. . ?* and the BSB satellite show *Cool Cube* before taking on the role of Jacqui Dixon in *Brookside*. She was on holiday with a friend's family in Pwllheli when she was called back for a second audition, which secured the part. Her parents dashed to Wales to drive her to the real-life Brookside Close: Alexandra was not unhappy about her holiday being disrupted.

MIKE DIXON

The eldest son of Ron and DD, Mike Dixon wears an old leather jacket, T-shirt and jeans, and sees himself as a modern-day James Dean or Fonz. He also has an eye for the girls and, in his time, made a play for Sammy Rogers and Beth Jordache, but neither fell for his charms.

Mike was academically bright and went to Brookside Comprehensive to study for his A levels. Sinnott, his arch-enemy there, spiked his drink with drugs at a party, so he planned to get his revenge by turning the tables on the school bully. Sister Jacqui bought drugs from Sinnott so that they could spike a drink for him, but she and Mike were arrested for possession. They escaped criminal charges and were cautioned.

Mike managed to get his revenge by offering Sinnott a can of Coca-Cola, which he had spiked with drugs. Moments later, the youth horrified classmates by throwing himself out of a classroom window. To Mike's relief, he survived the fall. Mike himself ended up in hospital after challenging Sinnott to a daredevil car race for a bet of £100. Mike crashed, but Sinnott finally agreed to call a truce.

However, Sinnott was back to his old tricks

> **Louisa Rix**, actress daughter of Whitehall farceur Brian (now Lord) Rix, played **ALISON DICKS**, the solicitor acting for Mandy and Beth Jordache during their murder trial in 1995. Louisa had previously starred on TV in the sitcoms *Colin's Sandwich* and *Side by Side*.

when guitarist Mike and his rock group performed at his polytechnic. Their singer Tina was doped up by Sinnott and stripped on stage. Mike also sank deeply into debt after buying a keyboard for the group on HP and started stealing from the till of his father's shop to keep up the payments.

Mike teamed up with his friend Keith Rooney in a venture organizing rave nights for teenyboppers at Barry Grant's nightclub, La Luz. It proved a great success and they even began selling videos of the raves to the teenagers, under the auspices of M&K Promotions.

Then, when his father had an affair with tarty Bev McLoughlin but felt remorse and returned to DD, Mike stepped in to ease Bev's heartbreak and slept with her. By the time Bev knew she was pregnant, she was back with Ron but kept from him the fact that her baby might not be his. When he found out, Ron walked out on her, but he later returned.

Greater responsibility fell on Mike's shoulders when Bev went into labour and gave birth to baby Josh. Ron and DD were sitting at the hospital bedside of Mike's brother, Tony, who was in a coma after a car crash and subsequently died. Fittingly, Mike delivered the baby, after being revealed to be the real father.

Ron refused to believe this when Mike's sister, Jacqui, forced Bev to confess – until blood tests proved it. Although Ron walked out on Bev, he eventually returned, happy to be with Bev and feeling that he could act as the baby's father.

Mike then made a play for teenager Beth Jordache but was rebuffed and supportive when she told him that she was a lesbian. Mike soon found comfort in the arms of Sarah Banks, estranged wife of Carl. Although she moved in with him for a while, the romance never lasted.

Paul Byatt (b. Liverpool, 22 December 1971) trained at the Liverpool Playhouse Youth Theatre and has performed on stage at the Playhouse, the Liverpool Empire and the New Brighton Floral Pavilion.

He has also worked on *Big Chance*, a project by *Brookside*'s parent production company Mersey Television, and had bit parts in programmes for the BBC, Granada Television and Channel Four.

Paul, who left St Edward's College, Liverpool, after passing A levels in physics, music, maths and general studies, joined *Brookside* in 1990. One of his two sisters, Michelle, played Tracy Corkhill's hairdresser friend Nikki White in the serial. The other, Sharon, acted solicitor Jonathan Gordon-Davies's secretary Coral, as well as appearing in *Bread*.

RON DIXON

A mobile shop in the Close signalled the arrival of Ron Dixon and family, and upset new resident Max Farnham, who was sure their presence would bring down property values and nicknamed them 'the Clampetts', after the ramshackle family in *The Beverly Hillbillies* on TV.

Ron began his working life as a labourer in a frozen-food factory in Kirkby and worked his way up to become production foreman. He took voluntary redundancy in 1988, used the money to buy a mobile shop – The Moby – and put down a deposit on no. 8 Brookside Close. The Moby sold a bit of everything. Ron believes in recycling, thinking that everything has a use – or will one day. As a result, the Close was soon littered with the Moby Dixons' junk.

Ron has often been exasperated by his three children. His youngest son, Tony, ruffled feathers by playing pranks on Max Farnham, and Mike and Jacqui were in trouble with the police for possessing drugs, although it turned out that Mike's arch-enemy Sinnott had planted them.

Ron's reluctant family chipped in to help in running the mobile shop, but he eventually achieved his long-term ambition of getting a proper shop when developers were planning to build Brookside Parade next to the Close, much to the consternation of some residents.

When they started building a footpath alongside his house to link up with the shops, Ron began his own campaign of resistance. But, when the developers offered him money and a shop rent-free for a year, in return for him stopping his protest, he had no qualms about accepting.

Dixon's Trading Post opened in October 1991. Ron employed Jackie Corkhill and Julia Brogan as assistants and falsely accused them of stealing money from the till when, in fact, the culprit was his own son Mike.

Ron's marriage began to crumble after DD's opposition to her brother Derek O'Farrell falling for the Farnhams' nanny, Margaret Clemence, and renouncing his vows as a Catholic priest. DD walked out on Ron when she found out that he had lent Derek and Margaret money to go on holiday together, although Margaret returned a week later. Ron then expressed disapproval at DD's decision to help pregnant schoolgirl Leanne Powell, Jacqui's friend, to arrange an abortion without her parents' knowledge. He was also shocked to discover that DD was opening a florist's shop, Deborah's, in Brookside Parade, using money she had secretly saved over the years.

Soon, he was looking for comfort elsewhere. Jackie Corkhill turned him down, but he had more luck with flighty Bev McLoughlin. DD, a devout Catholic all her life, witnessed Ron kissing Bev, suffered a nervous breakdown and retreated to a convent. Ron felt pangs of guilt and was ready to return to his wife, but she could not face him. Then, when he learned that Bev was pregnant and planning an abortion, he persuaded her to go ahead and have the baby, which he felt would cement their relationship.

Before the birth of Josh, on Christmas Day 1993 – Ron's birthday – the Dixons faced further tragedy with the death of Tony while travelling in a Rolls-Royce to Frank and Lyn Rogers's wedding reception, into which crashed a drug-crazed Jimmy Corkhill. Ron then moved in with Bev. The revelation that son Mike was Josh's real father led to Ron storming out on Bev and spending the night in his shop storeroom, before DD invited him back to the family home and planned a ceremony to reaffirm their marriage vows. But Ron could not go through with it, left DD standing at the altar and returned to Bev, willing to put aside the fact that his own son had slept with her and fathered her child.

Following the loss of Ron, the death of Tony, and Mike and Jacqui's decision to move out of 8 Brookside Close, DD left Ron for good – although only after Ron had discovered her at Tony's grave contemplating suicide. Bev moved into no. 8 with Ron – renaming it 'Bevron' – and promptly put him on a diet of healthy eating, much to his consternation.

Vince Earl (b. Birkenhead, Cheshire, 11 June 1944) began his career as a singer with Merseyside skiffle groups in the early sixties, often appearing on the same bill as The Beatles. His first group was the Vince Earl Talismen, but he found national success on television in 1975 with the Vince Earl Attraction, coming second to ventriloquist Roger DeCourcey and Nooky Bear in the talent show *New Faces*.

Two years later, Vince went solo as a comedian and appeared on TV in such programmes as *The Comedians*, *The Video Entertainers*, *Starburst* and *The Jimmy Cricket Special*. He was working as a stand-up comic on the cruise ship *Canberra* just before joining *Brookside*, in 1990. Vince has also acted in three Alan Bleasdale-written productions: on television in *Boys from the Blackstuff*; as a big-band heavy in the film *No Surrender*; and as a concert secretary on stage in *Turn for the Worse*.

Vince lives in Birkenhead, Cheshire, with his second wife, Irene. They have three children, Nicole, Stephen and Kimberley. Vince also has a son, Vince Jr, from his first marriage.

MAX FARNHAM

Quantity surveyor Max Farnham met his first wife, Susannah, when they were sixth-formers studying for A levels. At college, she became pregnant and left. Susannah was expecting a second child when Max began an affair with Patricia Crosbie. When she, too, became pregnant, a messy divorce followed. Max maintained he would have married Patricia anyway, but her pregnancy speeded up the event. He felt his marriage to Susannah was going stale and they were already becoming an old couple.

With baby Thomas, Max and Patricia moved into no. 7 Brookside Close in September 1990.

She worked for an advertising agency, and they needed a large income to pay for a live-in nanny and Max's maintenance payments to Susannah.

Shortly after moving into the Close, Max and Patricia were outraged by the arrival next door of the Dixon family, complete with their mobile shop. He felt they lowered the tone of the Close – and, perhaps, property values – and quickly nicknamed them 'the Clampetts', after the family of rustics in *The Beverly Hillbillies* TV series.

As he settled into the area, Max became a leading light in the local Round Table, with ambitions to become its president, and tried to set up a Neighbourhood Watch scheme in the Close, without much success. His two children from his first marriage, Matthew and Emily, were frequent visitors at weekends.

A new job with the electricity board gave Max a £3000 pay rise and enabled him to pay nanny Margaret Clemence more and keep Susannah happy. But he quit after a month, realizing that he had made a mistake taking the job. With no alternative employment, Max set about fitting a new kitchen and allowed some of the Dixons' property to be taken away when a council lorry arrived to clear the rubbish. When Ron Dixon found out, he declared war by setting up his own Berlin Wall between the properties.

Always weak willed, Max let ex-wife Susannah wind him round her little finger. First, she began arranging to see him under the guise of discussing their children's schooling. Then, he turned to her to be his wife for an evening at a Round Table event when Patricia refused to go.

Patricia found out and laid down the law to Max and Susannah about when they could see one another in future, but Susannah told her that she could win Max back whenever she liked. She tried to carry out the threat when Patricia was working away in London. With their daughter Emily ill, Max agreed that Susannah could stay over at the house but she must sleep on the sofa. Patricia promptly threw Max out of the house on Christmas Day 1992, but she asked him back a week later and revealed the tragic news that she had breast cancer.

When Margaret Clemence left the Close with her boyfriend, Derek O'Farrell, Max hired Polish immigrant Anna Wolska as Thomas's nanny, although Patricia was keen to give Margaret another chance on her return and seized on an opportunity to sack Anna.

When Susannah turned up with new boyfriend Andrew to announce they were emigrating to America with Matthew and Emily, Patricia must have thought her troubles were over. But Max, against the children moving so far away, followed Susannah to Florida and snatched them

back. Susannah returned to Britain for a showdown while Patricia was in London on business again. This time, she used her wily ways to get him into bed and persuade him that her plans were in the best interests of the children.

Max's father-in-law, David Crosbie – who by this time lived next door – learned of the incident and told Patricia on her return. This seemed rather hypocritical, considering David's own infidelity years earlier, but Patricia walked out and stayed with her parents. Although the decree absolute came through in October 1993, the Farnhams had sorted out their differences and remarried two weeks later.

But their marriage was tested again a few months later when Patricia became pregnant and, although she found out that the baby suffered from Down's syndrome, decided against a termination. Although Max had reservations about this, he showed an unusual strength of character by sticking by his wife. But, when baby Alice was born, Max rejected her and wished that Patricia had gone for an abortion.

By this time, his career had moved from surveying and estate agency. He went into partnership with wide-boy Barry Grant to open Grants restaurant. Shady Kenny Maguire pressed Max for protection money and, true to form, he crumbled. Barry came to the rescue by sorting out Kenny with a truckload of cement.

☆ ☆ ☆

Steven Pinder (b. Whalley, Lancashire, 30 March 1960), the son of a bank manager, worked in a foundry on leaving school so that he could save enough money to train as an actor, and attended The Drama Centre in London. He appeared on television in *Foxy Lady* as printer's apprentice Owen Buckley, *Crown Court* – in two different roles, as a policeman and a yobbo – *Now and Then*, *Scotch and Wry* and *C.A.T.S. Eyes*. He then joined *Crossroads* as Roy Lambert, the motel's garage mechanic as part of a YTS, before running a cornershop in the serial. He was in *Crossroads* for three years, until it finished in 1988.

Then, Steven played Tony in eight episodes of the afternoon soap opera *Hollywood Sports*, before joining *Brookside* as Max Farnham. He has also appeared in many TV commercials, including those for Harp lager and Bonus Print.

On stage, Steven was in *Deathwatch*, *Macbeth*, *The Miser*, *The Quest for the Rose and the Ring*, *Up 'n' Under* and *Watching*, playing Malcolm in a stage tour of the hit TV sitcom. During one lean period of his career, Steve worked in hotels and restaurants, washing dishes and waiting on tables. He and wife Taj, who had a baby daughter in 1990, live in London.

PATRICIA FARNHAM

Career-minded Patricia Farnham has always been the driving force behind her marriage to Max and for a long time had to deal with Max's ex-wife, his two other children at weekends and large maintenance payments. She became pregnant by Max while he was still married to Susannah, with one child and another on the way, and married him before the birth of their own son, Thomas. Later, she admitted that she had become pregnant deliberately so that he would not return to his wife. Although outwardly confident and slightly aloof, Patricia was actually insecure, worried that she might lose Max to another woman in the same way that she had taken the place of his first wife.

When Patricia and Max moved into no. 7 Brookside Close, she worked as accounts manager for a Manchester-based international advertising agency and hired Margaret Clemence as Thomas's nanny. Money problems were always prominent and, at first, the couple had to make do with only one car, which Max used for getting to work while Patricia relied on public transport. Eventually, Max bought her a car as a surprise birthday present.

Patricia had an early run-in with neighbour Josie Johnson after suggesting that she might be responsible for bills the Farnhams were receiving for catalogue goods. This had landed Patricia and Max on a credit blacklist, which prevented them buying a dishwasher. Josie responded with a kick in the shin and Max eventually found out that Jimmy Corkhill had ordered the goods when Sinbad was squatting in the house before they moved in. Sinbad took delivery, and Jimmy sold the items. More neighbour problems followed with the arrival next door of the Dixons and their mobile shop. Max wondered what sort of neighbourhood they had moved into and Patricia was dismayed at Ron's references to them as 'Maxie' and 'Pat'.

Patricia began to get disenchanted with her advertising job. After putting a lot of time and energy into a campaign for toxic waste, her boss switched her to another for impregnated mopheads. Offered promotion by moving to the agency's London office, Patricia went on a month's trial, pointing out to Max that he was out of work and she was the breadwinner.

Max found new employment and she did not take the job, but it was another visit to London for a presentation that presented Max's ex-wife, Susannah, with the opportunity to spend a night in his house, but he insisted she sleep on the sofa. Phoning home to say goodnight, Patricia was stunned to hear Susannah answer, slammed the receiver down and let the tears flow. At the same time, she discovered a lump on her breast.

On her return, Patricia threw Max out on the morning of Christmas Day 1992, despite his denials that he had slept with Susannah. But, realizing how much she needed him as she faced a life-or-death health scare, Patricia asked Max back a week later and revealed that she had breast cancer. This traumatic time brought the couple closer together.

Patricia had left her advertising job in August 1992 and became pregnant, but she suffered a miscarriage while acting as guest speaker at a Round Table lunch and set about busying herself by forming a public relations company with her old boss, Karyn Clark.

It looked as if Susannah's meddling with Max had finished when she turned up with a new boyfriend, actor Andrew, and announced that they were moving to America with Matthew and Emily. Max was against this and flew to Florida to get the children back, with the result that Susannah returned for a showdown. Patricia was away in London on business and Susannah used her charms to persuade Max to let her continue with her plans. The incident ended with Max and Susannah going to bed together.

Patricia's father found out and, on Patricia's return, told her what had happened. She walked out and moved in with her parents next door. Divorce proceedings went ahead swiftly and the decree absolute was issued in October 1993. By then, Max and Patricia were reunited and, just two weeks later, remarried.

A few months later, Patricia was elated to be pregnant again, only to be informed that she was carrying a Down's syndrome baby. But

BROOKSIDE

Max and Patricia decided against abortion and Alice Farnham was born on 19 August 1994. The couple experienced further anxiety when, in March 1995, as the Close was gripped by a virus, son Thomas fell ill and was taken into hospital fighting for his life. Fortunately, he pulled through and Patricia resolved to make the most of every moment of her life, having seen how precious life was. Switching careers, she opened a gift shop in DD Dixon's old florist's premises in Brookside Parade, which incensed Ron Dixon because he had been planning to knock through the wall of his Trading Post into the florist's and create a mini-mart.

Gabrielle Glaister (b. Moreton-in-Marsh, Gloucestershire) studied English and drama at Chichester College and trained as an actress at the National Youth Theatre.

She worked in repertory theatre in Ipswich, Coventry, Colchester, Hornchurch, Westcliffe, Bromley, Newbury and Leatherhead, acting in such plays as *Twelfth Night*, *The Caucasian Chalk Circle*, *Insignificance*, *Private Lives* and *Habeas Corpus*. Gabrielle also played the title role in *Daisy Pulls It Off* at the Globe Theatre, as well as appearing in *Great Expectations* at the Old Vic, *Dandy Dick* on a Compass Theatre national tour and *The Real Thing* on a British Council international tour.

She appeared in the film *The Class of Miss MacMichael*, and on TV in *The Ben Elton Show*, *The Franchise Affair*, *Casualty*, *Grange Hill*, *Rockliffe's Babies*, two series of *Blackadder* (as 'Bob'), *Happy Families*, *Jury*, *Jane Eyre*, *Have a Heart*, *Playaway*, *Houseparty*, *All at Number 20*, *Wish Me Luck*, *London's Burning*, *Mitch* and *Ben Elton – The Man from Auntie*. Gabrielle is single and lives in London. She plays the piano and sings mezzo soprano.

BARRY GRANT

Bad boy Barry Grant has lurched from one shady deal to another. Son of Bobby and Sheila, who moved to Brookside Close from their run-down council estate in 1982, Barry was later revealed to be the son of Bobby's mate Matty Nolan. By then, Bobby had walked out on Sheila and she had married Billy Corkhill and moved away to a new life in the south.

Eldest of the Grant children, Barry was a joiner by trade but showed no inclination to work for a living. His money-making schemes were usually on the wrong side of the law, but doting mother Sheila turned a blind eye to them. Barry's relationship with Bobby was difficult

and they often rowed, with Barry always ready to jump to his mother's defence. He was also ready to defend his sister Karen and, when her boyfriend 'Demon Duane' threw her out of his flat after accusing her of being a 'teaser', Barry went round and beat him up.

A string of women were loved and lost by Barry. He had an affair with Irene Harrison, wife of an amateur football club manager. Then, when neighbour Petra Taylor was grieving the death of her husband Gavin, Barry was quick to offer comfort. Eventually, she ran away and committed suicide in a North Wales hotel.

After getting jobs for a builder but being sacked for stealing materials, Barry and his childhood pal Terry Sullivan tried many get-rich-quick schemes together. They sold stolen perfume in a pub and started car-valeting and tool-hire businesses. When the pair became involved in a video enterprise run by local villain Tommy McArdle, Bobby threw Barry out of the house.

Worse was to come for Barry when he was beaten up by McArdle's cronies after trying to help fireman George Jackson's case in a warehouse robbery. McArdle had set up George, and Barry refused to give the villain's henchman, Victor, an alibi. After this, Barry moved to London. On the first of his subsequent short visits back to the Close, he learned of his mother's rape by a taxi driver and persuaded Tommy McArdle to have the rapist beaten up.

After another family tragedy, the murder of brother Damon, Barry's father turned to drink and lost his licence for drink-driving, which led to Bobby and Barry having a bitter argument and Barry walking out. Barry returned only to see his father leave the Close for good.

He decided to help his mother financially by

becoming involved with another crook, the stuttering Sizzler. Barry was 'employed' to seduce bookie's wife Penny Riozzi in a hotel room, but Sizzler videoed the session and used it to blackmail the woman so that he could gain control of her husband's betting shops. Barry, however, fell for Penny and tried to recover the tape by agreeing to do another job for Sizzler, trying to persuade Ma Johnson to let him have her gaming arcade. But she would not budge.

Back on the home front, Barry was jealous when his mother Sheila fell for Billy Corkhill, whom he referred to as 'the tea-leaf'. It was then that Barry started sleeping with Billy's daughter, Tracy, and she became pregnant but had an abortion without telling him.

In the middle of a feud between brothers Billy and Jimmy Corkhill and violent criminal Joey Godden – who had murdered their elder brother Frankie – Sheila revealed to Jimmy that her past had not been entirely whiter than white, and that Matty Nolan was Barry's real father. But it was some time before Barry learned the truth. Ironically, it was Barry who ended the feud between the Corkhills and Godden – after the thug had murdered Billy's and Jimmy's cousin Don – by threatening Godden with a shotgun.

Barry's darkest hour came after moving into no. 9 Brookside Close as Terry and Sue Sullivan's lodger. There was constant friction between Barry and Sue over the fact that Terry was not the real father of her baby son Danny and she had revealed the fact only after they had wed. As a life-long friend of Terry himself, he saw that as a betrayal. However, in 1991, when Terry stormed out of the house following a row with Sue, Barry stepped in to comfort her and the pair ended up having sex on the sofa.

After Sue threatened to tell Terry that Barry had slept with her, the bodies of Sue and baby Danny were found under scaffolding at the new Brookside Parade of shops. Graeme Curtis, a solicitor who had been pestering Sue at work, was found guilty of the murders and sent to jail, where he committed suicide.

But Barry had been on the scaffolding with Sue and Danny when they fell to their deaths and Sue's workmate Fran Pearson – who became another notch on Barry's bed post and was pregnant by him – found out the truth. Sue had been pregnant with Barry's child at the time of her death.

Barry made sure he told Terry before Fran did and took his friend to a deserted beach in Southport, where he revealed everything. He claimed that Sue had caught her foot on the scaffolding and he put his hand out to help her, although his mind was mixed up at the time.

Alan Igbon (b. Manchester) was GENE, who carried out a supermarket robbery with Billy Corkhill as getaway driver. He also played Loggo in *Boys from the Blackstuff*, Mike in *The Daughters of Albion* and Teddy in *G.B.H.*

Jane Cunliffe (b. Manchester, 1 June 1962) was tragic LAURA GORDON-DAVIES (née Wright), who died after falling down the stairs. Jane had previously acted in *The Practice*, *Albion Market* (as a student) and *Emmerdale* (as Carol Longthorn for eight episodes). She later took the role of Francesca Hamilton in 12 episodes of *Hollywood Sports* and voiced the part of Catherine Kovalic in 20 episodes of the French serial *Chateauvallon*, dubbed for screening in Britain.

Ricky Tomlinson (b. 26 September 1939) played trade unionist BOBBY GRANT, first husband of Sheila. Ricky had performed in clubs and as part of a country and western group, and acted in the TV play *United Kingdom* and *Boys from the Blackstuff*. He has since appeared in the films *Riff-Raff* and *Raining Stones*, and on TV in *Cracker* (as D.C.I. Wise).

Simon O'Brien (b. Garston, Liverpool, 19 June 1965) was DAMON GRANT in *Brookside* and the three-part spin-off *Damon & Debbie*. He has found further fame as an actor and TV presenter, in *Fraggle Rock*, *Young, Gifted and Broke* and *Rough Guide to the World*. He was also in the film *Dancin' Thru the Dark*.

Sue Johnston (b. Warrington, 7 December 1943) was SHEILA GRANT (later Corkhill), a devout Catholic who struggled to bring up her three children, Barry, Karen and Damon. Sheila gave birth to another daughter, Claire, in her forties. She suffered postnatal depression, battled to keep up son Damon's spirits as he fought unemployment, suffered the horror of rape, saw her marriage to Bobby break up, grieved over the fatal stabbing of Damon, then married Billy Corkhill and moved to Basingstoke. Just before joining the serial, when it began, Sue appeared in *Coronation Street* as bookie's wife Mrs Chadwick. Her many subsequent TV roles include Barbara Grade in *Goodbye Cruel World*, Ruth Parry in *Medics*, Grace Robbins in *Full Stretch* and Térèse Craven in *Luv*.

Offering Terry a shotgun, he told him to carry out his own justice, but Terry preferred to let Barry suffer for the rest of his life. Barry gave Terry a flat in Brookside Parade in return for silence over the events of that tragic day.

Barry's own troubles continued and he tried to kidnap Stephen, his son by Fran, but she fled to Greece to start a new life. His next conquest was Angela Lambert, who was separated from her husband and opened a hairdressing salon in the Parade. But she kept him in check and left in 1992 after a robbery at the salon.

Barry became co-owner of La Luz, a new nightclub opened next to the Parade shops on Christmas Day 1992. There was soon friction with his business partner, Joe Halsall, who objected to his plans to hold raves at the club.

Stephen McGann (b. Stephen Vincent McGann in Liverpool, 2 February 1963) was DAVID HARGREAVES, Karen Grant's student boyfriend. He later acted Johann Strauss in *The Strauss Dynasty*.

Ann Beach (b. Wolverhampton, Staffordshire, 7 June 1938) played Sue Sullivan's mother, MRS HARPER. On TV, she has portrayed Mrs Johnson in *The History of Mr Polly*, Sonia Barratt in *Fresh Fields* and *French Fields*, and Phyllis in *The Lifeboat*. She has two actress daughters, Charlotte (*Oranges Are Not the Only Fruit*) and Lisa (*Casualty*) Coleman.

Geoffrey Leesley (b. Manchester, 1 June 1949) played George Bladon in *Emmerdale* and Geoff Travis in *Albion Market* before acting JOHN HARRISON in *Brookside*. Geoffrey was also in *Coronation Street* and played Det. Con. Terry Wilson in five series of *Bergerac*, paramedic Keith Cotterill in four series of *Casualty* and Det. Supt. Frank Mathews in both series of *Waterfront Beat*.

Robert Beck (b. Chiswick, West London, 1 August 1970) was PETER HARRISON, who was cleared of raping Diana Corkhill, then acted Dan in *The Upper Hand*.

Amanda Burton (b. Londonderry, 10 October 1956) played glamorous accountant HEATHER HAVERSHAM, first married to cheating solicitor Roger Huntington, then to drug addict Nicholas Black. She left the Close to start a new life alone. Amanda has since appeared on TV as Margaret Daly in *Boon* and Dr Beth Glover in *Peak Practice*.

Barry found out that she had been fiddling the books, but she countered by framing him for a hit-and-run on Jimmy Corkhill. When it became clear that Barry was not responsible, Joe did a moonlight flit and he accepted the minority share in a 60/40 business partnership with the eccentric Oscar Dean.

In 1994, Barry fell for cheating M.P. Clive Crosbie's widow Penny – aunt of Patricia Farnham – and bought no. 5 Brookside Close, his family's former home. The only problem was that religious cult leader Simon Howe and his group were squatting there, so Barry took matters into his own hands and stormed the house, armed with a shotgun. But he was overpowered and held hostage, until Simon sent his 'disciples' away to Bristol and decided to blow up the house with a home-made bomb, determined that, if he could not have it, no-one else could either. He cleared Barry from the house just before the explosion and the only one hurt was Simon himself.

Barry continued his business enterprises by going into partnership with Max Farnham and opening a restaurant called Grants. Loyd Grossman and drag artist Lily Savage performed the opening ceremony in November 1994.

Life was looking rosy for Barry, until Penny was lured away from him by Max's business associate, Sam, while Barry was away in Spain with Terry. But, in the New Year, he was soon chasing another woman, Grants' hostess Emma Piper. She refused to jump straight into bed with him, eventually confessing that she was a virgin. When Emma told Barry that she would not sleep with him unless they were married, he bought her an engagement ring – but, before she could give him an answer, he left for Florida to find a holiday home near Fran and his son.

☆ ☆ ☆

Paul Usher (b. Liverpool, 20 April 1961) is the only surviving member of the original *Brookside* cast, although he had no acting experience before joining the serial, in 1982, and had previously worked in an abattoir and as a Bluecoat at a Pontin's holiday camp, entertaining the guests. Between appearances in the serial, he has followed a career as a singer, bass guitarist and songwriter, performing with various groups. Before joining *Brookside*, he had toured America with his group 20/20.

Paul, who is single, tries to take at least three months off from *Brookside* each year to recharge his batteries. In an attempt to keep in touch with reality, he has even lived in a caravan and taken a job at a garden centre, digging ditches, laying turf and shifting sand, as well as working as a farm labourer.

MICK JOHNSON

Moving into Harry Cross's bungalow as supposedly short-term lodger after leaving wandering wife Josie, likeable and easy-going Mick Johnson was Terry Sullivan's partner in a taxi business. They shared a cab and worked alternate shifts.

When Harry left for Las Vegas to be best man at his friend Ralph Hardwick's wedding to American Lana Costello, he offered Mick the chance to stay permanently. Mick asked for permission to have visits from his children, Leo and Gemma, and Harry added £2 a week to his rent for the privilege. Harry returned but later decided to leave the bungalow for good to live with his son and daughter-in-law in St Helens, Lancashire, so Mick stayed on as his tenant.

Josie started visiting when her relationship with her medallion-man boyfriend Tony was turning sour. Mick found this traumatic, but still hoped the marriage might work out, so he caved in to her advances and the couple decided to make a go of it again. But Josie flitted back and forward, seeing Tony again and setting herself and the children up in a flat, telling Mick that if they were serious about rejuvenating their marriage they would have to court each other all over again. When the stress began to show on their children, Josie moved back into the bungalow with Mick. Son Leo's move to the local school caused Mick and Josie anxiety when he suffered racial abuse and started playing truant.

Worse came for Mick in 1990 when he was badly beaten up by one of his passengers, who hospitalized him and kept him off work for several weeks. This plunged the Johnsons into a

Marji Campi, who was Harold Cross and Ralph Hardwick's friend BETTY HUNT, also appeared in the Phil Redmond serial *What Now?* and *Coronation Street*, as Jack Duckworth's fancy woman Dulcie Froggatt, before starring as Joyce Watson in the comedy series *Surgical Spirit*.

Rob Spendlove (b. London, 1 May 1953), who played Heather Haversham's unfaithful first husband ROGER HUNTINGTON, the solicitor who cheated on her with one of his clients, has since appeared on television in *That's Love*, *Hard Cases* and *TECX*, and the TV film *Closing Ranks*. He has also appeared in *Soldier Soldier* as C.S.M. Michael Stubbs.

Cliff Howells had already played a plumber in *Emmerdale Farm* when he took on the role of fireman GEORGE JACKSON, who was jailed for conspiracy to burgle after being framed by Tommy McArdle. His wife's campaign slogan 'Free George Jackson' became a rallying call for Brookside fans. There was even a record of the same name made by a country and western group called Blazing Saddles. Cliff left to return to the theatre but later popped up in *Coronation Street* as Terry Seymour, whose car Kevin Webster smashed up while taking it off for repair as an out-of-hours job to line his own pocket. He was also in *G.B.H.*

Anna Keaveney (b. Runcorn, Cheshire, 5 October 1949) played MARIE JACKSON, George's wife, who moved to Leeds to start a new life with him and their two young sons after his jail term. Anna has since appeared on TV in the comedy series *Divided We Stand*, *Emmerdale* (as Archie Brooks's mother, April), the Jimmy McGovern drama *Needle*, *Casualty* and *Peak Practice*, and in the film *Shirley Valentine*.

Veteran actor Ian Hendry (b. Ipswich, Suffolk, 13 January 1931) appeared in *Brookside* for a short time as old seaman DAVEY JONES, alcoholic father of Marie Jackson, Petra Taylor and Michelle Jones. Ian had starred on TV as Dr David Keel in *Police Surgeon* and his character was transferred to *The Avengers* when the cult sixties series began, although he left after the first series. Ian was also Erik Shepherd in *The Lotus Eaters*. He died on 24 December 1984.

financial crisis, as Josie continued her spend, spend, spend policy and refused Mick's demands to send mail-order goods. Josie took a part-time job at the infamous Fourstar Club to earn extra money. Mick did not want her to work in a nightclub, but she would not listen.

Two weeks before Christmas 1990, Mick was branded a hero by the local press when he took on a burglar who broke into the children's bedroom and, in the struggle, left the intruder unconscious and in need of hospital treatment. But police charged him with grievous bodily harm for using undue force. Mick's solicitor advised him to plead guilty, but he felt that he had done no wrong and was simply defending his home and family. He opted to go before a jury at a Crown Court and, in March 1991, was relieved to be found not guilty. On his return home, he discovered that Josie had 'borrowed' money collected by fellow cabbies to support him so that she could buy stolen children's clothes from Jimmy Corkhill for her new market stall.

The arrival of Mick's arrogant younger brother Ellis at the bungalow spelled disaster. Mick had virtually brought Ellis up after their father had walked out on the family, but Ellis was the one who always came up smelling of roses while Mick struggled to get through life. It was also Ellis who had introduced Josie to her other man, Tony. Days later, Josie invited her best friend Marcia Barrett to stay as well. Marcia was one of Ellis's old flames and he put the boot in at every opportunity when she became engaged to window cleaner Sinbad. Shortly afterwards, Mick's marriage to Josie finally crumbled when she walked out for good and went back to Tony.

Ellis showed some brotherly love when he gave Mick the deposit to buy the bungalow. But more trouble was around the corner when Josie's parents, the Christies, arrived and took Leo and Gemma back to Cardiff with them. Mick drove to Wales in Ellis's car to bring them back and, in his absence, Ellis borrowed his taxi without a licence to drive it. Mick's boss found out and sacked him, so Mick threw Ellis out.

New purpose came into Mick's life when he collected a petition to have the local Manor Park Primary School rebuilt after a fire in the spring of 1992 and he met Marianne Dwyer, the education department's representative. She told him, off the record, that the school had been designated for the axe a year earlier and the fire simply speeded up the process.

Ellis and Mick bought Pizza Parade in the new Brookside Parade of shops from Terry Sullivan, but it was targeted for a terror campaign by racist petrol station owner George Webb. He was responsible for graffiti at the takeaway and planned to petrol bomb the Johnsons' bunga-

low, but Ron Dixon had by then realized that Webb was a fascist and stopped him.

Ellis met Marianne Dwyer and they became engaged, although she grew more unsure about her choice of husband, while Mick was secretly jealous. Ellis and Marianne arranged a Valentine's Day double wedding with Sinbad and Marcia, but it ended up a disaster. Marcia decided she could not go through with it and Marianne jilted Ellis at the altar.

Josie was at that moment making a final attempt to get back together with Mick but, after Marianne fled the church, she ended up in Mick's arms. When Josie tried to take her children, Mick threw her out of the bungalow and looked forward to a future with Marianne.

His own domestic future was less secure when his money problems led the building society to threaten to repossess the bungalow. He let it go and moved into the flat above Pizza Parade with Marianne. Carol Salter helped in the takeaway and made it clear that she had designs on Mick, but he let her know that he was spoken for. Mick agreed to look after Carol's tearaway teenage son Garry when she went into hospital, but this did not please Marianne or Garry's father, who had just been released from prison.

Mick and Marianne's relationship became strained, especially when she experienced sexual harassment from her boss at work. She found a new job as personnel manager at Litrotech, where Brookside Close resident Eddie Banks was the union's shop steward, but she was sacked during a union dispute.

Worse was to come when Mick was arrested by the police as he turned up at the register office for his wedding, in November 1994. He was accused of a break-in at Litrotech after a cleaner made a mistaken identification. Eventually, Garry Salter – son of the real villain Greg – turned his father over to the police and the charges against Mick were dropped. Unfortunately, Marianne had already deserted Mick and accepted a new job in Glasgow.

☆ ☆ ☆

Louis Emerick (b. Louis Emerick Grant in Liverpool, 10 June 1953) had extensive TV experience before joining *Brookside*. He appeared in *Happy Families*, *The Practice* (as a garage attendant), *Albion Market* (as a landlord in two episodes), *Home to Roost*, *Celebration*, *Floodtide*, *There Was An Old Woman*, *A View of Harry Clarke*, *Last of the Summer Wine*, *Coronation Street*, *Children's Ward* and *Ball-Trap on the Côte Sauvage*.

The actor, who was once lead singer in a pop group and joined *Brookside* in 1989, was also in the film *The Fruit Machine* and various radio plays, and did a voice-over for two episodes of the four-part TV documentary series *Apartheid*. Louis's many stage appearances include *The Lion, the Witch and the Wardrobe*, *The Resistible Rise of Arturo Ui*, *Hamlet*, *Playboy of the West Indies* and *Rent Party*. Louis and wife Maureen have two daughters, Valerie and Zoe, and one son, Louis Jr, and live in Manchester.

BETH JORDACHE

Moving to Brookside Close gave Elizabeth Jordache, her mother Mandy and sister Rachel a new start after father Trevor was jailed for beating Mandy. When Mandy let him stay for a couple of nights after his release, Beth moved out and lived in the Harrisons' house.

Trevor was soon back for good and resumed his drinking and abusing ways. Beth decided the only way to end the family's hell was to kill him, so she and her mother mixed a lethal cocktail of weedkiller and tablets. But, when he drank the potion, he realized that he was being poisoned and started to attack Beth. Her mother, in desperation, grabbed a kitchen knife and plunged it into his back. Beth wrapped the body in bin bags and, with her mother's help, dragged it into the extension, before burying her father in the back garden.

Getting on with her own life, Beth qualified in medicine at Liverpool University and put her broken romance with Peter Harrison behind her. She found comfort in the arms of Margaret Clemence and found that her feelings toward Margaret were more than platonic. She let those feelings be known by giving Margaret a passionate kiss on Christmas Eve 1993.

Worried about her own feelings, Margaret rushed back to her parents in Oldham and, on her return, jumped into bed with Keith Rooney. But, after an evening out with Beth, the two returned to the Farnhams' house – where Margaret had previously been nanny to Thomas – and cuddled up in bed together for the night.

Beth accepted her lesbian feelings and agreed to be simply friends with Margaret. When the pair went to a gay bar one evening, Beth fell for a 30-year-old gay university lecturer called Chris. Margaret was still unsure about her sexuality and decided to join her estranged fiancé – former Catholic priest Derek O'Farrell – in Bosnia, after rekindling the flames on his return to Liverpool for young Tony Dixon's funeral.

Beth's sister, Rachel, spotted Beth and Chris cuddling on a day trip to New Brighton and neighbour David Crosbie caught them kissing at the Farnhams' house. When Mandy found out, Beth moved in with Chris, but there were tears when Beth's mother threatened to report the lecturer to the education authorities and Chris gave Beth her marching orders. Beth then moved back in with her mother. Both of them had to face the music when her father's body was discovered under the patio in January 1995. Although they fled to Dublin with Sinbad, they were eventually caught by police and taken back to Liverpool, for questioning. When the newspapers discovered that Beth was a lesbian, they portrayed her and her mother as man-hating females.

At the trial, in May 1995, Beth was sentenced to five years in jail after being found guilty with her mother of conspiring to murder. Her mother, additionally, was found guilty of murder and sentenced to life. Brookside residents mounted a 'Free the Jordaches' campaign.

☆ ☆ ☆

Anna Friel (b. Rochdale, Lancashire, 12 July 1975) became an instant pin-up when she took the role of Beth Jordache in *Brookside* in 1992. A book entitled *The Journals of Beth Jordache* was published in 1994. The actress started dating musicals actor Darren Day in the same year.

She had previously appeared on television in *Coronation Street* and *Emmerdale*, as well as in the hospital drama *Medics*.

MANDY JORDACHE

Battered wife Amanda Jordache arrived at no. 10 Brookside Close with her teenage daughters Beth and Rachel shortly after a couple called Shackleton bought the house. They were apprehensive about meeting other residents and talking about themselves but, when they did so, Mandy explained that her husband was dead.

The real story was that Mandy's husband, Trevor, had been imprisoned for beating her and raping Beth. The house had been bought as a refuge for them and other families in a similar position. This was the chance for the family to rid themselves of him and start a new life.

Unfortunately, Trevor tracked them down after being let out on parole. He claimed he was a changed man and begged Mandy to have him back. Against daughter Beth's advice, she caved in and let him return, but he was soon drinking again and beating up Mandy, whose excuses for her bruises quickly became lame.

After climbing into bed with Rachel and raping her, Trevor warned Mandy that he would kill her, the girls and himself if she said anything about that or about his past crimes. Mandy saw no alternative when Beth – always much stronger than herself – insisted that the only way to be rid of her father's evil ways was to kill him. In May 1993, they concocted a mixture of weedkiller and tablets to poison him, but he realized what they were doing and set upon Beth in the kitchen. Seeing his horrific rage and realizing that their lives were at risk, Mandy grabbed a kitchen knife and stabbed him in the back. Beth buried the body in the back garden.

Trevor was not supposed to be living with them anyway, so no-one was able to account for his whereabouts. Trouble came when his sister Brenna, who saw him in a different light and thought that Mandy had provoked his past violence, arrived looking for him. It was convenient when the police discovered a body that was so decomposed that Mandy could identify it as Trevor without anyone contradicting her. It was less convenient when Brenna asked for Trevor's signet ring, but Mandy persuaded Sinbad – who had befriended her, realized what had happened and laid a patio over the make-shift grave – to dig up the body and remove it.

Sinbad was keen to get closer to Mandy, but she was understandably reluctant to enter into another relationship. However, when he said he was seriously considering a chance to emigrate to Australia with his long-lost mother to live with his Uncle Jake, Mandy revealed her feelings for him, although she was still not ready to plunge headlong into a serious relationship.

Trouble seemed to be around every corner for the Jordaches, however. Roy Williams, Trevor's cellmate, turned up in early 1994 and blackmailed Mandy, who was worried that he knew something sinister had happened. She gave him £700 that Sinbad had collected for a fund to help Tony Dixon, who was dying in hospital

after a car crash. Sinbad went to a loan shark so that he could pay the money back and the loan was later transferred to Kenny Maguire, who increased the repayments – then persuaded Mandy to sleep with him to reduce the debt.

In January 1995, when Mandy took Beth and Rachel away for a holiday, next-door neighbour Eddie Banks found water leaking into his back garden and called the water board, which was about to dig up the Jordaches' garden to find the source of the leak. Convinced that Sinbad had hidden stolen goods under the patio, Eddie and Jimmy Corkhill started digging it up themselves and found Trevor's decomposed body.

Mandy and her daughters fled to Dublin with Sinbad to escape the law, but they were eventually caught by police and taken back to Liverpool to face the music. Beth and Sinbad claimed they were guilty of killing Trevor, but the police did not believe them and charged Mandy with murder. Sinbad paid Mandy's bail.

As they awaited the court case, Mandy found out she was pregnant, having consummated her relationship with Sinbad during their trip to Dublin. But this did nothing to reduce the sentence of life passed on her at the trial when she was found guilty of Trevor's murder. Mandy was also given seven years, to run concurrently, for conspiracy to murder, a charge that also resulted in Beth being jailed for five years.

☆ ☆ ☆

Sandra Maitland (b. Coventry, Warwickshire) trained at the Manchester Polytechnic School of Theatre, and appeared on television in *Casualty*, *Coronation Street*, *The Practice*, *Children's Ward* and *Kinsey*, before joining *Brookside* She also acted on a national tour with the Young Vic company.

She made a huge impact in *Brookside* as the battered wife who eventually meted out her own form of justice by stabbing her violent husband to death. The harrowing scenes of Mandy Jordache's husband Trevor beating her and Mandy and daughter Beth's subsequent murder of him were shown again in a one-off documentary, *The Jordache Story*, screened by Channel Four in 1994. Its intention was partly to show how children are affected by family breakdowns. Sandra lives in Manchester.

RACHEL JORDACHE

Younger sister of Beth, Rachel Jordache was elated when father Trevor returned to the fold after his spell in jail. But the schoolgirl was soon a victim of his crimes, when he climbed into Rachel's bed and raped her instead of Beth, whom he had abused before going to prison. When mother Mandy killed Trevor with a knife, aided and abetted by sister Beth, the pair decided not to tell Rachel, who was dismayed at the news that he had apparently just packed his bags and gone away.

Rachel began to cause her mother distress when she started smoking with a bunch of tearaways and was led into shoplifting. She also began answering her mother back and blamed her for letting her father sleep with her.

She only found out the truth surrounding her father's death when the police arrested Mandy and Beth. Rachel refused to have anything to do with them and took shelter with the Banks family next door, before pensioners David and Jean Crosbie offered her accommodation.

☆ ☆ ☆

Tiffany Chapman (b. Tiffany Jayne Chapman on 3 September 1979) was attending Oldham Theatre Workshop at the time she landed the role of Rachel Jordache. She appeared there as Rat in a production of *Dick Whittington*. She also acted in *Scrooge* with the Saddleworth Players at Millgate Theatre, Delph, near Oldham, as well as in school and church productions in Dobcross. The teenage actress has played netball for Greater Manchester, Lancashire Under-14s, Oldham Town Under-15s and Oldham Netball Club, who won the National Under-13s Championships.

MO McGEE

Sister of Rosie Banks, Mo McGee took a job behind the bar at Barry Grant's nightclub, La Luz, at the same time as Rosie was planning to buy a house in Brookside Close. She later joined a singles' club in the hope of finding Mr Right. She met barman Kevin there and started going out with him, but he was really more interested in Rosie.

☆ ☆ ☆

Tina Malone trained at Childwall Arts Theatre and has appeared in two feature films, as Edna Clotworthy in director Terrence Davies's *Long Day Closes* and as Mrs Crane in Frank Clarke's *Blonde Fist*, starring the director's sister, Margi Clarke. She was also on TV in *Harry Enfield's Television Programme*, *Terraces*, *Between the Lines*, *Sin Bin* and *Common as Muck*.

Tina's stage appearances include *Murder at Rathbone House*, *Marmalade's Magic Christmas*, the revues *A Spoonful of Sugar* and *Sentimental Journey*, *Lux 2*, *Cartoon Capers*, *Masquerade* and, at the Liverpool Playhouse, *Running for Cover*.

Gillian Kearney (b. Liverpool, 9 May 1972) was only 14 when she took the role of Damon Grant's girlfriend DEBBIE McGRATH in *Brookside* and the three-part spin-off *Damon & Debbie*. She has since appeared in the film *Shirley Valentine* (as the young Shirley), the TV movie *The Final Frame* and in the television police series *Waterfront Beat*.

Sheila Grier (b. Glasgow, 11 February 1959) played nurse SANDRA MAGHIE, who was held hostage with housemates Pat Hancock and Kate Moses by a crazed gunman. She had previously taken the role of Miss Richardson in *High Road*, in 1983, and since leaving *Brookside* has appeared on TV alongside Mark McManus in *Taggart* and as a barrister defending Kate Hughes on a death by reckless driving charge in *Emmerdale*.

Judith Barker was best known on TV as Janet Barlow (née Reid), Ken's second wife, in *Coronation Street*, and was Pauline Kent in *The Practice* before playing AUDREY MANNERS in *Brookside*. Audrey met her death after contracting the deadly virus that hit the Close in March 1995. Judith had previously acted EILEEN SALTER in the serial.

Brian Murphy (b. Ventnor, Isle of Wight, 25 September 1933) was best known on television as George Roper in both *Man About the House* and its spin-off, *George and Mildred*, before playing GEORGE MANNERS in *Brookside*, trying to woo back his wife but ending up a victim of the Close's deadly virus. He was later revealed to have carried the virus with him from Kenya. Brian also acted Ernest in the BBC radio serial *Citizens*.

Lawrence Mullin (b. Liverpool, 5 August 1953) had a long-running role in *Coronation Street* as Steve Fisher, boyfriend of Suzie Birchall, before other TV appearances in *Juliet Bravo*, *The Bill* and *The Chief*. In 1993, he joined *Brookside* briefly as STEVE MATHEWS, divorced husband of Lyn, Frank Rogers's fiancée.

Tony Scoggins (b. Anthony Scoggo in Liverpool) played Bobby Grant's friend MATTY NOLAN, who was revealed to be Barry Grant's real father. Tony was on TV in *Boys from the Blackstuff* and *Hearts and Minds,* and in the film *No Surrender*.

Edward Clayton (b. Shelfield, Staffordshire, 9 October 1940), who played ARTHUR PARKINSON of the Commonwealth and Empire Club, had already portrayed Stan Harvey in *Crossroads*. He was later seen as garage owner Tom Casey in *Coronation Street*.

Dicken Ashworth (b. Terence Dicken Ashworth in Todmorden, Yorkshire, 18 July 1946), who was computer buff ALAN PARTRIDGE, is one of the busiest actors around. He was in the films *Tess* and *Chariots of Fire*, and on TV in such programmes as *Juliet Bravo*, *Minder*, *The Gentle Touch*, *Nanny*, *Scab* and *Return to Treasure Island*. After *Brookside*, Dicken played Jeff Horton – father of Terry Duckworth's tragic wife, Lisa – in *Coronation Street*. His *Brookside* character married Samantha and they later emigrated to the Gulf state of Qatar.

Dinah May (b. Heswall, Cheshire, 9 September 1954), a former Miss Great Britain, who played SAMANTHA PARTRIDGE, later became film director Michael Winner's receptionist.

Julie Peasgood had made dozens of TV appearances when she joined *Brookside* as FRAN PEARSON, Sue Sullivan's friend. She has also performed with the RSC and later played Eden in the Carla Lane sitcom *Luv* and became TV critic for *Good Morning… with Anne and Nick*.

Stand-up comic Duggie Brown (b. Rotherham, South Yorkshire, 7 August 1940), brother of former *Coronation Street* actress Lynne Perrie, was RAY PIPER, who took over from Ron Dixon as compère at the Legion. Duggie, who shot to fame on TV in *The Comedians*, has also played two roles in *All Creatures Great and Small* and appeared in *The Bill*.

Tricia Penrose (b. Patricia Penrose in Liverpool, 9 April 1970) was W.P.C. EMMA REID, whose affair with Rod Corkhill ended his engagement to Kirsty Brown. At the age of 14, Tricia had acted Damon Grant's girlfriend RUTH in the serial and subsequently was Elsa Feldmann's friend Louise in *Emmerdale*, a Cotswolds hotel receptionist booking in Ken Barlow and Alma Sedgewick in *Coronation Street*, and barmaid Gina Ward in *Heartbeat*.

BEV McLOUGHLIN

Tarty sister of Lyn Matthews, Bev McLoughlin tore the Dixon family apart by having an affair with Ron, in whose shop she worked as an assistant. Bev later told Ron that she was pregnant. He persuaded her not to have an abortion, saying that a baby would cement their relationship. It was only much later that he found out the truth that the father of baby Josh was his own son Mike, who had stepped into his shoes when he felt remorse and thought he should return to wife DD. On finding that DD could not face seeing him and was staying longer at the convent to which she had fled, he installed Bev in no. 8.

When Ron took Bev to the Legion, where he had previously been compère, she flirted with his successor Ray Piper, who persuaded her to enter a talent contest.

It was only at the wedding of Frank and Lyn Rogers in December 1993 that DD found out that Bev was pregnant. She slapped Ron, and son Tony joined in. Hours later, tragedy struck as Tony travelled to the reception in the Rolls-Royce driven by Frank, which crashed and left the teenager in a coma. He later died.

On learning that Mike was the father of Josh, Ron left Bev again and returned to DD. But, with time to reflect, he returned to Bev, feeling that they were right for each other – despite her being the mother of his grandson.

Bev agreed to move into Ron's house after DD left Brookside Close in 1995 and set about feeding Ron 'healthy' meals, to his consternation, and installing hens in the back garden – as well as the sign 'Bevron' over the door.

☆ ☆ ☆

Sarah White (b. Liverpool, 21 March 1969) trained at the Rose Bruford College of Drama. She joined *Brookside* shortly after leaving drama school, but she also had a small speaking part in *Dante et Beatrice en Liverpool* for the French station Channel 7 and co-devised and performed *Fondant Fancies and Forbidden Fruit* at the Old Red Lion, Islington, London's celebrated fringe theatre venue.

KATIE ROGERS

Younger daughter of Frank and Chrissy, Katie Rogers and her sister Sammy and brother Geoff lived at no. 7 Brookside Close, then moved to no. 5 in May 1989 when the Grants' house went up for auction. Katie was the more introverted and intense child of the family – a quality she gained from her mother – and found a cause in the Green movement. Environmentally aware, she began collecting newspapers to be recycled.

She also tried to clean up a local brook but fell in and was rescued by two friends. She was taken to hospital and thought to have swallowed toxic waste. Her parents put aside their financial problems, seeing them pale into insignificance beside the threatened health of their daughter. Fortunately, she was not affected.

Katie became interested in dancing and attended classes with her friend Siobhan and also took up trombone lessons at school. Less happily, she was bullied at school by a girl called Bagga, who tried to make her steal money. On one occasion, she stole some loose change from her mother but eventually confessed to her actions.

When Frank and Chrissy's marriage broke up, Katie and her mother stayed with Gina, an old student friend of Chrissy. Katie pleaded with her mother to return to Frank, which she did, but not for long. On the day of sister Sammy's wedding to Owen Daniels – following the discovery by Katie's sister that she was pregnant – Chrissy left the Close for good. Katie watched from her bedroom window at no. 5 as Chrissy left with her cases after leaving her wedding ring on the bedside table.

Worse was to come when Frank decided to marry Lyn Mathews, the sister of one of his workmates who had been killed in a lorry crash while doing him a favour. On the wedding day, the couple left the register office ceremony to travel to the reception in a Rolls-Royce. With Frank at the wheel, they crashed into a wall after swerving to avoid a drug-crazed Jimmy Corkhill driving towards them. Frank was killed and Ron Dixon's son Tony – who was along for the ride – went into a coma and later died.

Katie blamed Lyn for Frank's death because she had allowed him to drink and drive, and he had only a short time earlier suffered a minor heart attack. Her innocence and mixed-up feelings were taken advantage of by religious cult leader Simon Howe, who worked at the garage. He provided Katie with a shoulder to cry on, enticed her into his group and slept with her. He persuaded Katie to let him and the group use no. 5 for meetings and Simon moved in with her.

She began to see through Simon when he ordered her to sleep with Terry Sullivan, who had also been entrapped by him. She ran out and stayed with Jacqui Dixon, while Simon and his group stayed on in her house as squatters.

Barry Grant bought the house – which had belonged to his parents before the Rogers family moved in – and sought to evict them,

Noreen Kershaw played KATHY ROACH, Jimmy Corkhill's former girlfriend and best friend of Sheila Grant. Noreen has appeared on TV in *Boys from the Blackstuff* (as the social security employee who had to deal with Yosser Hughes), in *Watching* (as Brenda Wilson's mother) and in the 'Alan Bleasdale Presents' production *Self Catering*. On stage, in Liverpool, she was the first actress to play Shirley Valentine. She lives in Manchester and is married to Australian-based theatre director Peter Oyston.

Eithne Browne (b. Huyton, Liverpool, 25 November 1954) portrayed CHRISSY ROGERS, first wife of Frank. The actress appeared in Liverpool and London's West End as Barbara Dickson's understudy in the Willy Russell musical *Blood Brothers*. She has acted on TV in *Albion Market*, *The Practice* (as Mrs McClusky) and *The Marksman* (starring as Muriel Brand, whose son was played by Kevin Carson – her son Geoff in *Brookside*).

Peter Christian (b. Dingle, Liverpool, 14 August 1947) played FRANK ROGERS. He appeared as Sammy in the original stage production of Willy Russell's *Blood Brothers*, at the Liverpool Playhouse, and spent six months in the London West End production of the show. He was also in Willy Russell's *Stags and Hens*, at the Young Vic. He had previously appeared in *Brookside* as FRANK BLACKBURN, a friend of Gavin Taylor, and was also on television in *Boys from the Blackstuff*, *Give Us a Break*, *Scully*, *The Brothers McGregor*, *Travelling Man* and *Truckers*.

Liz Gebhardt (b. Elisabeth Ann Gebhardt in Liverpool, 12 April 1945), who played MRS ROGERS in *Brookside*, had portrayed goody-goody Maureen Bullock in *Please Sir!* and *The Fenn Street Gang*, and an art student in the award-winning *The Naked Civil Servant*. She has also taken four different parts in *The Bill*.

Paul Barber was best known to television viewers as Del Boy's dippy mate Denzil in the sitcom *Only Fools and Horses...* before playing jailbird GREG SALTER in *Brookside*. Greg carried out a robbery at Litrotech for which Mick Johnson was mistakenly arrested. Paul also took the roles of Wesley in *The Brothers McGregor* and Malcolm in *The Front Line*.

breaking in armed with a shotgun. But he was overpowered and held hostage. After a while, Simon planted a home-made bomb in the house and released Barry just before it went off, hoping to destroy no. 5 so that no one could have it. Simon was the only one who sustained serious injuries and, although he recovered, he later died after gassing himself in Barry Grant's car. Life returned to normal for Katie and she later moved into a flat with Jacqui Dixon.

☆ ☆ ☆

Diane Burke (b. Liverpool, 17 July 1976) first became interested in acting while starring in a school production of *Cinderella*. She was encouraged by her drama teacher and invited to audition for the role of Katie Rogers in *Brookside* in 1988, taking over from Debbie Reynolds.

Diane, who lives in Huyton, attended Knowsley Hey School, in Liverpool, where she already knew her former screen brother Kevin Carson, who was also a pupil.

SINBAD (SWEENEY)

Abandoned at birth by his mother and brought up in a children's home, wily window cleaner Thomas Henry Edward Sweeney was nicknamed Sinbad after the fictional sailor because of his circular cleaning action, like that of a sailor dousing a porthole, and is noted for his shoddy work.

For many years, his alliance with Jimmy Corkhill spelled no good and usually involved enterprises well on the wrong side of the law, such as when they brightened up Brookside

Close with a huge Christmas tree – at the expense of a children's home. Another time, they offered residents cut-price turkeys for Christmas, although their customers had not realized they were being offered live birds.

Sinbad was love-struck when Caroline Choi moved into the Close and followed her to London when she left. But she rejected his advances and, when he returned to Liverpool, he found that another window cleaner had stolen his round. He started a new business, Sinbad Services, moved into his own flat, and built up his window-cleaning round again.

Romance came for Sinbad with an engagement to Josie Johnson's best friend, Marcia Barrett. Homeless, she moved in with Josie and husband Mick, who were also putting up Mick's smarmy brother Ellis, with whom Marcia had once had a relationship. Ellis constantly put down Sinbad and told Marcia she would be better off going back to him. Marcia resisted Ellis's advances and stuck with Sinbad, although she told him that she did not expect him to take Ellis's jibes lying down and be walked all over. Sinbad got his own back once by emptying a bucketful of window-cleaning water over Ellis's head.

Marcia encouraged Sinbad to search for his mother. Told that she was dead, but there was a surviving sister, Sinbad found Ruth Sweeney in Runcorn, Cheshire. She did not want to rake up the past and would rather he had not tracked her down. Eventually, she admitted to being his long-lost mother.

Elated, Sinbad proposed to Marcia by having a message, 'Marcia, will you marry me? Love Sinbad', put on the giant electronic scoreboard at Everton Football Club's ground. However, their relationship deteriorated when she told Sinbad that she could not have children. They split up but were reunited and planned a double Valentine's Day wedding with Ellis Johnson and Marianne Dwyer in 1993.

At the stag night, Ellis's brother Mick confided in Sinbad that he loved Marianne, and Sinbad told Marcia, who promptly tried to get Mick and Josie back together. Sinbad felt compelled to tell Marianne about how Mick felt and Marcia did not go through with the wedding. Marianne jilted Ellis at the altar.

Sinbad – who became caretaker of the Brookside Parade shopping centre after it was built in 1991 – later befriended Mandy Jordache, even helping to cover up Mandy's murder of her violent husband Trevor Jordache, who had served time for beating up Mandy and returned to terrorize her.

Although the battered wife had not confessed to killing Trevor, Sinbad found the knife that had done the deed and saw a pile of earth in the garden, where Mandy's elder daughter Beth had buried the body. He offered to build a patio, knowing that this would help to conceal the body.

More gory for Sinbad was digging up the body when Trevor's sister Brenna asked for his signet ring, following the discovery by police of a decomposed corpse that Mandy conveniently identified as her husband. He did the deed while Beth was celebrating her 18th birthday party at the La Luz nightclub.

Sinbad was fond of Mandy, but she avoided a relationship with him until his mother – who stayed in the extension at the Jordaches' house while suffering an illness – announced that she was emigrating to Australia to live with her brother Jake. Sinbad was invited, too, and he was tempted to go until Mandy revealed her true feelings for him.

But it was a blow when he found out that she had been sleeping with loan shark Kenny Maguire to pay off her debts. Planing revenge, Sinbad paid a final visit to Maguire – only to find that he had already been beaten up.

Then, in January 1995, Sinbad and Mandy fled the Close with Beth and Rachel when Trevor Jordache's body was discovered under the patio. They went to Dublin but were eventually caught by the police, who refused to believe Sinbad's confession that he had killed Trevor.

Mandy was charged with murder but allowed out on Sinbad's bail. While waiting for the trial, Mandy learned that she was pregnant with Sinbad's baby. It was a great shock when Mandy was jailed for life.

Michael Starke (b. Liverpool, 13 November 1957) is a former dustman who entered show-business as the front man in a comedy show band that toured the variety club circuit in Liverpool, Newcastle and Scotland. He became known as a comedian and impressionist. While performing in lunchtime theatre in Liverpool, he met *Brookside* casting director Dorothy Andrew, who gave him the role of Sinbad. His other television work includes *Boys from the Blackstuff* (as a gasman), *Tripods*, *Making Out* and *Watching*.

He was in the films *Distant Voices* and writer Alan Bleasdale's *No Surrender* (as a member of a punk group) and has appeared on stage in such productions as *Blood Brothers*, *One for the Road*, *The Resistible Rise of Arturo Ui*, *The Taming of the Shrew*, *She Stoops to Conquer*, *Hamlet*, *The Three Sisters*, *The Winter's Tale*, *No Holds Bard* and a tour of the musical *Be-Bop-a-Lula*.

TERRY SULLIVAN

A childhood friend of Jack-the-Lad Barry Grant, Terry Sullivan became a Brookside Close resident when he moved in with girlfriend Michelle Jones, whose sister Petra Taylor committed suicide after the death of her husband Gavin and a brief fling with Barry. Michelle lived with her elder sister, Marie Jackson, wife of George Jackson, who was jailed on a conspiracy to burgle charge after being framed by local villain Tommy McArdle.

Terry and Barry, who started a tool-hire business together, found themselves implicated in a casino robbery after McArdle used their car. Later, Terry was badly beaten up by McArdle's henchmen, and he split up with Michelle after her affair with dance teacher Richard de Saville.

Michelle and sister Marie moved to Leeds to start a new life, and Terry moved in with Pat Hancock and Sandra Maghie. He and Pat became firm friends and started a van-hire business. When they found themselves competing with another local firm for contracts, Terry met Vicki Cleary, whose brothers did not take kindly to the rivalry. The couple were together for more than a year but eventually split up. Terry

Alexandra Pigg (b. Sandra McKibbin in Liverpool), who played PETRA TAYLOR during the serial's first year, went on to star in the films *Letter to Brezhnev*, *Strapless* and *Chicago Joe and the Showgirl*, and has been on TV in *Making Out* and *Murder East, Murder West*.

was unlucky in love again, with croupier Alison, but found new romance after moving in as a lodger with solicitor Jonathan Gordon-Davies and meeting his secretary, Sue Harper. Their relationship blossomed and she encouraged him to get a taxi licence and go into a business partnership with the owner of a black cab. Mick Johnson later became Terry's partner.

Terry and Sue married and had a son, Daniel, but Sue's dark secret was that she had seen former lover Martin Howes for a one-night stand and that he was Daniel's father. Terry knew he had been lied to after a medical check showed that he was infertile. He threw Sue out of the house and went through a period of depression. The death of her mother brought the two back together and they started afresh.

But Terry's world fell apart when, in 1991, Sue and Daniel fell to their deaths off scaffolding next to the new Brookside Parade of shops. The following January, solicitor Graeme Curtis – who had been pestering Sue in the office – was found guilty of the murders and subsequently committed suicide in jail, but Terry found out only much later that Barry had been on the scaffolding with Sue on that day. At the time of her death, Sue had been pregnant – the result of Barry seducing her on the sofa one day at the house she shared with Terry.

Terry used the insurance money from Sue's death to buy Pizza Parade, the pizza parlour in Brookside Parade, although he later sold it to Mick Johnson. Terry also found romance with Fran Pearson, Sue's work friend who was also carrying Barry Grant's baby, but eventually gave her money to leave the country and start a new life. Before Fran left, Barry had kidnapped her and took Terry to a deserted beach in Southport, where he confessed that he had been with Sue on the scaffolding when she died, but she had caught her foot on it and fell as he held his hand out to save her. Dramatically offering Terry a shotgun, Barry invited him to mete out his own justice, but Terry preferred to let Barry suffer for the rest of his life.

Further romance came when Polish nanny Anna Wolska wanted Terry to marry her so that she could stay in Britain. But, when he fell for her in a big way, Anna decided that she could not go through with marriage.

Terry's mental state went rapidly downhill and, after selling Pizza Parade, he managed the garage, where he met Simon Howe, who sucked him into his religious cult, even trying to get him to sleep with young Katie Rogers. After being badly injured in an explosion that he had caused at the Rogers' house, no. 5, which Barry Grant had bought and hoped to take possession of, Simon kidnapped Barry and tried to get rid

of him by blowing up the house, but the plan misfired and Simon ended up in hospital.

The religious fanatic then slept rough in the woods, before persuading Terry to join him in a suicide pact. Simon took Barry's car, joined a hose to the exhaust and fed it into the vehicle, with him and Terry sitting in the front. Fortunately, Barry was on hand to pull Terry from the car, but Simon died.

Brian Regan (b. Liverpool, 2 October 1957) looked set for a career in professional football when he signed on as an apprentice for Liverpool. He was a goalkeeper, but left after suffering a slight injury and deciding to make acting his career. Brian became involved with the Liverpool Playhouse, while taking his A levels. Eventually, he gave up his exams to take a £26-a-week job as assistant stage manager there. He was at the Playhouse for six years, during which time he was promoted to stage manager and started acting.

His first major break was playing Kav in Willy Russell's *Stags and Hens*. Moving on to repertory theatres around the country, Brian acted in many plays, from Shakespeare's *Hamlet* to Jim Morris's *Blood on the Dole*. His first TV appearance took him back to his other love, football, when he played goalkeeper Stevie King in the children's serial *Murphy's Mob*. He joined *Brookside* as Terry Sullivan in episode six and soon became a regular in the cast.

Brian married long-time girlfriend Lisa Hunt, a secretary in the *Brookside* offices, in 1989. They have a daughter, Ashleigh Gemma, and two Rottweilers, and live in the Knowsley suburb of Liverpool.

Many celebrities have appeared as themselves in *Brookside*. They include astrologer RUSSELL GRANT opening a hospital fete, presenter PAULA YATES interviewed by student Karen Grant, a budding journalist, after judging the Liverpool University Rag Week Parade, Liverpool pop group THE FARM in a concert attended by Geoff Rogers and his girlfriend, SARAH GREENE as guest of honour at a charity fashion show, EAMONN HOLMES and LORRAINE KELLY interviewing Penny Crosbie on breakfast television, LOYD GROSSMAN and drag artist LILY SAVAGE opening Grants restaurant and MICHAEL PARKINSON interviewing Patricia Farnham and Jackie Corkhill on a chat show debating Mandy and Beth Jordaches' jail sentence and the campaign against it.

Back row: Reg Holdsworth (Ken Morley), Angie Freeman (Deborah McAndrew), Curly Watts (Kevin Kennedy), Raquel Wolstenhulme (Sarah Lancashire), Des Barnes (Philip Middlemiss), Andy McDonald (Nicholas Cochrane), Steve McDonald (Simon Gregson), Liz McDonald (Beverley Callard), Jim McDonald (Charles Lawson). Third row: Mike Baldwin (Johnny Briggs), Alma Baldwin (Amanda Barrie), Kevin Webster (Michael Le Vell), Rosie Webster (Emma Collinge), Sally Webster (Sally Whittaker), Jack Duckworth (William Tarmey), Phyllis Pearce (Jill Summers), Vera Duckworth (Elizabeth Dawn), Percy Sugden (Bill Waddington), Derek Wilton (Peter Baldwin), Martin Platt (Sean Wilson), David Platt (Thomas Ormson), Gail Platt (Helen Worth), Audrey Roberts (Sue Nicholls), Don Brennan (Geoff Hinsliff). Seated: Ken Barlow (William Roache), Emily Bishop (Eileen Derbyshire), Betty Turpin (Betty Driver), Bet Gilroy (Julie Goodyear), Rita Fairclough (Barbara Knox), Mavis Wilton (Thelma Barlow), Ivy Brennan (Lynne Perrie), Alf Roberts (Bryan Mosley). Front: Tracy Barlow (Dawn Acton), Vicky Arden (Chloe Newsome), Sarah Platt (Lynsay King), Nick Platt (Warren Jackson).

C oronation Street, Queen of the Soaps, was first broadcast by ITV at 7p.m. on Friday 9 December 1960. In the late fifties, books, theatre and cinema were already reflecting working-class culture in a way that had not been seen before and, with the *Street*, creator Tony Warren did the same for television, with a cast of finely drawn characters and realistic dialogue that made the programme a true reflection of working-class life in the north of England. He wrote 12 episodes, plus a 13th that would see the Street – in the fictional Manchester suburb of Weatherfield – bulldozed to the ground if it did not take off. He need not have worried: today, it is the longest-running serial on British television and still the most popular.

Made by Granada Television, the twice-weekly drama – admired for its high standard of writing and acting – gained an extra weekly episode in 1989, and viewers get the chance to see repeat episodes during the afternoons.

Its early, uncompromising characters included hairnetted harridan Ena Sharples, snooty publican Annie Walker and tart-with-a-heart Elsie Tanner. Also there in the first episode was Ken Barlow, played by William Roache, who is still in the programme today. There have been two *Street* spin-offs, the sitcoms *Pardon the Expression*, featuring Arthur Lowe as Leonard Swindley, and *The Brothers McGregor*, starring Paul Barber and Philip Whitchurch, who played half-brothers who broke up Eddie Yeats's engagement party.

VICKY ARDEN

Alec and Bet Gilroy became legal guardians of Victoria Arden after her parents were both killed in a car crash. She was the granddaughter Alec had found after discovering Sandra, his long-lost daughter from his first marriage, which had broken up very quickly.

Sandra had married a solicitor and lived in a plush house. Vicky went to private school and owned a horse, so holidays in a Weatherfield backstreet pub were not an obvious attraction. But meeting Steve McDonald was compensation. Alec tried desperately to stop her seeing Steve and she resisted his sexual advances until finally losing her virginity to him. This was a less important event for Steve than for Vicky because he two-timed her with nurse Alison Rathbone, with the result that both dumped him.

After Alec left Bet to become entertainments manager for a cruise line, based in Southampton, Vicky continued to return to the Rovers during her school holidays, treating Bet as a natural grandmother.

On reaching her 18th birthday in February 1995, Vicky inherited £240,000 left by her parents. To Bet's distress, Vicky immediately abandoned her studies and decided that money would buy her more than education ever could. After a visit to her grandfather in Southampton to explain her decision, Vicky returned looking bored and keen to confide in old flame Steve McDonald, although he was seeing hairdresser Fiona Middleton and Vicky was left out in the cold. She found a way back into his life by putting up money for his T-shirt company, but learned business the hard way by losing £1500 to produce an order for Costello's nightclub, which went bust without paying the bill.

Instead of putting Vicky off, this experience inspired her to enrol on a business studies course at the local technical college and become Steve's business partner, insisting that she had absolute control over the finances – which

annoyed Fiona. Fiona was even more annoyed when Vicky flew off to Dublin with Steve for a 'business' weekend and eventually dumped him, leaving Vicky to walk back into his arms.

☆ ☆ ☆

Chloe Newsome (b. Sheffield, South Yorkshire, December 1976) joined *Coronation Street* in 1991 at the age of 14. Chloe, who recalls her favourite scene in the serial as when Alec Gilroy had a tarantula loose in the Rovers Return kitchen, lives in Sheffield with her parents and – unlike her *Street* character – attended a comprehensive school.

TRICIA ARMSTRONG

Curly Watts thought he was on to something good when he caught single mum Tricia Armstrong's nine-year-old son Jamie shoplifting in Bettabuys supermarket in February 1994.

She was separated from her violent husband Carl Armstrong, a lorry driver, and started going out with Curly. When Jack Duckworth agreed to babysit Jamie one evening while the couple went out, Carl arrived on the doorstep and promptly thumped him, thinking he had met his estranged wife's new lover.

This was enough to put Curly off continuing the relationship and he saw no more of Tricia until she arrived in Coronation Street in 1995 to rent Deirdre Rachid's old house from Mike Baldwin.

Tricia caused a stir when she locked herself out and Jack rushed to her aid. Vera became suspicious when she realized that they already knew one another. Tricia then landed a job as cleaner at the Rovers Return. Although Curly thought there could only be trouble around the corner, he was getting over his broken engagement to Raquel Wolstenhulme and dated Tricia again. This caused some friction between the two women and Bet Gilroy eventually told Tricia to look for a new job or face the sack.

☆ ☆ ☆

Tracy Brabin worked in Theatre In Education companies, community theatre and rep., before leaving Loughborough University with a drama degree. To get an Equity actors' union card, she set up a company to tour schools with *The Road Safety Show*, playing Countess Crash Barrier.

The actress is best known on TV as Ginny in two series of *Outside Edge* and David Jason's girlfriend, Sandra, in *A Bit of a Do* – her first screen appearance. Tracy has also been on TV as a presenter of *But First This...* and *Corners*, and acted in *Hale & Pace*, *Mother Goose*, *Diamonds in Brown Paper*, *Aladdin*, *El C.I.D.* (as Fran), *Red Dwarf* (as Camille), *Family*, *In the Dark* and episodes of *Peak Practice*, as well

---

Kathy Jamieson, wife of John McArdle – who played Det. Con. Meadows in *Coronation Street* and Billy Corkhill in *Brookside* – was SANDRA ARDEN, Alec Gilroy's long-lost daughter from his first marriage, which ended in divorce. Shortly after Alec tracked her down, she and her husband died in a car crash, leaving Alec responsible for their daughter Vicky. Kathy previously played a potential buyer of Chalkie Whiteley's house in the *Street* and a policewoman in *Brookside*.

as playing the Duchess of York in the American TV drama *The Royal Romance of Charles and Diana* – Tracy was five months pregnant when she auditioned for the part!

Her stage roles have included Louise in *Road* at the Octagon Theatre, Bolton, and Tanzi in *Totterdown Tanzi* at Bristol Old Vic, as well as Sandra in *Stiff Options* and Amy in *The Fancy Man*, both on tour. Tracy has also co-scripted, with actress Beverly Hills, a sitcom provisionally titled *The Life of Riley*, about a women's weight-loss group on a northern council estate.

She lives in North London with actor Richard Platt – who plays barman James White in *Peak Practice* – and their daughter, Lois.

ALMA BALDWIN

Prepared to be treated like a doormat, Alma Sedgewick had an on-off romance with Mike Baldwin after beating him at a round of golf and seemed prepared to be kicked in the teeth again and again, as long as he always returned to her. Mike finally married Alma and settled down.

Alma Marie Sedgewick, born on 18 October 1944, co-owned Jim's Café in Rosamund Street with husband Jim and in April 1981, with their divorce imminent, decided that she would run the business herself. This meant telling Elsie Tanner, the manageress, that she was being demoted to waitress, although in reality she was doing the same job because Alma rarely showed her face.

With divorce proceedings against Jim under way, Alma went to live in Spain and fell for a property tycoon there. In June 1989, she was back in Weatherfield alone. She then took more

of an interest in the day-to-day running of the café and offered Gail Tilsley a 40 per cent share in the business as her partner.

Alma ruffled feathers immediately by dismissing Phyllis Pearce on the grounds that she was surplus to requirements. She also infuriated Gail when she fell for Mike Baldwin and disappeared for long lunches and shopping trips. Mike dropped Alma when he met estate agent Dawn Prescott. She moved into his new dockland flat with him but left him after Mike ripped off her brother in a property deal, which gave Alma the cue to return to the cockney Romeo.

She moved out of her flat above the café and in with Mike, but his affair with Jackie Ingram, widow of his former boss Peter, led to their break-up. Alma returned to her flat above the café but longed for him to go back to her.

In the meantime, she found romance with Ken Barlow, Mike's arch-enemy following his affair with Ken's wife and marriage to his daughter. Mike himself went through a short-lived marriage to Jackie. When Ken agreed to spend Christmas Day 1991 with estranged wife Deirdre and daughter Tracy, Mike – by now divorced from Jackie – visited Alma at her flat and slept with her. When Ken took Alma to a Cotswolds hotel over New Year, she confessed what had happened and fled back home. Mike then proposed marriage and the couple were finally wed on 19 June 1992.

Having her own business meant that Alma had something to occupy her mind when Mike was being particularly difficult or doing an especially dodgy piece of wheeler-dealing. But it was a shock when he told her that he had a son, Mark, from a relationship with florist Maggie Redman (née Dunlop). Alma found it even more difficult when Mike began taking an interest in Mark's life and insisted on sending him to private school, away from Weatherfield Comprehensive and teacher Ken Barlow. The decision came at a time when the Baldwins' own finances were tight and they needed every penny themselves.

In March 1995, Alma's first husband, Jim, died and left her £2000. Mike advised her to invest it and decide carefully how to spend it, but Alma went straight out and bought a car at a bargain price, much to his annoyance. Trying to downgrade the quality of the vehicle, Mike was even more miffed that it turned out to be a bargain and his recently bought Mercedes had been stolen and had parts from an Allegro in it.

Amanda Barrie (b. Shirley Ann Broadbent in Ashton-under-Lyne, Lancashire, 14 September 1939) was the granddaughter of theatre owner Ernest Broadbent. She was christened Shirley after Shirley Temple and, aged three, started dancing and singing at his theatre. Her first role was as a fairy on a Christmas tree. Later, she took up ballet and appeared in pantomime.

At the age of nine, when her parents split up, Amanda went to boarding school and, four years later, left school and moved to London to became a chorus girl. She made her professional debut in *Babes in the Wood* at the Finsbury Park Empire, earning £2.50 a week, was once a member of Lionel Blair's dance troupe and waltzed with Danny La Rue.

Since then, her many London West End stage performances have included *On the Brighter Side*, *See You Inside*, *A Public Mischief*, *Any Wednesday*, *Twelfth Night*, *Oh! Kay*, *Absurd Person Singular* and *Donkey's Years* (both alongside Paul Eddington) *Noises Off* and, with Julia McKenzie, *Stepping Out*. During a season at the Bristol Old Vic Theatre, Amanda was in the revue *Little by Little*, *The Beggar's Opera* and *Hobson's Choice*. She also played Sally Bowles in *Cabaret* in Johannesburg, South Africa, was in the fringe revue *Up the 80s* in London, and acted the Iron Lady in a national tour of *The Cabinet Mole*.

Her cinema roles have included a Glamcab driver in *Carry On Cabby* and the title role in *Carry On Cleo*, as well as the films *I Gotta Horse* and *One of Our Dinosaurs Is Missing*. Amanda made her TV debut as a dancer in the chorus, then as an actress in comedy sketches, for Morecambe and Wise in their first series, *Running Wild*, and was a hostess in the quiz show *Double Your Money*, presented by Hughie Green. She landed her first major TV acting role, as secretary Sandra, in the sitcom *The Bulldog Breed*, in 1960.

Amanda was in Jimmy Tarbuck's first television series and has since appeared on screen in *A Midsummer Night's Dream* (as Hermia), *Struggles* (alongside Tom Conti), *Are You Being Served?*, *Spooner's Patch*, *Sanctuary* and *L for Lester*. She joined *Coronation Street* in 1981 for just two weeks but returned in the same role as a regular eight years later. Amanda and her actor-director husband Robin Hunter married in 1967 and separated 13 years later, but they have never divorced. She lives in Covent Garden, London, and Manchester.

MIKE BALDWIN

Romeo Mike Baldwin came to Coronation Street from London, where he had begun building his business empire. He is known as a tough boss and has an eye for the ladies.

Born in Bermondsey, South London, on 16 February 1942, Mike worked as a tea-boy in a

radio factory after leaving school at 15, then set up a TV and radio repair shop in his family's home. After venturing into several other businesses, he moved into the rag trade with a denims factory in London's East End. Branching out, Mike decided to open another factory in the north of England and started Baldwin's Casuals, in Coronation Street, Weatherfield.

Shortly after his arrival in 1976, he began a relationship with Rovers Return barmaid Bet Lynch. He bought no. 5 Coronation Street and she moved in with him. When she became serious about Mike, he tried to get rid of her by saying his wife was due to arrive from London, but the woman turned out to be just another girlfriend, Anne Woodley. He eventually forced Bet out by selling the house.

A string of lovers followed, including Suzie Birchall, who worked in The Western Front, a denims boutique that Mike owned for a while. Mike also had a son, Mark, by Maggie Dunlop, and then rocked the Barlows' marriage by having an affair with Deirdre. It looked as if she would leave Ken for him but, when it came to the crunch, she ditched Mike.

As a result, Ken became his arch-enemy and even more furious when Mike began dating his daughter, Susan. The romance became serious and the couple planned to marry in May 1986. Ken refused to give Susan away but changed his mind at the last moment, although that did not alter his hatred for the cockney businessman.

Mike gave little encouragement to Susan in her idea to design children's clothes with a business called Hopscotch. It appeared that he simply wanted her to play the housewife, with a meal ready on the table when he arrived home. The marriage ended in 1987 when Susan became pregnant and decided to have an abortion.

Other romances followed, then café owner Alma Sedgewick came into Mike's life. She was willing to stick with him no matter what, with the result that she was ditched first for estate agent Dawn Prescott, then for Jackie Ingram. Mike had met Dawn when he was selling his factory to developer Maurice Jones and moving from his bachelor flat into a new one. She moved in with him but soon tired of his selfish, scheming ways. Alma returned to Mike and took Dawn's place.

He took a job at a textile factory owned by Peter Ingram, who subsequently died. Mike convinced Peter's widow Jackie that he was indispensable to her in running the business and they subsequently became lovers. The couple wed in 1991, but the marriage was over two weeks later, when Jackie discovered that Mike had used her money to help Alma to overcome financial problems at her café. Jackie gave him £100,000 to get him out of her life.

Mike subsequently prised Alma away from his old rival, Ken Barlow, married her on 19 June 1992 and opened a new business, MVB Motors, with mechanic Kevin Webster at the helm. Alma then had to absorb the news that Mike had a son, Mark, from his relationship years earlier with Maggie Redman (née Dunlop), whose husband had died. Mike began to take an interest in Mark's life, taking him out on trips and sending him to private school, at a time when Mike and Alma were facing financial problems.

Mike also used the link with Maggie to antagonize Ken Barlow, whom she was seeing. Maggie finally dumped Ken – who had been one of Mark's teachers at Weatherfield Comprehensive – after he became immersed in the whole saga. Then, in January 1995, Mike took great delight in not letting Ken into no. 1 Coronation Street to remove some family heirlooms after Deirdre left for Morocco and sold him the house for £15,000 plus the profit after he sold it on. But Ken got the upper hand for once, borrowing a spare key from Emily Bishop and taking what was his.

☆ ☆ ☆

Johnny Briggs (b. Battersea, South London, 5 September 1935) was evacuated to Guildford, Surrey, during the first year of the war, then to his uncle's in Winsford, Cheshire. While there, Johnny sang solo treble in a church choir.

Back in South London after the war, the 12-year-old auditioned for a place at the Italia Conti Stage Academy after his mother saw a newspaper advertisement. Out of 120 children auditioned, Johnny and five others were awarded scholarships. It was 1947, and Millicent Martin, Nanette Newman and Anthony Newley were all in his year at drama school. Johnny was soon in the chorus of an Italian opera company

that came to London each year, singing *La Bohème*, *Tosca*, *Falstaff* and *Rigoletto*.

He was also in the 1948 film *Quartet*, alongside George Cole, and *Cosh Boy*, with Joan Collins, and sang and danced in the London revue *Sauce Tartare*: Audrey Hepburn was a member of the chorus and Johnny and the glamorous star sang one number together. On leaving drama school, Johnny was offered a job at the Windmill Theatre, London, where Bruce Forsyth and Bill Maynard were resident comedians.

Johnny started National Service in 1953. He was in the Royal Tank Regiment as a gunner and unpaid acting sergeant, stationed in Germany, before returning to Britain as an instructor. A day after he left the army, his 15-year-old sister died of a brain haemorrhage and he stayed at home with his parents for a year after the tragedy.

Then, he joined a repertory company in High Wycombe, Buckinghamshire. Johnny made his TV debut in *The Younger Generation*, a series of 11 plays that also featured John Thaw, Ronald Lacey and Judy Cornwell. Going back into films, he appeared in *Sink the Bismarck!*, *HMS Defiant* (with Dirk Bogarde and Alec Guinness), *Doctor in Love*, *Devil-Ship Pirates*, *The Last Escape*, *Perfect Friday* and *The Best Pair of Legs in the Business*, as well as the big-screen versions of the TV hits *Love Thy Neighbour* and *No Honestly*.

By then, he was known to TV viewers as Det. Sgt. Russell in the legendary series *No Hiding Place*, appearing for three years of its seven-year run. He was also on television in *The Plane Makers*, *The Saint*, *Department S*, *Private Eye*, *Softly Softly*, *Z-Cars*, *The Avengers*, *The Persuaders*, *Love Thy Neighbour*, *My Wife Next Door*, *Thick as Thieves*, *No Honestly* and *Yus My Dear*, before landing the role of taxi firm boss Clifford Leyton in *Crossroads* in 1973. Three years later, Johnny switched to *Coronation Street* as wide-eyed Mike Baldwin.

His stage work includes *Parcel Post* and *The Kitchen* at the Royal Court Theatre, a tour of *Doctor in the House*, *Dial M for Murder*, *Hasty Heart*, *Boeing-Boeing* and *Wait Until Dark*.

> **Sam Kydd** (b. Belfast, **15 February 1915**), who played FRANKIE BALDWIN, father of Mike, appeared in **200 films**, including *The Blue Lamp*, *Father Brown*, *Reach for the Sky*, *The Thirty Nine Steps* and *I'm All Right, Jack*, as well as playing the lovable smuggler Orlando O'Connor, first in *Crane*, then the children's series *Orlando*. Sam also featured as a garage owner in *Crossroads*. He died on **26 March 1982**.

Johnny and first wife Carole had two children, Mark and Karen. He and second wife Christine – who met while he was working on *Crossroads* – have four, Jenny Lou, Michael, Stephanie and Anthony, and live in Stourbridge, Worcestershire. Their marriage hit the rocks when he took a 21-year-old former air hostess on holiday to Barbados in 1986, but Johnny and Christine were later reunited.

A keen golfer, Johnny takes part in many celebrity tournaments. He has a flat at Salford Quays, near the Granada Television studios, and a holiday home in Florida.

KEN BARLOW

Born in Weatherfield on 9 October 1939, Ken Barlow was the local boy made good, who went to university and was a bit of a rebel. He was the son of post office supervisor Frank Barlow and hotel kitchen help Ida.

As a student, Ken's first girlfriend was Susan Cunningham, and Albert Tatlock accused him of being 'a proper stuck-up little snob' when he was anxious about her visiting him in Coronation Street.

On 4 August 1962, Ken married Albert's niece, Valerie Tatlock, and they had twins, Peter and Susan. Ken went through various jobs, as a teacher, personnel officer, junior warehouse executive and taxi driver. When hairdresser Valerie was fatally electrocuted by a faulty hairdryer plug, Ken sent the twins to live with her mother in Glasgow.

His second marriage, to Janet Reid, in October 1973, ended in divorce. She returned to Ken's house in February 1977, pleading with him to

take her back, but he refused. However, he did allow her to sleep on his sofa for the night, only to find in the morning that she had committed suicide by taking a drugs overdose.

Ken appeared to have found happiness when, on 27 July 1981, he wed Deirdre Langton and became editor of a free local newspaper, the *Weatherfield Recorder*, going into partnership with the owner. When he later bought out his partner, Ken put their house up as collateral. Deirdre's affair with smoothie Mike Baldwin in 1983 was a result of Ken's obsession with his job and his increasing lack of interest in her, but they patched up the marriage, just as it looked as if she would leave him.

Six years later, Ken began running stories in his paper about private council meetings. Deirdre, then a councillor, was suspected of supplying him with them, but his source was council secretary Wendy Crozier. The two had an affair and Deirdre threw Ken out. His relationship with Wendy quickly soured and, when his paper was bought by a bigger group, he was dismissed and found himself with neither home nor job.

Trying to pick up the pieces of his life, he returned to teaching and rented the flat above Alf Roberts's Mini Market in Coronation Street, his only true home.

His life continued to be inextricably linked with that of Mike Baldwin when he fell first for Alma Sedgewick – who was then reunited with Mike and, shortly afterwards, married him – and then for florist Maggie Redman, who had given birth to the cockney businessman's son, Mark, a decade earlier. But the strain of this and Mike's increasing interest in the welfare of his son led Ken and Maggie to break up.

In 1994, hairdresser Denise Osbourne fell for Ken – and became pregnant by him. She miscarried but found that she had been carrying twins and the other baby was alive. But she began to feel claustrophobic with Ken around and, after Deirdre married Moroccan waiter Samir Rachid, she realised that Ken still held a torch for her and dumped him.

When Denise went into labour, she did not want Ken to know. But, as she prepared for the birth in hospital, she phoned him and he was there for the arrival of son Daniel on 4 January 1995. Ken then asked Mike Baldwin whether he could buy no. 1 Coronation Street, which Deirdre had sold to him, but – jealous of Ken's son – Mike refused, saying he was renting it out.

Ken was always on hand to help Denise with baby Daniel, but she soon went back to her previous position of not wanting a relationship with Ken, and upset him by neither registering Daniel in Ken's surname nor naming him as the father. Eventually, Denise realized that she did want to marry Ken, but by then it was too late. All he wanted was a part in Daniel's life.

William Roache (b. William Patrick Roache in Ilkeston, Derbyshire, 25 April 1932) is the only surviving member of the original *Coronation Street* cast.

The son of a doctor, William attended Rydal School, in North Wales, and began studying medicine, taking his first MB. He abandoned it as a career to join the army and, during five years in the Royal Welch Fusiliers, he served in Jamaica, British Guiana, Bermuda, Germany and Arabia, and reached the rank of captain. In Arabia, he lived with Bedouin tribesmen and was the only Briton among 125 non-English-speaking Arabs.

Resigning his commission, William decided to take up acting and, after writing hundreds of letters to producers, was given a small part as a doctor in the 1958 film *Behind the Mask*, starring Michael Redgrave, Tony Britton and Vanessa Redgrave, following it up with the role of a reporter in *His and Hers*, as well as appearing in *The Queen's Guards*.

William appeared in repertory theatre in Clacton, Nottingham and Oldham, then on television in *Skyport* (in which Doris Speed – later to play Annie Walker in *Coronation Street* – was seen pushing a tea trolley), *Knight Errant*, the sitcom *The Bulldog Breed* (as a naval officer) and *Biggles*, all produced by Granada TV.

He also played the lead in a Granada 'Play of the Week' called *Marking Time*, which led to his being spotted by *Coronation Street* creator Tony Warren and the serial's casting directors. William was cast as Ken Barlow when the programme began, in December 1960, and became one of its youngest actors. He won the 1983 Pye Television Award jointly with Anne Kirkbride and Johnny Briggs for their performances in the Ken-Deirdre-Mike love triangle story.

William, a director of Lancashire Cable Television, is divorced from his first wife, actress Anna Cropper, by whom he has a daughter, Vanya, and son, Linus, now a Royal Shakespeare Company actor who played William's screen son, Peter, for a time in *Coronation Street*. William and his second wife, actress Sara McEwen, have two children, Verity Elizabeth and William James. Their second daughter, Edwina, died in 1984 of a sudden viral attack at the age of 18 months. The family live in Wilmslow, Cheshire, and have a holiday home in Abersoch, North Wales.

William, who enjoys playing golf – and sometimes takes part in pro-celebrity tournaments – had his autobiography, *Ken and Me*, published in 1993.

TRACY BARLOW

Born in Weatherfield General Hospital on 24 January 1977, Tracy Lynette Barlow is the daughter of Ray and Deirdre Langton. Tracy's mother feared for the girl's life when a timber lorry crashed into the Rovers Return, but Tracy was later found wandering in a park. After divorcing Ray, Deirdre married Ken Barlow, who adopted Tracy. Growing up was a largely happy time for Tracy until the traumatic experience of her parents' divorce after Ken's affair with Wendy Crozier.

On finishing her GCSEs in 1993, Tracy accepted a job in Maggie Redman's flower shop, against the advice of Ken, who by then had returned to teaching, at Weatherfield Comprehensive, and wanted her to take A levels.

Tracy began to live her own life and moved into a flat with boyfriend Craig. She and Craig even lived with Deirdre for a while, but that arrangement did not work. The relationship itself eventually ended.

When her mother announced that she was wedding Moroccan waiter Samir Rachid, Tracy opposed the wedding but turned up at the last minute. Then, she could not believe that her mother was leaving for Morocco with Samir after he had been questioned by the immigration authorities and decided it was better to leave before being thrown out.

But Deirdre was back in March 1995 on hearing the terrible news that her daughter was in a coma in hospital after being plied with the drug Ecstasy at a party. Tracy suffered an allergic

---

Novelist Beryl Bainbridge played a BAN THE BOMB DEMONSTRATOR with Ken Barlow and his girlfriend, Susan Cunningham, in an early *Street* episode.

Noel Dyson played IDA BARLOW, mother of Ken, until her death under the wheels of a bus. Noel later took the role of Nanny in the sitcom *Father Dear Father*.

Linus Roache (b. Linus William Roache on 1 February 1964) was a child when he became the fourth of six actors to play PETER BARLOW, Ken's son from his first marriage, to Valerie. The real-life son of William Roache, who plays Ken, Linus has gone on to act with the RSC and appear on TV in *Saracen*, *Omnibus* (as Vincent Van Gogh), *Black and Blue* and *Seaforth*, as well as the films *Mister God, This Is Anna* and *Priest*.

reaction to the drug, which caused her kidney damage. Deirdre and Ken both offered kidneys for a transplant, but both proved unsuitable matches. In the meantime, she could look forward only to three days a week on a dialysis machine until a suitable donor was found.

When she was told that Samir was donating one of his kidneys, her relationship with him changed for the better. But tragedy struck on the night before the operation, in June 1995, when Samir was attacked and received a fatal blow to the head. His kidney saved Tracy, but her mother was left without a husband.

☆ ☆ ☆

Dawn Acton (b. Dawn Jean Acton in Ashton-under-Lyne, Lancashire, 15 March 1977) took over the role of Tracy Barlow at the age of 11 in 1988. The part had originally been played by Christabel Finch, then Holly Chamarette, who left *Coronation Street* nine months before Dawn joined. The idea was to make the change in actress less obvious to viewers. Dawn's hobbies are drawing, sewing and reading. She lives in Ashton-under-Lyne and, in 1994, helped her mother to set up the Fairfield Bakery, a bakery and sandwich shop in Audenshaw.

DES BARNES

Bookie Des Barnes lived with girlfriend Deborah Murray until he met builder's daughter Steph Jones in 1989 at the plush Midland Hotel in Manchester. After a whirlwind romance, he and Steph married on Valentine's Day 1990 and moved into no. 6 Coronation Street, first of the new houses on the old factory site to be sold.

The couple quickly made their mark, providing competition for the Duckworths with their slanging matches. Picking up Steph to carry her over the threshold of no. 6, Des promptly banged her head on the door. A row followed and ended with her locking him out. When they left for their honeymoon to Majorca the following day, Des dropped a suitcase, which then burst open in the street and caused more words.

Des and Steph proved to be a pair of practical jokers whose first victim was Kevin Webster. Steph won a bet with Des that she could shave off the mechanic's moustache, and he had to pay it off by walking into the Rovers Return and ordering a pint without his trousers on. A horrified Alec Gilroy threw him out.

Then, Des pretended to give Jack Duckworth racing tips. He started by leaving the Rovers and saying '*arrivederci*', which Jack presumed to be a hint. Jack found a horse running called Italian Boy, put a bet on it and the horse won. Further hints – and winners – followed. Then, Jack passed on a supposed tip to Don Brennan and Mark Casey. Jack and Don each lost £50 and Mark all his £100 holiday money. But Des insisted that, as a bookie, he could not give tips.

After going to the Boat Show in London, Des bought a boat for £500, installing it in his back garden so that he could do it up – and neglecting Steph, who arranged a skiing holiday by herself and insisted on going even after breaking her leg by falling off the boat.

It was only a year since their wedding, but the marriage appeared to be on the rocks as Des suspected that Steph's après-ski activities had extended to having an affair after spotting an amorous message on her leg plaster. Discovering that Clive Parnell, who had organized spare-time work for Steph promoting a new alcoholic drink in pubs, was also on the holiday, Des walked out. When she explained that Clive had pestered her but nothing had happened, Des believed her and apologized – although he confronted Clive, who then floored Des.

Steph later admitted that she was having an affair with Simon Beattie, an architect employed by Steph's firm. When she left him, during a boating holiday they were having with Gail and Martin Platt, Des burned all her belongings, along with his precious boat, as a symbol of the ashes of their marriage.

A court appearance to answer charges relating to this last act led to his meeting solicitor Lynette Campion. But, after a few dates, she made it clear that she simply saw him as 'a bit of rough'. It was left to design student Angie Freeman to help Des through his agony, but they kept their friendship platonic.

Dizzy barmaid Raquel Wolstenhulme came on the scene when she was looking for somewhere to live, but she left after Steph's reappearance in 1992. Steph also went on her way.

Des then fell for Lisa Duckworth, who had married jailbird Terry and had his baby, Thomas. Lisa ditched Terry and moved in with Des. Just as happiness seemed to have arrived for Des, it was snatched away from him when Lisa was killed by a car while crossing the road from the Rovers Return. Lisa's parents, Jeff and Doreen Horton, blamed Des for their daughter's death.

Raquel gave him the support he needed and fell back into his arms again. But, in 1995, Des proved the supreme rat by having an affair with Rovers barmaid Tanya Pooley – mistress of Des's boss, Alex Christie – leaving Raquel devastated and Des without a job. Tanya herself ran off with Bet Gilroy's boyfriend, trucker Charlie Whelan, although he realized his mistake, only to return and be rebuffed by Bet.

Des bounced back with a new job when Sean Skinner opened a bookmaker's in Rosamund Street and asked him to manage it. But he caused more trouble when Raquel agreed to marry Curly and, at their engagement party, forced her to admit that she did not love Curly. However, his own proposal of marriage was rejected by Raquel.

☆ ☆ ☆

Philip Middlemiss (b. Hartlepool, 1963) gained experience with the National Youth Theatre for eight weeks when he was 15 and later trained at LAMDA (the London Academy of Music and Dramatic Art), after being offered a choice of going there or to RADA.

During his last 18 months at drama school, he shared a council flat in Brixton, South London, with two graphic designers and fellow acting student Gary Webster, later to become Dennis Waterman's replacement on television in *Minder*. They were living there at the time of the Brixton riots.

Philip's first job was playing an eight-year-old boy in *Larkrise*. He followed it with stage roles in *A Tale of Two Cities* and *A Christmas Carol*, *Pinocchio* at the Theatre Royal, Stratford, East London, and a National Theatre tour of two plays, *Strippers* and *Trackers*, working with such stars as Jack Shepherd and Juliet Stevenson, and appearing in the Olympic Temple at Delphi in front of an audience of 15,000.

On television, he was in *Ladies in Charge*, *Closing Ranks*, *Inspector Morse* (as a villain), *Traffik*, *Christabel* (as a German soldier), *The Bill* and *Waterfront Beat* (as P.C. Barry Smith), before joining *Coronation Street* in 1990.

Philip shares a flat in South London with Gary Webster, with whom he also owns the Grants Arms pub in Ramsbottom, Lancashire. He enjoys watching Liverpool Football Club.

EMILY BISHOP

An upstanding member of the community, Emily Bishop has had occasional romances and plenty of heartbreak over the years. Born Emily Nugent, the daughter of a former Indian Army officer, on 18 October 1929, she was a helper at the Mission Hall and manageress of Gamma Garments, both bringing her into contact with the pompous Leonard Swindley, who was a lay preacher and ran the clothes shop. Because 1964 was a leap year, Emily proposed to him but stood him up at the altar on their June wedding day.

She then went to a marriage bureau and had dates with farmer Frank Starkey and hotelier Douglas Preston, to whom she became engaged. She split up with him when she realized he was only trying to get away from his domineering sister. Emily found brief happiness with Hungarian building worker Miklos Zadic in the spring of 1968. When he started a new job in Newcastle, she went with him but returned three weeks later alone.

It looked as if Emily had found true love when she met photographer Ernest Bishop. They married on Easter Monday 1972, worked together at Baldwin's Casuals and even fostered two black children for a while. But tragedy struck when Ernest, in his job as wages clerk, was shot dead in a robbery in 1978. Two years later, Emily married Arnold Swain in an October register office wedding but found out after three months that he was a bigamist and threw him out. The experience caused Emily to suffer a breakdown.

Curly Watts and Kevin Webster then lodged with her, before she took in pensioner Percy Sugden. Emily began seeing Arthur Dabner after meeting him at a dinner party given by Mavis and Derek Wilton. Mavis said he was separated, although Derek claimed he still saw his wife frequently. Emily did not take kindly to Mavis's warning, but Arthur confessed to her shortly afterwards that he was returning to his wife.

Losing her job as book-keeper at Mike Baldwin's factory when he sold up, Emily led the fight for redundancy payments. She filled part of her time with her work as a hospital visitor, before finding a new purpose in life as manageress of the charity shop in Coronation Street, but that closed after a short time.

Emily, as a churchgoer, seemed to have found her perfect match when, in 1994, she and Bernard Morton, vicar of St Saviour's Church, started seeing one another. She helped to guide him back on his religious path when he had a crisis of faith. He left St Saviour's and tried to live in a Church of England hostel but subsequently told Emily how much he needed her. When he proposed, she accepted.

But Emily had not told Bernard that two years earlier she had suffered a nervous breakdown. Percy's revelation about this to Bernard led to the former vicar confessing that his mother had also had a breakdown and he did not feel strong enough to go through the experience again. That was the last she saw of him.

☆ ☆ ☆

Eileen Derbyshire (b. Urmston, Manchester, 6 October 1930) is one of *Coronation Street*'s more reticent stars, shuns publicity and almost never speaks to the press. 'In the world of the soaps, she is a Garbo,' wrote *The Times*.

Eileen took a teaching degree in speech and drama, before training at the Northern School of Music and passing her London Royal Academy of Music exam. She had always wanted to be an actress and, passing Chorlton Repertory on a bus one day, she went in and asked for an audition. They had no vacancies but, thinking Eileen had come from London specially, gave her an audition. She was taken on as a student and later became an assistant stage manager there, before joining the Century Theatre's mobile company, performing in productions all over the country for two years. From there, she worked in repertory theatre throughout Britain.

Eileen first acted on radio at the age of 17 and has been in many broadcast plays since. After several small parts on television, she joined *Coronation Street* in December 1960 as an extra in episode three, returning a month later as Miss Nugent in episode 15, and has been with the serial ever since, although it was a year before the character was given a forename. Only William Roache has been in the *Street* longer.

During her early years in the programme, Eileen formed an on-screen double-act with Arthur Lowe, who played Leonard Swindley, Emily Nugent's boss at Gamma Garments. She missed the partnership when he decided to leave, finding fame in the *Street* spin-off sitcom *Pardon the Expression* and, later, in *Dad's Army*.

Eileen is married to retired engineer Thomas Holt and lives in a sprawling cottage in the Cheshire countryside. They have a son, Oliver, who read history at Oxford University before becoming a journalist in Liverpool. Eileen enjoys reading, listening to opera, going to concerts, and holidays in Vienna and Venice.

DON BRENNAN

Minicab driver Don Brennan was a fast worker when it came to romancing widow Ivy Tilsley. Born Donald Michael Brennan, he had been widowed himself six months earlier following his wife Pat's death from cancer. The couple had a son and two daughters.

One night in 1987, he picked Ivy up in his cab, got on with her and found that she helped him to face the future after his loss. Six months after their first meeting, Don proposed and the couple were married on 13 June 1988, with Jack Duckworth as best man. At first, Don proved to be a reliable and loving husband, although Ivy despaired of him when he got into scrapes.

One of his vices was gambling. Ivy was furious when he lost his cab to Mike Baldwin in a poker game just six months after their wedding. He and Jack Duckworth had beaten Mike at poker a couple of days earlier, taking £60 off him. He invited them to his flat for a another game, Alan

Bradley joined in and, when Jack and Alan were cleaned out, Mike produced £1000 in notes from his back pocket. Don threw his car keys in and Mike laid four kings on the table. Ivy, furious that Don had gambled his livelihood, bought the cab back with her savings.

Worse came when Ivy's son, Brian, was fatally stabbed, in 1989. She wanted him buried as a Catholic, with a mass, but his wife Gail did not, and Don told Ivy that it was Gail's decision. The couple drifted apart, but a Catholic priest consoled Ivy with the idea that he could still say a mass for her son, and the marriage survived.

Don took another gamble when he accepted a greyhound in lieu of a client's large taxi bill. The dog, Harry's Luck, ripped a hole in the Brennans' sofa and Don's attempts to train the animal for racing were worse than disappointing. The reason was that the dog was female and pregnant. Don ended up selling Harry's Luck and her five puppies for £800, which Ivy took as part of the money she had lent him to get his car back from Mike Baldwin.

Trouble loomed large for Don when his car was stolen by two youths while he popped into a betting shop, leaving the keys in the ignition. The car was then involved in a hit-and-run accident and he fell under suspicion. When he recognized one of the youths near a block of flats, he chased him, there was a scuffle, and the lad was injured. Don was charged with assault and fined £50, plus £70 costs. Spending £300 on repairs to the car rubbed salt into the wound.

Don showed the charitable side of his nature when Marie Ramsden, estranged wife of barmaid Tina Fowler's former boyfriend Eddie, took a lift in his cab with her baby son Jamie. Helping Marie to carry her shopping into her flat, he saw the poor conditions in which she was living and how she was finding difficulty in paying her bills. He helped her out, and wife Ivy, on realizing Marie's plight, invited her to stay over Christmas 1990. But Marie and Ivy failed to hit it off and Marie left suddenly.

Don and Ivy's marriage started crumbling when Ivy argued with her daughter-in-law over whether her grandchildren would still be called Tilsley when Gail married Martin Platt. Don told her he was fed up of hearing the Tilsley name. As his marriage went downhill, Don fell for Julie Dewhurst, whom he met as a passenger in his cab, then at Martin's stag night. Eventually, Don told Ivy about the affair and moved into bed-and-breakfast accommodation. When Ivy told him how much she missed him, he returned to her and Ivy pledged to put her memories of first husband Bert and son Brian behind her. Don met Julie again when she and Ivy unwittingly got into his cab together after an evening at a club. He visited her and suggested

they start seeing each other again but, having been let down by Don once, she was reluctant.

When Ivy suggested reaffirming their wedding vows, Don knew it was time to choose between the two women. He opted for Julie, but she rejected him and he drove away at speed, crashing on a bend and waking up in hospital with broken ribs and multiple fractures. Worst of all, the lower part of one of his legs was amputated. Blaming Ivy for what had happened, Don refused to go back to her and, on leaving hospital, moved into another B&B. Ivy turned to drink and, at Vera's request, he went to see her.

Angela Douglas (b. Gerrards Cross, Buckinghamshire, 29 October 1940), the late Kenneth More's wife, played Dennis Tanner's snake-charmer girlfriend EUNICE 'LA COMPOSITA' BOND.

Graham Haberfield (b. Chesterfield), who was Winston in the ITV comedy *The Dustbinmen*, played plumber JERRY BOOTH, Len Fairclough's business partner, for 684 episodes. Graham and the character died suddenly in October 1975.

Susan Jameson, who married James Bolam after acting his wife Jessie in *When the Boat Comes In*, was MYRA BOOTH (née Dickenson) in 61 episodes from 1963 to 1968, including the serial's longest, nine-minute scene, when Jerry discovered that Myra had run up massive debts. Susan also acted Kate in *Take Three Girls*.

Mark Eden, film actor and star of the sixties series *Crime Buster*, played baddie ALAN BRADLEY. He had previously appeared in the *Street* as Elsie Tanner's boyfriend WALLY RANDLE. Mark is married to *Street* actress Sue Nicholls.

Nightclub entertainer-turned-actress Lynne Perrie (b. Jean Dudley in Rotherham, South Yorkshire, 7 April 1931) played staunch Catholic IVY BRENNAN, shop steward in Mike Baldwin's factory and later a shelf-stacker at Bettabuys. In the sixties, she sang on the same bill as Sacha Distel, the Rolling Stones and The Beatles. She made her acting debut in the film *Kes*, playing the boy's mother, was on TV in *Slattery's Mounted Foot, Leeds United, Follyfoot, Mrs Petty, Queenie's Castle, The Intruder, Crown Court* and *It Was a Good Story, Don't Knock It*, and in the film *Yanks*. Lynne, the sister of actor-comedian Duggie Brown, appeared in *Coronation Street* from 1971 to 1994.

Jack Smethurst (b. Collyhurst, Manchester, 9 April 1932), who made his name as bigoted Eddie Booth in the sitcom *Love Thy Neighbour*, played conman PERCY BRIDGE, Stan and Hilda Ogden's lodger, for 12 episodes in 1980. He has also taken two other roles in the *Street*, as FRED CLARK, a bouncer at the Orinoco Club in 1961, who became a boyfriend of Elsie Tanner, and one of Eddie Yeats's wedding guests, JOHNNY WEBB, in 1983.

Gorden Kaye (b. Huddersfield, West Yorkshire, 7 April 1941) was hairdresser BERNARD BUTLER, Elsie Tanner's nephew for 38 episodes. He then found fame as café owner Rene in *'Allo, 'Allo*.

Margot Bryant (b. Hull, East Yorkshire, 1898) was timid, cat-loving MINNIE CALDWELL, who with Ena Sharples and Martha Longhurst made up the triumvirate of gossips in the Rovers snug. Margot, who had danced on stage in the Fred Astaire West End hit *Stop Flirting*, joined the *Street* in episode three and left in 1976, after 560 appearances. She died on 1 January 1989.

Sam Kelly (b. Manchester, 19 December 1943) played painter BOB CHALLIS, who was hired by the brewery to redecorate the Rovers in 1984. He also acted Warren in *Porridge*, Nazi Capt. Hans Geering in *'Allo, 'Allo*, Grunge in *Haggard* and Sam in *On the Up*.

Graham Fellowes played LES CHARLTON and became better known as pop star Jilted John, who had a top ten hit single of the same name in 1978.

Susan Brown (b. Susan Elisabeth Brown in Bristol, 6 May 1946) played milkman's wife CONNIE CLAYTON, whose elder daughter Andrea became pregnant by Terry Duckworth, which led to the family doing a moonlight flit. Susan has since appeared on TV as Helen in *Road*, Ruby in *Andy Capp*, Avril in *Making Out*, Jackie in *EastEnders* and Cilla in the series *September Song*.

Jane Hazlegrove (b. Susan Jane Hazlegrove in Manchester, 17 July 1968) played schoolgirl SUE CLAYTON, daughter of milkman Harry, before roles in *Albion Market* (as hairdresser Debbie Taylor), *Making Out*, *Waterfront Beat* and *Families* (as Lisa Shepherd).

Saying that she could not beat her problem without him, Ivy persuaded Don to stay, although he insisted that they had separate bedrooms and separate lives.

Don then took a fancy to hairdresser Denise Osbourne and gave her a much-needed £3000 loan for her hairdressing business, thinking that it would also buy her affections. When she rejected his advances, Don turned to Bet Gilroy and – although he spent a night with her – she sent him back to Ivy. Obsessed with Denise, he began making nuisance phone calls to her. Eventually, they were traced and Denise was shocked to find out they came from Don, to whom she had turned for help during her ordeal.

Having faced rejection from other women, Don pledged himself to Ivy again. But the marriage still did not work and Ivy finally ended it, leaving for a retreat, never to return. Settling down to life by himself, Don provided a refuge for Ivy's grandson, Nick Platt, when he fell out with his parents. But a new woman finally arrived in his life when he picked up Josie Clark in his cab. She did not have enough money to pay him but turned up in Coronation Street later with the cash. It marked the start of a new beginning for Don.

☆ ☆ ☆

Geoff Hinsliff (b. Leeds) trained at RADA after doing National Service and played mainly classical roles on stage during his early career. He has acted at the Old Vic and Royal Court theatres, as well as in the West End. Geoff appeared in the films *A Bridge Too Far* and *O Lucky Man!*, and on TV in such programmes as *Z-Cars*, *Softly Softly*, *Striker*, *Accident* and the first series of *Brass* (as George Fairchild).

He first appeared in *Coronation Street* in 1963 as a cycling friend of Jerry Booth, who wanted him as best man at his wedding, but wife-to-be Myra Dickenson wanted Dennis Tanner. Geoff also played a burglar who dated Bet Lynch in 1977. Ten years later, Bill Podmore – who produced *Brass* and had moved to the *Street* – asked Geoff to join the serial as cab driver Don Brennan. Typecasting was something that would have worried him earlier in his career but, at the age of 50 and after 30 years in acting, he decided he was willing to stick with one role.

But he took time off from the serial to star in the seven-part radio drama *September Song* in 1991, playing stand-up comedian Billy Balsam, whose act was based on that of the late Tom Mennard, who had portrayed Sam Tindall in *Coronation Street*. The series was later adapted for TV, with Michael Williams taking the role.

Geoff and wife Judith have two daughters, Gabrielle and Sophie, and live in Derbyshire. In his spare time, Geoff enjoys gardening.

JOSIE CLARK

Widow Josie Clark walked into Don Brennan's cab and his life just as he was getting used to living on his own, following an abortive affair with Julie Dewhurst and his wife Ivy's decision to leave him. Josie had the embarrassment of not being able to pay her fare, but she turned up in the Rovers Return later to hand over the cash and he bought her a drink, saying that she had restored his faith in human nature.

Don and Josie continued seeing one another and she expressed her desire to take the relationship further. Then, Don dropped a bombshell when he told Josie that he had been guilty of pestering hairdresser Denise Osbourne with nuisance phone calls in the middle of his earlier troubles, but she still felt that she wanted to be with him.

☆ ☆ ☆

Ellie Haddington trained at the Bristol Old Vic Theatre School and first appeared in *Coronation Street* as a girlfriend of Billy Walker in 1984, when he returned to look after the Rovers Return following the departure of his mother, Annie. Billy took her to the races and she joined him in after-hours drinking sessions.

Shortly before returning to the *Street* as Josie Clark, Ellie appeared on TV in a three-part *Cracker* story, *Wycliffe* and *In Suspicious Circumstances*. She had already featured in *Muck and Brass*, *Unnatural Causes*, *Loving Hazel*, *The Lorelei* and *Ball on the Slates* on television.

Ellie's theatre appearances include the title role in *Educating Rita* at the Octagon Theatre, Bolton, a one-woman show called *Female Parts* in Manchester, the title role in *The Duchess of Malfi*, also in Manchester, and parts in RSC productions of *Richard III* and *Mother Courage* and a National Theatre staging of *The Sea*.

JACK DUCKWORTH

Born in Rochdale, Lancashire, on 7 November 1934, John Harold Duckworth was the son of a bookie's runner and a barmaid. As a child, he was always in trouble and played truant from school. He did National Service, then found a job with a travelling fair. When it visited Manchester, he helped Vera Burton down from the big dipper when it got stuck. They fell in love, Vera thought she was pregnant and they married – but later discovered it was a false alarm.

Unemployed much of the time, Jack sang in the evenings in Manchester pubs and clubs, crooning the songs of his favourite singer, Elvis Presley. Vera worked in Mike Baldwin's fac-

Bill Kenwright (b. Liverpool, 4 September 1945) played GORDON CLEGG, the illegitimate son of Betty Turpin who was brought up by her sister Maggie Clegg. He went on to become a successful West End theatre producer with such shows as *Are You Lonesome Tonight?*

Malcolm Hebden proved a thorn in the side of Derek and Mavis Wilton as salesman NORRIS COLE in 1994. But, 19 years earlier, he was Spanish waiter CARLOS, who proposed to Mavis.

Stan Stennett (b. Pencoed, Mid Glamorgan, 30 July 1927), Hilda Ogden's chippie brother NORMAN CRABTREE, also played both Harry Silver and Sid Hooper in *Crossroads*.

Martin Shaw (b. Birmingham, 21 January 1945), later to find fame as Doyle in *The Professionals*, was hippie commune leader ROBERT CROFT, who moved into no. 11. Martin also starred on TV as Captain Scott in *The Last Place on Earth* and Chief Constable Alan Cade in *The Chief*.

Patricia Shakesby (b. Cottingham, East Yorkshire, 6 November 1942) played SUSAN CUNNINGHAM, Ken Barlow's student girlfriend when *Coronation Street* began. Patricia later acted Polly Urquhart in the nautical soap *Howards' Way*.

Bill Owen (b. William Rowbotham in Acton Green, West London, 14 March 1914) was CHARLIE DICKINSON. He is best known as Compo in *Last of the Summer Wine*, but has also been in *The Likely Lads*, *Taxi* and *Brideshead Revisited*.

American actor **Shane Rimmer**, who was the voice of Scott Tracy in *Thunderbirds*, was JOE DONNELLI, the murderer of Elsie Tanner's second husband, Steve.

Paul Shane (b. Rotherham, South Yorkshire, 19 June 1940) acted Alf Roberts's Post Office boss FRANK DRAPER in 1979, as well as a disc jockey, before finding fame as comic Ted Bovis in *Hi-de-Hi!*

Caroline Milmoe (b. Manchester, 11 January 1963) was tragic LISA DUCKWORTH (née Horton), who moved in with Des Barnes and was fatally hit by a car. She had previously played Sandra Lord in *The Practice* and Julie Jefferson in the first two series of *Bread*.

tory in Coronation Street and the couple moved to no. 9 opposite with their son, Terry, in 1983. Workshy Jack lost his job as a taxi-driver when he was breathalyzed and banned from driving for a year after an evening celebrating Vera's £260 bingo win. He had run into trouble with the law only months earlier when he was fined £150 for not having a TV licence.

He then tried selling shirts on a market stall, before Vera bought Stan Ogden's window-cleaning round and sent him out to work. He found the job had its compensations when he met Dulcie Froggatt, whose husband was often away working on an oil rig. The window-cleaning came to an abrupt end one night when he was climbing the ladder to Dulcie's bedroom window, fell off and broke an ankle.

When Fred Gee left his job as cellarman at the Rovers Return, Jack took over and found the working environment to his liking, spending many hours alone below the pub ensuring that the beer was of the finest quality.

Always fancying himself as a ladies' man, Jack once went to a video dating agency as singer Vince St Clair, complete with gold-plated chest medallion. Bet Lynch went to the same agency, saw his video and arranged a meeting, substituting a disguised Vera for her. Jack's loudmouth wife was also furious when he dated Rovers barmaid Tina Fowler.

Jack has always tried to bring Vera down to earth where family are concerned, having given up long ago on no-good son Terry, who got neighbour Andrea Clayton pregnant and ran off with an ex-army pal's wife.

When Terry sold his own son, Tommy – who was born to his tragic dead wife, Lisa, while Terry was in prison – to Lisa's parents, Jeff and Doreen Horton, after Vera had scrimped and saved to bring the baby up herself, Jack tried to play the diplomat with Jeff and Doreen instead of letting Vera get into a blazing row.

But Vera would not listen to him when, while attending her mother's funeral, she met Joss Shackleton, who claimed to be her real father and moved in with Vera and Jack. Joss even spun Vera a yarn that the family had royal blood and, when Jack pointed out that not even Joss's blood group was of the same type as hers, she still refused to listen.

Jack will always be a bit of a rascal but, deep down, he loves Vera. It is their constant bickering that keeps the marriage alive.

William Tarmey (b. William Cleworth Piddington in Ardwick, Manchester, 4 April 1941) grew up in the working-class Bradford district of the city. His father died during the war and his mother subsequently married her

Jack and Vera Duckworth's marriage has always thrived on their constant bickering.

next-door neighbour. On leaving school, Bill learned the building trade, was apprenticed to his stepfather and worked as an asphalt layer. At the same time, he did evening work as a singer in clubs and cabaret, appearing with show bands and as a session singer. While working at a club in Stockport, the owner decided his name was too long and billed him as William Tarmey, after the American singer Mel Tormé.

Bill had met his wife Alma ('Ally') when they were both 14 and members of a local church youth club. When they married, she ran a grocery and hardware shop. It did so well that Bill eventually gave up his work in the building trade to run it with her. He also got more singing work in clubs.

A friend who was a TV extra suggested that Bill could get similar work. Gradually, he was offered speaking roles. He has appeared on television in *Strangers*, *Crown Court*, *The Ghosts of Motley Hall*, *The Glamour Girls* and a BBC 'Play for Today', *Thicker Than Water*. In *Rising Star*, he sang with a group called Take Ten, with whom he often worked in clubs.

He joined *Coronation Street* in 1979, after several bit parts in the serial. Even after joining the *Street*, Bill had a bit part in Granada Television's production of *King Lear*, starring Laurence Olivier. He was sitting on a horse next to Olivier, who recognized him and asked, 'What the bloody hell are you doing here?' The actor replied, 'It's what they call experience, sir.' His *Street* partnership with Elizabeth Dawn extended into the recording studio with the 1989 single 'I'll Be With You Soon'. Three years later, he released *The Other Side of Me*, a tape containing his performances of 11 pop classics.

Bill, who has two children, Carl and Sara, has suffered heart problems for years and had his first heart attack in 1976 while appearing on stage as a singer in a nightclub. He had a heart bypass operation in 1987.

VERA DUCKWORTH

Blonde curls and a foghorn voice are the trademarks of Coronation Street's resident loudmouth, Vera Duckworth. Her quarrels with husband Jack are legendary, but everyone agrees that they were made for each other.

Born illegitimately in Moss Side, Manchester, on 3 September 1936, Veronica Burton left school aged 15 and met Jack when he was working for a travelling fair that visited the city. He rescued her from a big dipper that had jammed. They fell in love and, when Vera mistakenly thought she was having a baby, married.

In 1964, they did eventually have a son, Terry, who was to cause them more than a few worries, but he was really just a chip off the old blocks. Vera and Jack split up for a while, when she fell for bingo caller Don McMasters, but his wife came back on the scene and Vera went crawling back to Jack. At first, he sent her packing, but he later relented.

At work, Vera was always a loudmouth, complaining about conditions in the workplace. She was employed at Sir Julius Berlin's warehouse in Coronation Street until it was gutted by fire in 1975, when she joined Pickup's factory. Two years later, she became a machine operator at Baldwin's Casuals, where she proved to be a troublemaker, goading shop steward Ivy Tilsley into union battles with boss Mike Baldwin. When Mike sold the factory in 1989, Vera landed a job filling shelves at Bettabuys supermarket, where Curly Watts had just become trainee assistant manager.

Curly had moved in as Jack and Vera's lodger after Terry left home with Linda, the wife of old army pal Pete Jackson, in 1987. Two years earlier, milkman's daughter Andrea Clayton had become pregnant by Terry. As Vera's superior at Bettabuys, Curly had to write an assessment of his staff. His less than complimentary remarks about her led to Vera's dismissal and she threw him out of the house. But her reinstatement ensured Curly's return to his lodgings, where Vera treated him as a son.

More ructions followed at the supermarket when manager Reg Holdsworth fixed a raffle so that Rita Fairclough would win and Vera was sacked, essentially for broadcasting the fact. She complained to head office and a formal investigation followed, with Reg suspended.

When he persuaded Vera to withdraw the allegation, both were able to return to their jobs.

Vera was in her element when, at her mother Ivy's funeral, she finally met her father, Joss Shackleton, whom she had always known as 'Uncle Joss'. Desperate for somewhere to live, Joss persuaded Vera to let him stay with her and Jack, although Jack felt he was simply sponging. Then, Joss claimed that Vera's great-grandfather was Edward VII and she believed she was a direct descendant of royalty. Nothing Jack said could dissuade her, even when he pointed out that Joss was of a different blood group from her and could not be her father.

It was another feather in Vera's cap when son Terry married Lisa Horton – although he was in jail at the time and let out for the day, only to make an escape attempt – and Lisa gave birth to baby son Thomas, known to all as Tommy. With Terry in prison, Lisa became close to Des Barnes and eventually moved in with him, but tragedy struck when she was killed by a car while crossing the Street. Lisa's parents, Jeff and Doreen Horton, wanted custody of Tommy, but Vera was adamant that she would bring him up. After giving up work to do so, she was strapped for cash and Curly caught her shoplifting in Bettabuys but did not take any action.

The ultimate betrayal of all Vera's good intentions occurred when Terry was released from jail in December 1993 and promptly accepted £5000 from Jeff Horton in return for Tommy. The Hortons did not want a battle with Vera and, when she and Jack visited them in Blackpool, they were glad to let her see Tommy and assure her that she could do so at any time.

On a visit there in July 1994, Vera bumped into old flame Lester Fonteyne, who was working as an entertainer and staying in the same hotel. They went dancing together and Lester persuaded Vera to stay a few extra days. Rita Sullivan and Kevin and Sally Webster, on holiday in Blackpool themselves, were horrified to see

Nigel Pivaro (b. Manchester, 11 December 1959) played Jack and Vera's no-good son TERRY DUCKWORTH. He has also appeared in the films *The Revenge of the One-Armed Boxer* and *Meet Me Tonight in Dreamland*, the second produced by Mark Eden, who played Alan Bradley.

Diana Coupland, best known as Sid James's wife in the comedy series *Bless This House*, played MRS DUMBARTON. She later appeared in *Triangle* (as shipping line boss George Terson's mistress Marion), *One Foot in the Grave* and *The Trial of Klaus Barbie*.

Peter Adamson (b. Liverpool, 16 February 1930) acted LEN FAIRCLOUGH, who died in a motorway accident in 1983. Peter, who appeared 1797 times from episode 14, was sacked after selling stories to a national newspaper, following his acquittal on charges of indecently assaulting two girls. He then appeared on stage in Canada, before returning to Britain.

Peter Noone (b. Davyhulme, Manchester, 5 November 1947) played STANLEY FAIRCLOUGH, the first of three actors to take the role of Len's son, seen in a school playground scene in 1961, before finding fame as lead singer of the sixties pop group Herman's Hermits. He more recently guest-starred in *Family Ties*.

John Junkin (b. Ealing, West London, 29 January 1930) played BILL FIELDING, one of Elsie Tanner's boyfriends. As an actor, he has appeared in more than 20 films and his own series, *Junkin*. As a writer, he has scripted for Mike Yarwood.

Tracie Bennett (b. Tracey Anne Bennett in Leigh, Lancashire, 17 June 1961) caused a sensation as the Faircloughs' foster child SHARON GASKELL, who tried to seduce married Brian Tilsley. She has since appeared on TV in *Making Out* (as Norma) and the sitcoms *Rich Tea & Sympathy*, *Joking Apart* and *Next of Kin*. She also acted in the film *Shirley Valentine* (as Shirley's daughter, Millandra) and the West End stage hit *She Loves Me*.

Roy Barraclough (b. Preston, Lancashire, 12 July 1935), who was in the serial *Castlehaven*, the children's series *Pardon My Genie* and acted Cissie in Cissie and Ada (half of the old female gossips, with Les Dawson), took four different speaking roles in the *Street* before playing ALEC GILROY in 1972. In 1965, he was a GUIDE when Street residents went on a coach trip to Derbyshire's mines. A year later, he was window cleaner 'I-SPY' DWYER, who sold his round to Stan Ogden, and in 1967 he was a VACUUM CLEANER DEMONSTRATOR. He later played a BED SALESMAN. Alec Gilroy was first seen as steward of a working men's club, then theatrical agent and then manager of the Graffiti Club, before marrying Bet Lynch and becoming landlord of the Rovers Return. He left in 1992 and later starred as health-food-shop owner Leslie H. Flitcroft in *Mother's Ruin*.

Vera and Lester kissing, but Vera ultimately resisted the smooth-talking entertainer's attempts to lure her away from Jack.

Vera was taken in by another bad penny when Jack's brother, Cliff, arrived in 1994 asking for lodgings. He hinted that he was on the verge of dying and there would be money left to her and Jack in the will. But he had simply been cheating on his wife and was seeking refuge.

☆ ☆ ☆

Elizabeth Dawn (b. Sylvia Butterfield in Leeds, 8 November 1939) grew up in a Leeds council flat and began her working life in a clothing factory at the age of 15. She also had jobs on the light-bulb counter at Woolworth, in a shoe shop, as a cinema usherette in the evenings and as a club singer at weekends. It was then that she changed her professional name to Elizabeth Dawn.

Film director Alan Parker spotted Liz's talent and cast her as a sympathetic mother in a television commercial. Five years later, he included her in a commercial that so impressed comedian Larry Grayson that he asked Liz to play his neighbour Dot in *The Larry Grayson Show*.

She also appeared on television in *Z-Cars* (as a beautician), *Sam*, *Country Matters*, *Raging Calm*, *Mr Ellis versus the People*, *The Greenhill Pals*, *Speech Day*, *Daft as a Brush*, *All Day on the Sands*, *Sunset Across the Bay*, *Kisses at Fifty* and *Leeds United*. She was in the feature film *Who'd Be a Vet*, and joined *Coronation Street* in 1974, although the rest of the Duckworth family were not seen until 1979.

Tribute was paid to her characterization of Vera Duckworth when the late impersonator Dustin Gee mimicked her and Mavis Riley (as she then was) in a double act with Les Dennis. As well as appearing as Bill Tarmey's screen wife, Liz recorded a single with him called 'I'll Be With You Soon', released in 1989.

Liz married at 18 and had her first child, but she was divorced three years later. She split up with second husband Donald Ibbetson in 1984, but they have since reunited. Liz has four children, Dawn, Ann-Marie, Julie and Graham, lives in Salford, Lancashire, and had her autobiography, *Vera Duckworth – My Story*, published in 1993.

BET GILROY

Elizabeth Theresa Lynch, who rose from dolly-bird barmaid to landlady of the Rovers Return, was born in Clegg Street, Weatherfield, on 4 May 1940. Her father walked out when she was only six months old. Then, at 16, she had an illegitimate son, Martin, who was adopted at the age of six weeks. Bet worked as a shop assis-

As the financial responsibility of running the Rovers became too much for Bet, she did a moonlight flit. Alec Gilroy, concerned about losing his money, found her working as a waitress in Spain and took her back to Weatherfield.

A business partnership with Alec, whose name went over the door of the Rovers, meant that she could continue as landlady. Romance followed and the couple wed on 9 September 1987. It was an unlikely match but the marriage quickly became a success. Bet even became pregnant and the couple were distressed when she suffered a miscarriage.

Then, in 1990, the brewery announced that it wanted to turn the Rovers into a Yankee-style theme pub. In a protest that was reported on local radio, Bet and Alec locked themselves inside the premises and let regulars in through the back door. Although the brewery threatened repossession, boss Cecil Newton stepped to ensure that no changes were made.

Following the death of her parents in a car crash in 1991, Alec's granddaughter, Vicky Arden, started coming to stay with the couple during holidays from her private school. It appeared that, with Alec, Bet had found the happiness, family life and security that eluded her for so long, although there were signs that the former theatrical agent was beginning to get itchy feet.

He had already left Bet on her own so that he could take a troupe – including a glamorous exotic dancer called Tanya – on a tour of the Far East. While he was away, Bet went out socially with rival landlord Paul Rigby. Alec returned early, found them just back from a night out together and refused to believe that nothing had gone on between them. Both Bet and Alec went so far as to consult solicitors.

When Bet withdrew her services as wife and landlady, Alec sacked her. With no-one to look after him, he called in exotic dancer Tanya – real name Megan Morgan – with the result that Bet moved out of the Rovers and into the flat above Alf Roberts's cornershop.

To earn money, Bet took a bar job at the Flying Horse, but the landlady treated her like a skivvy, she could not take it and was sacked. Alec went to the Flying Horse to accuse Bet of informing the brewery about what had happened, but the landlady told him of Bet's sacking and said she understood why Alec had sent her packing. This transformed Alec and, realizing his love for Bet, he said she was the best thing that had ever happened to him. He found Bet at the flat, she told him that she had not informed the brewery and the couple made up.

But, in 1992, Alec could not resist the offer of a job as entertainments manager for a cruise line, based at Southampton. The couple prepared to

tant, then as a machinist at Elliston's raincoat factory, where she gave tearaway Lucille Hewitt a black eye for fiddling the firm's bonus scheme. Bet then worked in a launderette.

In 1970, Billy Walker took her on as a barmaid at the Rovers, to the disgust of his mother, landlady Annie, who regarded her as common. But Annie soon realized the blonde hair, ample bosom and quickfire banter pulled in customers.

Bet's son, Martin Downes, came in search of her in 1974. He arrived in the Rovers but, seeing Bet and regarding her as vulgar, left without introducing himself. When he died in a vehicle crash shortly afterwards while serving with the British Army in Northern Ireland, she unsuccessfully attempted suicide.

She had already had a romance with Len Fairclough when she fell for smoothie cockney Mike Baldwin, who had just arrived from London to open a denims factory. Bet moved into no. 5 Coronation Street with him. He soon tried to get her out by telling her that his wife was arriving from London. The 'wife' turned out to be just another mistress and Bet refused to budge. She finally had to leave when Mike sold the house to Ray Langton.

In 1985, Bet triumphantly moved from the flat over Alf Roberts's cornershop to the Rovers, after the brewery, Newton & Ridley, awarded her the tenancy, following Annie Walker's departure and a string of relief managers. Theatrical agent and club owner Alec Gilroy lent her money to take it.

But the pub and Bet almost went up in smoke when, in June 1986, a fire burned it down with Bet trapped in her bedroom. Kevin Webster helped to drag the landlady from a smoke-filled landing upstairs to her bedroom window, from which firemen managed to pull her to safety.

leave but, when moving day came, Bet could not bring herself to go and Alec set off alone. Alec accused her of breaking up the marriage, but Bet felt she could never leave the pub that had become a part of her life. Because Alec had sold the tenancy back to the brewery, Bet took on the role of manageress, with Newton & Ridley as her boss and its manager, Richard Willmore, pressurizing her to increase profits.

It looked as if serious romance was coming back into Bet's life in 1994, when she fell for trucker Charlie Whelan. But he allowed barmaid Tanya Pooley to seduce him and set off for Hamburg with her, before returning alone. He begged Bet's forgiveness but, unable to trust him again, she sent him packing.

☆ ☆ ☆

Julie Goodyear (b. Julie Kemp in Bury, Lancashire, 29 March 1942) was a fan of *Coronation Street* from its beginning in 1960 and was determined to act in it. Today, she is the serial's best-loved star.

The actress was born to George and Alice Kemp, but the couple split up when Julie was about five and, when her mother later married builder Bill Goodyear, Julie took his name. Her mother and stepfather then ran a real-life pub, the Bay Horse, in the Lancashire town of Heywood, where she has lived all her life.

When she was 17, Julie married 21-year-old Ray Sutcliffe after becoming pregnant with son Gary. But, within three years, the marriage was over and he emigrated to Australia without her.

Julie trained as a shorthand typist and took office jobs, in addition to selling washing machines, to earn enough money to keep her son. She had already shown an interest in singing, taking to the stage to perform 'Blue Moon' at the Bury Palais, only to be hit by a meat pie thrown by a member of the audience.

Modelling work led her into acting and, in 1966, she appeared in the ITV comedy series *Pardon the Expression*, the *Coronation Street* spin-off that featured former *Street* star Arthur Lowe and Betty Driver, who later joined the serial as barmaid Betty Turpin.

In the same year, Julie was cast in *Coronation Street* as Bet Lynch, one of the girls in Elliston's raincoat factory. By the time she had fulfilled her two-week contract, Granada TV had found out that she had no formal acting training or experience, and she was not asked back. Pat Phoenix, who played Elsie Tanner, advised Julie to train in repertory theatre and took her to the Oldham Coliseum, a training ground for many of the *Street*'s cast.

A year later, Julie returned to Granada but could not get another appearance in the one programme on which she had set her heart. She auditioned for other roles, but only at Granada, appearing in *The Dustbinmen*, *City '68*, *The War of Darkie Pilbeam* – a play by *Coronation Street* creator Tony Warren – and *Nearest and Dearest*. After a small part in *A Family at War*, director June Howson – about to take over as producer of *Coronation Street* – asked Julie whether she would be interested in becoming a regular member of the serial's cast.

Even then, when her dream came true, she showed a hint of the perfectionism and professionalism for which she was to become admired. The plan was to introduce a new character, but Julie pointed out that some viewers would remember Bet Lynch from the raincoat factory and that this must be her return. It was and, in 1970, she came back, working first in a launderette, then behind the bar of the Rovers.

Keeping her troubled private life away from the public gaze has been difficult for Julie, who is very critical of the British press. In April 1973, she married 42-year-old businessman Tony Rudman. Many of her fans turned up at the wedding and the shock proved too much for her second husband, who walked out on her at the reception. The marriage ended there.

Later, she became engaged to a *Coronation Street* director, Bill Gilmour, but he jilted her before they reached the altar. Then, on New Year's Day 1985, Julie married American businessman Richard Skrob in Barbados. They had met on a plane to New Zealand and she said he planned eventually to move from America to Britain. It never happened and, two years after the wedding, they were divorced. He later died, after marrying again.

By then, Julie had already experienced other personal traumas. In 1979, a routine check for cervical cancer showed that she needed surgery. She was given the all-clear after two operations.

It was this experience that motivated Julie to set up a charity fund to establish a laboratory to analyse smear tests taken throughout the Northwest. But, suddenly, she found herself accused of defrauding the charity by fixing a raffle so that the winner would sell the car prize and give the money back to the fund. In 1982, after a year on bail, which she described as the worst of her life, Julie was found not guilty.

The laboratory was still not built. Her mother pleaded with her not to carry on with the project after her year of misery, but Julie was determined to see it through. Today, the Julie Goodyear Laboratory, at the Christie Hospital, Manchester, is fully operational and detects the earliest stages of cervical cancer. It is one of Julie's proudest achievements. The others are her grandchildren, Emily Alice, Elliot Thomas and Jack William, children of son Gary.

MAUD GRIMES

Cantankerous, old, wheelchair-bound mother of Maureen Holdsworth, Maud Grimes stopped her daughter marrying first love Reg after taking an instant dislike to him. But, more than 20 years later, she failed to stop true love taking its course when Maureen and Reg met again and found their feelings had not changed.

In contrast to the crotchety front she now puts on, Maud was an outgoing, adventurous young woman. During the Second World War, she worked in a factory. Maud had a crisis of conscience when she met American serviceman Leonard Kennedy because she was already married to husband Wilfred, a British serviceman. She loved Leonard, but their time together was short because he was despatched to the French beaches. He was killed on the first day of the D-Day landings and his daughter, Maureen, was born to Maud shortly afterwards.

When husband Wilfred returned, Maud told him what had happened and he agreed to bring Maureen up as his own daughter. Maud and Wilfred loved one another and did not want the incident to ruin the rest of their lives.

When Maureen met Reg Holdsworth while she was working as a waitress in Llandudno, Maud did all she could to stop her seeing him – until the only solution was to move away from Weatherfield. Maureen wed another man and lived in Preston, but the marriage ended in divorce. More than 20 years after parting, Maureen and Reg met again at Bettabuys supermarket and carried on where they had left off.

They were determined this time that battleaxe Maud – now a widow – would not thwart their plans to marry, although she was adept at manipulating Maureen. Eventually, she had to accept the inevitable and the couple were married in January 1994. Reg had bought the cornershop in Coronation Street as a business for him and Maureen to run together, but he soon had to accept that Maud wanted to be in on the act, too. This helped Reg in his decision to take a job at Firman's Freezers and leave Maureen and Maud in charge.

Maud had by then befriended pensioner Percy Sugden and, when she was feeling a bit low, a comment from him that she would make someone a wonderful wife led Maud to think he was proposing marriage. She accepted and, after the initial shock, he went along with the idea. Then, she persuaded him to take her to Normandy in June 1994 for the 50th anniversary of the D-Day landings. Maureen joined them and Maud took her to the American cemetery and pointed to the grave of Leonard Kennedy, telling her

Lyn Paul acted a GIRL playing in the street before hitting the charts as a singer with The New Seekers.

Fulton Mackay (b. Paisley, Renfrewshire, 12 August 1922) played DR GRAHAM as a *Street* regular in 1961, before being dropped during an Equity actors' union strike. Fulton was later Chief Warden Mackay in *Porridge* and the Captain in *Fraggle Rock*. He died on 6 June 1987.

Joanne Whalley-Kilmer was a child when she appeared in two scenes in consecutive episodes as PAMELA GRAHAM, daughter of Rita Littlewood's then boyfriend Jimmy Graham, in 1974. Joanne also played a CUSTOMER trying on jeans in Sylvia's Separates in 1977, as well as Angela Read in *Emmerdale*. She has since appeared on TV in *A Kind of Loving*, *The Singing Detective*, *Edge of Darkness* and *Scarlett* (as Scarlett O'Hara), and in the film *Scandal* (as Christine Keeler).

Veteran TV and film actor Jack Watson (b. London, 15 May 1921) played BILL GREGORY, a boyfriend of Elsie Tanner in 1963 who returned 20 years later to whisk her off to a new life in Portugal. Jack, son of comedian Nosmo King, began his career as his father's stooge, Hubert.

Nick Stringer (b. Torquay, Devon, 10 August 1948) acted Rovers relief manager FRANK HARVEY, then community policeman Ron Smollett in *The Bill*.

Mollie Sugden (b. Keighley, Yorkshire, 21 July 1922) is known as lingerie-counter assistant Mrs Slocombe in *Are You Being Served?*, but also made appearances in the *Street* as Annie Walker's licensed victualler friend NELLIE HARVEY, from the Laughing Donkey, on and off from 1965 to 1977. Mollie also starred in *That's My Boy* and *My Husband and I*, the latter with her real-life husband, William Moore (who played Betty Turpin's husband, Sgt Cyril Turpin, in the *Street*).

Jennifer Moss, who played tearaway teenager LUCILLE HEWITT from the serial's early days until 1973, had previously acted on radio with other future *Street* stars, including Eileen Derbyshire, Arthur Lowe and Violet Carson. After leaving the programme, Jennifer married five times, suffered several personal tragedies and overcame alcoholism.

that he was her real father – a revelation that stunned Maureen. Maud explained that she wanted Maureen to know the truth. When Percy found out, he called off their wedding, not able to accept that she had conducted an affair behind her serviceman husband's back.

☆ ☆ ☆

Elizabeth Bradley was a member of the VAD (Voluntary Aid Detachment), part of the British Red Cross, during the Second World War and worked at a military hospital in the grounds of the Royal National Orthopaedic Hospital in London, where many children were treated. Her father, who worked in the Air Ministry, was killed three days before V.E. Day.

She has appeared in dozens of television programmes since the sixties, including *Dr Finlay's Casebook*, *Softly Softly*, *The Sweeney*, *Tales of the Unexpected*, *Shine on Harvey Moon*, *Juliet Bravo*, *The Bill* (in three roles), *Bergerac*, *Casualty*, *The Men's Room*, *Rides*, *Resnick*, *London's Burning*, *Memento Mori*, *An Ungentlemanly Act* and *A Little Bit of Lippy*, before joining *Coronation Street*. She was also in the films *An American Werewolf in London* and *Brimstone and Treacle*.

On stage, Elizabeth has acted at the National Theatre in *Caritas*, *The Crucible*, *Abingdon Square*, *Black Snow* and *Billy Liar*, and the Royal Court in *Touched*, *Restoration* and *Women Beware Women*, as well as West End productions of *The Three Sisters* and *Uncle Vanya*. As Florence Boothroyd in *Billy Liar*, Elizabeth was nominated for a Laurence Olivier Award as Best Actress in a Supporting Role.

MAUREEN HOLDSWORTH

While waiting on tables in a café in Llandudno, Maureen Grimes met Reg Holdsworth. He was on holiday in the North Wales resort back in 1968, dropped in for a cup of tea and asked her out. They became engaged three months later, but their plans were opposed by Maureen's domineering mother, Maud, who instantly disliked Reg. Maureen and Reg continued their romance in secret, so Wilfred and Maud Grimes decided to finish it once and for all by moving away. That was the last Reg saw of Maureen until she arrived as an assistant at Bettabuys supermarket, which he was managing.

During the intervening years, she had married Frank Naylor and lived in Preston, 50 km (30 miles) away. That had ended in divorce, as had Reg's marriage to Veronica Hardback. Maureen and Reg wasted no time in resuming their relationship, determined that Maud – now widowed – would not come between them this time. The

couple became engaged for a second time, although Maureen called off the wedding when she caught Reg with Debi Scott, widow of Bettabuys' former area manager, Brendan. She gave in when Reg pleaded with her to take him back and then let her own defences down for a night of passion with Curly Watts, who had been her fiancé's assistant at Bettabuys. But the wedding went ahead on 26 January 1994.

Brendan Scott had beaten Reg to buying Alf Roberts's Mini Market, in Coronation Street, but Brendan was now dead and Reg bought the business so that he and Maureen could work there together – although, in July 1994, he left Maureen and her mother in charge while he took a new job running Firman's Freezers.

☆ ☆ ☆

Sherrie Hewson (b. Sherrie Lynn Hutchinson in Nottingham) was brought up in the village of Burton Joyce, near Nottingham. Her father was in the gown business but also worked as a singer with big bands, and her mother was a model and beautician who also ran a boutique in Nottingham called Joy's. Sherrie started singing and tap-dancing at the age of seven in revues around the country. She found work as an usherette at the Nottingham Playhouse at the age of 17, before training at RADA.

Sherrie – who changed her professional name to Hewson in the seventies, when advised that Hutchinson was too long – became best known on television as part of Russ Abbot's act in such shows as *Russ Abbot's Madhouse*, *The Russ Abbot Show* and *Russ Abbot*.

Before joining *Coronation Street* in 1993, her TV appearances included *Love for Lydia*, *My Son, My Son*, *Flickers* (with Bob Hoskins), *Home, James!* (with Jim Davidson), *Lovejoy*, *Haggard* and *The Bill*. She is often seen in *It'll Be Alright on the Night* in her role as Christopher Beeny's wife in the sitcom *In Loving Memory*, in a scene in which the bed they are lying in collapses. Sherrie was also in the films *Carry On Behind*, in 1975, and *The Slipper and the Rose*, in 1976. Eleven years later, she appeared with *Street* actress Amanda Barrie in the West End stage production *Stepping Out*.

Sherrie and her British Aerospace executive husband Ken, who married in 1976, have a daughter, Keelie, and live in Surrey.

REG HOLDSWORTH

Some people wonder how bumbling Reg Holdsworth can hold down his position as manager of a supermarket, but the job runs in the family – his father was a grocer.

Reg's first love was Maureen Grimes, whom he

Reg came close to losing his job when he fixed a raffle so that Rita would win a trolleyful of goods. She donated them to a local hospital, but Vera Duckworth complained, resulting in Reg sacking her. She wrote to Bettabuys' head office and a formal investigation was launched by Reg's arch-enemy, Brendan Scott, whom he had once investigated himself. That had resulted in Scott's demotion, but he had worked his way back up and was now in a position to ruin Reg's career. Temporarily suspended, Reg persuaded Vera that it was in both their interests that she withdraw her allegations. She agreed, his job was secure and he reinstated her.

Reg's first love, Maureen, came back into his life at Bettabuys. She applied for a job as an assistant there and Reg saw it as a way of winning her back. Now called Maureen Naylor, she had also been married but was now divorced from husband Frank. The couple were finally together again, vowing that this time Maureen's mother would not stop true love taking its course. They became engaged, but Maureen broke it off after catching Reg with Debi Scott, Brendan's widow. He pleaded with her to have him back, they were engaged for a third time and, although Maureen subsequently admitted to a one-night stand with Curly Watts, the wedding went ahead on 26 January 1994.

Reg had bought the cornershop in Coronation Street, having previously left the Weatherfield branch of Bettabuys to become the firm's area manager. Alf Roberts had sold the shop to Brendan Scott – Reg's predecessor as area manager – but, when Brendan died suddenly, Reg took this second opportunity of acquiring a business for him and Maureen to run together.

He soon grew tired of working in such a small outfit and, in July 1994, left Maureen and her mother to run it while he became manager at Firman's Freezers, run by his old friend Eric Firman, who was best man at his wedding to Maureen. Later, he was able to offer Curly the job of his assistant there, reuniting the management team that had bumbled along at Bettabuys.

☆ ☆ ☆

Ken Morley quickly became a hit with viewers when he started hamming it up as supermarket manager Reg Holdsworth. But he switched to acting only after abandoning a career in teaching. He took a degree in English and drama at Manchester University and was in the films *Alfie Darling* and *Little Dorrit*, and on television in *Who Dares Wins*, *Quest*, *Bulman*, *The Return of the Antelope*, *All Passion Spent*, *Les Girls*, *The Management*, *Blind Justice*, *Chelmsford 123*, *Watching* and *You Rang, M'Lord?* He played scar-faced German army supremo Flockenstuffen in the BBC comedy series *'Allo, 'Allo* before joining *Coronation Street* in 1989.

met in 1968 on holiday in Llandudno, where she was a waitress in a café. He asked her out and they became engaged three months later. But Maureen's mother, Maud, took an instant disliking to Reg, then a humble shop assistant.

Following a two-week trip away from home on business, Reg returned to Weatherfield to be told by Maureen's timid father, Wilfred, that Maureen no longer wanted to see him – the family moved away shortly afterwards.

Concentrating on his job as an assistant at the Co-op, where he had started at the bottom in the supermarket business, Reg gained promotion and, in 1972, joined Thos Ellis and Goodwin, which three years later amalgamated to become part of Bettabuys. He took over as manager of the Weatherfield store in Albert Road. In 1989, Reg married Veronica Hardback. He took on Curly Watts as trainee assistant manager in the same year and treated him as his protégé.

Veronica threw Reg out when he had an affair with Bettabuys store detective Renée Dodds. He moved into the flat above Alf Roberts's shop in Coronation Street but was ejected from there, too, after Bettabuys started running a free bus service for customers, with a route that included the Street – and of course Alf's Mini Market. Tackling the problem head on, Reg ditched his fancy woman and transferred her to another branch. As a result, his wife took him back.

However, when he tried to woo Rita Fairclough, he told her that they had since separated and Veronica was in New Zealand. Curly's knowledge that she was simply visiting her sister there was a useful weapon when he had problems of his own with fiancée Kimberley Taylor, who worked at the supermarket, had broken off their engagement and wanted a transfer to the Bolton branch, against Curly's wishes.

CORONATION STREET

Richard Davies had found fame in the comedy series *Please Sir!* when he became cornershop owner IDRIS HOPKINS in the *Street*. He also played Max Johnson in the 1981 Welsh soap *Taff Acre*.

Prunella Scales (b. Prunella Margaret Rumney Illingworth in Sutton Abinger, Surrey, 22 June 1932) played bus conductress EILEEN HUGHES in 1961, before finding fame as Basil's wife Sybil in *Fawlty Towers* and Sarah in *After Henry*.

Tony Osoba, best known as grumbling McLaren in the comedy series *Porridge* and Det. Con. Chas Jarvis in *Dempsey and Makepeace*, played PETER INGRAM, who ran his own factory until his premature death, leaving the way for Mike Baldwin to step in as boss and woo his widow Jackie. He also acted in *Brookside*.

Ben Kingsley (b. Yorkshire) acted smooth-talking RON JENKINS, who tried to chat up Irma Barlow and had a fling with Ken Barlow's first wife, Valerie, in 1966. He later won a Best Actor Oscar as star of the film *Gandhi*.

Paula Wilcox (b. Manchester, 13 December 1949) played Ray Langton's wayward sister JANICE LANGTON, who arrived in the Street in 1969 after coming out of Borstal but went on her way two months later. Paula herself went on to star in the comedy series *The Lovers*, *Man About the House*, *Miss Jones and Son* and *Fiddlers Three*, as well as the Willy Russell stage play *Shirley Valentine*, in the West End. She also played Angela Heery, Diana Corkhill's lawyer, in *Brookside*.

Neville Buswell played RAY LANGTON, who worked in Len Fairclough's building business. The character snatched Deirdre Hunt from her fiancé Billy Walker, but their marriage ended in divorce. Neville, who appeared from 1966 to 1978, has never acted in Britain since and was last seen as a croupier in a Las Vegas casino. Granada has failed in its attempts to locate Neville – he is owed thousands of pounds in royalties for *Street* screenings.

Tony Anholt (b. Singapore, 19 January 1941), later to play Charles Frere in *Howards' Way*, was crooked model agency boss DAVID LAW, who ran off with registration fees from Gail Potter and her friend Tricia Hopkins.

Ken turned the character of Reg Holdsworth from a serious, hard-working supermarket manager into a comic figure. He said he saw Reg and his assistant, Curly Watts, as a team – 'two total prats in charge of a supermarket'. In 1995, he released a video, *Ken Morley Presents Party Time Karaoke*, in which he performed 14 classic songs, from 'Rock Around the Clock' to 'Dancing Queen'.

The actor's stage appearances include *The Adventures of Mr Toad*, *Volpone*, *Beaux' Stratagem*, *Insignificance*, *Comic Cuts*, *The Ragged Trousered Philanthropist*, *Dracula*, *Habeas Corpus*, *The Tax Exile* and *Pinnochio*.

Ken and wife Sue had a baby son, Roger, in September 1990. Ken's pride and joy is a matt-black Pontiac Le Mans Special nicknamed The Beast, one of a collection of classic cars.

ANDY McDONALD

Twin brother of Steve, Andrew Richard McDonald was born in Manchester on 26 June 1974 and proved to be the academic member of the family. His father, Jim, was in the army and most of Andy's childhood was spent moving from one base to another, until Jim returned to civvy street and bought no. 11 Coronation Street from Alf and Audrey Roberts in 1989.

Andy and Steve soon caused trouble by kicking a football through the window of Alf's shop. Father Jim confined them to the house and stopped their pocket money after Alf gave him a bill for £150. To add insult to injury, the boys escaped from the house by climbing out of a rear window and Steve started driving a digger from Maurice Jones's building site and crashed into the shop window.

Andy had a habit of losing his girlfriends to Steve, such as when he was seeing student 'Flick' Khan's younger sister, Joanne. This led to fisticuffs and Steve and Joanne ran away to the Lake District.

Then, Andy met Paula Maxwell on a visit to the library, where she was studying. Putting her education first, Paula cooled their relationship, so Andy told her to get lost. But the couple were quickly reunited and spent a long holiday touring Europe and planned to go to Sheffield University together – until Paula dropped the bombshell that she had been accepted at Manchester.

This inevitably led to a parting of the ways, and Andy started going out with shelf-filler Amy Nelson from Bettabuys supermarket, where he worked during an Easter holiday. He later found out that Amy had a young son, Dominic, but he got on well with the boy.

58

Andy decided to get a job at Bettabuys instead of going back to university. Amy opposed this idea but accepted his proposal of marriage. But she left on a holiday to Trinidad, got back together with Dominic's father, Errol, and did not return. Andy's plans to live in the flat above Jim's Café with his wife were scuppered and Bettabuys manager Curly Watts offered Andy a job as trainee manager and lodgings at his house, no. 7 Coronation Street.

When old flame Paula came looking for a holiday job in Bettabuys, Andy was pleased to recommend her to Curly, who asked her out on a date, only to be stood up. But Paula returned to her studies and Andy had only his career to think about. He gave up his job, decided to go to university himself and earned money by serving behind the bar at the Rovers Return.

☆ ☆ ☆

Nicholas Cochrane (b. Wythenshawe, Manchester, 16 December 1973) acted in school productions, including *My Fair Lady* and Willy Russell's *Our Day Out*, which was performed at the Forum Theatre, Manchester.

He had already appeared in *Coronation Street* as an extra – playing football in a street scene – when he was spotted at his comprehensive school, in Cheadle, near Stockport, and invited to audition for the role of Andy McDonald. Nicholas left school in 1990. His long-term ambition is to appear in films.

When, in 1993, Liz was offered the job of landlady of The Queens pub, in the heart of Weatherfield, Jim wondered what Newton & Ridley brewery boss Richard Willmore was really after. Liz had been a barmaid at the Rovers for only two years and now she was being offered the brewery's showpiece pub, with an up-market clientele.

Jim's jealousy ended up tearing the McDonald family apart and stripping Liz of her ambitions. After Jim thumped Willmore, he was barred from the premises, which inevitably led to him and Liz splitting up. His fury was heightened when he heard that Liz was having an affair with Colin Barnes, Des's romeo brother. Jim filed for divorce, but on New Year's Eve 1993 he and Liz came to their senses and decided to get back together. Liz lost her pub, but she and Jim had a marriage once more.

☆ ☆ ☆

Charles Lawson (b. Quentin Charles Devenish in Belfast, 17 September 1959) intended to join the Merchant Navy on leaving Campbell College public school, but a teacher persuaded him to consider acting and Charles trained at the Guildhall School of Music and Drama.

He has extensive theatre experience, appearing in *Murderers* for the National Theatre, *Henry VIII*, *Romeo and Juliet*, *The Comedy of Errors* and *The Shepherd's Tale* for the RSC, *Henry IV, Parts I* and *II* and *Henry V* for the English

JIM McDONALD

On leaving the army, Jim McDonald bought no. 11 Coronation Street from Alf and Audrey Roberts, and moved in with his family, wife Liz and teenage twin sons Andy and Steve.

Leaving the army was difficult for Jim, who insisted it had always 'been good' to the family. When he saw an advertisement for a recruiting sergeant based in Manchester, he was tempted, but Liz was adamant that he should make a clean break. She eventually told him to choose between her and the army, so he settled into civilian life and found work as a TV repairman.

He walked out on the job after a bust-up with Alf Roberts over Audrey's attempt to lure him into a compromising situation when he went to fix their set in the house they had bought, in Grasmere Avenue.

Jim bought a motorbike from Jack Duckworth, restored it and decided to turn his interest in bikes into a business, opening up a repair shop under the viaduct at the end of the Street. When he could not make a go of the business, Jim took a job as a mechanic under Kevin Webster at Mike Baldwin's garage, MVB Motors.

David Daker was Rovers Return relief manager GORDON LEWIS, before playing hotelier Harry Crawford in *Boon* and Ben Campbell in *Crown Prosecutor*.

Pop star **Davy Jones** (b. Manchester, 30 December 1945) was the first of two actors to play COLIN LOMAX, Ena Sharples's grandson. He appeared in one episode in 1961, aged 15, and went on to act in the first episode of *Z-Cars* and become lead singer of the sixties pop group The Monkees. More recently, he guest-starred in *Family Ties* on TV and was on stage in *Grease*, both in America.

Lynne Carol (b. Monmouthshire, 29 June 1914) played MARTHA LONGHURST for 295 episodes, from its early days until 1964, when Martha died in the Rovers snug, where she was usually seen with Ena Sharples and Minnie Caldwell. Lynne later appeared on TV in *The Newcomers* and in the film *Yanks*. Her late husband Bert Palmer acted Walter Biddulph, who sold The Kabin to Len Fairclough. Lynne died on 30 June 1990.

Shakespeare Company and *Diary of a Hunger Striker* for Hull Truck Theatre Company. Charles was in the films *Ascendancy, SS, I Cannot Answer That Question* and *Wilt*, and on TV in *Harry's Game, Four Days in May, Joyce in June, The Firm, Crown Court, The Monocled Mutineer, Upline, Bread* and *Valentine Falls*, before joining *Coronation Street* in 1989.

He and wife Susie, who have a daughter, Laura-Kimberley, separated in 1994, when Charles fell for Granada TV make-up artist Lesley Bond.

LIZ McDONALD

Wife of Jim and mother of twins Andy and Steve, Liz McDonald – born Elizabeth Jayne Greenwood – saw the move to Coronation Street as a chance to start a new family life after her husband's departure from the army.

However, Jim soon had ideas about taking up a recruiting sergeant's job in Manchester, and Liz told him that she had had enough of his army days. Johnny Johnson, who had once had a fling with Liz while Jim was away, intended to apply for the same job but decided not to when he heard that Jim was thinking of going for it. Liz eventually gave Jim an ultimatum: choose between her and the army. Jim decided to settle down in civvy street.

When son Steve ran off with Joanne Khan, sister of student 'Flick', Liz and Jim had no idea where they could have gone. A disillusioned Joanne returned to Weatherfield by herself, Liz borrowed Rita Fairclough's car and drove to the Lake District, where she found Steve, and took him home. She had to restrain Jim from beating Steve, and he calmed down only when she threatened to leave home with the boys.

After Tina Fowler left the Rovers Return, Bet Gilroy took on Liz as a barmaid, although Alec was apprehensive about her skills for the job and told her that she was entering showbusiness when she stepped behind the bar.

When Sally Webster went into labour and Kevin was out helping Alf and Audrey Roberts after their car broke down, Liz was on hand to deliver baby Rosie in the back seat of Don Brennan's minicab.

Liz suddenly saw her ambitions for a career being realized when Newton & Ridley boss Richard Willmore decided he liked her style behind the bar and offered her the licence of The Queens, the brewery's showpiece pub in the heart of Weatherfield. Jim wondered whether Willmore had ulterior motives for giving Liz her own pub when she had only two years' experience as a barmaid.

Liz jumped at the offer, not realizing that the move would bring the McDonald family to its knees. Jim's jealousy led him to thump Willmore, and Liz was summoned to the brewery. She thought that her short-lived reign at The Queens was over, but Willmore explained that the brewery had no quarrel with Liz, only Jim. She could carry on, but Jim was barred from the premises. She did so and found help behind the bar – and in the bedroom – from Colin Barnes, Des's smooth-talking brother.

Jim set divorce proceedings in motion, then Liz counter-petitioned, only for the couple to make up their differences on New Year's Eve 1993. Willmore told Liz she had to choose between the pub and Jim. She chose Jim and pressurized the brewery into paying her £2000 in compensation.

After picking up the pieces and working behind the bar at the Legion and the Rovers, Liz was offered a job in Sean Skinner's bookies. Sean's own marriage was on the rocks and he thought that Liz might be the woman to provide him with some comfort. When he made a pass at her, she turned him down and fled from the premises, but he later apologized and she continued in her new job.

Beverley Callard (b. Leeds), daughter of a concert pianist and a baker, made her stage debut at the age of seven as the boy lead in *Darius the Page Boy*.

On television, she has acted in *Emmerdale* – as Jackie Merrick's girlfriend Angie Richards – the Hinge and Brackett series *Dear Ladies, Hell's Bells* and *The Practice*. She also appeared with her teenage daughter Rebecca in both *The Booktower* and the BBC's 'Screen Two' film *Will You Love Me Tomorrow*.

She first appeared in *Coronation Street* in 1984, as June Dewhurst, a friend of Gail and Brian Tilsley, who with her husband (played by John Bowler, later to star in the comedy series *Watching*), enjoyed an evening out at the local casino with the couple. She returned to the *Street* as Liz McDonald five years later.

Beverley, who gave birth to her daughter at the age of 17 and previously acted under the name of Sowden, also has a son, Joshua, with her husband Steven and lives in Leeds. Daughter Rebecca has starred in *The Borrowers* and *September Song* on television.

STEVE McDONALD

A budding young businessman with an eye for the girls, Steven James McDonald was born in Manchester on 26 June 1974. Twin brother of the more academic Andy, Steve grew up to fancy himself as another Mike Baldwin.

When he fell for student 'Flick' Khan's younger sister Joanne, who was staying in Weatherfield during the summer holidays. the pair ran away to the Lake District, on Jim's motorbike. But, as life on the run became more difficult and the romance began to wane, Joanne hitched her way back to Coronation Street – and a father who had travelled from Canterbury in Kent. Steve's mother, Liz, drove to the Lakes to pick him up.

Steve's next venture was setting up a pirate radio station with brother Andy called Just Can't Wait, which broadcast from their father's bike shop on a home-made transmitter. Forced underground when the gossip they broadcast upset residents, they moved to Ken Barlow's flat, with the help of his daughter, Tracy. The police eventually stopped the broadcasts by confiscating the equipment when the brothers moved into Deirdre Barlow's house while she was on holiday.

When orphan Vicky Arden arrived at the Rovers Return for holidays from her private school, staying with her grandfather, Alec Gilroy, Steve liked what he saw and was soon leading her off the straight and narrow. She lost her virginity to him, but he had no qualms about two-timing Vicky with nurse Alison Rathbone. He ended up losing both of them.

By now, Steve was working in Mike Baldwin's T-shirt print shop and earning money on the side by running off cheaper shirts on the quiet. But Mike rumbled his game and Steve suggested that he start his own business in the print shop, paying rent, bills and rates to Mike.

Steve was in even more trouble when he ran up huge gambling debts, including £2000 at Sean Skinner's bookies. When Steve won £800 at dog racing, Sean was on hand to relieve him of the money to cover part of the debt. Steve called the police in but eventually withdrew charges.

The love of his life by this time was hairdresser Fiona Middleton, who moved into his luxury flat with him. On learning of his debts – including a credit card over its spending limit – she threatened to leave unless he acted more responsibly. He agreed and they moved into the more modest flat above Alma Baldwin's café.

Fiona was not so happy when, in April 1995, Steve's old flame Vicky invested some of her inheritance in his print shop, which he renamed Dun 2aT. Vicky lost £1500 that she gave Steve to produce an order for Costello's nightclub, which then went bankrupt without paying the bill. But Vicky continued investing on condition that she and Steve were business partners and that she had financial control. As a result, Fiona dumped Steve and he returned to Vicky.

☆ ☆ ☆

Simon Gregson (b. Simon Alan Gregory in Wythenshawe, Manchester, 2 October 1974) is a year younger than his screen 'twin' Nicholas Cochrane. Although he appeared in plays at primary school – playing the lead role in such productions as *The Simpleton* – Simon did no more acting until landing the role of Steve McDonald in *Coronation Street* in 1989.

Simon and Nicholas Cochrane both attended a comprehensive school in Cheadle, near Stockport, but hardly knew one another until they were both cast in the *Street*. Simon took his GCSEs in the summer of 1991.

Away from the studios, he enjoys tinkering with cars and owns a Suzuki Jeep. He also has a speedboat and enjoys water-skiing. In May 1995, Simon admitted to kicking a cocaine habit that had cost him £15,000 in 12 months.

Bill Maynard (b. Farnham, Surrey, 8 October 1928) was song agent MICKEY MALONE, before finding fame as the hopeless council handyman in *Oh No It's Selwyn Froggitt*, cunning boss Fred Moffat in *The Gaffer* and layabout Claude Jeremiah Greengrass in *Heartbeat*.

William Lucas (b. Manchester, 14 April 1925), who played Dr James Gordon in *Black Beauty* and *The New Adventures of Black Beauty*, acted Elsie Tanner's boyfriend DENNIS MAXWELL. William later played Stanley Webb in *Eldorado*.

Singer Michael Ball was MALCOLM NUTTALL, the boyfriend of Michelle Robinson who had a punch-up with rival Kevin Webster. Michael later starred in the West End musical hits *Les Misérables* and *Aspects of Love*.

Jean Alexander (b. Liverpool, 24 February 1926) will be remembered for ever as HILDA OGDEN. She left the role in 1987, after 23 years, and has subsequently appeared on television in *Boon*, *Last of the Summer Wine* (as Auntie Wainwright), the children's series *Woof!* and the sitcom *Rich Tea & Sympathy*, as well as playing Christine Keeler's mother in the film *Scandal*. A little-remembered fact is that Jean first appeared in *Coronation Street* as MRS WEBB – the landlady of Joan Akers, who kidnapped baby Christopher Hewitt – in 1962.

Bernard Youens (b. Bernard Popley in Hove, Sussex, 28 December 1914) played workshy STAN OGDEN from 1964 until his death on 27 August 1984, after 1200 episodes. The velvet-voiced Southerner was previously a Granada TV announcer.

Gabrielle Drake (b. Lahore, Pakistan), who played Dennis Tanner's Swedish girlfriend INGA OLSEN in 1967, later acted Lt. Gay Ellis in *UFO*, Kelly Monteith's wife in *Kelly Monteith* and motel manager Nicola Freeman in *Crossroads*.

Joanna Lumley (b. Srinagar, India, 1 May 1946) made her TV debut in *Coronation Street* as ELAINE PERKINS, appearing for eight episodes in 1973 as Ken Barlow's girlfriend before dumping him for a Liberal M.P. She went on to play Purdey in *The New Avengers*, Sapphire in *Sapphire and Steel*, Patsy in *Absolutely Fabulous* and Kate Swift in *Class Act*.

FIONA MIDDLETON

After joining Denise Osbourne's hairdressing salon in Coronation Street as a trainee, live-wire Fiona Middleton fell for budding businessman Steve McDonald after seeing him in a flashy new car and he offered to take her for a spin.

She was able to bring him down to earth when he splashed his money around and ran up gambling debts. When, in 1995, Steve proposed marriage, she turned him down but agreed to continue living with him, although she persuaded Steve to give up his penthouse flat and move into the more modest accommodation over Jim's Café in Rosamund Street, after his credit card was taken away from him.

Fiona was riled when Steve's former girlfriend, Vicky Arden, became involved in his life again by putting up money from her inheritance as capital for his T-shirt business. Finally, in June 1995, she threw Steve out of their flat.

By then, Fiona had her own business responsibilities. That month, she was made manager of the salon, after running it briefly while Denise took a short break following a row with Ken Barlow over his rights of access to son Daniel.

☆ ☆ ☆

Angela Griffin (b. Yorkshire), a former member of Leeds Children's Theatre and South Leeds Youth Theatre, played Tina in *Emmerdale*, Gail in *Under the Bedclothes* and Zoe in three series of *Just Us* before joining *Coronation Street*. She enjoys horse-riding, aerobics, swimming and badminton.

DENISE OSBOURNE

Hairdresser Denise Osbourne left her well heeled husband, Frank, to run off with Neil Mitchell. The couple married, but that relationship also ended and Denise sought a new life in Coronation Street, where she opened her own salon, Denise's. But she turned to Neil when work was needed on the premises. At first, he wanted to patch things up, but then he fell for design student Angie Freeman.

A new man came into Denise's life with the arrival of rag-trade businessman Hanif Ruparell, who wooed her with expensive meals. He was just looking for a good time, but Denise fell for him and was hurt when he rejected her.

Don Brennan, estranged from his wife Ivy, tried to buy love by lending Denise money for her business, but she made it clear that she was not interested in a relationship. Then, she started receiving nuisance phone calls in which the caller said nothing at the other end of the line. She even asked Don to stay with her one night in case more came – and was shocked to find out he was the culprit.

Denise found new love with Ken Barlow, who seemed to be making up with his third wife, Deirdre, just as her mother was taken ill and she had to leave the Street to care for her.

By the time she returned, Ken and Denise were an item. It was a shock to both of them when Denise became pregnant – and an even bigger one when she experienced the trauma of losing the baby, only to discover that she had been carrying twins and the other one was still alive.

But Denise had no expectations of Ken after the birth and even mistrusted his motives in wanting to fulfil his role as a father, especially after Deirdre announced that she was marrying Samir Rachid. With two broken marriages behind her, Denise was determined to maintain her independence and made it clear to Ken that she did not want to continue their relationship.

When she went into labour, she kept the news from Ken, but she had time to change her mind and he was there when baby son Daniel was born, on 4 January 1995. Ken gave Denise great support during the following weeks, but she still shut him out – and even registered the birth in her surname, without naming Ken as the father.

During her pregnancy, she had brought in stylist Jon Welch to run the salon and was hoping that he would buy her out, but he was unable to raise the cash. In 1995, after a picnic in the countryside with Denise and Daniel, Jon made a pass at Denise back at her flat but was rebuffed. He left the flat and the salon.

Denise, who had just refused Ken access to Daniel, was in a state of total confusion and, with Ken threatening legal action, left the Street with Daniel for a short break at the house of her sister Alison, which meant that her newly qualified assistant, Fiona Middleton, had to run the salon.

After having time to think, Denise returned to the Street and told Ken that she wanted to marry him but was shocked when he refused, saying that he no longer wanted to be a part of her life and was only interested in seeing Daniel. Denise, meanwhile, made Fiona manager of her salon so that she could concentrate on her son.

Denise Black (b. Denise Nixon in Portsmouth, Hampshire) read psychology at London University, then travelled to Gibraltar and the West Indies, before opting to be an actress. She found her first work at the Crucible Theatre, Sheffield, as a cat in a play called *Miniatures* and subsequently acted in fringe theatre.

After getting her Equity actors' union card in 1980, Denise went on a year-long tour of South America, Israel, Greece and Yugoslavia with the Actors Touring Company, performing *Measure for Measure*, *Don Quixote*, *Berlin Berlin* and *The Tempest*. Then, she returned to Britain and the Newcastle Playhouse to act the lead role of a female Spanish leader in *Pasionaria*, in which she aged from 14 to 42.

Two of the actresses with whom she was working – Josie Lawrence and Kate McKenzie – shared an interest in singing with Denise, who had been performing jazz standards with a guitarist. So they formed Denise Black and the Kray Sisters and started touring.

As a result of her association with Josie Lawrence, Denise was seen on TV in *Saturday Live* and *Josie*, as well as landing parts in *Casualty*, the *Sherlock Holmes* series (as a Welsh maid), *The Bill*, the BBC 'ScreenPlay' *Dead Romantic*, *A Touch of Frost* and *Between the Lines*. She was also in the National Film and Television School production *Play Dead*, which was screened on Channel Four.

The actress found that television was a way to finance her work in the theatre. Her other stage appearances have included two productions of *Twelfth Night* – playing Olivia at the Edinburgh Fringe Festival and Maria for the Cambridge Theatre Company – *Romeo and Juliet* (as Juliet), at the Grove Theatre, and the Carib Theatre Company production *Streetwise*, which won her a Best Supporting Actress award. She also appeared in an improvised show at the Donmar Warehouse, in which Julian Clary starred as a Scholl sandal and Denise played another shoe in the shop!

Married to musician Paul Sand, she has two children, son Sam and daughter Dandy. Denise and Paul met when she auditioned for a part in a touring production. In 1995, she was producer of a new musical, *Mad and Her Dad* – with the music written by Paul – at the Lyric Theatre, Hammersmith, and took the role of unlucky-in-love Madelaine, searching for her father.

PHYLLIS PEARCE

Chasing fellow pensioner Percy Sugden has become a full-time occupation for Phyllis Pearce, of the blue-rinse hairdo. Born in Gorton Close, Weatherfield, on 7 February 1921, Phyllis visited Coronation Street when grandson Craig Whiteley moved there with his grandfather on the other side of the family, Chalkie.

When her own home, in Ondurman Street, was demolished, Phyllis asked Chalkie if she could move in with him. He refused and, after winning £3500 on the horses, he emigrated to Australia, where Craig was already living.

Soon, Phyllis was working for Gail Tilsley in Jim's Café, but she was sacked when owner Alma Sedgewick decided to take a more active interest in the business. Phyllis was already chasing Percy Sugden, whose war memories she listens to avidly, but he has always insisted that he is not interested in her. This has not stopped her infatuation.

☆ ☆ ☆

Jill Summers (b. Eccles, Lancashire, 10 December 1910) has been in showbusiness all her life. Her father was a circus tightrope walker and her mother a revue artist. Almost inevitably, she took to the stage as a child and performed a musical comedy double act with her brother, before becoming a stand-up comedienne, performing in almost every theatre in Britain.

As an actress, Jill appeared on television in such programmes as the serial *Castlehaven*, *How We Used to Live*, *Stay with Me Till Morning*, *This Year, Next Year* and the Alan Bennett play *Sunset Across the Bay*. She also had her own TV series, *Summers Here*, featuring a different star guest each week. Jill first appeared in *Coronation Street* in 1972, as Hilda Ogden's

> **Ray Brooks (b. Brighton, East Sussex, 20 April 1939) played NORMAN PHILLIPS** and went on to star in such programmes as *Big Deal*, *Running Wild* and *The World of Eddie Weary*.
>
> **Veteran actress Doris Hare (b. Bargoed, Mid Glamorgan, 1 March 1905) turned down the part of Ena Sharples in 1960** because she did not want to commit herself to a long-running role. But, nine years later, she played ALICE PICKENS, who agreed to marry grumpy Albert Tatlock, mainly for financial reasons, until the vicar was delayed for the wedding ceremony and the pair had time to think better of it. Doris's best known to television viewers as Mum in *On the Buses*.
>
> **Warren Clarke appeared in just six episodes – as three different characters.** He was KENNY PICKUP, one of Lucille Hewitt's boyfriends, in 1965, and student TIM JORDAN, another of her lovers, two years later, before returning in 1968 as GARY BAILEY, Elsie Tanner's nephew. He has acted in the films *A Clockwork Orange* and *O Lucky Man!*, and on television in *The Manageress*, *Gone to the Dogs* and *Gone to Seed*.

fellow cleaner, Bessie Proctor, at a nightclub where Rita Fairclough (then Littlewood) sang. Ten years later, she returned as Phyllis Pearce.

In 1984, her second husband, a doctor, died and she credits the *Street*'s cast with helping her through her grief. Jill is particularly liked by children, who see her as a grandmother figure. She is almost ten years older than the character she plays, lives in Yorkshire and has an adopted son and two grandchildren.

GAIL PLATT

After marrying Brian Tilsley twice, mothering his two children and having an affair with his cousin, Gail Tilsley sought a life without dependence on men. But her relationship with toy-boy Martin Platt and the birth of their son David gave her a different perspective on love – until Martin, too, cheated on her.

Born in Weatherfield on 18 April 1950, Gail was the illegitimate daughter of Audrey Potter and never knew her father. The experience of growing up without a father and with a mother who had an eye for the men left Gail with a feeling of insecurity.

She took a job in the Mark Brittain Warehouse, then moved to Sylvia's Separates, managed by Elsie Tanner. When Mike Baldwin bought the boutique, he turned it into a shop selling denim fashions, The Western Front, and Suzie Birchall worked there.

Gail shared the flat above the corner shop with Tricia Hopkins and, in 1976, began to get nuisance phone calls where the caller said nothing. Gail reported the calls to the G.P.O. and telephone engineer John Lane came round that evening, promising to deal with the caller when he next rang. As the pair sat in the flat and the hours passed with no calls, it became apparent to Gail that she was sitting in the same room as the phantom caller. Emily Bishop's suspicions about an engineer coming round in the evening led to the police arriving. Lane explained that he would not have hurt Gail, but he was clearly obsessed with her.

Shortly afterwards, Gail moved into Elsie Howard's house and lost her virginity to an older man, Roy Thornley, only to discover that he was married. She ditched him but found herself cited as co-respondent in a divorce action. Gail was let off the hook after Elsie informed the cheating man's wife that he had also been sleeping with his boss, Sylvia Matthews.

Happiness seemed to have arrived when Brian Tilsley gatecrashed a party at Elsie's house. Four months later, the couple were engaged, they married on 28 November 1979 and son Nicky was born on 31 December 1980. Facing financial problems, the couple sold their house and moved in with Brian's mother, Ivy, a Catholic who resented the fact that her son had not married someone of the same religion. Gail pressed Brian to find somewhere else for them and their toddler, but he was content to stay.

In April 1985, Gail walked out on her husband and moved into a small flat. Brian persuaded her to return and they moved into a council house, but their relationship was still not working. A year later, Gail had an affair with Ian Latimer, Brian's Australian cousin, who was visiting Britain. When Gail discovered she was pregnant, she told Brian that it could be Ian's child. He left her and moved in with his new girlfriend, Liz Turnbull. When blood tests proved it could not be Ian's baby, Brian said it made no difference, and divorce followed.

Shortly after the birth of their daughter, Sarah Louise, on 3 February 1987, Gail started seeing carpenter Jeff Singleton, and Brian was concerned about another man standing in as his children's father. In desperation, Brian seized son Nicky and took him away. The police mounted a nationwide search and Brian planned to take his son to Ireland. But, knowing that he would probably be found and seeing that Nicky was beginning to miss his mother, Brian took him home after four days.

The couple reconciled their differences and, in February 1988, remarried. But they started to drift apart again and Brian began seeing other women. One evening exactly a year later, Gail told him that she did not love him and wanted a divorce. He went out to a disco, picked up a young blonde and was stabbed to death on his way out by a gang of youths. By then Gail had become a partner in Jim's Café, with 40 per cent of the business. She had enough experience of running the café and looking after husband Brian's garage-business accounts to believe she could make a go of it.

Gail, to her own surprise, began a relationship with young Martin Platt, who had worked on and off at the café. They became closer as he took Nicky out for kickabouts in the park with his football. Against the wishes of Gail's mother, Audrey, and mother-in-law, Ivy, Martin moved into Gail's house and Gail became pregnant. Feeling that she could not cope with another child and that a baby would tie Martin down, she planned to have an abortion. As she set off on a train to have the termination, a last-minute dash by Martin resulted in him persuading Gail to keep the baby. Gail gave birth to second son David on Christmas Day 1990 and the couple married on 27 September 1991.

Martin seemed right for Gail, but their happiness was disrupted by the arrival of his fellow student nurse Carmel Finnan as a lodger in 1992. She was besotted with Martin and believed he loved her, too. When she eventually told Gail that she was too old for Martin and he did not love her, Gail threw the student out. Worse was to come when Carmel returned a few weeks later, claiming to be pregnant by Martin. Gail agonized over the situation, but the arrival of Carmel's grandfather from Ireland put her mind at rest. Carmel was not pregnant and had a history of mental illness.

Life went back to normal in the Platt household until Nick's increasing tension with Martin drove a wedge between the couple. At a Christmas party in 1994, Martin slept with a nurse, Cathy Power, and the revelation of this three months later led Gail to think she could never trust a man again and would be better off without Martin. But the couple were eventually reunited and, again, picked up the pieces of their marriage.

☆ ☆ ☆

Helen Worth (b. Cathryn Helen Wigglesworth in Leeds, 7 January 1951) is one of *Coronation Street*'s more private stars, trying to keep out of the limelight and rarely giving interviews. Her grandmother ran a boarding house for music-hall stars in Bradford, and Helen – brought up in Morecambe, Lancashire – soon caught the acting bug. She began dancing lessons when she was three to correct a tendency to walk with her toes turning inward, and her school mounted Shakespearean productions. Aged ten, she was in both the Granada Television news magazine *Scene at 6.30* – chosen to read some excerpts from a book – and an episode of *Z-Cars* in which Glenda Jackson had one line. Years later, in a TV quiz show, contestants spotted Helen but not Glenda!

As a 12th-birthday treat, Helen's parents took her to London and she auditioned for the part of one of the children, Birgitta, in the West End production of *The Sound of Music*, at the Palace Theatre. She landed the role and stayed in London with chaperones for nine months.

Helen finished her schooling in Morecambe, then returned to London to attend the Corona Stage Academy, before working in repertory theatre in Northampton, Hornchurch, Watford and Richmond-upon-Thames. She was in BBC radio's rep. company for a year, playing roles ranging from a two-year-old to a grandmother, and had small parts in the films *Oliver!* and *The Prime of Miss Jean Brodie*. On TV, she acted in *Doctor Who* and *The Doctors*, before joining *Coronation Street* in 1974, at the third attempt.

Helen married actor Michael Angelis in 1991, after 12 years of living together. They have a cottage in Cheshire and a flat in London.

MARTIN PLATT

When easy-going Martin Platt was taken on to help in Jim's Café by Gail Tilsley, she had no idea that one day she would fall for him, set up home together and have his child.

Born at 14 Malton Street, Weatherfield, on 2 June 1968, Martin took a confectionery course at Salford Technical College after gaining two

---

Stratford Johns, who played Charlie Barlow in *Z-Cars*, *Softly Softly*, *Barlow at Large* and *Barlow*, acted MR POWELL in *Coronation Street*.

Louise Harrison (b. Louise Anna Imogen Harrison in Manchester, 26 November 1962) was DAWN PRESCOTT, first working for conman Alan Bradley in his home-security business, then as an estate agent, before moving in with Mike Baldwin. She previously appeared in *Gentlemen and Players* and later acted Lisa Barras in *The Sharp End* and, since 1991, W.P.C. Donna Harris in *The Bill*.

William Ivory played Tina Fowler's boyfriend EDDIE RAMSDEN, whose girlfriend had left him with baby son Jamie. William previously acted a burglar called Jed in *Emmerdale* and later played D.C. Mark Divine in *Resnick*, Greg in *Chef!* and Andrew Jackson in *Between the Lines*. He also wrote the TV sitcom *Common as Muck*, which included his on-screen *Street* girlfriend Michelle Holmes.

GCSEs from Weatherfield Comprehensive. He spent a year unemployed before getting a job as a waiter at the café in 1985. He served such awkward customers as Percy Sugden, washed up and swept the café, and enjoyed a laugh with Phyllis Pearce, who worked there before owner Alma Sedgewick took a more active interest in the day-to-day running of the business.

Schoolgirl Jenny Bradley fell for Martin, who at first resisted her advances. When he saw that she was upset, he agreed to take her out and assured her legal guardian, Rita Fairclough, that he would not take advantage of her. He drove Jenny in Rita's car to a talent contest in Rochdale and finally gave in when Jenny asked him to let her take the wheel on the way home. As a result, the car crashed and turned over.

Then, Martin fell for Sally Webster's younger sister, Gina Seddon – and was caught in bed with her by Kevin and Sally, who had returned home thinking they could hear burglars upstairs.

Martin left the café to work for Alan Bradley's burglar-alarm company. When Rita Fairclough's scheming lover was arrested after trying to defraud her, Martin took night work at a petrol station, then became a hospital porter.

In 1989, after the death of her husband, Brian, whom she was planning to divorce for a second time, Gail fell into the arms of Martin, who had previously been simply an affable young man who was a reliable employee. He was a generation younger than Gail, but the reaction of some Street residents – especially Gail's mother-in-law Ivy – was not enough to split them up.

Martin was good for Gail and got on well with her two children, Nicky and Sarah Louise. They also had their own baby – David, born on Christmas Day 1990 – although it took a last-minute chase by Martin on a train to persuade Gail not to go ahead with an abortion during the early weeks of her pregnancy. Giving up his job at the hospital, Martin returned to the café, putting up with Alma's disappearances and being a good listener when she went through romantic traumas with Mike Baldwin.

Martin and Gail finally wed on 27 September 1991 and, after spending a while as a house-husband, Martin decided to carve out a career for himself and became a student nurse. Over Christmas 1992, Martin and Gail's marriage came close to ending when fellow student Carmel Finnan stayed with them and, obsessed with Martin, tried to seduce him. She even slept in the same bed as him when he was so drunk that he thought it was Gail there, although they never had sex. When Gail discovered what had been happening, she sent Carmel packing.

But Carmel returned from her family home in Ireland shortly afterwards, saying she was pregnant and Martin was the father. Gail now found it difficult to accept that nothing had happened, until Carmel's grandfather arrived from Ireland and explained that she was disturbed and a similar incident had happened before. The marriage settled down, but life became difficult when stepson Nick grew away from Martin, comparing him unfavourably with his real father.

With a wedge driven between him and Gail, Martin gave way to temptation at the hospital's staff party at Christmas 1994 and slept with nurse Cathy Power. When, three months later, he told Gail what had happened, it came as a bombshell. She showed no wish to talk about it, feeling that the marriage was over and she was better off with just her children.

For weeks, Gail distanced herself from Martin, but the pair were finally reunited after he passed his nursing exams and took the family away to North Wales for a weekend caravan holiday. The couple put the incident behind them and, once again, picked up the pieces.

Sean Wilson (b. Ashton-under-Lyne, Lancashire, 4 April 1965) had ambitions to become a graphic designer and, on leaving schoool, worked for an advertising agency but left after a week because he was being used as a dogsbody.

He started in showbusiness by building sets at Oldham Coliseum as a YTS trainee. Then, he joined Oldham Theatre Workshop and appeared in the musical *The Gas Street Kids*, before teaming up with a friend to do a cabaret act around pubs and clubs to gain his Equity actors' union card. Oldham Theatre Workshop asked him back to play the son in Brecht's play *The Mother*. He then spent a year in community theatre, in the Manchester area and at the Edinburgh Festival, during which he co-wrote a play called *The Bogeymaster*.

He appeared on television in *Crown Court* (as a National Front skinhead), *Travelling Man* and the Channel Four film *Mozart's Unfinished*, in which he played the young Mozart because of his uncanny likeness to the great composer. Trying to get into *Coronation Street*, Sean auditioned for the roles of Terry Duckworth and Kevin Webster but was turned down. It was third time lucky when he was offered the part of Martin Platt in 1985.

Sean's parents split up when he was a child, and his mother married again, but he did not get on with his stepfather and left home at the age of 16. He is single and lives in his real father's old three-bedroom semi in Ashton-under-Lyne. A keen artist, Sean's drawings have sold in the town's arts centre. He presented *Street* actress Jill Summers, who plays Phyllis Pearce, with a portrait of herself to mark her 75th birthday.

DEIRDRE RACHID

Behind the big glasses of Deirdre Rachid lies a string of emotional tragedies that have transformed the quiet, young secretary into an independent, determined woman. Born in Weatherfield on 8 July 1955, Deirdre is the daughter of Donald and Blanche Hunt. On leaving Bessie Street School, she took a typing course at Weatherfield Commercial College. She was first seen in the Rovers Return at a party in 1972. A year later, she left her job as a clerk-typist at Cresta Insurance to work for Len Fairclough in his builder's yard, organizing Len and partner Ray Langton.

Working evenings as a barmaid at the Rovers, she found romance with publican's son Billy Walker, 20 years her senior. They became engaged, but she backed out a month before the wedding. Deirdre then fell for Ray Langton and they married on 7 July 1975. Daughter Tracy Lynette was born on 24 January 1977, with Emily Bishop as godmother. The marriage faltered less than two years later, when Deirdre found out that Ray was having an affair with waitress Janice Stubbs. Ray then took a building job in Holland and the couple divorced.

In 1979, friendship with Ken Barlow turned to love and the couple married at All Saints' Church on 27 July 1981 and honeymooned in Corfu. All seemed well until Deirdre had an affair with Mike Baldwin two years later and he even proposed marriage. As Ken became more obsessed with his work as editor of the *Weatherfield Recorder* and less interested in Deirdre, she found comfort in the arms of the cockney romeo. When she told Ken, he ordered her to leave, but she begged him to let her stay

67

and promised she would never see Mike again. The couple made up and set off for a second honeymoon, in Malta.

Deirdre gave up her job as an assistant in Alf Roberts's shop when she beat him in the local elections to become an independent councillor. Dedicating herself completely to the job caused friction with Ken. He had an affair with council secretary Wendy Crozier, who was leaking him confidential information for his newspaper. Deirdre threw Ken out and later found romance with odd-job man Dave Barton, shady entrepreneur Phil Jennings, who turned out to be married, and mechanic Doug Murray, who did a moonlight flit after stealing Mike Baldwin's car.

Desperate for money, Deirdre took a job as a shelf-stacker at Bettabuys supermarket. It looked as if she might have Ken back as Christmas 1993 approached, but her mother was taken ill, which meant leaving the Street for several months to care for her. On her return, she found that Ken had fallen for hairdresser Denise Osbourne. Even more of a shock was the fact that Denise was pregnant with his child.

Deirdre needed a holiday and, going to Morocco, found sun, sand and a young waiter called Samir Rachid. She returned to Weatherfield, borrowed money from Emily Bishop, her next-door neighbour and longtime friend, and sent it to Morocco so that Samir could finance a two-week trip to Britain. Wanting to stay together, the couple extended the visit indefinitely and Samir worked illegally as a waiter. When the authorities discovered this, the only way Deirdre could find of keeping him in the country was to marry him. She insisted that she loved him and the register-office wedding took place on 25 November 1994.

Jill Kerman (b. Mill Hill, North London, 4 July 1946), who was John Alderton's fiancée in *Please Sir!*, took the role of MAGGIE REDMAN (née Dunlop), mother of Mike Baldwin's son Mark.

Geoffrey Palmer (b. London, 4 June 1927) acted the REGISTRAR at the marriage of Dennis Tanner and Jenny Sutton in 1968. He later played Jimmy in *The Fall and Rise of Reginald Perrin*, Ben in *Butterflies* and Lionel in *As Time Goes By*.

Windsor Davies (b. Canning Town, London, 28 August 1930), Battery Sergeant Major Williams in *It Ain't Half Hot Mum* and Oliver Smallbridge in *Never the Twain*, played a RETURNING OFFICER in Annie Walker and Len Fairclough's 1966 local government election battle.

The immigration authorities thought that the wedding must be a sham and questioned both Deirdre and Samir. To pre-empt being thrown out of the country, Samir decided to return to Morocco. The only way that Deirdre could stay with him was to leave the country and start a new life there with him. So, on 30 December, after Deirdre had given her house to Mike Baldwin, who put £15,000 in her Moroccan bank account in return, the couple left.

Three months later, Deirdre was back after hearing that daughter Tracy – who had opposed the marriage to Samir – was lying in a coma in hospital after being plied with the drug Ecstasy at a party. Tracy pulled through but had suffered kidney damage and needed a transplant. Deirdre and Ken both offered kidneys but theirs were not suitable matches. Until a donor could be found, Tracy was reliant on a dialysis machine three days a week. Samir offered one of his kidneys and the operation was set for 2 June 1995. But, the evening before the operation, Samir was found dying next to a canal after apparently being attacked by a gang. One of his kidneys brought Deirdre's daughter back to full health, but she had lost her third husband.

☆ ☆ ☆

Anne Kirkbride (b. Oldham, Lancashire, 21 June 1954), dubbed 'Sexy Specs' by some newspapers, actually wears contact lenses and shirts and jeans away from the studios, and is a million miles away from Deirdre. She is the daughter of cartoonist Jack and brother of author John. A bit of a dreamer as a child, she once went missing while on a family holiday to North Wales aged seven and was eventually found in a small, empty chapel, standing in the pulpit giving a sermon in a convincing Welsh accent, trying to speak the language.

One of Anne's heroes was the American comedian Spike Jones and she learned his zany routines off by heart. She was also a *Monty Python* fan, imitating all the characters' voices, too. Aged 11, Anne joined the Saddleworth Junior Players, her first part playing a tulip in a competition for local drama clubs. Anne had no lines to say, but her group won. She joined Oldham Rep. straight from school, starting as a student, graduating to assistant stage manager and then becoming an actress. In between productions there, Anne stage-managed a charity performance of *Snow White*.

Anne landed a part in a Granada Television play, *Another Sunday and Sweet FA*, written by Jack Rosenthal, playing a girl on the touchline at a football match, wearing hot-pants and a yellow bob-cap. Enjoying her theatre work and resistant to change, she had to be forced by her father to audition for the play. As a result, she auditioned for the pilot episode of a new series and, aged 18, was offered a bit part in *Coronation Street*, as Deirdre Hunt. She soon became a regular and has had some of the programme's most dramatic storylines. She, William Roache and Johnny Briggs jointly received the 1983 Pye Television Award for their performances in the Deirdre-Ken-Mike love triangle.

In October 1983, Anne was fined £250 after pleading guilty to possessing cannabis. She said she was not a user of the drug: cannabis found by police at her home had been left by a friend.

Anne lives in Didsbury with her husband, actor David Beckett, who played her screen boyfriend Dave Barton. They married in 1992. Two years later, she was hastily written out of the *Street* when diagnosed as having a rare form of cancer but later received the all clear. Away from the studios, Anne enjoys photography, gardening, swimming, reading and walking.

ALF ROBERTS

First seen in the Street as a friend of Ken Barlow's father Frank, post office supervisor Alf Roberts went on to become a local councillor and gain respect in the community.

Born on 8 October 1926, he served in the Royal Corps of Signals during the Second World War and married Phyllis Plant a year after being demobbed. As an independent councillor for Weatherfield, straight-laced Alf was a friend of Len Fairclough and even known to go to a strip club with Ray Langton and Ernest Bishop. Phyllis died in 1972 and, shortly afterwards, Alf proposed to cornershop owner Maggie Clegg, but she turned him down. He ran against Len Fairclough to become Mayor of Weatherfield, won and asked Rovers Return landlady Annie

Walker to be mayoress, an offer she accepted. Still looking for romance, Alf courted Donna Parker, who worked in the post office canteen and disappeared with £500 he lent her to start a hairdressing business. He later married Renée Bradshaw, who had taken over the shop and took early retirement. It was a bitter blow when in 1980, after just two years of marriage, Renée died in a car accident. Old-fashioned Alf inherited the shop and ran it until 1994, his only concession to modern times coming when he turned it into a Mini Market.

It appeared to be third time lucky in marriage when he wed Audrey Potter, mother of Gail Platt, in 1985. He soon became wise to her tactics of doing very little and spending money on shopping sprees. Alf considered himself to be very careful and responsible with money, and was not prepared for his hard-earned cash to be frittered away.

Alf, who received a bit of a jolt when he had a heart attack in 1987, lost his job as a Weatherfield councillor when Deirdre Barlow, who had worked on his shop till, stood against him and won. He and Audrey later moved from no. 11 Coronation Street to Grasmere Avenue but continued to run the shop and let out the flat above. Eventually, Audrey persuaded Alf to sell the shop to Brendan Scott, who died months later. Alf took it back but again sold, this time to former Bettabuys store manager Reg Holdsworth.

When Alf became Mayor of Weatherfield again, in 1994, he faced the problem of how Audrey would rise to the occasion of being his mayoress. Her term of office got off to a bad start when she refused to take part in a local tree-planting, fearing that she would get soil on her shoes. Eventually, Alf dispensed with her as mayoress and, looking for a woman of sobriety to fill her shoes, asked Rita Fairclough to step in. Not wishing to ruffle feathers, Rita declined, but Rovers Return barmaid Betty Turpin breached the gap, to Audrey's bemusement.

☆ ☆ ☆

Bryan Mosley (b. Leeds, 25 August 1931) served with the RAF in Air Traffic Control, during which time he started acting at the Byre Theatre, in St Andrews. After National Service, he trained at Bradford Civic Theatre under Esmé Church, whose other students included Tom Bell, Robert Stephens and William Lucas. Bryan then toured with the New Pilgrim Players, putting on plays in churches, abbeys, pubs and prisons, before working in repertory theatre at York, Perth, Derby and Harrogate.

His television appearances include roles in *Skyport*, *The Plane Makers*, *The Saint*, *Z-Cars*, *The Avengers*, *No Hiding Place* (in which Johnny Briggs played Det. Sgt. Russell), *Play of the Week*, *Crossroads* (as Denis Rutledge), *The*

Madge Hindle (b. Blackburn, Lancashire, 19 May 1938) was cornershop owner RENÉE ROBERTS (née Bradshaw), who died in a car crash. Madge had already starred as Lily in the sitcom *Nearest and Dearest* and later appeared in *The Two Ronnies*, *Lost Empires*, *First of the Summer Wine* and *The Rector's Wife*. Daughter Charlotte is a TV presenter.

Milton Johns, who played short-lived shopkeeper BRENDAN SCOTT, acted villains in *Z-Cars* and *Softly Softly* before switching to comedy in *Foxy Lady*, *The Good Life* and *Butterflies*.

Harold Goodwin (b. Wombwell, South Yorkshire, 22 October 1917) played Vera Duckworth's estranged father, JOSS SHACKLETON, who claimed to have royal blood. Harold is the veteran of 100 films, including *The Dam Busters*, *The Bridge on the River Kwai* and *The Prince and the Showgirl* (alongside Laurence Olivier and Marilyn Monroe). He has also had about 600 TV roles, including Harry in the sitcom *Oh No It's Selwyn Froggitt*.

Violet Carson (b. Manchester, 1 September 1898) was hairnetted harridan ENA SHARPLES, who frequented the Rovers snug with Minnie Caldwell and Martha Longhurst. Violet, who previously found fame on radio as 'Auntie Vi' in *Children's Hour*, was made an OBE, left the serial in 1980 and died on 26 December 1983.

Terence Hillyer acted bookie SEAN SKINNER, Des Barnes's boss who chased Steve McDonald for £2000 in debts, but he had played TERRY GOODWIN, the violent husband of Suzie Birchall, in 1983. In between, Terence acted henpecked landlord Steve Harvey in *Families*, as well as appearing in *Boon*, *The New Statesman*, *The Tenpercenters* and *Small World*.

Reginald Marsh (b. London, 17 September 1926) played bookie DAVE SMITH, who had a fling with Elsie Tanner. He was also Bob Molesworth in *Emmerdale* and appeared in *Crossroads*.

Patricia Routledge (b. Birkenhead, Cheshire, 17 February) was SYLVIA SNAPE, who ran Snape's Café in Rosamund Street, in 1961. She is best known as Hyacinth Bucket in the sitcom *Keeping up Appearances* but also starred in Alan Bennett's *A Woman of No Importance*.

Villains, *Doctor Who*, *It's a Square World*, *The Arthur Haynes Show*, *The Dick Emery Show*, *The Worker* and *Queenie's Castle*.

An expert fencer and fight arranger, who started fencing in the Air Force at the age of 18, Bryan was a founder member of the Society of British Fight Directors in the sixties. He had first used his skills during repertory days in Perth, when he directed the fights in *Othello*. He did the same at the Theatre Royal, York, and taught fencing in schools around Leeds. The actor appeared in a sword fight with Ian Hendry on television in *The High Game* and also made his mark in films, fencing with Terence Stamp in *Far from the Madding Crowd* and on a rooftop with Michael Caine in *Get Carter*, which brought a very nasty end for his character.

Bryan was also in the films *A Kind of Loving*, *Billy Liar*, *This Sporting Life*, *Rattle of a Simple Man*, *Up Jumped a Swagman*, *Privilege* and *Charlie Bubbles*, swung from a huge chandelier, sword in hand, in an unscreened TV commercial for a cereal, and appeared with Morecambe and Wise in a commercial for Watney's.

As a fight director, Bryan coached such stars as Robert Hardy and Tom Courtenay, as well as a young Neil Diamond, who was starting out on his career and needed to look like a fencer for a photosession on the roof of his agent's offices.

With no sword in sight, Bryan first appeared in *Coronation Street* in episode 64 in 1961, although the role of Alf Roberts had already been played for two episodes by actor Gordon Cowan. He appeared on and off for the next two years and, when he was asked back in 1967, became a permanent fixture.

Bryan and wife Norma – who met at a Leeds youth club when they were 12 – have six children, Jacqueline, Simone, Helen, Jonathan, Bernard and Leonard, and live near Shipley, West Yorkshire. During the week, he stays in a Salford flat near the Granada Television studios. His three sons all work in the theatre, and daughter Jacqueline is a set designer and actress who once had a small part in *Coronation Street* and appeared in *Children's Ward*.

AUDREY ROBERTS

Flighty Audrey Roberts is the mother of illegitimate Gail Potter but gave up her flirtatious ways after meeting cornershop owner Alf Roberts. Realizing she was not getting any younger, and looking for security at last, she married Alf and has mellowed just a touch. Married life suited Audrey in that she did not need to earn a living. When Alf called on her to help in the shop, her heart was never in it – and

often she was not, either. Audrey enjoys spending Alf's money, especially on new clothes.

Aspiring to a posh new home, she persuaded Alf to buy a house in Hillside Crescent. They vacated no. 11 for the McDonalds to take over and arrived outside their new home, only to find out that they could not move in because of a hiccup in the home-buying chain. To Audrey's dismay, she and Alf moved into the flat above the cornershop, which she saw as dingy. Eventually, they moved to Grasmere Avenue.

By then, she had revealed that, as well as Gail, she had an illegitimate son called Stephen, who lived in Canada. The confession came when he was involved in a car accident and Audrey travelled to Canada to see him. It was also news to Gail that she had a brother, whom Audrey had conceived when she was 16 and given away for adoption to a couple who later emigrated.

When Alf was elected Mayor of Weatherfield in 1994, Audrey soon tired of the ceremonials. She began staying in the plush limousine with chauffeur Brian Bowes, and used it for non-official duties. Seeing that she was not prepared to fulfil her duties as mayoress, Alf enlisted Rovers Return barmaid Betty Turpin to take over. Audrey did not complain until there was a royal occasion that Alf was due to attend, so Alf simply told her that she *and* Betty could go and he would stay at home.

Sue Nicholls (b. The Honourable Susan Frances Harmar Nicholls in Walsall, 23 November 1943) is the daughter of former Tory M.P. Lord Harmar Nicholls. At her Staffordshire boarding school, she excelled at languages and looked like going to Oxford University. But she auditioned to train at RADA, which had turned her down two years earlier, and was accepted.

Sue then went into repertory theatre with actor-manager Charles Vance's Group of Three, whose name referred to three rep. companies. She worked in Wolverhampton and Weston-super-Mare, starting as an assistant stage manager, making tea and acting bit parts. Special memories of her days in rep. include media mogul Eddy Shah as a stage manager and the theatre in Weston-super-Mare burning down, causing the production of *To Dorothy a Son* to move to a local town hall. Sue also appeared in *Alfie*, *Don't Start without Me*, *How the Other Half Loves*, *Time and Time Again*, *Absurd Person Singular* and *Middle Aged Spread*. She acted in the RSC production of *London Assurance* on Broadway, and was in the films *Expresso Splasho!* and *The Nightingale Saga*.

On TV, she first found fame in *Crossroads*. She auditioned for the role of Jill Richardson before the programme started in 1964, but gave it too strong a Birmingham accent. Instead, the producers offered her the part of waitress Marilyn Gates. Her boyfriend of the time, actor Malcolm Young, also appeared in the serial during its early days, as Phillip Winter.

Sue's *Crossroads* character once had to stand in for a nightclub singer and perform 'Where Will You Be', written by Tony Hatch, composer of the *Crossroads* theme music. Asked to record the song for real, Sue found herself with a Top 20 hit and left the serial to follow a career as a pop singer. Her follow-up single, 'All the Way to Heaven', was not so successful and her performances in cabaret began to frustrate her, so she returned to the theatre and did a summer season with Bob Monkhouse in Bournemouth.

Soon, Sue was back on television, appearing in *Not on Your Nellie*, *Jangles*, *Rentaghost* (as the witch), *Pipkin's*, *Tycoon*, *The Duchess of Duke Street*, *Wodehouse Playhouse*, *Doctor on the Go*, *Village Hall*, *The Professionals*, *Up the Elephant and Round the Castle* (as Jim Davidson's amorous neighbour Wanda Pickles) and *The Fall and Rise of Reginald Perrin* (as Perrin's raunchy secretary, Joan Greengross).

She appeared in *Coronation Street* as Audrey Potter on and off for six years before becoming a regular in 1985. Sue is married to actor Mark Eden, who played *Street* baddie Alan Bradley. They have homes in London and Manchester.

> **Kenneth Cope, a regular in *That Was the Week That Was*, played jailbird JED STONE, Minnie Caldwell's lodger, before starring as Marty Hopkirk, the dead half of *Randall & Hopkirk (Deceased)*. He later presented a special *Coronation Street* tribute to Margot Bryant, the actress who played Minnie, on her death in 1989.**

PERCY SUGDEN

Snooper extraordinaire Percy Sugden pokes his nose into everyone's business under the guise of looking after the welfare of other Street residents, but his interfering ways often infuriate. Born in Weatherfield on 8 April 1922, widower Percy trained as a commis chef in a hotel and served in the Royal Army Catering Corps. He came to Coronation Street as caretaker of the community centre, a job he did until reaching retirement age. His niece, Elaine Prior, married Bill Webster – father of Kevin – and moved away to Southampton.

Percy then took a job as a lollipop man but came a cropper when he tried to rescue long-time admirer Phyllis Pearce as she turned back on a crossing to pick up some apples and a car hit him, injuring his leg. Phyllis, who had continued to chase Percy despite his protestations, was full of praise for her gallant hero. Phyllis was happy to push Percy around in his wheelchair afterwards, but Street residents were not so happy at the trouble he caused in it, especially Alec Gilroy, who fell over it three times. Percy was furious when he found out that he would not only get no compensation for the accident, but was being dismissed from his job as a lollipop man because he had lied about his age when applying for it and was too old.

Although he always resisted Phyllis's advances, Percy was happy to see pensioner Maud Grimes – mother of Maureen Holdsworth – and pushed her around Weatherfield in her wheelchair. The pair decided to marry. In 1994, as he was planning a trip to Normandy for the 50th anniversary of the D-Day landings, Maud asked if she could go with him. He agreed, and her reason became clear when, in the American cemetery, she pointed to the grave of American serviceman Leonard Kennedy and told her daughter that he was her real father, which was a shock to Maureen and Percy. Unable to accept what Maud had done all those years before while her own serviceman husband was away fighting for his country, Percy called off the wedding.

☆ ☆ ☆

Bill Waddington (b. Oldham, Lancashire, 10 June 1916) is the son of a builder father and a mother who owned seven butcher shops and a pub. Because she was busy with her business, he was partially fostered by a couple called the Robinsons until they died when he was seven. At the age of 14, Bill left school to work in one of his mother's butcher shops. He learned to play the ukulele, and his talent as a comedian was spotted in his army days during the Second World War. After serving in the cookhouse, Bill joined *The Blue Pencils*, the first concert party recruited from the forces at the start of the war to entertain the troops. Then, he went into the *Stars in Battledress* concert party and starred in the BBC wartime radio show *Ack Ack Beer Beer*. It was his first of more than 800 broadcasts in comedy and variety programmes.

After the war, he continued his career as a stand-up comedian and character actor, topping the bill at the Royal Variety Performance in 1955, before the present Queen Mother. Bill was also principal comedian on the bill with American stars including Frankie Laine, Lena Horne and Dorothy Lamour when they performed on the British stage. His agent was Lew Grade, who became the boss of ATV, one of the first ITV companies in Britain.

On television, Bill appeared in *A Family at War*, *Dear Enemy*, *Talent*, *Fallen Hero*, *The Mating Season*, *Cousin Phyllis* and *Second Chance*. He has had five different roles in *Coronation Street*, first playing a drunken businessman compelled to roll around laughing at one of Stan Ogden's unfunny jokes. In 1980, he acted George Turner, best man at the wedding of Emily Bishop and Arnold Swain, who turned out to be a bigamist. He also appeared in the serial as a money-lender and a customer in The Kabin, before becoming Percy Sugden in 1983.

The role came just after Bill's stage partnership with *Carry On* star Sid James came to an end following the actor's sudden death, then the death from cancer of Bill's second wife, actress and singer Lillian Day. Working on the programme, he met old friends from music-hall days such as Betty Driver and Jill Summers, as well as Tom Mennard and Len Marten, who have since died. There are five Percy Sugden Appreciation Societies, including one at Cambridge University.

Bill is twice divorced and had two daughters, secretary Denise and actress Barbara – who appeared in *Coronation Street* as the daughter of one of Annie Walker's rival publicans – by his second wife, Lillian. Bill and Lillian once managed a 60-ha (150-acre) farm and racing-horse stud in Cheshire. He eventually sold it but still breeds thoroughbred racehorses.

The actor has written two books, an autobiography titled *The Importance of Being Percy* in 1992 and *Percy's War*, to tie in with the 50th anniversary of the D-Day landings, in 1994.

RITA SULLIVAN

Newsagent Rita Sullivan has had more than her fair share of heartbreak. Her marriage to Len Fairclough ended with his death in a car accident, her relationship with scheming Alan

then tearaway teenager Sharon Gaskell, who tried to seduce married Brian Tilsley when he drove her home after babysitting for him.

But the marriage came to a sudden end when Len was killed in a motorway accident. There was also the unwelcome realization that he had been driving to Bolton and another woman – his mistress, Marjorie Proctor.

When Rita took in papergirl Jenny Bradley following the death of her mother, Jenny's father Alan arrived and fell for her. Soon they were living together, but Rita was reluctant to marry, so he eventually moved in with another woman. Rita pleaded with him to return, and he did so, only to defraud her by using the deeds on her house to remortgage it and get money to start his burglar-alarm business. She found out, confronted him with her discovery and he tried to murder Rita by smothering her with a cushion.

The police caught up with Alan, his case came to court and a charge of attempted murder was changed to one of assault. For that and the other charge of fraud, he was deemed to have served enough time – seven months – in custody. He then returned to Coronation Street to work as a labourer for builder Maurice Jones. A shocked Rita had a nervous breakdown and disappeared. Bet and Alec Gilroy found her in Blackpool, singing in a hotel and having suffered a complete memory loss. Alan – accused of murdering Rita after her disappearance – followed, chased her and was fatally hit by a tram.

She then kept her distance from men and found the attentions of supermarket manager Reg Holdsworth slightly comic. He did not relinquish his attentions until sales rep. Ted Sullivan started romancing her as he was planning his retirement. He asked her to marry him, but her world caved in when she learned that Ted had a terminal brain tumour. The couple continued with their plans and wed on 5 June 1992. Ted died peacefully just a few months later while watching a bowling match, but Rita was thankful for the time she had shared with him.

She put a brave face on her lot in life and went back to working full time in The Kabin, having put Mavis and Derek Wilton in charge of it during her happy months with Ted.

Bradley ended when he tried to murder her and her second marriage, to kindly Ted Sullivan, ended in his death from a brain tumour. Not surprisingly, Rita is wary of men, but she is philosophical and never wallows in self pity.

Born in Manchester on 25 February 1932, Rita Littlewood had her eye set on a career in showbusiness from the age of four, when she began singing and dancing at family parties. Two years later, her father Harold walked out on the family. She worked in a grocer's on leaving school at 14 but later ventured into showbusiness, appearing all over the north of England and the Midlands in pantomimes and revues.

Rita became a dancer at the Orinoco Club, in Weatherfield, where Dennis Tanner was assistant manager, and later took to the stage in various clubs as a singer, with Alec Gilroy as her agent. She had an affair with construction worker Harry Bates, who was separated, and they lived together as man and wife. Rita, known to everyone as 'Mrs Bates', also acted as a mother to Harry's two children, Terry and Gail.

When widowed Ken Barlow became deputy headmaster of Bessie Street School, he called her in when he was having problems with Terry and the pair soon struck up a friendship. When she subsequently met Len Fairclough, Harry beat her up and threw her out of the house.

Rita and Len built up The Kabin newsagent's business together and, after his second proposal, married on 20 April 1977. The marriage proved rocky and, at one stage, Rita walked out on Len, following his developing relationship with Elsie Tanner. But Len tracked Rita down to a launderette in Blackpool and begged her to return.

The couple found a family life they would otherwise have foregone together when they took in two foster-children, first John Spencer,

☆ ☆ ☆

Barbara Knox (b. Oldham, Lancashire, 1938) was the daughter of a foundry worker and, on leaving school at 15, worked as a post office telegraphist, then in offices, shops and factories. As a schoolgirl, she had longed to act. After performing in amateur theatre, she joined Oldham Rep. and worked extensively in repertory theatre. She also appeared in radio programmes with Ken Dodd, Jimmy Tarbuck, Ray Alan, Mike Yarwood, Les Dawson and Freddie

Shirley Stelfox (b. 11 April 1941) played MARGOT SUTCLIFFE, owner of the Bill and Coo Dating Agency, which matched Bet Lynch with Jack Duckworth, who made a video in the guise of club entertainer Vince St Clair. She later returned as SHIRLEY HENDERSON, owner of a Blackpool hotel and friend of Lisa Duckworth's parents. Shirley, who also acted Madge Richmond in *Brookside*, Carol May in *Making Out*, Helen in *Civvies* and Lucy in *Get Back*, is married to actor Don Henderson.

Angela Pleasence (b. Daphne Anne Angela Pleasence in Chapeltown, Sheffield), actress daughter of the late actor Donald, was MONICA SUTTON, one of the hippie commune who took over Elsie Tanner's empty house in 1967. Monica was sister of Jenny, who later married Dennis Tanner. Angela's many subsequent television parts include Catherine Howard in *The Six Wives of Henry VIII* and the title roles in *Saint Joan* and *Charlotte Brontë*.

George Waring (b. George Edward Waring in Eccles, Manchester, 20 February 1927) played Tom Meek in *Castlehaven* before joining *Coronation Street* as ARNOLD SWAIN, who bigamously married Emily Bishop. George later acted Wilf Padgett in *Emmerdale*.

Arthur Lowe (b. Hayfield, Derbyshire, 22 September 1915) played pompous LEONARD SWINDLEY, who ran Gamma Garments for 198 episodes from programme three, before starring as Swindley in the spin-off comedy series *Pardon the Expression* and playing Captain Mainwaring in the classic sitcom *Dad's Army*. Arthur, who also starred as Irish priest Father Duddleswell in the comedy series *Bless Me Father*, and in the title role of a headmaster in *A. J. Wentworth, BA*, died on 15 April 1982.

Pat Phoenix (b. Patricia Noonan in Manchester, 26 November 1923) was ELSIE TANNER, *Coronation Street*'s first sex-siren, who was married three times. Pat also wed three times, the last two to screen husband Alan Browning and, shortly before her death on 18 September 1986, to actor Anthony Booth. After leaving the *Street* in 1983, she starred in her own situation-comedy, *Constant Hot Water*, as a seaside landlady.

Davies, and on television in *Emergency – Ward 10*, *Mrs Thursday*, *Never Mind the Quality, Feel the Width*, *The Dustbinmen* and *A Family at War*, as well as having a small part in the 1969 film *Goodbye, Mr Chips*.

She became exhausted with her busy routine of weekly repertory theatre, doing funny voices in weekend radio shows and making occasional television programmes, and in 1969 had a serious operation and nearly died. She gave up showbusiness but, three years later, was offered the role of Rita Littlewood in *Coronation Street*. She declined, but her daughter Maxine, by first husband Denis, persuaded her to accept the part.

The actress had actually played Rita as early as 1964 for two episodes, when the character's cabaret act took her to the Sporting Club, and Dennis Tanner – who, as assistant manager at the Orinoco Club, knew Rita – invited her to stay at his mother's house.

Barbara achieved her ambition of making a record when, in 1973, she recorded an LP called *On the Street Where I Live*. She won the *TVTimes* 1989 Best Actress on TV award, following her performances in the sensational Rita Fairclough-Alan Bradley saga. Early on in her *Street* career, Barbara also took on other work as both actress and singer, but collapsed through overwork in 1975. She also underwent two operations to remove cancerous growths on her face in the mid-eighties.

After divorcing her first husband, Denis Mullaney, in 1977 after 23 years of marriage, Barbara married businessman John Knox and took his name, but the couple split up in 1994. Barbara lives in Worcestershire.

BETTY TURPIN

Betty Preston – renowned for her hotpots at the Rovers Return – was born in Weatherfield on 4 February 1920 and worked in a mill on leaving school. She had a job in a munitions factory during the Second World War, then became a school meals assistant. Betty had an illegitimate son, Gordon, whom her sister Maggie Clegg brought up as her own, and she later married police sergeant Cyril Turpin.

In 1969, Betty became a barmaid at the Rovers Return, moving into the flat above the cornershop in Coronation Street, which was owned by her sister, who harboured Betty's secret.

She had already undergone the ordeal of being held hostage by Keith Lucas, who had once gone to prison as a result of Cyril arresting him. Arriving home, Cyril tackled the man, who had an iron bar, and was stopped from killing him only by the intervention of Len Fairclough.

After a row with Annie Walker in 1970, Betty left the Rovers and temporarily took a job at the Flying Horse, even playing in the darts team against the Rovers, but she soon returned.

It was a great loss to Betty when Cyril died of a heart attack in 1974, and she went through a period of confusion afterwards and moved in with her sister, Maggie, at the cornershop. When the Hopkins family moved into the shop, with a view to buying it, they found Gordon Clegg's birth certificate and tried to blackmail Maggie into reducing the price of the premises. Instead, she told Gordon the truth and the Hopkins did a moonlight flit, in February 1975.

Two years later, Betty stormed out of the pub again after Annie accused her of stealing money and suggested she consult a psychiatrist to help with her 'problem'. Betty was on the verge of taking the case to court when she finally agreed to return to the pub. She was also one of three women who had the dubious privilege of being asked to marry cellarman Fred Gee, who was told by brewery Newton & Ridley that he could become landlord of the Mechanic's Arms if he had a wife. Like Bet Lynch and Flying Horse barmaid Alma Walsh, Betty turned him down.

Gordon introduced Betty to his fiancée, Caroline, in 1982, but upset his mother by marrying without letting her know. There was another ordeal for Betty later in the year when she was mugged by a girl from Ken Barlow's youth club and ended up with a broken arm. In 1985, Betty became a grandmother when her daughter-in-law gave birth to Peter and spent a few months of the following year with Gordon and Caroline in London.

When, in 1992, the Rovers was forced to stop selling food in the pub because the kitchen did not meet legal standards, Betty's job was effectively made redundant and she left in tears. But, once the kitchen was done up and modern equipment installed, she returned. Two years later, Betty was flattered to be asked by Alf Roberts to be his mayoress when he was Mayor of Weatherfield and his wife, Audrey, was reluctant to take part in official visits. But there was a potentially embarrassing situation when Alf was invited to a royal occasion, which provided an opportunity for hobnobbing and bragging afterwards. Audrey was adamant that she would go, but Betty was equally determined, so Alf let them go together and stayed at home.

It was a shock for Betty when on 8 May 1995, the 50th anniversary of V.E. Day, Billy Williams came to the Rovers for a drink. It was the first time they had seen each other since the night they had spent together 50 years earlier at the end of the Second World War. Both Betty and Billy had written to each other afterwards but the letters had not reached their destination.

Betty was stunned to find out that, in one of them, Billy had asked her to marry him.

Betty Driver (b. Leicester, 20 May 1920) moved to Manchester with her family when she was two. Her theatre-struck mother, a talented pianist who never had the chance to turn professional, encouraged Betty to take part in concerts for the elderly, singing around the Manchester area. Aged nine, Betty joined the Terence Byron Repertory Company, in Longsight, Manchester, appearing in pantomimes and such shows as *Daddy Long-legs* and *The Silver King*. A year later, she landed her first professional job, at a theatre in Burnley, then toured in the revue *Mixed Bathing*, meeting other young performers including Tessie O'Shea and Beryl Reid.

The offer of a role in the 1934 George Formby film *Boots! Boots!*, in which she had a few lines of dialogue and a big production number in which she sang and tap-danced with the star, turned to disappointment. Formby's forceful wife Beryl, who managed his career and danced in the film, apparently could not bear the idea of a sweet child stealing the limelight from her and had the scene and Betty's dialogue edited out.

At the age of 14, while performing in a revue at the Prince of Wales Theatre, London, Betty was

Jack Howarth (b. Rochdale, Lancashire, 19 February 1896) was grumpy pensioner ALBERT TATLOCK, uncle of Ken Barlow's first wife, Valerie. Jack went to school with Gracie Fields and started acting at the age of 12. He directed the original British stage productions of *Dracula* and *Frankenstein*. As well as appearing in 18 films and 100 TV programmes, Jack was on radio as Mr Maggs in *Mrs Dale's Diary* for 14 years before joining *Coronation Street* when it began, in 1960. He died on 31 March 1984.

Christopher Quinten (b. Middlesbrough, 12 July 1957) was BRIAN TILSLEY, Gail Platt's first husband and father of Nick and Sarah Louise. Chris had already appeared in the film *International Velvet*, alongside Tatum O'Neal, and on TV in *Warship*, *Target*, *The Pink Medicine Show*, *The Little Big Show* and *Quatermass*, before joining *Coronation Street* in 1978. Eleven years later, Chris left to marry American chat-show host Leeza Gibbons and moved to Los Angeles, hoping to launch a Hollywood career. But the couple split up after a year and Chris returned to Britain.

spotted by Archie Pitt – former husband of Gracie Fields – and his agent brother Bert Aza. Bert became her agent and Archie put her into the hit show *Mr Tower of London*, which had originally starred Gracie Fields. After seeing Betty dancing and singing in a show called *Jimmy Hunter's Brighton Follies*, film producer Basil Dean cast her in the 1938 film *Penny Paradise*. She followed this with roles in the pictures *Let's Be Famous* and *Facing the Music*.

During the Second World War, she teamed up with bandleader Henry Hall and sang in his radio programme *Henry Hall's Guest Night* on and off for more than seven years. Betty's other radio work included her own show, *A Date with Betty*, and she performed in variety and with the troops entertainment organisation ENSA as part of Henry Hall's show. Betty made records, including 'The Sailor with the Navy Blue Eyes', 'MacNamara's Band', 'Pick the Petals of a Daisy' and 'September in the Rain'.

At the age of 32, she married South African singer Wally Petersen, who left a double act with his brother to join Betty's act. After a while, Wally decided to move back to South Africa and set up a theatrical agency. Betty went with him but returned a few months later, the marriage over after seven years.

William Moore (b. Birmingham) played **CYRIL TURPIN**, Betty's policeman husband who was killed, and later acted a character called Jackson in *Emmerdale*. He is married to actress Mollie Sugden, who played Annie Walker's licensed victualler friend Nellie Harvey.

Doris Speed (b. Manchester, 3 February 1899) was Rovers Return landlady **ANNIE WALKER** from the first episode, in 1960, until ill health forced her to retire in 1983, after 1746 appearances. Doris, who had previously acted in *Shadow Squad* and *Skyport* (as the trolley-pushing tea lady), as well as the film *Hell Is a City*, died on 16 November 1994.

Ken Farrington (b. Kenneth William Farrington in Dulwich, South London, 18 April 1936), who was **BILLY WALKER**, son of Jack and Annie, later acted Major Frances in *Danger UXB* and Morrison in *A Killing on the Exchange*, and starred in the first series of *Trainer*.

Kevin Lloyd (b. Kevin Reardon Lloyd in Derby, 28 March 1949) played **DON WATKINS** in the *Street* before taking the role of DC 'Tosh' Lines in *The Bill*.

Subsequently, she appeared on stage in *The Lovebirds*, *Pillar to Post* and *What a Racket* (starring Arthur Askey). She was on television with James Bolam in *Love on the Dole* and as the canteen manageress with Arthur Lowe in *Pardon the Expression*, the sitcom spin-off from *Coronation Street*, in which Arthur recreated the character of Leonard Swindley. While throwing him in one programme, she dislocated her hip and injured her back. She lost her confidence and decided to retire from showbusiness.

Betty, sister Freda and their father took over a pub, the Cock Hotel, in Whaley Bridge, Derbyshire, and then the Devonshire Arms, in Cheshire. In 1969, *Coronation Street* producer H. V. (Harry) Kershaw asked Betty to play barmaid Betty Turpin in the serial. Five years earlier, she had auditioned for the part of Hilda Ogden, but someone thinner was wanted. Now, she was making her comeback after her period in the wilderness. Today, Betty and sister Freda live near Altrincham, in Cheshire, with their boxer dogs Totti and Polly, and cat Abby. Betty is godmother to *Street* star William Roache's son, William Jr.

CURLY WATTS

The ups and downs of executive stress in Curly Watts's career have more than been matched by the highs and lows he has experienced with women, having lived with one and had two broken engagements.

Born on 4 July 1964, Norman Watts – nicknamed Curly because of his straight hair – left school with eight O levels and two A levels. His first job was working for Rita Fairclough as a paper-boy in The Kabin. He had ambitions to be a fighter pilot but was rejected because of his poor eyesight. Turning down a university place, he emptied dustbins to earn money but still took an interest in literature and astronomy.

Slow on the uptake with girls, he dated Elaine Pollard and Tina Wagstaff while he was lodging with Emily Bishop, before finding a steady relationship with factory worker Shirley Armitage in 1987. They lived in the flat over Alf Roberts's Mini Market and, on their first night together, he insisted that she switch the light off, adding, 'It's all right for you – I haven't broken my duck yet.'

Curly returned to full-time education and was set to prepare for college exams on the day that Shirley had planned a surprise party to mark their first anniversary together. She invited all their friends round, ready for his return to the flat but, when he arrived, Curly turned angry, threw everyone out and told Shirley that he needed to revise for the next day. Shirley left for her parents' home, never to return. Without any income, Curly was thrown out of the flat and moved in with Jack and Vera Duckworth, following the departure of their wayward son Terry. In 1989, after passing his college exams, Curly became trainee assistant manager at Bettabuys supermarket, in Weatherfield – under manager Reg Holdsworth.

He fell for shelf-filler Kimberley Taylor, who was from a church-going family and, when they became engaged in 1990, she insisted that they did not go to bed together until they were married. Continual interference from Kimberley's parents – and the discovery that she was having an affair with a building society manager – led to the break-up of their relationship.

But another Bettabuys employee, dizzy Raquel Wolstenhulme, was soon chasing Curly and not so concerned to protect her own moral well-being. He accompanied her to Buxton, where she was the Weatherfield entrant in a Miss Bettabuys beauty competition. But the romance was short lived, after a photographer offered her work in London. Having lost another woman and moved out of the Duckworth residence into no. 7 Coronation Street, Curly fell for his housemate, design student Angie Freeman, but she cooled the relationship after a night of passion when they were both feeling down.

Desperate for love, Curly joined a dating agency and was matched with Kimberley Taylor. They decided they must be right for one another and became engaged again. Kimberley finally called off the wedding after realizing that she had competition for her affections from the observatory Curly had built in his attic.

When Reg Holdsworth became Bettabuys' area manager in 1993, Curly succeeded in taking over as boss at the Weatherfield store, but his assistant, Elaine Fenwick – who had failed to land the job herself – was out to bring him down. She reported to head office an incident where Curly took no action after Vera Duckworth, penniless and trying to feed her grandson Tommy, tried to steal goods by hiding them in the baby's pushchair.

He was still having no luck in love, except for a one-night stand with Maureen Naylor when she briefly walked out on her fiancé, Reg Holdsworth. At the supermarket, there was constant friction between Curly and Elaine, although she became very drunk at the Bettabuys Christmas party in 1993 and made amorous advances to him. Elaine invited him to her room but collapsed into a drunken sleep before he could have his way with her.

Two months later, Curly started dating single mum Tricia Armstrong after catching her son, Jamie, shoplifting. But that ended when her violent ex-husband, Carl, came back on the scene.

Elaine then made Curly's life hell at Bettabuys by landing the job of area manager herself when Reg Holdsworth left the company to take over Alf Roberts's Mini Market, in Coronation Street. Curly's Bettabuys days were numbered and, in October 1994, he was sacked after being told that Elaine and Kimberley had complained that he had sexually harassed them.

An attempt to earn cash by working for Des Barnes at the bookmakers in Rosamund Street proved a disaster, but Curly appeared to land on his feet by getting a job with Soopascoopa. He also had Raquel's shoulder to cry on and thought he had finally found his true love when she agreed to marry him. But Des Barnes, whom Raquel had ditched after he cheated on her with rival barmaid Tanya Pooley, stepped in to ruin Curly's happiness. At the couple's engagement party, Des cornered Raquel and forced her to admit she did not love Curly. Raquel realized that she could not marry Curly, whose heartbreak led him to snap at Soopascoopa and get reprimanded. He walked out.

Picking up the pieces of his life, Curly accepted Reg Holdsworth's offer to make him his assistant at Firman's Freezers.

☆ ☆ ☆

Kevin Kennedy (b. Kevin Patrick Kennedy in Manchester, 4 September 1961) trained at the Manchester Polytechnic School of Theatre and has appeared on stage in *Ducking Out* at the Greenwich Theatre and in London's West End (alongside Warren Mitchell), *Hamlet* at the Crucible Theatre, Sheffield, and *No Sex, Please – We're British* on tour in 1989, playing the lead role of Runnicles. He has also acted in various radio plays.

On television, Kevin made his debut as a team helper in *Cheggers Plays Pop* as a teenager. After drama school, he acted on the small screen in the Hinge and Brackett series *Dear Ladies* (playing a punk rocker), *The Last Company Car* and *Keep on Running*. He joined *Coronation Street* as Curly Watts in 1983 and appeared on and off for two years, before becoming a regular. MENSA made Curly an honorary member of its elite society because he is the egghead of the *Street*, which its members voted top TV programme.

The actor's uncle played with Shep's Banjo Boys and four of his family were in brass bands, so music is in the blood. For a while, he played guitar with Johnny Marr and Andy Rourke from The Smiths in a group called the Paris Valentinos, then – after drama school – in an Irish band called The Borderline, before forming his own country group, The Bunch of Thieves, who played as support for Ken Dodd at Birmingham's National Exhibition Centre. He has also performed in Nashville, the home of country and western music and still occasionally plays with Irish band The Men They Couldn't Hang, whose lead singer is Kevin's cousin, Cush, as well as joining Galway group The Saw Doctors on stage.

Kevin's first wife, Dawn, who met him when she was working as an extra, gave birth to son Ryan in January 1987 and the couple wed seven months later, with Michael Le Vell – who plays Kevin Webster in the *Street* – as best man. The couple later divorced and Kevin became engaged to girlfriend Claire Johnson in 1994.

KEVIN WEBSTER

Born in Weatherfield on 3 September 1965, Kevin Webster trained as a mechanic at Whitehead's Garage on a Youth Opportunity Programme, only to find that the business had no intention of giving him a job at the end of it.

Hitch-hiking near Bolton one day, Kevin met Alf Roberts, who was trying to repair a fault with his car. Kevin fixed it and Alf suggested he approach Brian Tilsley to see whether there was a job going at his garage and he was taken on.

Than, Kevin's father – property repair man Bill – started renting Rita Fairclough's yard, which had belonged to her late husband, Len, and the family moved into no. 11 Coronation Street. When Bill married Percy Sugden's niece, Elaine Prior, they moved to Southampton and Kevin became a lodger with Hilda Ogden.

His first girlfriend was Mandy Whitworth, but the relationship fizzled out and he met posh teenager Michelle Robinson on a blind date set up by Terry Duckworth. When Terry subsequently taunted him by suggesting that he was

still a virgin, Kevin claimed that he had slept with Michelle, who promptly dumped him.

But the young mechanic literally made a splash when he drove past Sally Seddon in a street, soaking her as he went through a puddle. Hilda disapproved of the relationship, knowing Sally's mother as a rough type. Eventually, she came to see that Sally was not a chip off the old block and gave Kevin her blessing, which meant a lot to him. Kevin and Sally married in October 1986 and moved into the flat above Alf Roberts's cornershop. When Hilda left the Street to live in Derbyshire as Dr Lowther's housekeeper, they bought her house, no. 13.

Before their marriage, Kevin and Sally returned from a pop concert late one night to find the Rovers Return on fire. Fearing for landlady Bet Lynch's life, Kevin climbed in through her bedroom window and rescued her from the smoke.

After Brian Tilsley's murder, Kevin and Sally had hopes of buying the business but could not raise the money. Tom Casey took over the garage and made Kevin the boss, then foisted his son Mark on to him as a mechanic. Kevin had to put up with Mark's bad time-keeping and irresponsibility. After seeking an assurance from Tom Casey that he had complete control over the day-to-day running of the business, Kevin sacked Mark but later reinstated him. The two became good friends until Tom gave the garage to Mark as a 21st-birthday present. Kevin was stunned but, for a while, he and Mark managed to work together.

Financial pressures began to hit the Websters shortly after the birth of their daughter, Rosie, at Christmas 1990. The crunch came when Kevin, trying to earn extra money by doing 'foreigners' – freelance repairs for customers – crashed a car that he was working on. The owner, Terry Seymour, made it clear that he expected Kevin to pay the £1250 bill. Pressurizing Mark to put it through the garage's insurance, Kevin also let slip a remark about Jenny Bradley, who had been seeing Mark but, unknown to him, had found a new boyfriend. Mark sacked Kevin, who was taken on by another local garage, Walker's. In the end, Sally's mother paid the £1250 being demanded by Seymour.

Later, Mike Baldwin hired Kevin as boss at his new business, MVB Motors, at the end of Coronation Street. Kevin had several assistants, until Jim McDonald proved to be steady and reliable. But Jim's son, Steve, led Kevin into trouble when he borrowed Mike's car and drove without a licence. Stopped by the police, he gave Kevin's name and, as a result, Kevin was charged with aiding and abetting him and felt lucky to get away with a fine.

When Sally announced to Kevin that she was pregnant again, in the spring of 1994, he walked out, worried about the financial pressures. But Kevin came round to the idea and was present at Sophie's birth on 2 November 1994.

Michael Le Vell (b. Michael Turner in Manchester, 15 December 1964) trained at Oldham Theatre Workshop and has appeared on stage in *Kes*, *Joby*, *No More Sitting on the Old School Bench*, *Dick Whittington* and *Jack and the Beanstalk*. Michael – who had to change his professional name because there was already an actor called Michael Turner, who played J. Henry Pollard in *Crossroads* – acted on TV in *My Son, My Son*, *Fame Is the Spur*, *The Last Song*, *The Hard Word*, *A Brother's Tale* and *One by One*. He played newspaper delivery boy Neil Grimshaw in the *Street*, in 1981, before joining as Kevin Webster three years later.

Being in the *Street* has given Michael the chance to realize one of his biggest ambitions, playing in celebrity soccer teams at Wembley twice, Anfield, Goodison Park and Old Trafford. He is a Manchester United and Oldham Athletic supporter, having begun to follow Oldham's fortunes while living in the town.

Michael's wife is actress Janette Beverley, who played dizzy Sharon in the comedy series *Sharon and Elsie*, and Sister Diane Meadows in *Children's Ward*. She also appeared in *Coronation Street* twice, first as a mugger of Betty Turpin, then as Curly Watts's girlfriend Elaine Pollard. Michael and Janette live in Saddleworth, West Yorkshire.

bill for a car he crashed when doing work outside the garage, unknown to Mark Casey, who had taken over as boss. Sally's attempts to get the disgruntled car owner to agree to accept the money over a period of time failed, but her mother bailed the couple out with money she received after the death of Sally's father.

The seemingly perfect couple found their marriage threatened when Sally started childminding and was befriended by one of her clients, divorcé Joe Broughton. He fell for Sally and tried to persuade her that Kevin – who was due in court for allegedly aiding and abetting Steve McDonald in driving a car without a licence – was a no-hoper and he could offer her more.

Eventually, when Kevin found out, he sent Joe packing and the Websters were able to get their life back to normal. They even managed a holiday in Blackpool when Rita Fairclough – who had adopted them as a good cause, never having

SALLY WEBSTER

Brought up in a rough area of Weatherfield by feuding parents, Sally Seddon left behind her unhappy childhood when she met and married garage mechanic Kevin Webster. His landlady, Hilda Ogden, initially disapproved of their relationship, but she eventually read their tea leaves and told Sally and Kevin that they would have a happy life together.

Sally worked as an assistant in Alf Roberts's cornershop and, after lodging with Hilda, the couple moved into the flat above it. When Hilda left no. 13, they bought it. Taking on Kevin and Mark Casey, his mechanic at the garage, at banger racing, Sally proved herself to be the fastest, which particularly upset Kevin.

Sally gave up her job working on the till at Alf Roberts's Mini Market when she became pregnant in 1990. On Christmas Eve, she had a baby girl, Rosie, born early and delivered by Liz McDonald in the back of Don Brennan's cab.

With financial pressures already mounting, Sally and Kevin found themselves with a £1250

Peter Armitage was BILL WEBSTER, Kevin's father. The actor has since been seen on television in *Chimera*, *G.B.H.*, *Sam Saturday* (as Jim Butler), *Heartbeat*, *Medics*, *Casualty* and *Peak Practice*.

Sue Devaney (b. Ashton-under-Lyne, Lancashire, 2 July 1967) played DEBBIE WEBSTER, Kevin's sister. She subsequently appeared on TV in *Jonny Briggs*, *Exclusive Yarns*, *The Real Eddy English*, *About Face* (as Maureen Lipman's daughter), *Haggard*, *Spatz*, *The Bill*, *Heartbeat* and *Casualty* (as paramedic Liz Harker). She also formed the funk duo the Dunky Dobbers with former *Street* actress Michelle Holmes.

had a real family of her own – gave Sally and Kevin £5000 after being moved by their struggles to make ends meet.

Then, on 2 November 1994, the couple's second daughter, Sophie, was born. They originally named her Lauren, but Rosie was insistent that she was called Sophie. Rita opened a building society account for the baby with £1000.

Sally Whittaker (b. Middleton, near Oldham, Lancashire, 3 May 1963) was, by her own admission, a plain and chubby teenager with spectacles, but she has matured into a slim blonde who wears contact lenses and is one of *Coronation Street*'s finest actresses.

She grew up in Somerset and started acting at the age of 13 with Oldham Theatre Workshop, then trained at the Mountview Theatre School, North London, for three years. Sally began her career as one of two dancers touring with *The Metal Mickey Road Show* – which involved tap-dancing in leotards – and worked with the Abbadaba Theatre Company, performing old-time music hall in London and, for a month, on America's West Coast with director Robin Hunter, estranged husband of Amanda Barrie, who plays Alma Baldwin in *Coronation Street*. She also acted in the pantomime *Beauty and the Beast* at Oldham Coliseum.

On television, Sally appeared in *Juliet Bravo*, as a 15-year-old middle-class heroin addict called Wendy, then in an episode of *The Practice* as a teenager who found it difficult to cope with the fact that her mother had epileptic fits. The actress also appeared in *Hold Tight!*, as well as commercials, then joined *Coronation Street* in 1986. During one break from the serial, she returned to the stage to star in *A Taste of Honey*, at the Octagon Theatre, Bolton.

Sally and her fiancé, television scriptwriter Tim Dynevor – who in 1994 became a storyline writer on *Emmerdale* – have homes in Bowdon, Cheshire, and near Hampstead Heath, in North London. In April 1995, they celebrated the birth of a baby daughter, Phoebe. Sally enjoys horse-riding, keep fit and walking.

Richard Beckinsale (b. Nottingham, 6 July 1947) made his TV debut in April 1969 as P.C. WILCOX of Tile Street Police Station, one of the arresting officers when Ena Sharples was caught for shoplifting. Richard later found fame in the comedy series *The Lovers*, *Rising Damp* and *Porridge*. He died of a heart attack on 19 March 1979. Daughters Samantha and Kate are both actresses.

DEREK WILTON

As a furniture rep., Derek Wilton arrived at The Kabin in 1976 and spent the next 12 years playing with Mavis Riley's emotions until they finally married.

Born in Harrogate, North Yorkshire, on 8 August 1936, Derek started his working life as a sales rep. for Fresher Air Chemicals. Later came the job of furniture rep. and he started dating Mavis after that first visit to The Kabin.

But he let Mavis down many times, with the comic pair going through a series of setbacks and misunderstandings. Turning up in his new job as a confectionery company rep., he persuaded Mavis to order a huge quantity of Easter eggs for The Kabin. He won a salesman of the month award, but she was almost sacked. Derek intended to give his prize – a canteen of cutlery – to his mother, but Rita Fairclough told him diplomatically that Mavis probably deserved it more. He gave it to her, she invited him to supper and, when Mavis ventured to suggest that his mother might have liked the cutlery, Derek agreed and promptly took it back.

Victor Pendlebury met Mavis and became Derek's rival for her affections. However, she accepted Derek's proposal of marriage, in September 1984, and they looked set for the altar, only to jilt each other on the big day. Derek then married Angela Hawthorne, daughter of his boss. The marriage foundered and Derek returned to Mavis, whom he wed on 9 November 1988. After living in the flat above The Kabin, the couple decided they needed a place of their own, but the deal fell through when Derek lost his job selling toys and novelties, most of them in the worst possible taste. Victor offered Derek a job as a sales rep. for his company, Pendlebury Paper Products.

Victor still tried to win Mavis from Derek, sending him away on an overnight business trip to Bedford so that he could visit her. Derek returned to find Victor rubbing her foot. But Victor conceded defeat, made Derek Northwest area manager and moved to his Darlington office, returning later with a wife of his own, who bore an uncanny resemblance to Mavis.

In March 1990, Derek and Mavis moved out of the Kabin flat and into no. 4 Coronation Street, part of the new housing development. The death of Mavis's beloved budgie, Harriet, marred the move, but Derek gave her the send-off that Mavis wished, burying the budgie in the garden after storing her in the fridge.

Derek finally saw Victor disappear from his and Mavis's lives when he was sacked. For a while, he worked as assistant school caretaker at

Weatherfield Comprehensive. He took over as caretaker but was sacked after a break-in. The governors decided to reinstate him but were amused to receive a letter from Mavis defending her husband. On learning of this, he resigned. Derek horrified Mavis when he told her he was returning to work for his first wife, Angela.

Then, Norris Cole came into the lives of Mavis and Derek. When Derek and Norris went to a sales meeting for EnviroSphere, a pyramid-selling organization, Derek was taken in and spent £2000 on start-up products. Norris started on a smaller scale but earned money, while Derek saw his 'investment' disappear.

Norris brought more misery to the Wiltons when he persuaded Derek to buy a Mile Muncher exercise machine. When Mavis, who had dismissed it as a toy and a waste of money, secretly tried it out and was thrown from the machine, Derek had ideas of getting compensation, but Mavis eventually admitted that she was wearing the wrong footwear and Derek backed down.

☆ ☆ ☆

Peter Baldwin (b. Chichester, West Sussex, 1933) grew up in the tiny village of Chidham, near Chichester, close to the sea. During the war, Peter and his younger brother, Christopher, moved to his grandparents' home near Horsham, where his mother was a teacher.

In 1946, Peter was given his first toy theatre and he was soon collecting them and planning a career for himself on the stage. On moving back to Chichester, he joined the local dramatic society and successfully applied to train as an actor at the Bristol Old Vic Theatre. But, before he could go there, he had to do two years' National Service, serving in the army at Aldershot.

His first repertory theatre job was with the West of England Theatre Company, based in Exmouth, Devon, which toured in productions all over the West Country. In the same company was Thelma Barlow, who became Peter's screen wife almost 30 years later in *Coronation Street*. The pair also played the husband and wife never on stage at the same time in *The Way of the World* at the Bristol Old Vic in 1967.

On television, Peter has appeared in *Bergerac*, *Agatha Christie's Miss Marple* and *Seven Deadly Sins*. He also played the husband of a feminist in three series of *Odd Girl Out*, a sitcom about women's liberation. He first played Derek Wilton in *Coronation Street* in 1976 and acted in the serial on and off for 12 years before becoming a regular member of the cast.

In the theatre, he acted alongside Edward Fox in *Dance of Death* and appeared in the stage version of the later television series *Ever Decreasing Circles*, playing the lead role of Howard, which went to Stanley Lebor on screen, although Peter auditioned for it. Peter's many other stage appearances have included *The Browning Version*, *The Inspector Calls*, *You Never Can Tell*, *Macbeth* and *Romeo and Juliet*, in which he met his actress wife Sarah Long, who went on to become a presenter of *Play School*. They had two children, Julia and Matthew, but Sarah suddenly died of cancer just before Christmas 1987, while Peter was doing one of his occasional stints in *Coronation Street*. After the funeral, he battled on, fulfilling his commitment to another five weeks in the *Street*, performing some hilarious scenes with Thelma Barlow at a time of great personal grief. Six months later, he joined the cast full time.

Peter's childhood interest in toy theatres was revived when he got one out one Christmas to perform a nativity play for his daughter. He worked for many years at Pollock's Toy Museum while resting between acting jobs. When the museum opened a shop, Pollock's Toy Theatres, in Covent Garden, London, in 1980, he became the part-time manager and later, with his brother, took it over. The shop specializes in 19th-century toy theatres. Peter, who has homes in North London and Manchester, staged an exhibition of toy theatres at the National Theatre in 1988 and has written a book, *Toy Theatres of the World*.

MAVIS WILTON

Born in Weatherfield on 7 April 1937, Mavis Riley had a strict Methodist upbringing and was Emily Nugent's best friend at school. Father Tom retired from his job at a stable after being injured and, with wife Margaret, bought an off-licence in Grange-over-Sands – even though the couple were teetotal! Mavis returned to Weatherfield in 1969 and lived with her Aunt Edith. A qualified secretary, she worked for Brittain's mail-order firm alongside Emily.

At Emily's wedding to Ernest Bishop, in April 1972, Mavis met plumber Jerry Booth. They started seeing one another and Jerry intended to propose marriage, but the couple's relationship finished when the builder told her that he was a divorcé. Mavis fled in shock to Grange-over-Sands but returned to work as a vet's receptionist, then in Maggie Clegg's cornershop.

She had a romantic encounter with Spanish waiter Pedro when some of the Street's women won a prize trip to Majorca and, when she heard that he was coming to Weatherfield, went to meet him and was confronted by British-based Spanish café waiter Carlos, who had set him up in an attempt to rile Jerry. Going out to dinner that evening, Carlos produced a ring and proposed. Mavis accepted, but backed out when she found that he wanted her to marry him only so that he could obtain a work permit.

Mavis became Rita Fairclough's assistant in The Kabin newsagent's in June 1973. With the job went the flat above the shop, and Mavis lived there with her beloved budgie, Harriet.

Derek Wilton came into Mavis's life when he arrived at The Kabin as a furniture rep. in 1976. Romance blossomed and Derek even proposed buying a house together, but she realized he was not proposing marriage and told him to go. But he returned after landing a job as a rep. working for a confectioner's and was to enter Mavis's life, on and off over the years, vying for her affections with Victor Pendlebury, a town hall planning officer whom she met at night school when she was attending literary classes.

Mavis and Victor wrote a prize-winning short story for radio, and Mavis's talents extended to writing a novel, *Song of a Scarlet Summer*, with the characters based on local residents. Victor asked Mavis to live with him in a trial marriage, but she refused, preferring the real thing instead.

Derek reappeared and asked Mavis to marry him. She agreed, but Victor also asked for her hand in marriage. She agreed to that, then changed her mind again. So Derek and Mavis set the wedding for September 1984, but neither of them could go through with it and, on the day, both failed to turn up at the church.

A year later, Mavis was stunned to hear that Derek had married someone else – Angela Hawthorne, his boss's daughter – but now felt trapped in a loveless marriage. Then, in 1986, Derek left his wife and Angela cited Mavis as co-respondent in the divorce case, although she persuaded Angela that she and Derek had not slept together. Derek then upset Mavis by moving to Cornwall, where he had bought a business. But he returned to Weatherfield as area manager for a stationers. Derek proposed again – through the letterbox of The Kabin – and the couple finally married on 9 November 1988.

Despite failed attempts by Victor to woo Mavis back, she and Derek have proved to be a comic match that is likely to survive anything. Victor paid her the ultimate compliment when he married a woman who was a Mavis clone, although the real Mavis was appalled by her.

But there were other men standing by, ready to drive a wedge between Mavis and Derek. Roger Crompton met her at evening art classes and Derek accused her of getting up to no good with him, although Mavis appeared jealous when he started seeing Rita Sullivan.

When bad penny Norris Cole sold Derek a Mile Muncher exercise machine, Mavis tried it out and ended up with concussion in hospital. Derek dropped his efforts to get compensation for damages when Mavis admitted she had been wearing the wrong footwear.

☆ ☆ ☆

Thelma Barlow (b. Middlesbrough, Cleveland, 19 June 1937) never knew her father, who died of pneumonia five weeks before her birth. She grew up without any males in the house, which left her terrified of men.

Thelma spent the first seven years of her working life as a secretary in Huddersfield, but decided to try acting and took speech and drama lessons at evening classes. Soon, she was appearing in amateur productions, before joining Joan Littlewood's Theatre Workshop in East London.

For many years, Thelma acted on stage, appearing in mainly classical productions. Then, she broke into television, in plays and serials such as *Vanity Fair*.

She took the role of Mavis in *Coronation Street* for the first time in 1972. Thelma had previously worked with screen husband Peter Baldwin on stage, first with a touring theatre company in the West Country, then at the Bristol Old Vic, where they played husband and wife in *The Way of the World*, in 1967.

Divorced from designer Graham Barlow, by whom she has two grown-up sons – off-licence manager Clive and theatre director James – Thelma has a flat in Manchester and a cottage in Giggleswick, North Yorkshire, where she enjoys pottering around in her organic garden. She was a close friend of the late chat-show host Russell Harty, who also lived in Giggleswick. Thelma wrote a book called *Organic Gardening with Love*, published in 1992.

RAQUEL WOLSTENHULME

Bettabuys supermarket shelf-filler Raquel Wolstenhulme fell for assistant manager Curly Watts after he was dumped by fiancée Kimberley Taylor. He decided that her obvious charms, made freely available, compensated for her lack of brains. When she represented the Weatherfield branch in the supermarket's national beauty competition in Buxton, Derbyshire, Raquel was distraught at not coming in the top three, but Curly was there at her hotel to commiserate with her afterwards.

More successful was her modelling of design student Angie Freeman's clothes in a college fashion show. A photographer offered her work in London and she gave Curly the elbow, telling him that they no longer mixed in the same circles. But Raquel later returned to Weatherfield, having been duped with false promises.

She found a job as a barmaid at the Rovers Return and, looking for accommodation, moved in with Des Barnes, who had just split up with his wife, Steph. She proved a good shoulder to cry on for Des but left for a room at the Rovers when Steph returned, albeit briefly.

Raquel was thrilled when footballer Wayne Farrell, star striker of County F.C., began seeing her. But she finally caught him with Serena Black, ditched him and agreed to go out with cricket fan Gordon Blinkhorn, who taught her the theory of the game. When they planned a holiday to France, Raquel took French lessons with Ken Barlow, but Gordon became jealous and she left him.

Raquel was on hand to give Des the emotional support he needed after the death of his live-in lover Lisa Duckworth. It seemed that Des and Raquel's relationship would work out this time, until wandering Des could not resist the advances of barmaid Tanya Pooley, Raquel's bitchy rival at the Rovers. Raquel's discovery of this proved to be her greatest heartbreak and she could not bring herself to forgive Des.

It was Curly Watts's turn to provide a shoulder to cry on and this led to the Street's two losers in love becoming engaged. Curly was elated, but Des was around again to bring grief to other people's lives. At the couple's engagement party, he confronted Raquel and made her admit that she did not love Curly. She knew this was true and could not go through with marriage. It was now Curly's turn to be heartbroken.

☆ ☆ ☆

Sarah Lancashire is the daughter of TV scriptwriter Geoffrey Lancashire, who wrote 74 episodes of *Coronation Street* over seven years, as well as *The Lovers* and *Foxy Lady*. Sarah, who trained at the Guildhall School of Music and Drama and sang with a dance band, first appeared in the *Street* in 1987, as nurse Wendy Farmer, who answered the Duckworths' advertisement for a lodger, but Vera thought she might be too much for Jack's blood pressure.

The actress was also on TV in *Dramarama*, *Celebration*, *Watching* (as a mechanic), *Bradley*, *My Secret Desire* and the Maureen Lipman series *About Face* (as Maureen's daughter), as well as playing Linda in *Blood Brothers* on the West End stage.

Sarah and her husband, music lecturer Gary Hargreaves, have two sons, Thomas and Matthew, and live in Oldham, Lancashire.

Michael Elphick (b. Chichester, West Sussex, 19 September 1946) played DOUGLAS WORMOLD, son of landlord Edward. Douglas tried to buy the original Kabin and persuade residents of Coronation Street to sell their homes. Michael followed his four 1974 *Street* episodes with the roles of Sam in the comedy *Three Up, Two Down*, Ken Boon in *Boon* and a seedy Fleet Street reporter in *Harry*.

Geoffrey Hughes (b. Liverpool, 2 February 1944) had already appeared in the films *The Virgin Soldiers* and The Beatles' *Yellow Submarine* (as the voice of Paul McCartney), before playing lovable rogue EDDIE YEATS in *Coronation Street*, lodging with Stan and Hilda Ogden, before leaving Weatherfield to marry Marion Willis. Geoffrey has since starred in the sitcoms *The Bright Side* and *Keeping up Appearances* (as Onslow).

Standing: Tiffany Raymond (Martine McCutcheon), Robbie Jackson (Dean Gaffney), Bianca Jackson (Patsy Palmer), Natalie Price (Lucy Speed), Nigel Bates (Paul Bradley), Debbie Bates (Nicola Duffett), Clare Tyler (Gemma Bissix), Carol Jackson (Lindsey Coulson), Sonia Jackson (Natalie Cassidy), Alan Jackson (Howard Antony), Nellie Ellis (Elizabeth Kelly), Dr Harold Legg (Leonard Fenton), Geoff Barnes (David Roper), Michelle Fowler (Susan Tully), Ruth Fowler (Caroline Paterson), Mark Fowler (Todd Carty), Pauline Fowler (Wendy Richard), Vicki Fowler (Samantha Leigh Martin), Arthur Fowler (Bill Treacher), Martin Fowler (Jon Peyton Price), Grant Mitchell (Ross Kemp), Peggy Mitchell (Barbara Windsor), Sharon Mitchell (Letitia Dean), Phil Mitchell (Steve McFadden), Kathy Mitchell (Gillian Taylforth), Roy Evans (Tony Caunter), Janine Butcher (Alexia Demetriou), Ricky Butcher (Sid Owen), Pat Butcher (Pam St Clement), Della Alexander (Michelle Joseph), David Wicks (Michael French), Binnie Roberts (Sophie Langham), Sanjay Kapoor (Deepak Verma), Steve Elliot (Mark Monero). Sitting: Billy Jackson (Devon Anderson), Blossom Jackson (Mona Hammond), Jules Tavernier (Tommy Eytle), Ethel Skinner (Gretchen Franklin), Steven Beale (Stuart William Stevens), Cindy Beale (Michelle Collins) with Lucy Beale (Eva Britten-Snell), Ian Beale (Adam Woodyatt) with Peter Beale (Francis Britten-Snell), Gita Kapoor (Shobu Kapoor) with Sharmilla Kapoor (Gagendeep Rai).

EastEnders, created by its original producer Julia Smith and script editor Tony Holland under the working title *East 8* (the postal district of Hackney, in London's East End), hit BBC1 screens for the first time at 7p.m. on 19 February 1985 with the words of Queen Vic landlord Den Watts: 'Stinks in here.' 'Dirty' Den, Arthur Fowler and Ali Osman were seen breaking down the door of Reg Cox's flat, where they found the old man slumped in his armchair, dead. That first scene set the tone for what was to come. Following in the style of Channel Four's *Brookside*, *EastEnders* aimed to reflect the Britain of the Eighties. A year before, the BBC had bought Elstree Studios, where the programme is made, and built an outdoor set of Albert Square, Walford, London E19, on a piece of wasteland there.

At first scheduled against *Emmerdale Farm* (now *Emmerdale*), the residents of Albert Square lost the battle for viewers. With a change of transmission time for its two weekly screenings, *EastEnders* soared in the TV ratings and even challenged *Coronation Street*, although it beat the ITV serial usually only after adding the audience for its Sunday omnibus edition. The combined figures produced an audience of 30 million for the Christmas Day 1986 episode, when Angie Watts walked out of the Queen Vic pub after husband Den announced he was divorcing her. In April 1994, the programme went thrice weekly. A 'prequel', *Civvy Street*, screened as a one-off programme in 1988, told the story of Albert Square during the Second World War.

DEBBIE BATES

Part-time flower stallholder and mother of Clare, Debbie Tyler met Nigel Bates at his birthday party. Nigel was seen as a loser by most people, but Debbie wanted to mother him.

When her violent husband Liam returned in 1994, Debbie told Nigel that she wanted only him and the couple moved into a new flat in George Street. But Liam threatened to stay in Walford until he won custody of Clare and found refuge in the new Roach Motel opened by market inspector Richard Cole.

As the custody battle continued, Nigel asked Debbie to marry him as soon as her divorce came through. They won custody and wed at St John's Church on 12 July 1994, with Clare as bridesmaid and Grant Mitchell as best man. Debbie bought her ivory fabric wedding dress with lace collar just 24 hours before the event. Although Nigel was anxious to have children with Debbie, she was more concerned to continue her work at the betting shop, but walked out when her boss, Stan Dougan, made an unwelcome pass at her. Shortly afterwards, she was fatally hit by a car while crossing the road.

☆ ☆ ☆

Nicola Duffett (b. Portsmouth, Hampshire) trained at the Arts Educational School and appeared on TV in *You the City*, *Perfect Scoundrels*, *The Bill*, *Laugh Baby Laugh*, *Maigret* and *Hot Dog Wars*. She also played Ruth Hadley in *Shadow of the Noose* and Elvira Barney in *In Suspicious Circumstances*, in addition to supplying the voice of Ruby Kumara in the satellite TV serial *Jupiter Moon*, and acting prostitute Jackie Bast in the film *Howards End*.

Divorced from theatrical agent Andy Easton, by whom she has a daughter Jessica, Nicola married actor Ian Henderson – who plays Callum in the TV comedy series *Second Thoughts* – in the Bahamas in August 1994. The couple live in London. Nicola, who suffered two miscarriages during her first marriage, also had an ectopic pregnancy two months before her second wedding and doctors feared she had an ovarian cyst. She suffered another tragedy with the death of her father, Jack, a commander in the Royal Navy, at the age of 59 in 1993. He had suffered from Alzheimer's disease.

NIGEL BATES

Bumbling but lovable Nigel Bates is one of life's losers, although he proved he was not the wimp some thought when he stood up to wife-to-be Debbie Tyler's ex-husband. He had met Debbie at his birthday party. What he did not know was that she had a daughter, Clare, and began to wonder about her curious behaviour, such as cutting short evenings out.

Eventually, the truth came out, but this did not deter Nigel. Nor did the arrival in Walford of Debbie's first husband, Liam, although he made life difficult for the couple by threatening to win custody of Clare. But nothing was going to thwart Nigel and Debbie's happiness and the couple married on 12 July 1994.

When his friend Grant Mitchell was shunned by everyone else in Albert Square after hospitalizing his brother for sleeping with his wife, Nigel offered him shelter. Grant repaid Nigel by setting up an incident that changed his reputation. One day while Nigel was walking with Clare, Janine Butcher and Sonia Jackson, some thugs started to threaten him. He made a stand and the yobs disappeared. This all happened in front of the girls and transformed the way they saw him. But Nigel's life was torn apart by the death of Debbie in a road accident on 22 June 1995.

☆ ☆ ☆

Paul Bradley graduated in drama from Manchester University, where he shared a hall of residence with *Young Ones* stars Rik Mayall and Adrian Edmondson, who were his friends. Paul appeared in *The Young Ones*, as Warlock, in 1984 and, nine years later, in the first series of the Mayall-Edmondson comedy *Bottom*, as a burglar. In between, he was seen on TV in *The Bill*, *The Comic Strip Presents...*, *Travelling Man*, *The Gift*, *Secret Desire*, *T-Bag*, *The Manageress*, *Boon*, *Red Dwarf*, *Stop That Laughing at the Back*, *The Kate Robbins Show*,

Jeff Rawle (b. Birmingham, 20 July 1951), who took the title role of the TV comedy series *Billy Liar* and, more recently, was George in *Drop the Dead Donkey*, played an AIDS COUNSELLOR at the Terrence Higgins Trust, counselling Mark Fowler.

David Roper (b. David Anthony Roper in Bradford, West Yorkshire, 20 June 1944) played P.C. Sadler in *Coronation Street* in 1974, went on to star in the comedy series *The Cuckoo Waltz* and appeared in *Families* and *Brookside* (as Sam Bishop), before joining *EastEnders* as GEOFF BARNES, who fell for Michelle Fowler.

Tara Moran played café assistant Christine Carter in *Coronation Street*, Chelsea Richards in *Families* and newly qualified nurse Mary Skillett in *Casualty*, before joining *EastEnders* as FELICITY BARNES, Geoff's daughter.

Births, Marriages and Deaths, *Smith and Jones* and *Murder Most Horrid*. He also devised, co-wrote and starred in his own comedy series, *Bradley*, and played Len Bigwell in *Titmuss Regained*, before joining *EastEnders* in 1992.

On stage, Paul has acted acted in *A Midsummer Night's Dream* and *Twelfth Night* for the New Shakespeare Company at the Open Air Theatre, Regent's Park. He was a member of Peter Gill's first company at the National Theatre, in 1985.

In his spare time, Paul plays guitar in The Kippers, whose other members have performed on records by Peter Gabriel, Van Morrison and The Pogues. Paul met his girlfriend, stage manager Lynn Nelson, in 1987, when they were both touring in *The Taming of the Shrew*. They live in Dalston, East London, and have a son, Matty, and a daughter, Maude.

CINDY BEALE

WEST SOHO
LONDON'S

Convent girl Cindy Williams was first seen in the Square working on her mother's hat stall. When she was snubbed by Queen Vic barman Simon Wicks, who ditched her for Donna Ludlow, she became hardened and resolved to behave in a similar way, which gave her a reputation for sleeping around.

Ian Beale fell for Cindy, but she was using him to make Wicksy jealous. After a one-night stand with Wicksy upstairs at the pub after closing time, Cindy became pregnant. Wicksy refused to accept that the baby was his, so she let Ian believe that he was the father.

Her marriage to Ian in a register office on 12 October 1989 was marred by Cindy's rows with Ian's family. Married life did not start well for the couple – who lived first in Ian's father's towerblock flat, then Colin Russell's old flat at no. 3 Albert Square – and nothing improved after the birth of baby Steven two weeks after the wedding. On seeing the baby, Wicksy changed his mind, made it clear that he wanted to be with Cindy and Steven, ditched Sharon Watts and moved into the B&B with Cindy.

Ian was devastated when, in August 1990, Cindy told him that she loved Wicksy, who was Steven's father, and Ian's family made life difficult for Cindy and Wicksy. The pair left for a new life in Devon four months later. But, in 1992, Cindy was back, spending Christmas with Ian after being dumped by Wicksy. Ian had tracked her down to a small London bedsit and started wooing her back. They made a new start and, on 9 December 1993, Cindy gave birth to twins Peter and Lucy. 'Tricky Dicky' Cole tried to bed Cindy, but she resisted his advances.

But life was not happy for Cindy as she struggled at home with Steven and the twins while Ian, finding it difficult to recover loans, teetered close to bankruptcy in his finance business. Eventually, she poured her heart out to Gita Kapoor, who found her about to hit Steven in her frustration. Ian could only tell her that he had plans to buy the old Chinese takeaway and open it up as a fish-and-chip shop.

On her trips to the local swimming pool, Cindy fell for 19-year-old lifeguard Matt and slept with him. When he tried to persuade her to leave Ian, she dumped him and decided that she should make the most of her marriage. But, in May 1995, Cindy had a one-night stand with David Wicks, Simon's half-brother.

☆ ☆ ☆

Michelle Collins (b. Hackney, East London) grew up in Islington, North London, and attended the Cockpit Youth Theatre – where *The Life and Loves of a She-Devil* star Julie T. Wallace was a friend – and Mountview Youth Theatre in her spare time. On leaving school with five O levels, aged 16, she studied drama and theatre arts and an English literature A level at Kingsway Princeton College, where Steve McFadden – later to play Phil Mitchell in *EastEnders* – was then studying social science. Until acting work came along, she worked as a waitress and in London Zoo's gift shop. When Michelle saw an advertisement placed by a pop group looking for a singer, it turned out to be Sex Pistols manager Malcolm McLaren seeking someone for his group Bow Wow Wow. She failed the audition, but appeared in the promotional video for Squeeze's 'Up the Junction' single and in *The Crimson Island*, at the Gate Theatre, Notting Hill. Michelle became a backing singer with Mari Wilson and the Wilsations, as well as a backing singer, under the name Candide, in The Marionettes, recording singles and appearing on TV in *The David Essex Showcase*, *Video Entertainers* and *Riverside*.

Gaining her Equity actors' union card through her singing work, she finally found acting work and appeared in such programmes as *Morgan's Boy*, *Marjorie and Men*, *The Manageress*, *Bergerac*, *Good Neighbours*, *Going to Work* and *Lucky Sunil*. She played Sophie, Ray Brooks's daughter, in two series of *Running Wild*, Carol – a nurse from London who had an affair with a Jewish doctor – in eight episodes of *Albion Market*, and model agency booker Pru Murphy in the daytime fashion soap *Gems*, as well as appearing in the films *Empire State*, *Hidden City* and *Personal Services* (as waitress Jackie), before joining *EastEnders*.

During her two years away from the programme, she had a short, unhappy stint as co-presenter of *The Word* and recorded a single, the Temptations classic 'Get Ready'. She released another single, 'Ain't No Right Or Wrong Way', in 1993. After returning to *EastEnders*, Michelle broke off her engagement to her boyfriend of three years, Nick Fordyce.

IAN BEALE

Son of Pete and Kathy Beale, Ian has come a long way since his carefree days riding round on a motorbike. The introverted teenager has been transformed into a sharp businessman. At the same time, the caring nature of his youth has been replaced by a hard, businesslike attitude. While Ian was growing up, his father tried to

toughen him up, so he took up boxing and bought the bike. But he went too far when he bought a lethal knife to tackle potential muggers. Although always closer to his mother than his father, Ian lost his cool and attacked Kathy when it was revealed that Donna Ludlow was the daughter she had conceived after being raped at the age of 14.

After joining Sharon Watts, Simon Wicks and Kelvin Carpenter in a rock group, The Banned, which played at the community centre, Ian started on the right track when he attended catering college and gained a City and Guilds qualification. He had already helped Sue and Ali Osman out in the Square's café and, on leaving college, developed his own business, Beale's Catering, complete with liveried vans and a Jeep, and a team of waitresses. He had contracts to supply the Queen Vic and the Dagmar.

When Ali was unable to pay his debts, Ian also ran the café. Then, he branched out with his Beales on Wheels delivery service, supplying lunches and buffets to local pubs and eventually sold the café to a consortium of his mother Kathy, aunt Pauline Fowler and Frank Butcher, before starting the Meal Machine. He was soon employing young Hattie Tavernier as his office assistant and Mark Fowler's friend Joe as chef. When Ian found out that Joe was HIV positive, he sacked him and took on Steve Elliot.

The recession hit Ian's business and he had to lay off Steve, reduce Hattie's hours and establish a more modest business working from home. Continuing money problems meant that Ian had to take a job back at the café.

Ian's love life was also full of setbacks. In his youth, he had a short romance with Sharon Watts, then moved into a flat with girlfriend Tina, but that relationship did not last. He fell for flighty market-stall worker Cindy Williams and the couple lived together in his father's highrise council flat after his parents' divorce.

Cindy had a one-night stand with Simon Wicks, son of Ian's father by first wife Pat, and became pregnant, but Wicksy refused to accept that the baby was his. She allowed Ian to believe that he was the father. He was delighted and they married on 12 October 1989, with Wicksy as best man. Baby Steven was born two weeks later.

As he built up his catering business, Ian began to neglect Cindy. When Wicksy saw the baby, he wanted both Cindy and his son. Cindy told Ian that she was starting a new life with Wicksy. Ian drove off, crashed and ended up critically injured in hospital. Suffering a breakdown, Ian refused to accept that Steven was not his, but a blood test revealed the truth. Desperate for money, Wicksy accepted Ian's

Anna Wing (b. Anna Eva Lydia Catherine Wing in Hackney, London, 30 October 1914) played LOU BEALE, harridan mother of twins Pauline Fowler and Pete Beale, until the character's death in 1988. She had appeared in such TV series as *The Chinese Detective* and *Flying Lady*, and later acted Gran in a one-off remake of *The Grove Family* and Mrs Tutt in the comedy series *Bonjour la Classe*.

Peter Dean (b. Hoxton, East London, 2 May 1939) played PETE BEALE from *EastEnders'* first episode until 1993, when his character was killed in a car crash with new love Rose Chapman. Peter previously played villain Jack Lynn in *Law and Order* and was in *Target, Shoestring, Minder, Shine on Harvey Moon, The Zoo, Coronation Street* (as lorry driver Fangio Bateman) and *Big Deal*.

Sean Maguire (b. Ilford, Essex), who played young footballer AIDAN BROSNAN, went on to present *O-Zone*, act in the drama *Dangerfield* and have hit singles with 'Someone to Love', 'Take This Time' and 'Suddenly'.

Sophie Lawrence played Frank Butcher's daughter DIANE BUTCHER, who left for Paris in 1991 but made a brief return three years later when her baby was born. Sophie, who at the age of ten acted in *Bugsy Malone* in the West End, joined *EastEnders* in 1988 and later had a hit single with 'Love's Unkind'.

Mike Reid (b. London, 19 January 1940), who shot to fame as a stand-up comic in *The Comedians*, was secondhand car dealer FRANK BUTCHER. Mike began his TV career as an extra in such series as *The Saint* and *The Baron* and hosted the children's series *Runaround*, played Arthur Mullard's brother in *Yus, My Dear* and had a Top 10 single with 'The Ugly Duckling'. He left *EastEnders* in 1994, after six years.

Edna Doré played MO BUTCHER, Frank's widowed mother, who had Alzheimer's disease. Veteran actress Edna had previously appeared on TV in *The Brothers, The Liver Birds, Doctor in the House, Doctor at Large, Open All Hours, Tenko* and *Casualty*. After leaving *EastEnders*, she played Grace Taplow in *Love Hurts* and Iris Cromer in *Westbeach*.

offer of work in his catering business. Ian, intending to kill himself and Wicksy, broke the brake cables on his delivery van. They crashed, but both escaped unhurt.

In December 1990, Cindy and Wicksy moved away from the Square to start a new life in Devon and Ian buried himself in his work. He had the sympathy of most residents, but their patience began to grow thin as he became more cynical and bitter. He took to kerb-crawling around King's Cross to pick up prostitutes and had an affair with an older woman.

When, in 1992, Ian wanted to cash in insurance policies he had taken out with Cindy and needed her signature, he tracked her down to a small London bedsit after she had been ditched by Wicksy. He started seeing Cindy again and eventually persuaded her to return to the Square, where they started afresh.

Cindy became pregnant again, giving birth to twins Peter and Lucy two months prematurely, on 9 December 1993. But, for Ian, life still did not run smoothly. His mother fired him from his job at the café when she found he was using it as a base for his own business, the Meal Machine. He bounced back with a new venture, Ian Beale Finance, gained a reputation as a loan shark and saw his popularity in the Square plummet to new depths. When the business almost went bankrupt because he found it difficult to recover loans, Ian opened a fish-and-chip shop in the former Chinese takeaway premises. As he concentrated on building up his new concern, he failed to notice that Cindy was falling for Matt, a lifeguard at the local swimming pool. Ian never knew about the affair, but Cindy played with fire when she fell for David Wicks.

☆ ☆ ☆

Adam Woodyatt (b. Woodford, Essex, 28 June 1968) was brought up in Chingford, Essex, before moving with his parents to Wales, where he had a Saturday job in a butcher's shop. He was about to become an apprentice butcher when he heard of auditions for *EastEnders*, and landed the role of Ian Beale from episode one.

He had previously played one of Fagin's gang in a West End revival of the musical *Oliver!*, and Ragamuffin, alongside Felicity Kendal, in Tom Stoppard's *On the Razzle*, at the National Theatre. Adam appeared on television in *The Baker Street Boys* (as Shiner), and *The Witches of Grinnygog* (as Dave Firkettle).

In 1990, he escaped unhurt when his new £15,000 Sierra Cosworth, driven by a friend, was involved in a car crash. It happened at the same time as his *EastEnders* character was in intensive care, recovering from a van crash. Adam plays football for Walford Boys' Club, a charity team made up of members of the *EastEnders* cast. On FA Cup Final day in 1987, he played in goal for the David Frost XI. Adam, who lives in Hertfordshire with his girlfriend Beverley Sharpe and their daughter Jessica, born in 1994, also enjoys playing snooker.

PAT BUTCHER

Pat Harris was a good-looking teenager who hung out with Angie Watts and let all the boys congregate around them. At the age of 16, Pat won a Miss Butlin's beauty contest in Clacton-on-Sea. It was there that she lost her virginity to Frank Butcher, who was at the contest with his fiancée, June. He simply introduced himself, took her back to her chalet and they made love.

After Frank's marriage, he and Pat occasionally rekindled the old flames, but he would not leave his wife and she simply played the field, gaining a reputation as a slut. Two of her boyfriends were Den Watts and Kenny Beale. Kenny's brother Pete married Pat when he thought she was pregnant, although she turned out not to be.

During their marriage, they had two sons, David and Simon, although Pat had affairs with several other men – including Pete's brother Kenny, Brian Wicks and Den Watts – so she knew that her husband was probably not the boys' father.

Spurred on by his mother Lou, who had always been against the marriage, Pete left Pat and she married Brian Wicks on the rebound. Brian drank increasingly and beat Pat, who eventually walked out on him and returned to Albert Square, where son Simon had gone to be with Pete Beale, the man he believed to be his father.

She worked behind the bar at the Queen Vic pub and, in her low-cut tops, became a hit with the locals. She also had a room at the pub and went back to the days of putting herself around.

In February 1988, old flame Frank Butcher told Pat that his wife had died and he was free to marry her. So, when Angie and Den split up, Pat and Frank took over the tenancy of the pub and, on 22 June 1989, married. It appeared to be a marriage of convenience. His four children – two sons and two daughters – needed a mother; she was fat, 40 and lonely. But it helped to calm down Pat, known for her fiery personality.

Frank bought the B&B, the Square car lot and became a sleeping partner in the café. With these commitments, he and Pat gave up the pub, he devoted his energies to the car lot and Pat concentrated on running the B&B.

Pat was uneasy at first about taking in husband Frank's mother Mo as she battled against Alzheimer's disease, but she gradually warmed to her and gave her the care and attention she needed. But, as Mo's health deteriorated, it was decided that Frank's sister Joan, in Essex, could give her more care. Mo died in December 1992.

Life was on the way downhill for Pat and Frank. In May 1992, the recession forced them to sell the B&B and move into a small flat at no. 43b Albert Square. This came on top of Frank's daughter Diane running away from home and son Ricky marrying Sam Mitchell in what turned out to be a major mistake.

Then came Pat's worst moment. On Christmas Eve 1992, by this time driving for her own taxi firm, PatCabs, Pat took a fare after drinking a couple of gin and tonics and ran over a young woman, Stephanie Watson, who later died in hospital. The following summer, Pat was sentenced to six months in jail for drink-driving.

She came out after three months to find Frank's family in turmoil. Ricky had split up with Sam, Diane was pregnant in Paris and Janine was proving too much for her elder sister Claire. Janine moved in with Frank and Pat, and showed herself to be a spoilt brat, although she was being bullied at school.

Further cash problems caused Frank to sell the taxi firm, by now called F&P Cabs, and the couple moved next door to no. 41 Albert Square before selling the first flat. Frank could not pay both mortgages and Pat took a cleaning job at the Queen Vic. Frank eventually accepted a ridiculously low offer for the flat from Phil Mitchell, who also bought his share of the café.

Frank's money problems signalled the end of the couple's marriage. Hoping to claim a massive sum on insurance, Frank conspired with Phil Mitchell to burn down the car lot. The torching went wrong and a homeless boy died in the fire. In April 1994, Frank left the Square, escaping manslaughter charges and racked with guilt. Ricky became obsessed with looking for him, and Diane returned to the Square briefly to help, with baby son Jacques in tow.

Four months earlier, Pat's son David Wicks had come back to her. He said he wanted to make up for the lost years but was, in reality, running away from debts. Another bad penny had arrived on Pat's doorstep. In February 1994, David's parole officer came to the Square and told Pat that he had been convicted for VAT fraud and had defaulted on his maintenance payments. Pat herself took out a loan from Ian Beale's finance company to meet the mortgage repayments and gave David £500 when he claimed that heavies were threatening to break his legs unless he paid up. He also reopened Frank's car lot as Deals on Wheels, with Ricky as his business partner.

Pat, still doing cleaning jobs to earn more cash, started stealing and was caught taking money from Sharon Mitchell's purse. But kind-hearted Sharon paid off Pat's loan to Ian and gave her the money she needed to cover her debts. In December 1994, Pat took over running the Queen Vic, following the break-up of Grant and Sharon Mitchell's marriage, but walked out five months later, fed up of Grant and Phil's mother Peggy continually interfering.

She thought she had found herself a new admirer in Geoff Barnes, the college tutor who was also Michelle Fowler's boyfriend, but Pat misread the signals and felt a fool. However, Pat was not wrong about the interest shown by car dealer Roy Evans, after lampooning him for selling David a dodgy motor. As the couple became closer, Pat refused Roy's offer to take her and Janine on a cruise and dumped him, but the couple were reunited when Pat realized how much she missed her new man.

Pam St Clement (b. Harrow-on-the-Hill, Middlesex, 12 May 1942), whose father came from London's East End, lived in Stepney for a while, within the sound of Bow Bells. Previously a journalist and teacher, Pam trained as an actress at the Rose Bruford College of Speech and Drama, London, and Rolle College, Devon.

Pam is one of the most experienced all-round actresses in *EastEnders*, having worked extensively in theatre, film and television. Her stage appearances include *Once a Catholic*, *Macbeth*, *Troilus and Cressida*, a tour of Strindberg and Chekhov plays with the Prospect Theatre Company, and a world tour and season at the Aldwych Theatre, London, with the RSC.

She has featured in such films as *Our Cissie*, *The Hunchback of Notre Dame*, *Doomwatch*, *Hedda*, *The Nation's Health*, *The Bunker*, *Scrubbers*, *Biggles* and *Czechmate*. Her many TV appearances include *Thomas and Sarah*, *The Onedin Line*, *The Fenn Street Gang*, *Van Der Valk*, *Follyfoot*, *Within These Walls*, *Enemy at the Door*, *Emmerdale* (as Mrs Eckersley), *Minder*, *Bottle Boys*, *Shoestring*, *Private Schultz*, *Together* (the live ITV serial, as Noreen Mullin), *Angels*, *We'll Meet Again*, *Ladykillers*, *The Chinese Detective*, *Partners in Crime*, *C.A.T.S. Eyes* and two BBC 'Play for Todays', *Not for the Likes of Us* and *King*.

Pam, divorced from husband Andrew Gordon in 1976 after seven years of marriage, was one of 18 showbusiness personalities to identify themselves as lesbian or gay in defending actor Ian McKellen's decision to accept a knighthood in the 1991 New Year Honours List. Pam and her partner, Jackie Reed, live in Radlett, Hertfordshire, and the Norfolk village of Mundesley. The actress enjoys music, cinema, food and drink, and travelling.

RICKY BUTCHER

Son of secondhand car dealer Frank, Ricky Butcher arrived in Albert Square when his father married Pat Wicks and took over the Queen Vic pub from Den and Angie Watts. He was not noted for his intelligence and was fined £75 after knocking down Pauline Fowler while driving a car with only a provisional licence.

Ricky fell for hairdresser Marie, then Shireen Karim, whose father was against their relationship. Ricky was finally sent packing when the

Karims closed their shop and moved. On leaving school without a single GCSE, Ricky started working at Grant and Phil Mitchell's garage and, shortly afterwards, met their younger sister, schoolgirl Sam. At first, the brothers were protective toward Sam and did not want Ricky to go out with her. When the couple announced their engagement, in May 1991, both families banned the teenagers from seeing each other.

They responded by eloping. Sam left school one day, walked round the corner into Ricky's van and the pair made off for Gretna Green. Grant and Phil found a route map that gave away their destination. They set off north, with Frank and Pat joining in the chase. Ricky and Sam discovered there was a two-week wait at the register office in Gretna Green and Sam accidentally bumped into Pat at a petrol filling station. But Pat was sympathetic and the wedding ceremony went ahead on 4 July 1991. Forced to accept the situation, Ricky's father, Frank, and Sam's mother, Peggy, arranged a blessing at St Stephen's Church, Walford.

But the marriage was rocky and ended after 18 months. Although Ricky wanted it to work out, Sam was too young and impressionable. She won the Miss Queen Vic competition in April 1992, but Ricky blew his top when, two months later, he discovered that she had been duped into modelling topless. Then, Sam had an affair with a yuppie called Clive, left the Square in February 1994 and, planning to further her fledgling career as a model, started with a job on a cruise liner.

Frank ran away shortly afterwards, having put Phil Mitchell up to torching his car lot in an effort to get the insurance. But a homeless boy was killed in the blaze, and Frank faced manslaughter charges. After moping around for a while, Ricky became David Wicks's business partner when he reopened his father Frank's car lot, under the name Deals on Wheels, although he found himself being used as the grease monkey and returned to Phil Mitchell's garage.

But he did find love with Square newcomer Bianca Jackson, although again he faced opposition from her family and his own – unaware that her father was David Wicks, his own stepbrother. Ploughing on blindly, Ricky moved into Bianca's bedsit with her. But Bianca's best friend, Natalie Price, wanted to get her own claws into Ricky and seduced him. Ricky did not put up a fight and, when Bianca caught them kissing in the garage, she ditched him and, in February 1995, Natalie left the Square.

☆ ☆ ☆

Sid Owen (b. David Owen) was nicknamed Sidney as a child because he was plump and it rhymed with kidney, as in steak and kidney pie. Aged nine, he was an extra in the film *Oliver!*. Later, he went to drama school, starting on the same day as John Alford, who played Robbie in *Grange Hill*. He then had a prominent role in the 1985 film *Revolution*, starring Al Pacino.

Sid, who has a flat in Wanstead, East London, enjoys playing football and listening to the music of the Rolling Stones and Fleetwood Mac. He was engaged for a while to Amanda Berry, sister of former *EastEnders* star Nick.

Danniella Westbrook (b. Essex, 5 November 1973) acted on stage in *Joseph and the Amazing Technicolor Dreamcoat* at the Royalty Theatre and on television, in *To Have and to Hold*, *Grange Hill* and *Agatha Christie's Miss Marple* before joining *EastEnders* as SAM BUTCHER (née Mitchell). She had previously appeared in the serial as an extra, rollerskating across Albert Square. She has since played Timothy Spall's niece Dawn in the series *Frank Stubbs Promotes* and *Frank Stubbs*, and returned to *EastEnders* in 1995.

Paul Medford (b. London) was KELVIN CARPENTER, a member of Albert Square's ill-fated rock group The Banned. In real life, he released a hit record, 'Something Outa Nothing', with fellow-*EastEnder* Letitia Dean. He has since found success presenting children's television programmes. and as a star of London stage musicals, including *Five Guys Named Moe*.

Oscar James (b. West Indies, 25 July 1942) played builder and handyman TONY CARPENTER, who was separated from wife Hannah. Angie Watts had a brief fling with Tony to get back at husband Den. Oscar, who moved to Britain in 1975, previously appeared in *Emmerdale* as teacher Antony Moeketsi, who taught Seth Armstrong to read.

Cheryl Hall, who played CHRISTINE, made her name as Wolfie Smith's girlfriend Shirley in the sitcom *Citizen Smith*. She married Robert Lindsay, who played Wolfie, but the couple subsequently divorced. She has since appeared on television in *The Men's Room*, *Inspector Morse*, *The Chief* and *The Bill*, and worked with the RSC. Cheryl was elected a Labour county councillor for Ramsgate South, in Kent, in 1993.

Ian Reddington (b. Sheffield), who had appeared on TV in *Casualty*, *The Bill* and *Inspector Morse*, was RICHARD COLE – 'Tricky Dicky' – who made conquests of Rachel Kominski and Kathy Beale. A Sheffield Wednesday soccer fan, he recorded a single, 'If It's Wednesday, It Must be Wembley'.

Louise Plowright (b. Cheshire, 1956) played hairdresser JULIE COOPER. Her other TV appearances include *London's Burning*, *Palmer*, *Beaver Road*, *Families* (as Linda) and *Do the Right Thing*. Her sister Rosalind is a famous opera singer.

June Brown (b. Needham Market, Suffolk, 16 February 1927) played DOT COTTON, the Square's minder of morals and mother of villainous Nick Cotton. She was previously on TV in *The Sweeney*, *Oranges and Lemons*, *Churchill's People*, *South Riding*, *The Prince and the Pauper*, *Angels*, *The Duchess of Duke Street*, *Couples*, *A Christmas Carol*, *Shadows*, *The Ladies*, *Young at Heart*, *The Bill*, *Minder*, *Lace* and *Relative Strangers*.

John Altman (b. Reading, Berkshire, 2 March 1952) was NICK COTTON, who murdered pensioner Reg Cox in 1985, and blackmailed both Colin Russell over his gay relationship with under-age Barry Clark, and Kathy Beale about her rape at the age of 14, before becoming a drug addict and killing publican Eddie Royle. John played George Harrison in the film *The Birth of the Beatles*.

Kathryn Apanowicz (b. Horsforth, Leeds, 3 June 1960) found fame as bullying nurse Rose Butchins in *Angels* before playing MAGS CZAJKOWSKI. As a child, Kathryn was a regular in the TV talent show *Junior Showtime* and acted in the film *Bugsy Malone*. Later, she appeared in the soap *Rooms* and *The Black Stuff* (the original 'Play for Today'). After leaving *EastEnders*, Kathryn presented her own daily show for a Leeds radio station.

Bill Treacher (b. London, 4 June 1937) played ARTHUR FOWLER, who suffered a nervous breakdown and later had an affair with Christine Hewitt. Bill had appeared on TV in *Angels* and *Grange Hill*, and was Sidney the milkman in the radio soap *Mrs Dale's Diary*. An original *EastEnders* cast member, he left in 1995.

STEVE ELLIOT

Smart Steve Elliot's first job in Albert Square, in October 1991, was working as a chef for Ian Beale's catering business. As the recession hit Ian's business, Steve was laid off, but romance with Hattie Tavernier – Ian's office assistant – blossomed and she proposed to him.

A wedding date was set for June 1993, but Steve ran away a few days beforehand, leaving Hattie a hastily scribbled note. She followed him to Portsmouth, where he was to set sail on a cruise ship, having landed a new job. Her pleas failed to change Steve's mind and she returned home, harbouring the secret that she was pregnant with his baby, which she later miscarried.

Steve eventually returned and shared a flat with Mark Fowler. In early 1994, he opened a hairdresser's in George Street, which Della Alexander ran. When he found her unresponsive to his advances, Della revealed that she was gay. Switching his attentions to Ruth Aitken, she told him there was no chemistry between them. Deciding to close the hairdressing salon in 1995, Steve put new energy into opening a bistro in Kathy Mitchell's café in the evenings.

Mark Monero played a schoolboy called Arthur in the fifth series of *Grange Hill*, in 1982. He later acted in *The Paradise Club*, *The Firm* and *The Bill*, before joining *EastEnders*.

ROY EVANS

Selling a dodgy car to David Wicks at Deals on Wheels in December 1994 led to car salesman Roy Evans getting a tongue-lashing from David's mother, the formidable Pat Butcher. Widower Roy was so intrigued by her that he invited her out to dinner, although her new-found independence – following the disappearance of her husband Frank, and her new job running the Queen Vic – made her reluctant, especially after she had mistaken college tutor Geoff Barnes's friendliness for something more. But Pat soon found Roy to be a good partner and, after refusing his offer to take her and Janine on a cruise, realized how much she missed him. The two were reunited.

Tony Caunter (b. Hampshire) trained at LAMDA and spent three years in the RAF, working on aircrew selection before becoming an actor in 1959. Before joining *EastEnders* in December 1994, at the age of 57, he had appeared in about 300 television productions, including *The Saint, United!, The Baron, The Avengers, Department S, Queenie's Castle, The Sweeney, The Professionals, Pennies from Heaven, Blake's 7, Doctor Who, Gems, High Road, Minder, Howards' Way, London's Burning, Tumbledown, Bust, The Chief, Boon, The Bill, Lovejoy, Stay Lucky, Kinsey, West Beach, Anna Lee* and *May to December.*

In the cinema, Tony has appeared in *The Hill, The Ipcress File, Twist of Sand, Mind of Mr Soames, Cromwell, Mr Quip* and *Killing the Beast.* His stage plays include *Plays for England,* at the Royal Court, *Caligula* at the Phoenix Theatre, *Chips with Everything,* in the West End and on Broadway, and tours of *Ross* and *Wait Until Dark.* Tony and his teacher wife Frances have three sons and one daughter.

MARK FOWLER

As a teenager, moody Mark Fowler became involved with Nick Cotton on the shady side of the law. Harassed by Nick, he ran away to Southend, where he lived with an older woman. Eventually, his family tracked him down, but he had no wish to return home permanently and drifted across the country.

Mark turned up in Albert Square again in 1990, fell for teenager Diane Butcher and decided to stay. He appeared elusive and unapproachable but, in 1991, he eventually revealed to Diane the dark secret that he had been diagnosed HIV positive as the result of an earlier relationship with a woman. Diane told Mark she loved him and pledged to stand by him. She persuaded him to see a counsellor at the Terrence Higgins

Trust. Mark's ex-girlfriend, Gill, then arrived in the Square for a short visit to tell Mark she had AIDS and he subsequently asked Diane to marry him. She turned him down and, shortly afterwards, left for a new life in France.

On Boxing Day 1991, Mark finally told his parents the secret he had kept from them, although Rachel Kominski – his new girlfriend – had advised him against it. Old flame Gill came back into his life the following April, but her own days were running out as she battled against AIDS. Just a day before her death, Mark and Gill married. At the hospice where Gill spent her final days, he met Ruth Aitken, who was visiting a friend dying of AIDS. She helped Mark to come to terms with his HIV status.

The flames of romance flickered, but Mark sent Ruth away, feeling he could not put her through the agony he had endured with Gill. When she returned to Mark, love blossomed, although he was cautious because of his fears for the future. Then, Mark had a short relationship with fun-loving student Shelley Lewis, who shared a house with his sister, Michelle. He then fell for Ruth again, who moved in with Michelle, and Mark married her on 20 April 1995.

☆ ☆ ☆

Todd Carty (b. Ireland, 1963) began his career in London at the age of four, working in commercials, radio, theatre, television and films. He made his stage debut in the title role of *Lionel,* based on the life of Lionel Bart, at the New London Theatre, Drury Lane.

As a child, he appeared on television in *Z-Cars, Our Mutual Friend, Drummer, Headmaster, Focus on Britain* and *The Idle Bunch* – both for German TV – and *We're Happy,* for the Irish network RTE. He featured in the films *Professor Popper's Problems, Please Sir!, The Gang's OK* and *The Magic Trip.*

During his teens, Todd played heart-throb Tucker Jenkins in both the BBC children's serial *Grange Hill* for five years and the spin-off serial *Tucker's Luck,* written by *Grange Hill* creator Phil Redmond. He also played Oswin in the science fantasy film *Krull* and turned to comic roles in such pictures as *What's in It for You, A Question of Balance, Serve Them Right* and *The Candy Show.* As well as doing voice-overs for TV commercials and narrating programmes such as *Scene in New York* and *The Jungle Creatures,* he played Tucker in *Grange Hill – Tucker's Return* on stage at the Queen's Theatre, Hornchurch, Essex.

Todd, who is single, joined *EastEnders* in 1990, taking over the role of Mark Fowler from actor David Scarboro, who committed suicide two years earlier while suffering from depression.

PAULINE FOWLER

Downtrodden mother Pauline Fowler is the twin sister of the late Pete Beale and daughter of the late Lou. Never one to let her problems get on top of her, Pauline prefers that the world knows all her troubles.

She had even more to contend with when she became pregnant in her forties with son Martin, wayward son Mark ran away from home and husband Arthur faced unemployment, then a prison sentence, for stealing cash to pay for daughter Michelle's wedding. The money Pauline earned from working at the Bridge Street launderette was crucial for the family's survival. After Arthur's conviction, she took additional jobs to pay back the stolen money.

Arthur suffered a nervous breakdown and served a short prison sentence for his crime. He was a different man when he returned home, and it was difficult for Pauline to adjust. However, Pauline is a battler. That quality has certainly been passed on to daughter Michelle, who refused to name the father of baby Vicki. However, Pauline eventually guessed that it was Den Watts and told Michelle that she knew, but kept the secret to herself.

Pauline joined sister-in-law Kathy Beale and Frank Butcher in buying the Square's café, of which she became manager. But Pauline's extended visit to her brother Kenny in New Zealand, in 1992, after he was involved in a car crash, gave Arthur the opportunity to develop his friendship with Christine Hewitt. It turned to romance and when, the following year, Pauline found out, she hit her husband over the head with a frying pan and threw him out. Arthur

eventually decided to make another go of their marriage and returned to Pauline.

She was not averse to accepting the attentions of another man herself when her first love – singer Danny – came back to see her and started taking her out for drinks and flattering her. A distant relative of the Fowlers, busybody Nellie Ellis met Arthur and Pauline at Pete Beale's funeral in December 1993, then moved in with them. Arthur was relieved when she went to live with Jules Tavernier and then in sheltered accommodation.

☆ ☆ ☆

Wendy Richard (b. Middlesbrough, Cleveland, 20 July 1946) was brought up in London, where her parents ran a pub and restaurant. After her father committed suicide when Wendy was 11, she helped her mother to run a guest house. Wendy trained at the Italia Conti Stage Academy but started her career as a singer, recording the no. 1 hit 'Come Outside' with Mike Sarne in 1962. She then played supermarket manageress Joyce Harker in the BBC serial *The Newcomers* and clippie Doreen in *On the Buses*, as well as appearing on television in *Harpers West One*, *The Arthur Haynes Show*, *Dixon of Dock Green*, *Danger Man*, *No Hiding Place*, *Joe Nobody*, *The Making of Jericho*, *Z-Cars*, *Please Sir!*, *The Fenn Street Gang*, *Not on Your Nellie*, *Hugh and I*, *Both Ends Meet*, *Hog's Back*, *Spooner's Patch*, *Dad's Army* and *West Country Tales*.

Then Wendy landed the role of busty sales assistant Miss Brahms in the comedy series *Are You Being Served?*, which made her instantly recognizable. She also appeared in the film and stage versions. When casting the new BBC soap opera *EastEnders*, producer Julia Smith did not intend to use well known actors and actresses, but she remembered working with Wendy in *The Newcomers* and thought she was right for the role of Pauline Fowler.

Wendy was in several *Carry On* films, *Doctor in Clover* and big-screen versions of *Bless This House* and *On the Buses*. On stage, she was in *No Sex, Please – We're British*, *Let's Go Camping* and a tour of *Blithe Spirit*.

Her personal life has often been less than happy. Wendy attempted suicide at the age of 28 after her mother's death. By then, she had already been married once, to Leonard Black for just five months. She later wed advertising executive Will Thorpe, but the marriage lasted only 18 months and she accused him of beating her. Wendy married third husband Paul Glorney, a carpet fitter, in 1990, but they split up four years later. Wendy lives in Baker Street, London, and enjoys gardening, tapestry and collecting ornamental frogs and clowns.

RUTH FOWLER

At a hospice where his girlfriend Gill was dying of AIDS, Mark Fowler met Ruth Aitken, who was down from Scotland visiting a friend also dying of the disease. Mark married Gill a day before her death. He offered Ruth a place to stay and found that she helped him to come to terms with losing Gill and the fact that he was HIV positive.

But, when Mark fell head over heels in love with Ruth, he began to feel he could not put her through the agony that he himself had endured with Gill, so he sent her away.

That did not stop her returning to the Square and moving in with Mark's sister, Michelle. Love blossomed, although Mark was still cautious about having a relationship with Ruth. She seemed settled in Walford and heard, in January 1995, that she had landed a job in the local crèche.

Ruth and Mark decided they wanted to spend the rest of their lives together and, on 20 April 1995, married near Ruth's home in Scotland – although only after telling her strict parents, John and Susan, that Mark was HIV positive. They had been apprehensive about Ruth marrying in the first place and John, a minister, refused to attend the wedding ceremony.

☆ ☆ ☆

Caroline Paterson is an actress who shies away from publicity and is happiest when returning to her native Scotland to help with the running of the 7.84 theatre company. As well as *EastEnders*, her television appearances include *A Touch of Frost*, *Taggart*, *Cardiac Arrest* and *Finney*.

ALAN JACKSON

Alan Jackson, his common-law wife Carol and her four children moved from Walford Tower into Dot Cotton's old home in Albert Square at the beginning of 1994. Alan and Carol had been together for five years and, for the previous two, since he had been laid off from a local car plant, Alan had been unemployed.

Younger than Carol, Alan was closer to the children's ages and tended to get on particularly well with them. The youngest child, Billy, was the only one he had fathered himself.

He showed his support for stepson Robbie when Grant Mitchell accused him of stealing from the pub – then Alan told Robbie off himself outside.

He found occasional work on Mark Fowler's market stall and as a mechanic at David Wicks's new car lot/garage business.

But, at home, Alan almost came to blows with Carol when she finally revealed to him that David Wicks was the father of her daughter, Bianca. Alan and David brawled after Alan heard that Bianca had tried to seduce David, not knowing he was her real father. After Bianca found out about her parentage, she became more difficult and started rowing.

☆ ☆ ☆

Howard Antony had no previous television experience when he joined *EastEnders*, but he had appeared in director Stanley Kubrick's Vietnam War film *Full Metal Jacket*.

A trained marksman with a green belt in karate, Howard also enjoys athletics, football and cricket.

Susan Tully (b. Highgate, North London, 20 October 1967), who appeared in *Grange Hill* as the rebellious Suzanne Ross for four years, joined *EastEnders* as MICHELLE FOWLER when it began in 1985. Her character gave birth to baby Vicki after sleeping with Den Watts, experienced a loveless marriage to Lofty Holloway and almost wed college tutor Geoff Barnes. Susan left in 1995.

Pat Coombs (b. Patricia Doreen Coombs in Camberwell, South London, 27 August 1926) played Brown Owl MARGE GREEN. She is best known as the star of such sitcoms as *Beggar My Neighbour*, *Lollipop Loves Mr Mole*, *You're Only Young Twice*, *The Lady Is a Tramp* and *In Sickness and in Health*.

Elizabeth Power, TV presenter Michael Aspel's estranged third wife, was MRS (CHRISTINE) HEWITT, who had an affair with Arthur Fowler and worked as a chef in Kathy Beale's café-turned-bistro.

Tom Watt (b. Thomas Erickson Watt in Wanstead, East London, 14 February 1956) appeared as wimpy LOFTY HOLLOWAY, who married Michelle Fowler, then left the Square after the couple split up. Tom has since appeared on TV as a presenter of *Night Network* and acted in the wartime drama *And a Nightingale Sang*, *Boon* and the 'Comedy Playhouse' pilot *Stuck on You*, as well as in the film *Patriot Games*. He has also written a book about soccer called *The End*.

BIANCA JACKSON

Hot-headed Bianca Jackson is a chip off the old block, very like her mother, Carol, who always believed everything she was told by men. On moving to the Square, Bianca was just 16 and working on a YTS hair and beauty course.

Market inspector 'Tricky Dicky' Cole quickly bedded her, but he soon tired of the teenager young enough to be his daughter. He ditched Bianca, then rubbed salt into the wound by flirting with her mother. Spurred on by her best friend, Natalie Price, Bianca took the number of his credit card and ran up a huge bill. She also flirted with David Wicks to make Richard jealous, causing Bianca's mother to tell David for the first time that he was her daughter's father.

Then, Bianca fell for jilted Ricky Butcher – but both families were against the relationship. She did not know that her father was David Wicks, who was the son of Ricky's step-mum, Pat. Her mother was only 14 when she became pregnant with Bianca, and David had run away.

Bianca moved into a bedsit, with David secretly paying the rent. Ricky then moved in with her, but Bianca took a job at Ian Beale's fish-and-chip shop and began to go out more with her new friend, Tiffany Raymond. Meanwhile, her other 'friend', Natalie, made a play for Ricky and, when Bianca found them kissing in the garage where he worked, she ditched him.

But Bianca unwittingly forced the truth about her parentage out of David Wicks when he saved her from the clutches of a man who plied her with drink in a club one evening and hoped to bed her. As they left a taxi in Albert Square, David told the man to get lost and took a drunken Bianca to his car lot to sober up. She threw herself at him and he could only stop her by revealing that he was her father.

Patsy Palmer (b. Julie Harris) appeared regularly as an extra in *Grange Hill* and was in commercials for Phileas Fogg and Clearasil before joining *EastEnders*. The actress is a single mother who has a son, Charley, by her former boyfriend, cab driver Alfie Rothwell. Charley, claims Patsy, helps her to rehearse her lines for the serial. East End girl Patsy lives in Bethnal Green with her mother and stepfather.

BLOSSOM JACKSON

Alan Jackson's grandmother, Blossom, came to live with the Jackson family at no. 25 Albert Square in April 1994 and soon found a friend in neighbour Jules Tavernier, who had been left by himself when his son, Celestine, and his daughter-in-law Etta moved to Norwich.

Mona Hammond (b. Tweeside, Clarendon, Jamaica) moved to Britain in 1959 on a Jamaican scholarship and worked for Norman and Dawbarn Architects. Keen on acting, she attended evening classes at the City Literary Institute for two years and won a scholarship to RADA.

Mona joined *EastEnders* as Blossom in 1994, but she had previously appeared in the serial eight years earlier as the midwife who delivered Michelle Fowler's daughter, Vicki.

Her other TV appearances have included *In the Beautiful Caribbean*, *Past Caring*, *Playboy of the West Indies*, *Hard Cases*, *Black Silk*, *Juliet Bravo*, *Coronation Street*, *Last of the Mohicans*, four episodes of *Desmond's*, *Us Girls* and *Making Out*. On stage, Mona has acted at the Royal Court Theatre in *Play Mas*, *Sweet Talk* and *A Hero's Welcome*, and the National Theatre in *The Crucible* and *Peer Gynt*, as well as playing Mrs Jefferson in the Royal Shakespeare Company's Mermaid Theatre production of *The Great White Hope* and a small role in *Macbeth* at the New York Festival.

CAROL JACKSON

Carol Jackson's family have lived in the East End for years and moved to Albert Square in January 1994 after Carol took over Dot Cotton's job at the launderette. Hers has been a hard life. Divorcée Carol has four children – Bianca, Robbie, Sonia and Billy – all by different men.

The eldest, Bianca, was born when Carol was only 15. The youngest, Billy, was the only one fathered by Carol's common-law husband, Alan. They had been together for five years on moving into Dot Cotton's old house, no. 25.

Like her daughter Bianca, Carol Jackson is headstrong. She flipped her lid when Bianca started flirting with David Wicks, who, unknown to Bianca, was her real father. Carol felt it necessary to reveal this to David. More happily, the Jacksons enjoyed a rare spending spree when Carol won £1000 at bingo.

When Bianca fell for Ricky Butcher, Carol disapproved of the relationship but had no intention of revealing to Bianca that David Wicks, Ricky's stepbrother, was her real father. Bianca then moved into a bedsit with Ricky.

It fell to David to tell Bianca that he was her father after she threw herself at him when he saved her from the clutches of another man on a drunken night out. As a result, all her children wanted to know the truth about their parentage.

☆ ☆ ☆

Lindsey Coulson, brought up in Tottenham, North London, appeared in such television programmes as *The Bill*, *Think About Science* and *A Bear Behind* before joining *EastEnders*. She was also in demand for voice-overs and storytelling on cartoons and children's series.

She is married to her agent, Phillip Chard, and has a daughter, Molly Claire, whom she had in a birthing pool. Lindsey is also a supporter of Greenpeace and interested in natural medicine.

ROBBIE JACKSON

Teenage tearaway Robbie Jackson was technically still at school when his family moved to Albert Square in 1994, although there was always some doubt about when he was actually there. Robbie was soon causing trouble. He decided it would be fun to steal a Mercedes from Frank Butcher's car lot and go joyriding, but he crashed and ended up in hospital.

On his 16th birthday, when he actually intended to go to school, Robbie was followed by a stray dog. He tried to take it to the police station, which made him late for school, with the result that he was expelled because of his poor attendance record. Then, he was caught by Grant Mitchell after stealing vodka from the pub.

☆ ☆ ☆

Dean Gaffney (b. 14 February 1978) appeared on television in *The Bill*, *Oasis* and *The Young Indiana Jones Chronicles*, as well as in the film *The Power of One*, before joining *EastEnders*.

GITA KAPOOR

Gita met Sanjay Kapoor at college and they started going out together, against the wishes of her parents. Their feelings that he was not good enough for Gita seemed justified when his clothing import business went bankrupt. By then, Gita was pregnant with their first child, daughter Sharmilla. But she heard that he was doing well again after setting up in Bridge Street market and decided to mend fences.

But she could see Sanjay's old ways were still there when he lost the £800 he had saved up for the deposit on a flat in a poker game. Unknown to Gita, Sanjay borrowed the money from market inspector Richard Cole and they moved into a flat at no. 43 Albert Square.

But their happiness was again short-lived when Gita returned home one day in January 1994 to find Sanjay in bed with her sister, Meena. She promptly left the Square but returned in May after losing her job and Sanjay moved into Richard Cole's Roach Motel.

Then, Gita became the victim of a race-hate campaign – her door was spray-painted, nasty parcels were put through her letter box and a brick was hurled through her window. The taunts became worse when a local councillor died and the fascist British Party mounted a high-profile campaign for the by-election.

During the campaign, violence erupted and Sanjay was arrested for beating up a youth who tried to attack Gita. He ended up behind bars, but Gita realized that she could now forgive him for the upset he had previously caused and the couple were reunited on his release.

☆ ☆ ☆

Shobu Kapoor trained at the Drama Studio and has since worked in repertory theatre in Watford and Bolton, in addition to touring Britain and India in *Women of the Dust*. On TV, Shobu played Nasreen in the second series of *Family Pride*, before joining *EastEnders*.

Judith Jacob (b. 13 December 1961) was student nurse Beverly Slater in *Angels* before taking the role of CARMEL JACKSON in *EastEnders*. Her real-life baby daughter Aisha played her niece. Since leaving, she has done little TV, apart from *Jackanory* and a children's series called *Radio Room*. She formed a production company called Bibi with six other actresses, and their first play, *On a Level*, opened in London in 1993.

SANJAY KAPOOR

Market trader Sanjay Kapoor met opposition from wife-to-be Gita's family when they started going out together. They thought she could do better for herself, so he set out to prove he was a success by building up a business importing clothes from abroad. But it collapsed and Gita's family felt justified in their original opinion of him. Sanjay turned to drink and gambling, and Gita – pregnant with their first child – left him.

In an attempt to win her back, Sanjay asked market inspector Richard Cole to help him. He gave Sanjay a prime pitch in the Bridge Street market and Sanjay started selling designer clothes again, but on a smaller scale. Richard also gave him free accommodation while he saved up the deposit for a flat.

Gita heard that Sanjay was making a real effort to sort himself out and tracked him down to Albert Square, although they still fought like cat and dog and he stepped off the straight and narrow again by losing the £800 deposit he had saved for a flat to Nigel Bates in a poker game at the Queen Vic pub. Secretly borrowing the money for a flat at no. 43 Albert Square from Richard, Sanjay was able to move in with Gita and their newborn baby daughter, Sharmilla.

Just as they were settling down, Gita's elderly mother died. Gita's sister, Meena, spent a lot of time at their flat, comforting her sister, but there was friction between Meena and Sanjay. On one occasion, Sanjay returned to find Meena by herself, weeping. He comforted her and the two began to get closer. This led to them sleeping together and, in January 1994, Gita returned home to find them in bed together and walked out on Sanjay. She returned four months later after losing her job, forcing Sanjay to move into the Roach Motel. But the couple were reunited

after Sanjay beat up a racist who tried to attack Gita during a local by-election campaign, in which the British Party adopted a high profile.

Deepak Verma trained at the Central School of Speech and Drama, gaining experience in a variety of productions, including *The Merchant of Venice*, *Uncle Vanya*, *Twelfth Night* and *Lady Windermere's Fan*. He subsequently appeared in a three-part *Taggart* story on TV and in the National Film and Television School production *Flying Colours*, in the lead role.

DR HAROLD LEGG

A friendly G.P., Dr Harold Legg is the son of a wealthy Jewish doctor who moved out of the East End to Finchley, North London, when Oswald Mosley started his marches. Dr Legg trained at Bart's Medical School for seven years. During the Second World War, his young wife, a nurse, was killed by a German bomb that fell on Albert Square during the Blitz. He has never remarried. Dr Legg is well past retirement age but continues to serve the residents of Albert Square, who regard him as a pillar of the community. He lives in Islington and rents rooms above his surgery.

☆ ☆ ☆

Leonard Fenton (b. London) lived in Stepney until he was 13. He qualified as a civil engineer and was commissioned into the Royal Engineers during National Service. Then, he worked for five years with a firm of consulting engineers, before turning to acting. He trained at the Webber Douglas Academy, supporting himself by teaching maths at Westminster Polytechnic.

Leonard worked in repertory theatre and acted with the RSC in *London Assurance*, *Major Barbara* and *Twelfth Night*, at the Royal Court Theatre in plays by Wesker, Arden, Antrobus and Brenton, and at the National Theatre in such productions as *A Month in the Country*, *Don Juan*, *Much Ado About Nothing* and *Serjeant Musgrave's Dance*. At the Royal Court Theatre, he was also in a production of Samuel Beckett's *Happy Days*, directed by the playwright. Leonard also performed in a programme of Samuel Beckett's work at the 1984 Edinburgh Festival, as part of a tribute to the writer.

His other London stage appearances include Lindsay Anderson's West End productions of Chekhov's *The Seagull* and the Ben Travers farce *The Bed Before Yesterday*, Marguerite Duras's *The Square* and Wolf Mankowitz's *The Irish Hebrew Lesson*. His TV appearances include *Mrs Thursday*, *The Brief*, *Beryl's Lot*, *The*

> **Matilda Ziegler played DONNA LUD-LOW, the daughter Kathy Mitchell had at 14 after being raped. Matilda has since appeared on TV in *Mr Bean* (with Rowan Atkinson) and *My Good Friend* (as Betty).**
>
> **Peter Cleall (b. Finchley, North London, 16 March 1944) played boat-owner MALCOLM, who shopped on-the-run Clyde Tavernier following the murder of Queen Vic landlord Eddie Royle. Peter had made his name as troublemaker Eric Duffy in the sitcoms *Please Sir!* and *The Fenn Street Gang*, and appeared in *Mr Big*, *The Losers*, *A Tale of Two Cities*, *Spooner's Patch* and *Growing Pains*.**

Brothers, *Owen MD*, *Z-Cars*, *Colditz*, *Secret Army*, *The Fourth Arm*, *Shine on Harvey Moon* (as the Austrian Jew Erich Gottlieb) and *The Bill*. Leonard had two spells with BBC radio's repertory company and was in the films *The Third Man on the Mountain*, *Brown Ale With Gertie*, *Devil-Ship Pirates*, *Happy Days*, *Witchcraft*, *Up the Creek*, *Panic*, *Give My Regards to Broad Street* and *Morons from Outer Space*.

He and his wife, cellist Madeleine Thorner, have four children and live in North London. An accomplished artist, Leonard works in watercolour and paints landscapes. In 1984, the National Theatre included ten of his paintings in an exhibition by actors who paint and, five years later, he had an exhibition of his work at the Primrose Hill Gallery, in North London.

GRANT MITCHELL

Grant Mitchell lashes out first and ask questions later, although Sharon Watts thought she had found a sensitive, humorous side to him when they married. Brothers Grant and Phil arrived in Albert Square when they bought the garage, as well as Sharon Watts's flat, in February 1990.

Grant started going out with Sharon and gave her driving lessons. It was as she was setting off for her mother Angie's wedding in America that Grant confessed his interest in Sharon. In 1991, when he thought Queen Vic landlord Eddie Royle was making a play for Sharon, Grant attacked him in a jealous fit.

Following Eddie's death, Grant's money enabled Sharon to take over the tenancy of the Queen Vic with a temporary licence. The couple were married on Boxing Day 1991 and Sharon was officially installed as Queen Vic landlady the following month.

The marriage proved stormy. Grant wanted to start a family, but Sharon preferred to concentrate on running the pub. In 1992, he set it alight to get the insurance money to pay off some heavies, not realizing that Sharon was inside. She ended up in hospital. In March 1993, Grant hit Sharon during a row, the police arrived, Grant attacked them and ended up in prison for a short spell. Sharon turned to Grant's brother, Phil, for comfort and slept with him.

An old army pal, Dougie Briggs, turned up in 1994, trying to persuade Grant to take part in a robbery. He refused and Dougie took Sharon and Michelle Fowler hostage, accidentally shooting Michelle in the leg before running off.

When Grant heard Sharon's taped confession, in a conversation with Michelle, that she had slept with Phil, he hospitalized his brother and ostracized Sharon. She pleaded for a second chance, but he forced her to sign divorce papers before Christmas 1994 and Sharon left to visit her mother in Florida. She returned three months later seeking a settlement. It included Grant's mother, Peggy, buying her share of the pub.

☆ ☆ ☆

Ross Kemp (b. 21 July 1964) trained as an actor at the Webber Douglas Academy, in London, before appearing on stage in *Staircase*, *Fur Coat and No Knickers*, *The Wizard of Oz* and *Mr Punch* at the Palace Theatre, Westcliff, and in *A Pin to See the Peep Show* at the Redgrave Theatre, Farnham. On television, he was in *Playing Away*, *Claws*, *Emmerdale* (as Dolly Skilbeck's illegitimate son Graham Lodsworth, on the run from the army), *The Money Men*, *London's Burning* and *The Chief*, before joining *EastEnders* as Grant Mitchell in 1990.

Ross, who lives near Brentwood, Essex, enjoys playing rugby and golf.

KATHY MITCHELL

Life has been tough for Kathy Mitchell. She grew up in the slum area of Walford and, at the age of 14, was raped. As a result, she had a baby who was adopted, and she kept the ordeal secret even from first husband Pete Beale. Kathy was only 17 when she fell for Pete, after his marriage to Pat Harris (now Butcher) had failed. They quickly married and had a son, Ian.

Kathy's secret threatened to come out into the open when she was blackmailed by thug Nick Cotton after he broke into Dr Legg's surgery and found notes revealing her rape. She was happy with Pete and faithful to him, but their life changed after two earth-shattering events in 1988. First, her secret daughter, Donna Ludlow, turned up demanding Kathy's love and acceptance, despite Kathy's wish to bury the past. Unstable Donna had a brief romance with Ian in an attempt to get close to the family, then tried suicide by taking a drugs overdose and died choking on her own vomit.

Then, in July 1988, Kathy was raped for a second time, by James Willmott-Brown, landlord of The Dagmar, the upmarket pub where she had just taken a job behind the bar. One night, she agreed to have a drink with him in his flat above the bar after closing time, thinking he was lonely and in need of a chat. However, he was not interested in talking and attacked her.

After her ordeal, The Dagmar was mysteriously burned to the ground. No-one said anything, but Den Watts's gangland connections were believed to be behind it. (Den was then managing Strokes wine bar for the Firm after leaving the Queen Vic.) Willmott-Brown was jailed for three years for Kathy's rape, but Pete partly blamed Kathy, whom he had not wanted to work at the pub. The couple drifted apart, Kathy had a breakdown and, in January 1989, moved out of the council flat she shared with Pete.

Later that year, Kathy had a short-lived affair with market trader Laurie Bates and was then pursued by Eddie Royle after he became new landlord of the Queen Vic. But she was not ready for romance again, returned to being a Samaritan, helped Ian to run the Square café and moved into the basement flat at no. 3 Albert Square. She, sister-in-law Pauline and Frank Butcher eventually bought the café from Ian.

A ghost from the past returned to haunt Kathy when, in January 1992, Ian was outbid at an auction for the pizza parlour by James Willmott-Brown, who was out of prison after just a year and had also bought a flat at no. 43 Albert Square. He was convinced that Kathy really loved him and was returning to claim her hand in marriage! It took a few weeks of ex-husband Pete's threats and Kathy's attempts to spell out the truth that she thought him totally worthless before he left the Square for good.

Kathy later had a fling with market inspector 'Tricky Dicky' Cole and new romance came into her life when she fell for Phil Mitchell on a 1993 trip to Paris. They began to live together early the following year and, in March 1994, Phil bought Frank Butcher's share of the café for Kathy. When Kathy had nightmares about Willmott-Brown, Phil searched for him, only to discover he was in prison for another rape. Kathy began to see the shady side of Phil when she learned that he had been responsible for

torching Frank Butcher's car lot, killing a vagrant who was there at the time. But marriage was on the cards. Phil and Kathy's engagement party was ruined by a taped confession by Sharon Mitchell that she had slept with Phil. Grant beat Phil up so badly that he was hospitalized and almost died. But the brothers made up – and so did Phil and Kathy. They married in a register office on 28 February 1995, with Pat Butcher and Grant Mitchell as witnesses.

Gillian Taylforth (b. London, 14 August 1955), daughter of a master printer and a cleaner at the *Daily Mirror*'s offices, had her first taste of acting at the age of nine, when she and a cousin won a seaside fancy-dress contest as Andy Capp and Flo. On leaving school, Gillian trained as a secretary and began evening classes at the Anna Scher Theatre School, of which sister Kim was already a member. Gillian turned professional and filled in time between jobs by working as a personal secretary. She was a secretary in a firm of solicitors for nine years, leaving when her acting work became more regular.

Gillian made her television debut as a schoolgirl with two lines in *Eleanor*, a BBC 'Play for Today', and has appeared in *Zigger Zagger* (alongside sister Kim), *The Rag Trade*, *The One and Only Phyllis Dixey*, *Thunder Cloud*, *Little Girls Don't*, *Watch This Space*, *Hi-de-Hi!*, *Big Jim and the Figaro Club*, *Shelley*, *Sink or Swim*, *On Safari*, *The Gentle Touch*, *Minder* and *Fast Hand*. She also stepped into a role in the film *The Long Good Friday* offered to sister Kim, who had to go to America. After auditioning for *EastEnders*, Gillian had to wait two months before she heard she had landed the part of Kathy Beale. The producer was worried that she looked too young to play a mother, but finally decided she was right for the part.

A great Frank Sinatra and Fred Astaire fan, Gillian treasures her collection of their records, has seen all their films and used to send the two stars cards on their birthdays. Judy Garland is another of her screen idols. Gillian, who lives in North London, made newspaper headlines when she dated *EastEnders* actor Nick Berry, who played Wicksy. Since then, she has lived with businessman Geoff Knights and, in January 1992, they had a daughter, Jessica.

There were more headlines exactly two years later when she and Knights lost a libel action against *The Sun*, which alleged that the couple were found by police having oral sex in a car on the hard shoulder of a motorway. They had to pay £500,000 costs. Away from the glare of publicity, Gillian enjoys dancing, keep fit, reading, music, swimming and cooking.

PEGGY MITCHELL

Fearsome Peggy Mitchell, who had been against her daughter Sam's ill-fated wedding to Ricky Butcher, moved to Albert Square in 1994 to sort out her sons. By then, she had split up with boyfriend Kevin, who had joined her on the chase to Gretna Green three years earlier in an abortive attempt to stop Sam's wedding.

On Peggy's arrival in the Square in 1994, Phil was in hospital, after Grant had found that he had slept with his wife, Sharon, and taken his revenge. But the brothers told their mother that he had fallen downstairs.

In December 1994, Peggy was baffled as to why Sharon walked out on Grant, and gave her a frosty reception when she returned three months later, looking for a divorce settlement. There was also friction between Peggy and Pat Butcher, who took over the running of the Queen Vic after Grant and Sharon's break-up. In May 1995, Pat walked out, fed up with Peggy stepping on her toes all the time. Peggy then bought Sharon's share of the pub.

Barbara Windsor (b. Barbara Ann Deeks in Shoreditch, East London, 6 August 1937), veteran of ten *Carry On* films, joined *EastEnders* to take over the role of Peggy Mitchell, played for several episodes by actress Jo Warne in 1991, when the character returned to sort out her feuding sons and help out at the Queen Vic.

Evacuated to Blackpool during the war, Barbara later joined a dancing school, Madame Behenna's Juvenile Jollities. She also won a scholarship to Our Lady's Convent School,

where she decided she would become a nun on leaving. But an interest in acting intervened and Barbara joined the Aida Foster Stage School, making her debut as one of the Aida Foster Babes in a pantomime at Golders Green in 1951. A year later, she made her West End debut as Sadie Kate in *Love from Judy*, which ran for two years at the Saville Theatre.

TV work followed with a series of *Dreamers Highway*, as well as *The Jack Jackson Show* and *6.5 Special*, before she made an impact on stage as Rosie in *Fings Ain't Wot They Used T'Be*, which opened at the Theatre Royal, Stratford, East London, in December 1959, transferred to the Garrick Theatre three months later and ran for two-and-a-half years. Barbara's later stage successes included *Oh! What a Lovely War* – her New York theatre debut, in 1964 – and West End roles in *Twang!*, *Come Spy with Me*, *Sing a Rude Song* (playing Marie Lloyd), *The Threepenny Opera* and *Carry On London*.

By then, she had made a name for herself in films. The 1.49m (4ft 11in) actress made her big-screen debut in 1954, in *The Belles of St Trinian's*, and followed it with *Lost*, *Too Hot to Handle*, *On the Fiddle*, *Flame in the Streets* and *Hair of the Dog*, before getting starring roles in the Edgar Wallace thriller *Death Trap* and *Sparrows Can't Sing*, a film version of the play *Sparrers Can't Sing* staged by Joan Littlewood's Theatre Workshop. Joan had hired Barbara for the musical *Fings Ain't Wot They Used T'Be* after spotting her singing and doing impressions in a nightclub. The film caused a sensation in America because it was the first to carry subtitles because of the cockney accents.

After taking a dramatic role in the film *Crooks in Cloisters*, she appeared in her first *Carry On* film, *Carry On Spying,* in 1964. She was in nine others: *Carry On Doctor*, *Carry On Camping*, *Carry On Again, Doctor*, *Carry On Henry*, *Carry On Matron*, *Carry On Abroad*, *Carry On Girls*, *Carry On Dick* and *That's Carry On*. Barbara was one of the most popular members of the comedy team, although she still appeared in other films, including *Chitty Chitty Bang Bang*, *The Boy Friend*, *Not Now Darling*, *Comrades* and *It Couldn't Happen Here*.

The actress has also made many television appearances over the years. and was best known in the sixties as one of the dressmakers at Fenner Fashions in the sitcom *The Rag Trade*. One of Barbara's most popular later roles was as Saucy Nancy in *Worzel Gummidge*. She made her *EastEnders* debut in the episode shown on 27 October 1994, which attracted 25.3 million viewers, the soap's top rating for seven years.

Barbara, who divorced husband Ronnie Knight after he fled to the Costa Del Sol to avoid criminal charges – he later returned – then married chef Stephen Hollings, 19 years her junior, who runs her Buckinghamshire pub and restaurant.

PHIL MITCHELL

Garage owner and mechanic Phil Mitchell tries to keep younger brother Grant in line. Both were over-protective toward their teenage sister Sam when she fell for Ricky Butcher, whom they employed at the lock-up garage under the railway arches. They treated her as sweet and innocent, blind to the fact that she was a flirt.

Phil and Grant organized an illegal MOT racket. When they asked Arthur Fowler to deliver the fake certificates, his son Mark did so instead and was arrested by police. The brothers stepped in to defend Mark's plea of ignorance.

Phil had a short affair with a woman called Anne but ditched her after finding out she was married. Then he went through a marriage of convenience with Russian immigrant Nadia. When brother Grant went to jail in 1993, Phil provided his wife, Sharon, with comfort and bedded her. Sharon loved him but fell straight back into Grant's arms on his release.

Phil, meanwhile, fell for divorcée Kathy Beale. He even told her about Sharon. But it was another couple of months before she found out that he was married. His relationship with Kathy became difficult when the Home Office were investigating Nadia and she needed to live with Phil to prove that theirs was a genuine marriage. On Christmas Day 1993, after plenty of alcohol, Nadia lured him into bed, although Kathy refused to believe it when Nadia told her.

In 1994, Frank Butcher – facing financial ruin – sold his share in the Square's café to Phil and took him up on his suggestion that he could torch the car lot for him to claim the insurance. But a vagrant died in the fire and Frank left the Square riddled with guilt. Phil stayed.

Back on the home front, Phil proposed to Kathy, who accepted, but he had to buy off Nadia so that she would agree to a divorce. She accepted the money and fled to Germany. The marriage plans were then threatened when Grant found out that Phil had slept with Sharon. Grant played the taped confession at Phil and Kathy's engagement party in October 1994 and, as Phil ran away, chased him to the garage, where he beat him up so badly he was hospitalized, fighting for his life. Remarkably, the brothers made up with each other afterwards.

Despite Phil's deceit over Nadia and the revelation that he had slept with Sharon, he and Kathy found they had a strong relationship and the

Phil Mitchell won the hand of divorcée Kathy after his marriage of convenience.

couple married quietly in a register office on 28 February 1995, with Pat Butcher and Grant as witnesses.

☆ ☆ ☆

Steve McFadden won the Derek Ware and Patrick Crane awards at RADA and, while there, appeared on stage in *Entertaining Mr Sloane*, *Twelfth Night* and *The Threepenny Opera*. Since then, he has played the title role in the Pentabus Theatre Company's production of *The Ballad of Johnny Reece*. He was in the films *Rossinanti* and *Buster*, and on television in *The Firm*, *Minder*, *Hard Cases*, *Vote for Them*, *The Bill*, *Saracen*, *Bergerac*, *All Change* and the BBC TV film *Ligmalion*.

Steve, who holds a certificate in stage fighting, enjoys boxing, karate, snooker, sailing, horse-riding, climbing and playing football.

ETHEL SKINNER

Kindly Ethel Skinner was born in Camden, North London, and worked in service for many years, arriving in the East End as undermaid to a wealthy family in Hackney. She lost all her family in the Blitz when a bomb hit their house but enjoyed several romances during the war years, before marrying husband William, a docker, in 1947. After his death, Ethel gave all her love to her dog Willie, spending much of her pension on him. After a hip operation, Ethel moved out of her rent-free flat at Dr Legg's premises to lodge with Dot Cotton because she could not cope by herself. Later, she went into a home. When the Square celebrated Ethel's 80th birthday, Nellie Ellis threw a spanner in the works by revealing she was, in fact, only 79!

☆ ☆ ☆

Gretchen Franklin (b. Gretchen Gordon Franklin in Covent Garden, London, 7 July 1911) was born into a theatrical family. Her comedian father formed a double act with her mother, who died when Gretchen was only four. She was brought up by her grandmother, went to a convent school and then worked in a shop.

Gretchen started her stage career as a £2-a-week chorus girl in a Bournemouth pantomime. She worked in vaudeville, cabaret and musical comedy, before becoming a successful West End revue artist in the *Sweet and Low* series with Hermione Gingold at the Ambassadors Theatre. After the Second World War, Gretchen turned to acting, initially in a BBC television comedy revue. She was sacked when the producer heard her telling everyone how silly the show was but went on to become a familiar face on television.

Her TV appearances include *Danger UXB*, *George and Mildred*, *Quatermass*, *Some Mothers Do 'Ave 'Em*, *Fox*, *Potter*, *The Dick Emery Show*, *The Other 'Arf*, *Maybury*, *Blackadder*, *In Loving Memory* and *The Victoria Wood Show*. Gretchen also played Alf's wife Else in the pilot of *Till Death Us Do Part*, in the 'Comedy Playhouse' slot in 1965, and Myrtle Harvey (née Cavendish) in *Crossroads*. On TV, she has appeared as mother to Ronnie Corbett and Yootha Joyce, mother-in-law to Dick Emery, aunt to Leonard Rossiter and Thora Hird, and housekeeper to Irene Handl. She has also acted on stage in *Hedda Gabler*, *Hay Fever*, *Logan* and *Little and Large*.

The actress, whose writer husband Caswell Garth is now dead, joined *EastEnders* when it began in 1985 but now makes only occasional appearances. At home in Barnes, London, Gretchen enjoys gardening and embroidery.

JULES TAVERNIER

Born in Trinidad, Jules Henry Hercules Tavernier came to Britain to visit his son and his family in 1968 and decided to stay. He is the wise, old man who dispenses good advice and recalls days gone by, including tales of his involvement in the 1937 oil field strikes. Fancying himself as a bit of a singer, Jules agreed to be in the Queen Vic's quiz team as long as he could perform in the pub one night.

In June 1992, when Jules's son Celestine landed a job in Norwich and left the Square with his wife, Jules stayed on. Two years later, he found a new friend in Blossom Jackson, who moved

Letitia Dean (b. Wild Hill, near Potters Bar, Hertfordshire, 14 November 1967) played Den and Angie Watts's adoptive daughter SHARON MITCHELL (née Stretton). Letitia, who previously played Lucinda in *Grange Hill*, Dawn in *Brookside* and a drug addict in *The Bill*, had a Top 20 hit single, 'Something Outa Nothing', with fellow *EastEnder* Paul Medford. She left the serial in 1995.

Nejdet Salih (b. London, 23 December 1958) was ALI OSMAN, owner of the Square's café. Nejdet, who in real life went out with *EastEnders* actress Linda Davidson, then married girlfriend Sue Steven in 1989 but was divorced three years later, has moved to America since leaving the serial in 1990.

Sandy Ratcliff (b. London, 2 October 1950) was SUE OSMAN, wife of Ali. After modelling, Sandy made her acting debut as a schizophrenic, in the 1971 Ken Loach film *Family Life*. Sandy, a heroin addict who was in the original cast, has hardly worked since leaving *EastEnders*.

Michael Melia (b. 1945), son of thirties boxing champion John, played Queen Vic landlord EDDIE ROYLE, murdered by Nick Cotton. He had previously appeared in *Coronation Street* and *Hollywood Sports* and later played boxer Freddie Mills in *In Suspicious Circumstances*, and Brian Phillips in *The Detectives*.

Paddy Joyce, who was JOHN ROYLE, Eddie's father, played rag-and-bone man Tommy Deakin in *Coronation Street* during the sixties and seventies.

Linda Davidson (b. Lynda Davidson in Toronto, Canada, 18 June 1964) played punk single mum MARY SMITH and has since acted Anita Pilsworth in *First of the Summer Wine* and Kitty in the second series of *House of Eliott*, as well as acting in *Casualty*, *The Bill* and *The Full Wax*.

Michelle Gayle (b. Michelle Patricia Gayle in London, 2 February 1971) played Fiona Wilson in the BBC children's serial *Grange Hill* before joining *EastEnders* as HATTIE TAVERNIER. After leaving the serial, Michelle concentrated on her career as a pop singer, releasing singles including 'Lookin' Up', 'Sweetness' and 'I'll Find You'.

into Dot Cotton's old house with her grandson Alan's family. As Jules and Blossom saw more of each other, Nellie Ellis – the Fowlers' aunt who had moved in with Jules – began to feel unwanted and left for sheltered accommodation.

☆ ☆ ☆

Tommy Eytle is a showbusiness all-rounder who performs in cabaret in Britain, Holland, Denmark, Norway and Sweden when not acting. Before joining *EastEnders* in 1990, he was on TV in *The Bill*, *Snakes and Ladders* and the series *Never Say Die* (as Jack). Tommy was in the films *Day of the Fox*, *Elsa the Lioness*, *The Hijackers*, *Man Friday*, *Beyond the Sunrise*, *Blue Smoke* and *Red Mountains*. His West End plays include *The Death of Bessie Smith*, *As Time Goes By*, *One More River*, *Toys in the Attic*, *South* and *Playboy of the West Indies*. He was also in *Measure for Measure*, *The American Clock* and *Ma Rainey's Black Bottom* at the National Theatre, *Leave Taking* at the Liverpool Playhouse, *Split Second* at the Lyric, Hammersmith, *A Blow to Bute Street* at the Sherman Theatre, Cardiff, and *Take Back What's Yours* at the Warehouse Theatre, Croydon.

Anita Dobson (b. London, 29 April 1949) was ANGIE WATTS, wife of Queen Vic landlord 'Dirty Den' until they parted and Angie managed The Dagmar, before leaving to run a bar in Marbella and, later, marry again in New York. Angie has since been on TV as star of the comedy series *Split Ends* and a stripper in *The World of Eddie Weary*. She had a 1987 hit single with 'Anyone Can Fall in Love', a vocal version of the *EastEnders* theme.

Leslie Grantham (b. Camberwell, South London, 30 April 1947) was one of the most written about stars of the eighties when he played Queen Vic landlord DEN WATTS. Revelations that he had served 11 years in jail after murdering a taxi driver in 1966 made headlines. After leaving *EastEnders*, with his character shot dead by underworld gangsters, Leslie starred as fight promoter Eddie Burt in *Winners and Losers*, Danny Kane in *The Paradise Club* and conman-turned-cop Mick Raynor in *99-1*, as well as acting in the West End play *Rick's Bar Casablanca*.

Nick Berry (b. North London, 16 May 1963) played barman SIMON WICKS ('Wicksy'), who fathered Cindy Beale's baby son Steven. Nick's single 'Every Loser Wins' reached no. 1 in 1986 and, when he starred as P.C. Nick Rowan in *Heartbeat*, he had a hit with the title song. He wed model Rachel Robertson in 1994.

Shirley Cheriton (b. London, 28 June 1955) found fame as nurse Katy Betts in *Angels*. As yuppie DEBBIE WILKINS in *EastEnders*, she was nurse Andy O'Brien's girlfriend but left the Square to marry Det. Sgt. Rich. Shirley had a five-year affair with Ross Davidson, who played Andy. She has since appeared on television in *Three Up, Two Down* and *Grace and Favour* (as Miss Prescott).

DAVID WICKS

Smooth-talking David Wicks, son of Pat Butcher from her first marriage to Pete Beale, was reunited with his mother at Pete's funeral at Christmas 1993, having left home 16 years earlier. It was the first time they had spoken since.

David, who had already served 18 months in prison for VAT fraud, stayed in Albert Square – leaving behind his wife and two children – and proved a tower of strength to his mother. But she found out about the conviction and his failure to keep up maintenance payments when David's parole officer visited the Square.

There was a bigger shock for David when he bumped into Carol Jackson, his old flame from teenage years. Because Bianca started flirting with David, Carol shocked him by revealing that he was Bianca's father. At the time, he had run away, leaving 14-year-old Carol pregnant. Bianca did not know that he was her father.

Then David conned £500 out of his mother by claiming that heavies were threatening to break his legs. His next money-making scheme was to re-open Frank Butcher's car lot as Deals on Wheels, with Ricky as his business partner.

But David found himself playing the concerned father when Bianca was led astray by her friend Tiffany Raymond and picked up in a club by a man who plied her with drink and took her back to the Square to bed her. David sent him on his way and took a drunken Bianca to the car lot to sober up. As she tried to throw herself at him, David admitted he was her father. He was not so bashful when, in May 1995, bored housewife Cindy Beale had a one-night stand with him.

☆ ☆ ☆

Michael French has a background in musicals, having appeared in *West Side Story*, *Les Misérables* and *Godspell*, before making his TV debut in *EastEnders*. He is single, lives in London and enjoys playing tennis and squash, horse-riding and skiing.

Back row: Kelly Windsor (Adele Silva), Dolores Sharp (Samantha Hurst), Luke McAllister (Noah Huntley), Angharad McAllister (Amanda Wenban), Bernard McAllister (Brendan Price), Jessica McAllister (Camilla Power), Biff Fowler (Stuart Wade), Eric Pollard (Christopher Chittell), Alan Turner (Richard Thorp), Alice Bates (Rachel Tolboys), Caroline Bates (Diana Davies), Kathy Tate (Malandra Burrows), Nick Bates (Cy Chadwick), Kim Tate (Claire King), Frank Tate (Norman Bowler), Zoe Tate (Leah Bracknell). Front row: Scott Windsor (Toby Cockerell), Vic Windsor (Alun Lewis), Viv Windsor (Deena Payne), Donna Windsor (Sophie Jeffery), Seth Armstrong (Stan Richards), Betty Eagleton (Paula Tilbrook), Robert Sugden (Christopher Smith), Sarah Sugden (Alyson Spiro), Victoria Sugden (Jessica Heywood), Jack Sugden (Clive Hornby), Annie Sugden (Sheila Mercier), Rachel Hughes (Glenda McKay), Chris Tate (Peter Amory), Linda Glover (Tonicha Jeronimo), Jan Glover (Roberta Kerr), Ned Glover (Johnny Leeze), Dave Glover (Ian Kelsey), Roy Windsor (Nicky Evans).

Emmerdale began life as *Emmerdale Farm*, first broadcast on 16 October 1972 and created to help fill the increased number of daytime broadcasting hours on ITV. Its remit was to cater for mothers, pensioners and shift workers at home during the day. Soon, however, more and more people were watching and the programme was moved to a teatime slot. Eventually, in 1977, it gained a place in the evening schedule in some regions, although it was another 11 years before every other ITV company did likewise.

Creator Kevin Laffan centred the story around Annie Sugden, newly widowed and facing up to life running a Yorkshire Dales farm with the help of her two bickering sons, Jack and Joe. The programme's slow, leisurely pace was one of its main attractions, but in the late eighties and early nineties new producers moved the action away from the farming and made the stories more raunchy. This was reflected by the change of title, in 1989, to *Emmerdale* and more emphasis was given to the new owners of Home Farm, the Tates.

The village of Beckindale also changed its name to Emmerdale, in 1994, following a tragic plane crash over it the previous Christmas. This was done to mark both a new beginning for the village and recognize the contribution made by the farm and the Sugden family down the years. Actress Sheila Mercier, who plays matriarch Annie Sugden, is the sole surviving member of the original cast.

SETH ARMSTRONG

Poacher-turned-gamekeeper Seth Armstrong is most likely to be found propping up the bar at The Woolpack, ready to take part in the banter with his dry sense of humour. He is instantly recognizable in his Barbour jacket, wellingtons and woolly hat, plus eccentric whiskers and gummy grin.

Seth – who with his late wife, Meg, had two sons, Jimmy and Fred – was first seen in 1978 as an odd-job man, looking after the boiler in the village school, digging graves and solving the vicar's electrical problems. He was also the wiliest poacher in Emmerdale, but his knowledge of the woods made him an asset to N.Y. Estates, which the following year appointed him gamekeeper at Home Farm and, in doing so, kept his illicit activities at bay.

The death of George Verney, the owner of the old manor house just outside Emmerdale, brought massive death duties and the sale of the estate. The locals no longer had a paternal lord of the manor and were wary of N.Y. Estates, which bought the three farms. David Thatcher, the first estate manager, realized he could win them over by getting Seth on his side. Thatcher was succeeded by Richard Anstey, then local farmer Joe Sugden, who took charge temporarily, but the job was – to his surprise – given permanently to Alan Turner, who was lazy and a little too fond of alcohol.

Despite being workshy and slightly devious, Seth did not deserve the fate that was bestowed on him when a gang of poachers and badger-baiters beat him unconscious, leaving him for dead. He slowly recovered from head injuries and damaged ribs in hospital. Returning to his job at N.Y. Estates, Seth was soon back in the old routine. He was given responsibility for looking after a new fish farm and, when Alan Turner bought The Woolpack in 1991, Seth thought his boss's new responsibilities would make it easier for him to get away with even less work. He reckoned without secretary Elizabeth Feldmann, whom Alan made fish farm manager. Immediately, she gave Seth a timetable that made clear what he should be doing and when – and allowed him less time to put his earnings back into Alan Turner's pocket at The Woolpack.

Seth's long-suffering wife Meg died in 1993, leaving him a tin full of valuable pre-decimal banknotes that dodgy Eric Pollard bought for £20 from Seth and sold for £500. Pollard handed over the profit only after his wife, Elizabeth, pressurized him to do so. Concerned not to go home to an empty cottage after Meg's death, Seth craftily found food and accommodation first with Elizabeth Feldmann and Alan Turner, then with Nick Bates and Archie Brooks. Just when Nick and Archie though he was moving in for good, Seth announced that he was returning to his own cottage.

After the Emmerdale plane crash on 30 December 1993, Alan Turner was deeply concerned about Seth's safety, since he had banished him from The Woolpack's Dickensian Evening. When Seth eventually appeared with Samson, the horse, Alan was close to tears. Seth's own home had been destroyed, along with Smokey. He had found safety with widow Betty Eagleton, an old flame of his from the Second World War who had been snatched away from him by Wally Eagleton.

Seth also made national newspaper headlines, with the bonus of a fully paid for private prostate operation, which he had been diagnosed as needing during the previous year. The journalist who feted him, Gavin Watson, gave him a new dog, Charlie, but he was left to find a new home in a hut on the game reserve. Nick Bates invited Seth to live at Mill Cottage, until Betty Eagleton offered him accommodation.

Frank Tate had by then employed him as guide at his model farm. Seth resigned on hearing that Kim Tate – standing in after husband Frank's heart attack – had appointed Dave Glover as gamekeeper. He made Dave's life difficult by switching back to poaching and apparently killing the mythical 'Beast of Beckindale', and Kim felt duty-bound to give him back his job as the Heritage Farm warden.

Seth was soon rekindling the flames with Betty Eagleton and the couple set a wedding date for December 1994. When it came to the big day, they decided there was no need to exchange vows at their age and they would simply live together. So they cancelled the wedding breakfast and organized a forties fancy-dress knees-up for villagers instead.

☆ ☆ ☆

Stan Richards (b. Stanley Richardson in Barnsley, South Yorkshire, 8 December 1930) grew up in a mining village near Barnsley and worked as a Ministry of Labour clerk on leaving school. When he was transferred to London, he hated the city so much that he was allowed to move back to the North. A piano player since the age of ten, he passed his Trinity College of Music exams and started his showbusiness career as a dance-band pianist.

Gradually turning to acting, he formed a comedy and musical quartet called Melody Maniacs in 1952. They toured northern clubs and cabaret venues, then Stan went professional as a solo entertainer 16 years later. He still performs his cabaret act today, and is in demand as an after-dinner speaker.

After acting in two plays for BBC radio, Stan's talents were spotted by director Ken Loach, who cast him in his TV play *The Price of Coal*. Stan followed it with roles in *Coronation Street, The Cuckoo Waltz, Crown Court, All Creatures Great and Small* and *Last of the Summer Wine*, and was the subject of *This Is Your Life* in 1991. He also appeared in the films *Yanks* and *Agatha*, and has played Seth Armstrong in *Emmerdale* since March 1978. For the role, he takes out his false teeth – his toothless grin and large moustache are his trademarks.

Stan's wife of more than 40 years, Susanna, died in 1994. They had six children – Alan, Keith, Irvin, Joan, Dawn and June. The actor lives in Barnsley.

Away from the studios, Stan – who also has five grandchildren and a great-grandson – is likely to be found wearing a pinstripe suit and driving his sleek Saab with carphone. He enjoys reading and playing the piano, and speaks fluent French and German.

CAROLINE BATES

Caroline Bates moved to Emmerdale with daughter Kathy and son Nick in 1984, when she became Alan Turner's secretary at N.Y. Estates. She lived in the tied cottage, no. 17 Main Street, which came with the job, and proved to be longer-lasting than Alan's string of previous assistants, who had to endure his drinking, gambling and amorous advances.

She was still getting through the trauma of splitting up with her schoolteacher husband Malcolm and hoped that she might be reunited with him. But, in 1987, he turned up in Emmerdale with the news that his new girl-friend was pregnant and demanded a divorce.

Alan and Caroline began a business venture together by opening a game farm. As romance developed between them, the couple were engaged, but the wedding did not go ahead. Caroline left the village and later returned to see Alan, who had by then taken over The Woolpack, to demand compensation for her cottage, in which she had been the sitting tenant. Alan had been able to buy it as the office for the fish farm only because they had intended to live there together. Trying to avoid spending any money, Alan took Caroline out for a picnic and asked her to marry him, but she said she wanted a financial settlement, not a marriage proposal. She helped out in the pub restaurant for a while but then returned to Scarborough, to look after her ailing mother. Caroline continued to return to Emmerdale to see her children.

On a visit in 1993, Alan again proposed marriage. She turned him down but assured him of her most loyal friendship. Later, she introduced him to the drop-in centre, where he met his

Jean Heywood (b. Jean Murray in Blyth, Northumberland, 15 July 1921) was Dolly Skilbeck's mother, PHYLLIS ACASTER, who did not take to Amos Brearly's giving Dolly away at her wedding to Matt. Jean had already featured on TV as Bella Seaton in *When the Boat Comes In* and Miss Kay in *Our Day Out*, and later played Dolly McGregor in *The Brothers McGregor* and housekeeper Mrs Alton in *All Creatures Great and Small*.

David Fleeshman (b. Leeds, 11 July 1952) played nasty CHARLIE AINDOW, the crooked councillor who had an affair with Dolly Skilbeck. When she became pregnant, he abandoned her and she had an abortion. David previously appeared in six episodes of *Emmerdale* as BARRY HILL and has also been in *Boys from the Blackstuff, Edge of Darkness, Coronation Street* (as estate agent Peter Haines), *The Practice, Brookside* (as David Hurst) and *EastEnders* (as Mr Soames). He is married to *Brookside* actress Sue Jenkins.

Tom Adams (b. London, 3 September 1938) appeared in many films before becoming known on television as Dr Wallman in *General Hospital*, Daniel Fogarty in *The Onedin Line* and Ken Stevenson in *Strike It Rich*, before taking the role of MALCOLM BATES, Caroline's former husband, in *Emmerdale*.

Peter Denyer became known as the dunce Dennis Dunstable in *Please Sir!* and *The Fenn Street Gang*. He later turned up in *Emmerdale* as a character called BATTY, before taking the roles of both gay Michael and Michael-lookalike Graham in the sitcom *Agony*, and lonely-heart Ralph Dring in the comedy *Dear John*.

Susan Wooldridge (b. London), who later acted Daphne Manners in *The Jewel in the Crown* on TV, played MARGARET BECKETT.

Cricketer IAN BOTHAM appeared as himself in February 1995 to open the refurbished Woolpack pub.

Veteran entertainer Max Wall (b. Maxwell George Lorimer in Brixton, South London, 12 March 1908) played ARTHUR BRAITHWAITE, a friend of Sam Pearson, as well as appearing in *Crossroads* as Walter Soper, cousin of Arthur Brownlow, and *Coronation Street* as Elsie Tanner's friend Harry Payne. Max died on 22 May 1990.

Ronald Magill (b. Hull, East Yorkshire, 21 April 1920) played Woolpack landlord AMOS BREARLY, complete with bushy sideburns, for more than 18 years, from the serial's start in 1972, and has made several comeback appearances. He was previously on TV in *Special Branch* and *Parkin's Patch*, and appeared alongside John Gielgud and Charlton Heston in the 1970 feature film *Julius Caesar*.

Tony Pitts (b. Sheffield, 10 October 1962), who played teetotal ARCHIE BROOKS from 1985 until the character's death in the Emmerdale plane disaster of 1993, was working as a mechanic in Sheffield when film director Ken Loach – maker of *Kes* – gave him a leading role, Alan Wright, in the film *Looks and Smiles*. He also appeared on TV in *Bingo!*, *Welcome to the Times* (as a psychopathic killer with a shaved head) and *Rainy Day Women*.

Stephanie Cole (b. Solihull, Warwickshire, 5 October 1941) played MRS BULSTRODE and went on to act Dr Beatrice Mason in *Tenko*. Her subsequent TV appearances include the Alan Bennett *Talking Heads* monologue *Soldiering On*, and the role of geriatric tyrant Diana in the sitcom *Waiting for God*.

wife-to-be Shirley Foster, who tragically died after a post office raid that went wrong.

In December 1994, Caroline's mother died and she decided to stay in Emmerdale, although she ditched Eric Pollard, who had been romancing her, after finding out that he had been cooking the books at The Woolpack and had almost succeeded in stealing the pub from Alan Turner.

☆ ☆ ☆

Diana Davies (b. Manchester, 20 July 1936), the daughter of a big-band musician, took a modelling course before beginning her acting career as an extra. She appeared in non-speaking roles for Granada Television for 11 years, before winning the role of Freda Ashton's friend Doris in the popular 1970–1 series *A Family at War*. This led to the part of cornershop assistant Norma Ford, one of Ken Barlow's many girlfriends, in *Coronation Street*, when *A Family at War* director June Howson took over as producer of the serial. She left after 18 months, remembered by many as 'Di the Thigh', after her mini skirts.

Diana was cast as battered housewife Letty Brewer in *Emmerdale* for four episodes before returning as Caroline Bates, known originally only as Mrs Bates. She has also appeared on TV in *The Liver Birds*, *Send in the Girls*, *Juliet Bravo*, *Enemy at the Door*, *Shoestring*, *All Creatures Great and Small* and *Medics*, and was Mum in the Lyons cakes commercials in the seventies. A highlight of Diana's stage career was appearing alongside Glenda Jackson in the West End hit *Rose*. Diana was also in a national tour of *Gaslight*.

Divorced from husband Peter, she has a grown-up son, Stephen, part-owns a show horse, Tom Cobley, with Christie Littlewood and lives in Manchester with her sister, illustrator Jill Barton, whose third book, *The Pig in the Pond*, was shortlisted for the Kate Greenaway Award.

NICK BATES

Brother of Kathy Tate and son of Caroline Bates, Nick Bates experienced the heartbreak of his parents' broken marriage.

Nick was hailed a hero when he foiled a robbery at Emmerdale post office in 1988, but he could not resist pocketing some of the loot and entrusting it to his then girlfriend, Clare Sutcliffe, who promptly disappeared.

When Eric Pollard and Phil Pearce found out what he had done, they tried to blackmail him, but Nick had the last laugh when he shopped the pair for trying to steal antique fireplaces from Home Farm. Phil confessed, but Eric maintained his innocence and there was no firm evidence to point the finger at him.

Nick eventually found love with Elsa Feldmann. When they discovered she was pregnant, Nick was determined to stand by her, but Elsa's fiercely protective mother and brother assured him that he was not needed and they would help her to bring up the child. When Elizabeth Feldmann eventually realized that Nick really loved her daughter, she allowed him to move into their cottage with them. Later, Nick planned to move to Demdyke Cottage, intending it as a home for him and Elsa, but she said she was too young to set up home with him. Her mother, who had become more trusting of Nick, persuaded her to join him there.

Shocked by the cost of baby clothes and accessories, Nick took an extra job as a newspaper delivery boy, in addition to his work as a gardener at Home Farm, to earn money. He was intent on being with Elsa when their baby was born, so went with her to an antenatal class to see a film about childbirth. The gory production caused him to pass out and he became disenchanted with the whole idea of childbirth.

The couple planned a Valentine's Day wedding in 1991, but Elsa went into labour prematurely on the way to the register office and gave birth to baby daughter Alice Rose. In the absence of a midwife, vet Zoe Tate delivered her.

Nick and Elsa grew further apart and she never adapted to life as a mother, resenting the demands it made on her. Eventually, on Christmas Eve, she walked out on her fiancé, taking Alice with her, although Elsa later returned the baby to Nick when she found that caring for Alice prevented her from having a social life. It was left to Nick to care for Alice, which he did admirably. He was helped by Archie Brooks, who moved in with him in April 1992 and acted as a childminder. It was a trying time for Nick three months later when a distraught woman turned up claiming that Alice was really her daughter following a mix-up at the hospital, but this proved to be a hoax.

Nick found new love with Julie Bramhope, who herself had a daughter, Rebecca. They suffered two worrying moments, first when her ex-lover, Brian, turned up to see the baby he did not even know he had fathered after being traced by the Child Support Agency and ordered to pay maintenance, then when Nick and Julie were babysitting Lynn Whiteley's son, Peter, who became ill with meningitis. Nick bundled Peter's belongings out of the door in case Alice should become infected, which caused friction with Lynn. The relationship with Julie ended when she opted to return to her ex-boyfriend. Then, Alice went missing, feared dead, in the

Emmerdale plane crash on 30 December 1993. Nick himself was left deranged by the disaster and in need of hospital treatment, and his friend Archie was dead. Elsa rushed back from Leeds and, after learning of her mother's death in the disaster, feared the worst for her daughter. But Alice was eventually pulled out of the rubble of Nick's home, which had been destroyed.

Although Elsa tried to get custody of Alice, using the false rumour that Nick was gay as part of her character assassination, Nick won the court battle in 1994. He found new accommodation in the old nursery at Home Farm once occupied by Dolly Skilbeck and her son, Sam. He also found new love with single mum Paula.

☆ ☆ ☆

Cy Chadwick (b. Leeds, 2 June 1969) appeared in the ITV children's programme *The Book Tower* at the age of 13 and the schools series *How We Used to Live* two years later. After leaving Leeds Intake High School, where he studied drama, Cy appeared in *On the Boat*, a four-part English-language programme made in Germany. He returned to Britain and, at the age of 16, joined *Emmerdale* in September 1985. He has also done voice-overs for commercials.

The actor took four months off from *Emmerdale* in 1989 after the break-up of his relationship with *Emmerdale* actress Sara Griffiths (who played his screen girlfriend Clare Sutcliffe) and two burglaries at his home. At the time, Cy confessed that he had also spent tens of thousands of pounds on clubbing, gambling and buying a sports car, cameras and hi-fi equipment.

Cy, who lives in Leeds, enjoys photography and listening to pop music. Apart from ambitions to direct pop videos, he manages a group called Baby Boys. In 1992, he released his own pop single, 'The Love Game'.

Stuart Wolfenden (b. Rochdale, Lancashire, 7 February 1970) was a thug called CHUCK, after his *Coronation Street* role as car mechanic Mark Casey.

Julie Dawn Cole (b. Guildford, Surrey, 26 October 1957) had already played nurse Jo Longhurst in *Angels* when she arrived in *Emmerdale* in 1978 as PIP COULTER, who with Steve Hawker took Sam Pearson hostage at gunpoint in his workshop while they were on the run from the police. The pair had robbed The Woolpack and released Sam after one-and-a-half hours, when Annie provided a getaway car for them. Julie later appeared briefly in *EastEnders* as Geraldine.

NELLIE DINGLE

Mother of the terrible Dingle clan, Nellie rules her family with an iron fist and has no qualms about speaking her mind, shouting everything at the top of her voice. The Dingles swore revenge on Luke McAllister after their son Ben died in a fight with him at a rave party in Emmerdale. The whole village hated the Dingles, so Nellie was in her element when they won a free meal at the Woolpack re-opening in February 1995.

Sandra Gough (b. Manchester) has been an actress since the age of 12, when she landed a role in the 'Children's Hour' serial *The Whittakers*. On leaving school, she worked as an extra for Granada Television and acted with the Library Theatre company, in Manchester.

In 1964, Sandra joined *Coronation Street* as Stan and Hilda Ogden's daughter Irma, who married David Barlow and had a baby boy. Four years later, she left when the characters emigrated to Australia. In 1970, David and the baby were killed in a car crash and Sandra returned to the *Street* as Irma. Her contract was terminated by Granada the following year after she had missed rehearsals. Unknown to the TV company, she was caring for her mother, who was dying of a rare bone disease, and suffered a nervous breakdown as a result of the stress.

In the eighties, Sandra played Sheri in the soap *Hollywood Sports*, before joining *Emmerdale* for a short run as Doreen Shuttleworth, barmaid at the Malt Shovel, local rival to The Woolpack. She returned to the serial in 1994 as Nellie Dingle. Sandra has also been on TV in *Foxy Lady*, *Travelling Man*, *How to Be Cool*, *All Creatures Great and Small*, *Medics*, *Cracker* and *The Wanderer*, and in the films *The Dresser* and *The Rise and Rise of Roy 'Chubby' Brown*.

Twice-divorced Sandra's first marriage – to Spaniard Miguel Major – was annulled after a week and the second ended after two months.

TINA DINGLE

Wayward Tina Dingle has always been a worry for her mother, Nellie – she was expelled from school for assaulting a teacher and then became involved in the brawl with Luke McAllister, which led to a feud between the two families. When 16-year-old Tina Dingle first caught sight of Luke in 1994, she wanted him. But his involvement in the fight in which her brother, Ben, died meant that she had to distance herself and side with her own family.

Once relations between the two families cooled down and Luke's parents returned to London, she accepted a lift from Luke and the pair were soon all over one another. It appeared to be a relationship of pure lust, but Luke brought out the loving, caring side of Tina, which had been lost after years of living among her rough family. But she did everything possible to make sure Luke's sister, Jessica, did not return. On hearing an answer-machine message that she was coming, Tina set up Jessica's boyfriend, Biff Fowler, with her friend Sadie so that Jessica would discover them together.

Jessica was disgusted that Luke was going out with Tina and even more shocked when Tina announced that she was pregnant, which led to her own family throwing her out. Luke then proposed marriage and she accepted.

Jacqueline Pirie (b. Stirling, 10 October 1975) made her TV debut with a brief appearance in *Crossroads* at the age of 11 and later was a regular in *Palace Hill*. Before joining *Emmerdale* in 1994, she was a presenter of Sky Television's children's programme *The DJ Kat Show*, chatting to the fluffy host. She also made a film, *Chasing the Deer*, starring Brian Blessed. Her hobbies are oil painting and swimming.

ZAK DINGLE

Father of Ben Dingle, who died in a fight with Luke McAllister, Zak Dingle was as determined as the rest of his rough family to get even with the doctor's son. But causing trouble for the whole of Emmerdale seemed to be the Dingles' aim. They wreaked havoc at The Woolpack's celebrations to mark the death of the mythical 'Beast of Beckindale'. A confrontation with Ned Glover there led to Zak challenging him to a bare-knuckle fight. The Dingles thought all their wrongs were about to be righted but, after a bloody battle with heavy blows on both sides, the pair rolled down a bank into a stream, where Ned delivered the final punch.

☆ ☆ ☆

Steve Halliwell (b. Stephen Harold Halliwell in Bury, Lancashire, 19 March 1954) was an apprentice engineer, gardener and worker in a cotton mill and paper mill before training at Mountview Theatre School.

He appeared as a Russian courier in the feature film *The Fourth Protocol* – the Frederick Forsyth thriller starring Michael Caine – and has made dozens of television appearances, including roles as P.C. Goole in two *All Creatures Great and Small* Christmas specials, Stephen in *Brookside*, Peter Bishop in two series of *The Practice* and Bob Cairns, barman at The Queens pub alongside Liz McDonald, in *Coronation Street.*

Steve, who is divorced from first wife Susan Woods, is married to artist Valerie and lives in Burnley, Lancashire. He has a daughter, Charlotte Jane, from his second marriage, and two stepsons, John James and Nicholas William.

BETTY EAGLETON

An old flame of Seth Armstrong, Betty Eagleton walked back into his life in 1994. It was exactly 50 years since Wally Eagleton had beaten Seth to claim her hand in marriage.

Seth found refuge with her after the Emmerdale plane disaster the previous Christmas, months after her husband had died, although she had already walked out on him after a confrontation in which she told scrap-dealer Wally to choose between her and his old rag-and-bone horse, Samson. Seth himself had just lost his wife, Meg. Betty also landed a job in Emmerdale, cleaning for Dr McAllister and his wife.

The next summer, Eric Pollard persuaded Betty to rent out her land for a rave party. It left her with debts of £19,000, but she refused to sell Pollard the field, which had been his aim. She was too shrewd to let Pollard get one over her.

Betty and Seth drew closer and announced their engagement, although their marriage plans were confirmed only after Betty's elderly father had met and approved his daughter's husband-to-be.

However, the wedding set for December 1994 did not go ahead. The couple decided at the last minute that they were too old to be exchanging vows and would simply live together. They turned the wedding breakfast into a forties fancy-dress party for the villagers.

☆ ☆ ☆

Paula Tilbrook has played dozens of roles on screen during her career. Her films include *Wetherby*, *A Private Function*, *Yanks* and *Resurrected*, and on television she has appeared as Mrs Tattersall in *Open All Hours*, Mrs Enright in *Last of the Summer Wine*, Mrs Ashby in the TV movie *Walter* (starring Ian McKellen and shown on the first evening of Channel Four, in 1982), Mrs Tibbett in two series of *Sharon and Elsie*, Paula in *In Sickness and in Health*, Aunt Flo in *Andy Capp* (alongside James Bolam) and Violet Rokeby in *Lovejoy*.

She also played Betty Hunt in *Brookside* and widow Vivienne Barford, who took a shine to Alf Roberts, in *Coronation Street*. She had previously appeared in the *Street* as a friend of leg-

---

David Beckett played D.I. FARRAR, who led the search for missing Robert Sugden in 1995. David previously appeared in *Coronation Street* as handyman Dave Barton, who went out with Deirdre Barlow, played by Anne Kirkbride. Although they split up on screen, the couple married in real life. David also played Det. Chief Insp. Webb in *Families*.

Naomi Lewis (b. Manchester, 24 March 1971) played ELSA FELDMANN, who walked out on fiancé Nick Bates and left him to care for their baby daughter, Alice. Naomi, who had previously appeared in *Lost Empires* on TV, acted on stage in the West End musical *Buddy*.

Veteran actor Donald Morley (b. Richmond-upon-Thames, Surrey) played both ALEC FERRIS and FRANKLYN PRESCOTT in *Emmerdale*. He had previously appeared as Babbage in the sixties soap *Compact* and Walter Fletcher in *Coronation Street*. More recently, he took the role of Mrs Slocombe's husband, Cecil, in the sitcom *Grace and Favour*.

Patricia Brake (b. Bath, Avon, 25 June 1942), was in the early TV soap *Home Tonight* as a teenager and, after playing SARAH FOSTER in *Emmerdale*, took the role of Ronnie Barker's long-suffering daughter Ingrid in both *Porridge* and *Going Straight*. She was later Gwen Lockhead in the ill-fated *Eldorado*.

endary Rovers Return landlady Annie Walker. Paula's stage appearances include the title role in a National Theatre production of *Effie's Burning*, which she recreated on television.

BIFF FOWLER

Luke McAllister's biker friend Biff Fowler found romance in Emmerdale with Jessica McAllister's friend Dolores Sharp, although Dolores worried that she might be pregnant. When Biff found a new girlfriend in Jessica McAllister, Luke fell for Dolores. Trouble came when Biff was involved in a fight with the terrible Dingles when they confronted Luke outside the local school, the culmination of their threats to get their own back for the death of Ben Dingle in a punch-up with Luke.

When Jessica's parents announced they were leaving Emmerdale to return south, she and Biff ran away together and 17-year-old Jessica lost her virginity to him. Biff moved into the McAllister home but fell out with Luke and left when Luke's fiancée, Tina Dingle, falsely claimed that he had made a pass at her.

☆ ☆ ☆

Stuart Wade (b. Halifax, West Yorkshire, 1 August 1971), younger brother of actor Danny Coll, joined the Actors' Workshop Youth Theatre in 1987 and performed there in productions of *Amadeus* (as Mozart), *'Tis Pity She's a Whore* (as Giovanni), *Romeo and Juliet* (as Romeo), *One Flew over the Cuckoo's Nest* (as Billy), *Kiss of the Spider Woman* (as Molina, alongside *Pie in the Sky* TV star Joe Duttine) and *Hamlet* (in the title role), as well as taking the lead in the musicals *Lock up Your Daughters*, *Roberta* and *A Funny Thing Happened on the Way to the Forum*. A fitness fanatic, Stuart enjoys playing squash, swimming and horseriding. He lives on the outskirts of Halifax.

that included flashing horns. Seth 'killed' it and was offered back his old job as a reward.

When it became known that Kathy and Chris Tate had split up because of his affair with Rachel Hughes, Dave decided to make a play for Kathy, first giving her flowers, then taking her out for a drink. Kathy insisted they go to The Woolpack to show that she was staying in Emmerdale with her head held high.

Chris Tate was furious when he heard that his father, Frank, had made Dave assistant farm manager. However, he felt easier about Kathy's new relationship after she accepted his £120,000 divorce settlement.

☆ ☆ ☆

Ian Kelsey joined *Emmerdale* in 1994 and soon made friends with another newcomer, Noah Huntley, who plays Luke McAllister. The two quickly found a bachelor flat together near the *Emmerdale* studios, just outside Leeds. Before joining the cast, Ian made a film version of *Black Beauty*, alongside Sean Bean.

DAVE GLOVER

Like his father Ned, easy-going Dave Glover is not afraid to get his hands dirty. He settled quickly in Emmerdale and found friends in Luke McAllister and Biff Fowler. Dave gained employment as gamekeeper at the Home Farm estate but was baffled by stories about the 'Beast of Beckindale', created by Luke and Biff. This mythical tale was perpetuated by Seth Armstrong, who was anxious to reclaim his old job as Heritage Farm warden and set up a 'meeting' with the beast, which was no more than Samson the horse with an electronic rig-out

JAN GLOVER

The backbone of the Glover family, Jan has stood by them through thick and thin. She is willing to do any job to bring money into the household and found bar work at The Woolpack after moving to Emmerdale.

When husband Ned accepted a challenge to a bare-knuckle fight with Zak Dingle, Jan tried to persuade him that he was getting too old to contemplate such an event. What, she asked, would be the consequences to the Glover family if he lost or of the law if he won? Ned was all set to withdraw when daughter Linda revealed she had been sexually menaced by the Dingles at school. This made Ned determined to teach Zak Dingle a lesson for life, which he duly did.

Roberta Kerr already had experience of soaps when she joined *Emmerdale* in 1994. She played Sally Haynes, who lived with Harry Cross's son Kevin, in *Brookside*. The character had a strained relationship with Harry until Sally announced that she was expecting his first grandchild. She went into premature labour and the baby died at the hospital after a period in an incubator. The scenes provided some of Harry Cross's most moving moments in the serial.

Roberta later caused a storm in *Coronation Street* as Wendy Crozier, who had an affair with Ken Barlow, which resulted in the break-up of his third marriage, to Deirdre. She was the council secretary who leaked stories to Ken Barlow, editor of the *Weatherfield Recorder*. Married to actor Graeme Kirk, who plays Kenton Archer in the radio serial *The Archers*, Roberta has a son, Jack.

LINDA GLOVER

After doing well in her GCSEs, Linda Glover gave up all ideas of continuing her education when her family moved to Emmerdale and she sought work locally. Her love of animals helped her to land a job as vet Zoe Tate's assistant, although she accepted a pittance of a salary.

It was Linda's admission that she had been sexually menaced at school by the Dingles that made her father, Ned, determined to go through with the bare-knuckle fight to which Zak Dingle had challenged him. In 1995, Linda was shocked to find out that her new boyfriend, Danny, was the son of wealthy Lady Weir.

☆ ☆ ☆

Tonicha Jeronimo (b. Horsforth, West Yorkshire) danced as a child until she had a knee injury at the age of 13, so she switched to acting, joined the Scala Kids Agency and went to drama classes. She made her TV debut in *Emmerdale* in 1994, after taking her GCSEs.

NED GLOVER

Strong as an ox, former tenant farmer Ned Glover arrived in Emmerdale with his family and mobile home, which he had won in a fight. He found work at the farm, under Jack Sugden. Like other villagers, Ned hated the Dingles. A confrontation with Zak Dingle at The Woolpack led to a challenge to a bare-knuckle fight. Wife Jan tried to persuade him not to go through with it, but daughter Linda's revelation that she had been sexually menaced at school by the Dingles hardened his resolve and he turned up at what transpired to be a well publicized event. After a bloody battle with some heavy blows struck by both sides, the pair rolled down an embankment into a stream, where Ned finished the fight with the final blow. This action won Ned the gratitude of all of Emmerdale.

☆ ☆ ☆

Johnny Leeze (b. Yorkshire) is a former army sergeant who worked as a tank recovery mechanic and later became a club entertainer. As an actor, he appeared in *Coronation Street* as milkman Harry Clayton, whose family arrived in 1985 but stayed only six months, doing a moonlight flit after daughter Andrea had become pregnant by Terry Duckworth. His many other television appearances include roles in *Strike, Strangers, Open All Hours, Last of the Summer Wine, Juliet Bravo, All Creatures Great and Small, Stay Lucky, Chimera, Resnick, Heartbeat, Harry, Cracker, Seaforth* and *Common as Muck*. He also played a photographer in the film *Ladder of Swords*. Before joining *Emmerdale* as Ned Glover, Johnny made a number of appearances in the serial as an extra.

RACHEL HUGHES

The daughter of Kate Hughes, who married second husband Joe Sugden in 1989, Rachel Hughes was an awkward teenager who grew up to lure both Pete Whiteley and Chris Tate away from their wives.

Shortly after arriving in Emmerdale from Sheffield, Rachel showed her support for animal rights by running in front of the guns at a pheasant shoot in an attempt to stop it and released veal calves from their crates.

Then she caused a sensation by having an affair with Pete Whiteley, to whom she lost her virginity on her 18th birthday. Pete eventually ended the relationship and, when his pregnant wife Lynn found out, the couple moved to Birmingham.

Rachel then concentrated on her A levels and passing her driving test. She decided to take a year off studying, before going to university, and was offered the job of receptionist at Tate Haulage. On the first day of her new job, Rachel missed the bus and Pete Whiteley, returning to Emmerdale to be with her, was on hand to drive her to work. She resumed her relationship with Pete but, after an argument in The Woolpack, she stormed out with his car keys, preventing him from driving while drunk. Rachel's mother, Kate, slapped Pete across the face and told him to stay away from her daughter. After a few more drinks, Kate insisted on driving home with her friend Fran. Pete was walking along the road and she accidentally ran him over, accepting Fran's advice to speed back to Emmerdale Farm as if nothing had happened. Pete was dead, Kate admitted her involvement and was jailed for causing death by reckless driving. Rachel and brother Mark were looked after by Joe and his mother, Annie. Lynn's son, Peter Jr, was born on the day of his father's funeral.

Kate was guilt-ridden for killing her daughter's lover, but Rachel admitted she did not really love Pete. Rachel told Annie of her own guilt for taking Pete's car keys, but Annie insisted she must get on with her life.

She was then attracted to Michael Feldmann, a man more of her own age, but he did not seem interested, so Rachel resolved to start 1991 by revamping her image. She chose a new hairstyle, but Michael said he preferred her the way she was. However, the flames of romance started flickering when Rachel was sacked from her job at Tate Haulage after Frank Tate spotted her reading brochures during office hours. Michael commiserated and the two shared a cuddle.

Only a week later, Zoe prised Michael away from Rachel and spent a night with him. But the pair were soon back together and Michael even proposed marriage, which Rachel accepted but then realized it was the last thing on her mind – she was an ambitious young woman.

When Rachel went away to Leeds University, she and Michael grew apart and she eventually broke off the engagement, which he took badly. She then fell for medical student Jayesh Parmar, brother of Sangeeta, with whom she shared a house in Leeds. But, when Michael was jailed for aggravated burglary at Home Farm, Rachel stood by him, writing letters and visiting him.

When stepfather Joe Sugden started dating her bitter enemy, Lynn Whiteley, Rachel threw a gin-and-tonic over Lynn in The Woolpack, where Lynn worked behind the bar. Joe and Lynn's romance eventually cooled. Tragedy struck Rachel's family when, on 30 December 1993, brother Mark became one of the victims of the Emmerdale plane disaster.

The following year, she fell for another married man, Chris Tate, who was left paralyzed in the tragedy. His marriage to Kathy had been wavering and he found in Rachel someone who did not simply give him pity. On Bonfire Night

1994, Chris and Kathy's third wedding anniversary, Kathy saw her husband kissing Rachel at Frank Tate's party. The couple's affair scandalized the village when it became known that Rachel was pregnant with Chris's baby. Then, in March 1995, Chris proposed to Rachel. When, on 8 June, Rachel was told that Joe had died in a car crash, she went into premature labour and gave birth to a baby boy, whom she called Joseph as a memorial to her stepfather.

☆ ☆ ☆

Glenda McKay (b. Glenda Rose McKay in Leeds, 2 February 1971) was born in TV's 'Jimmy's', St James's Hospital, Leeds, daughter of a Scottish father and Hull-born mother. Her mother chose the name Glenda after reading an article about actress Glenda Jackson and her role in the film *Women in Love*.

By the time Glenda left school in 1989 with ten O levels and four A levels, including one in theatre studies, she had already played Pepper in the musical *Annie* at the Grand Theatre, Leeds, aged 12, and appeared in Ken Russell's film version of D. H. Lawrence's *The Rainbow*. Ironically, Glenda was cast in the role of Gudrun, whose grown-up character Glenda Jackson played in *Women in Love*, which Lawrence had written first. Glenda Jackson played her mother in this film.

Since joining *Emmerdale* at the end of 1988, Glenda has appeared on TV in *Stargazers*, in which she flew on the wing of a plane, and in a *Krypton Factor* special featuring soap stars. Up against *The Bill*'s Jon Iles, *Coronation Street*'s Philip Middlemiss and *Brookside*'s Annie Miles, she came third – but won the assault course, and the series' second-best women's time of 1990. Three years later, Glenda presented Yorkshire Television's *Parish Pump*, a type of *It's a Knockout!* for the county's villages.

Glenda, who is single and lives in Leeds, enjoys swimming, runs up to 24 km (15 miles) a week and works out regularly at the gym.

JESSICA McALLISTER

Bernard and Angharad McAllister arrived in the Dales from London in 1993, hoping that the move north would spell the end of 17-year-old daughter Jessica's relationship with boyfriend Danny, a tearaway they considered to be a bad influence on her. But she was immediately running up the phone bill by calling Danny every day, much to her parents' consternation. Eventually, she dumped idealistic Danny and their no-sex-before-marriage relationship for the more hunky appeal of leather-clad biker Biff

Coral Atkins found fame in ITV's popular series *A Family at War* in the seventies but gave up acting to start a children's home. She returned to TV in 1993, aged 56, playing divorcée RUTH JAMESON (née Simpson), an old flame of Frank Tate, who nearly married him. She had previously appeared in *Softly Softly* alongside Norman Bowler, who plays Frank.

James Aubrey (b. Klagenfurt, Austria, 28 August 1947) played REV. BILL JEFFRIES, a contrast to his role as Gavin Sorenson in *A Bouquet of Barbed Wire* and its sequel, *Another Bouquet*. His other TV appearances include *The Cleopatras*, *The Sweeney*, *Lovejoy*, *The Men's Room*, *Selling Hitler*, *Inspector Morse* and *Casualty*. He had starred in the film *Lord of the Flies* at the age of 16.

Veteran actor Bernard Archard (b. 1922) acted the elderly but shortlived character LEONARD KEMPINSKI, who married Annie Sugden in 1993, only to die in a car accident shortly afterwards during the village's dramatic plane crash. Bernard was star of the long-running series *Spycatcher* in the fifties and sixties.

Lesley Manville played teenager ROSEMARY KENDALL, who had a crush on Joe Sugden while staying at Emmerdale Farm for a while. She has gone on to appear in *Coronation Street* and such series as *Soldier Soldier* and the nannies drama *Tears Before Bedtime*, as well as the film *High Hopes*.

Brian Deacon (b. Oxford, 13 February 1949) was the HON. NEIL KINCAID, master of foxhounds and owner of a London stockbrokers, who had an affair with Kim Tate. Brian, brother of actor Eric Deacon, has appeared in such programmes as *Public Eye*, *Churchill's People*, *Bleak House* and *Mr Palfrey of Westminster*, as well as classical productions on stage and television.

Amanda Wenban (b. Sydney, Australia, 24 May 1955) took the part of teacher ANGHARAD McALLISTER after her role in *Families* as tart-with-a-heart Jackie Williams and appearances in Gold Blend coffee commercials. Amanda began her career as a dancer, training at the Royal Ballet School and performing with the London Festival Ballet for ten years.

Martin Dale (b. Bradford, West York-shire, 15 November 1930) played SGT. IAN MACARTHUR for 13 years. The actor began his working life in the police force and started entertaining as an ama-teur. He turned professional as a singer and compère in northern clubs, and branched out into acting on TV in *All for Love*, *Close to the Edge*, *United Kingdom* and *Edge of Darkness* (as a policeman). Martin died on 21 August 1994.

Kathleen Byron (b. London, 11 January 1923), who acted IRENE MADDEN in *Emmerdale*, has appeared in such TV series as *Emergency – Ward 10*, *The Avengers*, *The Professionals* and *General Hospital*, as well as the live daytime soap *Together*. She has also been in dozens of films, including *Tom Brown's Schooldays*.

Fred Feast (b. Scarborough, 5 October 1929) played cricketer MARTIN in *Emmerdale* before taking on the role of barman Fred Gee in *Coronation Street*.

Conrad Phillips (b. Conrad Philip Havord in London, 13 April 1925) took the role of N.Y. Estates manager CHRISTOPHER MEADOWS. He was best known in the title role of *William Tell*, appeared in more than 30 films and was on TV in *Howards' Way* and a late-eighties remake of *William Tell* called *Crossbow*, this time playing Tell's elderly mentor Stefan.

Ian Sharrock (b. Darley, North York-shire, 20 December 1959) was JACKIE MERRICK, illegitimate son of Jack Sugden and Pat Harker, teenage lovers who split up when Pat married Tom Merrick but were later reunited and mar-ried. Jackie wed Kathy Bates but tragical-ly died in 1989, when he accidentally shot himself. Ian appeared in the film *Candle-shoe* at the age of 12 and, later on TV in the title role of *Smike*, the controversial play *Scum* and *She-Wolf of London*.

Lynn Dalby, who was Adam Faith's long-suffering mistress in the hit series *Budgie*, continued playing floozies in such pro-grammes as *On the Buses*, *Return of The Saint* and *Emmerdale*, in which she took the part of RUTH MERRICK. Lynn, who moved to Australia in 1984 and remarried following her divorce from actor Ray Lonnen, also appeared in *Crossroads* as office secretary Rita Hughes.

Fowler, who had already slept with Jessica's friend Dolores. Jessica's parents were horrified.

When Bernard and Angharad decided to leave Emmerdale and their troubles behind, and move south, Jessica was devastated. She and Biff ran away and spent a night of passion together, dur-ing which the 17-year-old lost her virginity.

Jessica then gave in and left Emmerdale with her parents, but she soon returned and was shocked to find Luke and Tina Dingle together. Tina tried to get rid of her for good by pairing off Biff with her friend Sadie so that Jessica would discover them and leave. But Jessica stayed and took it upon herself to organize household management and delegate chores.

☆ ☆ ☆

Camilla Power (b. 13 November 1976) trained at the Sylvia Young Theatre School and appeared with screen brother Noah Huntley in the children's TV serial *Moonacre*, as Maria Merryweather, the reincarnation of the Moon Princess, returning to resolve the animosity between two families that has lasted for genera-tions and bring happiness to Moonacre Valley.

Before joining *Emmerdale* in 1993, she was also on TV in *Over the Rainbow*, *Physics for Fish*, *Soft Soap*, *Not the End of the World*, *The Mystery of the Keys*, *Bonjour la Classe*, *The Chronicles of Narnia* and *The Silver Chair*. She was in the film *A Summer Story*, as well as the radio production *History – Lost and Found*. Camilla's hobbies include horse-riding.

LUKE McALLISTER

Motorbike-mad Luke McAllister arrived in Emmerdale in December 1993, when his doctor father Bernard and teacher mother Angharad uprooted themselves from London to start a new life in Yorkshire. His father was returning to work as a G.P. after becoming disillusioned with cutbacks at a hospital where his chances of becoming a consultant were bleak. He filled a gap in the Emmerdale community after the vil-lage's many years without a G.P. Luke's mother became headmistress of the local school.

Luke soon found a soulmate in fellow biker Biff Fowler, who slept with Dolores Sharp, a school-friend of Luke's sister, Jessica. When Biff switched his affections to Jessica, Luke took up with Dolores. That romance turned sour when she caught him kissing Linda Glover – but she ditched him, too.

Trouble was in store for Luke during the sum-mer of 1994, when he and his friends organized a rave party in a field owned by Betty Eagleton. Ben Dingle, his rough family and friends started

causing trouble. Luke confronted him, a scuffle broke out and Ben fell to the ground. Luke was arrested and charged with actual bodily harm. When Ben died in hospital, it looked likely that this would be changed to a manslaughter or even murder charge. Eventually, it was proved that Ben's death had been caused by a rare condition and Luke walked free.

The Dingle family swore to take revenge. Intimidation and threats followed, until the Dingles confronted Luke outside the local school. Biff Fowler, Dave and Roy Glover, and Scott Windsor were all involved in the fight that followed. This led to the decision by Luke's parents to leave the village, although another factor was Kathy Tate's obsession with Bernard, following her break-up with husband Chris.

Luke refused to leave Emmerdale and stayed on in his parents' house. This gave him the opportunity to bed Tina Dingle, to whom he had been attracted since their first meeting. The feud between the two families had prevented the pair from taking things further, but the departure of Luke's parents cleared the way. In April 1995, Tina announced she was pregnant and she subsequently accepted Luke's marriage proposal.

Noah Huntley (b. Noah Cornelius Marmaduke Huntley on 7 September 1974) is one of eight children – he has six sisters and one brother – who grew up on a large farm in the Sussex countryside. His greatest hobby used to be off-road biking, which made him ideal for the part of Luke, but an accident in which he ruptured his pancreas forced him to give it up.

Before joining *Emmerdale*, Noah starred with Camilla Power – who plays his sister in the soap – in the children's TV serial *Moonacre*, an

Jane Hutcheson (b. Stockport, Cheshire) played SANDIE MERRICK, the Hotten Market auctioneer who had an illegitimate baby, Louise, whom she gave up for adoption but later took back. Jane had a small part in *Coronation Street* and played another character in *Emmerdale* before taking the role of Sandie. She has since appeared as a lawyer in *The Bill*.

Jack Carr was the third actor to play TOM MERRICK, Pat Sugden's former husband, appearing in *Emmerdale* at around the the same time that he had a brief spell in *Coronation Street* as policeman Tony Cunliffe, who lodged with Betty Turpin and took a fancy to Rita Fairclough. He has also been in *Truckers*, *Chancer*, *The Chief*, *Medics* and *The Bill*.

Jenny Hanley (b. Gerrard's Cross, Buckinghamshire, 15 August 1947), daughter of actor Jimmy Hanley and actress Dinah Sheridan, was BRIDDY MIDDLETON, who ran some stables. She had previously played the wife of Harry Hawkins (*Emmerdale* actor Norman Bowler) in *Softly Softly* for five years and went on to present the children's magazine programme *Magpie*.

Paul Jerricho (b. 18 November 1948) has plenty of experience in soaps. He played Matt Taylor in *Triangle*, DANNY MOORCOCK in *Emmerdale* and later appeared as Robert Hastings in *Howards' Way*. He was also in the films *Force 10 from Navarone*, *The Empire Strikes Back*, *The Thirty-Nine Steps* and *Cry Freedom*.

Annie Hulley, who acted auctioneer's assistant KAREN MOORE, who had an affair with Joe Sugden, later appeared in the short-lived serial *Eldorado* as Joanne Gallego, a character looking for her daughter, who had been abducted by the child's father.

Toke Townley (b. Margaret Roding, Essex, 6 November 1912) was SAM PEARSON, father of Annie Sugden and chairman of the village cricket team, from the first episode until the actor's sudden death from a heart attack on 27 September 1984, after more than 800 appearances. Toke was a factory clerk until turning professional at the age of 32. He had appeared in almost 30 films, usually playing country bumpkins.

adaptation of Elizabeth Goudge's novel *The Little White Horse*, playing Robin, the swashbuckling shepherd who lives in a cave in the forest and saves the Princess of Moonacre. Luke also made a commercial for Flora, which was being screened at the time he joined the soap. He sees his *Emmerdale* character as 'a cool dude, but a bit naïve at times'.

ERIC POLLARD

Dodgy dealer Eric Pollard has been objectionable to the locals ever since he was brought in to revitalize Hotten Market in 1986. He lost his job as head of the auctioneering business the following year, when he was suspected of fiddling the books and arranging private deals on the antiques' sales. Joe Sugden, regional manager of N.Y. Estates – responsible for the market – noticed discrepancies in the accounts. As a result, Pollard mounted a hate campaign against new head auctioneer Sandie Merrick – who had been his assistant – and drunkenly threatened her with a poker in her home at the old mill.

He then set up as a private antiques dealer but returned to his old job in May 1989, when Hotten Council bought the market from N.Y. Estates. He achieved this by pulling strings on the council and remained in debt to markets committee chairman Charlie Aindow.

One of Pollard's many scams was to steal antique fireplaces from Home Farm with builder Phil Pearce, but he performed one of his greatest dodges by leaving Phil to take the blame and go to jail. He also teamed up with city-slicker Denis Rigg, who was just as devious, but Denis was later killed by a bull.

The tables were turned on Pollard in 1990, when he fell for young Debbie Wilson, who gained his trust and became engaged to him. As market manager, he was not allowed to have his own business, so he gave Debbie £2000 to open an antiques shop, only to see her run off with the money, which he had borrowed from Charlie Aindow. He then vied with Aindow for Dolly Skilbeck's affections. Aindow had arrived in Emmerdale to ask Pollard to pay back the £2000 he had lent him. In a desperate effort to get the cash, Pollard fiddled the market takings. Dolly was never interested in him, but he interfered in her relationship with Aindow by telling her that the councillor was married.

Pollard married Elizabeth Feldmann in October 1992, although she was unaware that he was still married to his first wife, Eileen. Elizabeth appeared to tame Pollard, persuading him to give back some of the money he took from naïve Mark Hughes in return for his Triumph Spitfire sports car. He had sold it to Mark for an excessive £900, but it needed a lot of work to make it roadworthy. Again, Elizabeth persuaded him to make amends after he gave Seth Armstrong just £20 for £500 worth of old bank notes in 1993.

Elizabeth was not so honest when she came across a muddy bracelet at the fish farm. It was Roman and worth a fortune, but she thought it must legally belong to Frank Tate, on whose land it lay. However, because it gave her the chance to pay off debts and set up a trust fund for granddaughter Alice, Elizabeth let Pollard sell it for £15,000.

After a burglary at Home Farm, Pollard paid the price for his apparent good deed in helping to convict Steve Marshal and stepson Michael Feldmann. On his release from jail, Steve tampered with the brakes of Pollard's car, which crashed on a bend, careered off the road and went up in flames. Fortunately for Pollard, Nick Bates was on hand to pull him from the inferno.

But he was up to his old tricks again when he stole cheques from the Home Farm cheque book, for which Elizabeth was responsible in her work for Frank Tate. When Elizabeth found out, on Christmas Eve 1993, she threw him out of the cottage in full view of a group of carol singers performing outside The Woolpack opposite. A week later, on the night of the Emmerdale plane disaster, Elizabeth was dead.

Then, Eric's first wife, Eileen – known as Pollock – arrived in the village. Because he had failed to divorce her before marrying Elizabeth, she blackmailed him into giving her a share of the insurance money. Ready to cash in on the tragic events, Pollard sold an oil painting donated to the air crash disaster fund for £175,000 and sanctimoniously presented the fund with only £1500. Frank Tate discovered the fraud on reading an article in *The Times*.

Fuelled by his stepfather's insistence that Elizabeth's body be cremated and not buried, her son, Michael – who never got on with him – believed he might have used the disaster as a cover for murdering his mother, but Michael's allegations were never substantiated.

During a row with Michael at the cottage, Pollard was knocked to the floor, unconscious. Not knowing whether he was dead or alive, Michael fled in Pollard's car, which was later found at the airport. Pollard, who was very much alive, was relieved at the thought that this thorn in his side might now be out of the country.

Turning to another money-making venture, he colluded with Councillor Hawkins to investigate the possibility of setting up an open prison on widow Betty Eagleton's land. The whole village, led by Frank Tate, opposed the idea. But, in an attempt to get Betty to sell the land, Pollard persuaded her to let it out for a rave party, which he said would make her a huge profit. But he was determined that it would be a total failure and force her to sell the land. The event was a disaster. Local yob Ben Dingle died after provoking a fight with Luke McAllister, and Betty was left with debts of £19,000, but she still refused to sell the land.

Pollard then planned a robbery at stately Briardale Hall, which housed valuable artefacts. He executed the robbery to perfection, getting away with £500,000 in stolen goods and securing an alibi by arranging a dinner date with Alan Turner and spiking his drink with a drug that sent him to sleep.

Pollard began romancing Caroline Bates, but she ditched him in disgust when she found that he had been cooking The Woolpack's books after offering to help Alan Turner to sort out his financial problems. With Alan drinking heavily, Pollard had persuaded him to sign over the pub to him. Frank Tate joined in the character assassination by arranging to have Pollard's car crushed in front of the pub's customers.

☆ ☆ ☆

Christopher Chittell (b. Christopher John Chittell in Aldershot, Hampshire, 19 May 1948) began his career with the National Theatre in 1963, playing – in his own words – 'choirboys, candleholders and acolytes'.

His first film was *To Sir with Love*, as a toerag called Potter, and he subsequently featured in *The Charge of the Light Brigade*, *Golden Rendezvous* and *Zulu Dawn*. He has appeared on television in the children's series *Free-*

Kathy Staff (b. Dukinfield, Cheshire, 12 July 1928), who played WINNIE PURVIS in *Emmerdale*, acted customers in *Coronation Street* shops for years before landing the part of shopkeeper Vera Hopkins in the serial. She then took on the role of Nora Batty in *Last of the Summer Wine*, in addition to playing Miss Dingwall and Doris Luke in *Crossroads*.

James Whale provided the voice of the RADIO ANNOUNCER who brought the news of the death of Stephen Fuller, Dolly Skilbeck's ex-boyfriend. The radio disc jockey is now best known for his night-time ITV shows, including *Whale On*.

Alan David, who was a regular in the sit-coms *The Squirrels* and *Foxy Lady*, played DICK ROBERTSHAW in *Emmerdale* and was later in *Making Out*.

Victor Winding (b. London, 30 January 1929), who played TAD RYLAND, also acted garage owner Victor Lee in *Crossroads* and had previously portrayed Det. Chief Insp. Fleming in *The Expert*.

Liz Smith, who played HILDA SEMPLE, is the veteran of many films and TV programmes, cornering the market in 'old bags'. On television, she played Patricia Hodge's geriatric mother in *The Life and Loves of a She-Devil* and Les Dawson's daughter in *Nona*. Her films include *The Pink Panther*, *The French Lieutenant's Woman* and *A Private Function*.

Louise Jameson (b. Wanstead, East London, 20 April 1951) had already appeared on television in such series as *Cider with Rosie*, *Z-Cars*, *The Omega Factor* and *Boy Dominic* when she joined *Emmerdale* as SHARON. Later, she found fame as Blanche Simmons in *Tenko*, Jim Bergerac's girlfriend, Susan, in *Bergerac* and teacher-turned-cabbie Janet in *Rides*.

Bernard Kay (b. Bolton, Lancashire, 23 February 1938) played ROBERT SHARP, father of Joe Sugden's first wife, Christine. He later appeared in *Crossroads* as garage boss Harry Maguire, before returning to *Emmerdale* as an elderly recluse called METCALFE, who left his neighbouring farm to Matt Skilbeck, a reward for Matt's help. Bernard also acted a character called Cyril in *Coronation Street*.

EMMERDALE

Andy Rashleigh (b. East London, 23 January 1949) played P.C. Woodhouse in *Coronation Street* for eight episodes, a trades union officer in *The Practice*, Colin Arnold in *Albion Market*, a policeman in *Gems* and Chef in *Crossroads*, before local farmer TED SHARP in *Emmerdale*, who kidnapped Dolly Skilbeck in 1989. He was later D.S. Pryde in *EastEnders* and Eliot Creasy in *Jupiter Moon*, and has written episodes of *Crossroads* and *The Archers*.

Jean Rogers (b. Perivale, Middlesex, 2 February 1942) took over as DOLLY SKILBECK (née Acaster) from Katherine Barker in 1980. She was known on TV as Nurse Rogers in *Emergency – Ward 10* and Julie Shepherd, Meg Richardson's personal secretary, in *Crossroads*. Dolly split up with husband Matt, later became pregnant by councillor Charlie Aindow, had an abortion and left in 1992.

Frederick Pyne (b. London, 30 December 1936), who acted MATT SKILBECK from 1972 until 1989, started his working life as a farmer in Cheshire and Cambridgeshire. He also appeared in *Crossroads* and, since leaving *Emmerdale*, has worked exclusively in the theatre.

Peter Ellis (b. Bristol, 30 May 1936) played a character called STAN, before finding greater fame as Chief Supt. Brownlow in *The Bill*. He has also appeared in the films *An American Werewolf in London*, *Agatha* and *Remembrance*.

Tim Healy (b. Newcastle upon Tyne, 29 January 1952) made one of his earliest TV appearances in *Coronation Street*, and followed it with parts in *Emmerdale*, as a character called STEVEN, *When the Boat Comes In*, *Crown Court* and *Minder*. Fame came in the role of foreman Dennis in *Auf Wiedersehen Pet*. Since then, he has been on TV in *A Perfect Spy*, *Casualty*, *Boon*, *A Kind of Living*, *Boys from the Bush* and the TV movie *Flea Bites*.

Andrew Burt (b. Wakefield, West Yorkshire, 25 May 1945) was the first actor to play JACK SUGDEN. He left the serial in 1974 and has since appeared in *Dixon of Dock Green*, *Crown Court*, *Blake's 7*, *Juliet Bravo*, *Doctor Who*, *The Gentle Touch*, *London's Burning*, *The Bill*, *EastEnders* and *Agatha Christie's Poirot*.

wheelers, *The Tomorrow People* and *Tucker's Luck*. Outside acting, his experience includes helping to run a restaurant, dealing in antiques and diving for treasure, although he laments that he never recovered anything of value.

Christopher, who enjoys skin-diving, cricket and watching rugby, met wife Caroline Hunt, from Leicestershire, while he was working in South Africa during the seventies. They married in 1979, have two children, Benjamin and Rebecca, and live in Nottinghamshire.

ANNIE SUGDEN

The calming influence on her family and all those in Emmerdale who seek her advice, Annie Sugden was first seen coping with a rundown farm and battling sons Jack and Joe after the death, in 1972, of her husband Jacob, who had drunk away the farm's profits in The Woolpack. She also had a daughter Peggy, who had just married farmhand Matt Skilbeck.

Daughter of Sam Pearson, whose family had farmed at Emmerdale for more than 1000 years, Annie was of tough Yorkshire stock and set about making Emmerdale Farm pay, keeping the peace between her sons and offering her daughter motherly advice. She had been making important decisions about the running of the farm before Jacob's death and soon proved that she could make it a success. Annie, Jack, Joe and Matt set up a new, limited company, with Henry Wilks joining the board.

Tragedy has never been far from Annie and her family. It struck with Peggy's sudden death from a brain haemorrhage in May 1973, three months after giving birth to twins Sam and

Sally. Later in the year, the twins were killed in an accident on a level crossing.

In 1986, son Jack's wife Pat died in a car accident, and Joe – who had already experienced the heartbreak of divorce – saw his second wife, Kate, go to jail after killing Pete Whiteley in a hit-and-run accident. The last incident was typical of the way Annie approached such problems. Returning from a holiday in Scotland, she took the news of Kate's arrest in her stride, saying everyone must rally round as a family.

Annie was not immune to drama herself. In 1988, Matt and Dolly Skilbeck hired Phil Pearce to renovate Crossgill, the farmhouse left to them by an elderly recluse called Metcalfe. Phil carelessly left rags to burn indoors and the building was razed to the ground with Annie inside. Fortunately, Phil rushed through thick smoke to rescue her. A year later, Annie needed friendly advice when her reliance on tranquillizers turned to addiction. Henry Wilks advised her to flush them down the toilet.

Another series of dramatic events for Annie and her family began with the news, in 1993, that Emmerdale Farm was suffering subsidence as a result of the old lead-mine working. Forced to leave their home of three generations, they bought Hawthorn Cottage.

Annie, feeling that son Jack and his girlfriend (now wife) Sarah were not consulting her, refused to move into Hawthorn Cottage and temporarily took up residence with Kathy and Chris Tate at Mill Cottage. Only after Annie's old friend Amos Brearly's suggestion that the house be renamed Emmerdale did Annie agree to move in.

On a holiday at Amos Brearly's villa in Spain, Annie met his wealthy friend, tax exile Leonard Kempinski. Their announcement of marriage came as a shock to Jack and Joe, but the wedding went ahead on 28 October 1993 – with the Rev. Donald Hinton stepping in to conduct the ceremony – and Annie looked forward to a second marriage that she hoped would be happier than her first. But less than two months later, as Joe drove Annie and Leonard off to the airport to whisk them away to another holiday in the Spanish sun, the car careered off the road as a result of the horrific plane crash over Emmerdale. Leonard was found lying dead next to Annie, who went into a coma – existing on a life-support machine – and only regained consciousness after Jack and Sarah brought their newborn baby, Victoria, to the hospital.

Sheila Mercier (b. Sheila Betty Rix in Hull, East Yorkshire, 1 January 1919), the sister of Whitehall farceur Brian (now Lord) Rix, trained as an actress at the Stratford-upon-Avon College of Drama under Randle Ayrton, widely considered the greatest Lear of his generation. She was spotted by the great actor-manager Sir Donald Wolfit, who picked her to tour in his Shakespeare Company shortly after war broke out in 1939.

During the war, she worked with RAF Fighter Command in the WAAF, rising to the rank of adjutant. When peace came, Sheila made her television debut as Mrs Moss in *Exercise Bowler*, on the BBC in 1946, then returned to repertory theatre and was soon working for her brother, by this time an actor-manager.

After seasons in Hull, Warrington, Bexhill, Tonbridge, Ilkley, Margate, Huddersfield and Bridlington, she acted in his famous Whitehall farces, including *Chase Me, Comrade!* and *Uproar in the House*, from 1955 to 1969. She also appeared in one-off television productions with the Whitehall Theatre company, as well as two series, *Dial Rix* (1962) and *Six of Rix* (1972), and two films, *The Night We Dropped a Clanger* and *The Night We Got the Bird*.

Sheila joined *Emmerdale* when it began as *Emmerdale Farm* in 1972, playing the pivotal character, Annie Sugden. Although in recent years she has cut down on her appearances in the programme – she works in the studio one week a month and takes a three-month winter break – Annie remains the matriarchal figure in the village. When the programme celebrated its 1000th episode, in 1985, she was a 'victim' of Eamonn Andrews on *This Is Your Life*.

Her husband, former actor Peter Mercier, whom she met while working in repertory theatre, died in 1993, after 42 years of marriage. Their son, Nigel David, is a TV sound engineer and video editor at LWT. In her 1994 autobiography *Annie's Song: My Life & Emmerdale*, Sheila revealed that she also has a daughter, Monica Janet, whom her parents forced to give away for adoption after she suffered the ordeal of rape on the night before her 21st birthday. The actress lives in Hawkhurst, Kent.

JACK SUGDEN

Elder son of Annie, Jack Sugden left Emmerdale Farm after constantly rowing with his father, Jacob, about intensive farming. He did not believe in it and left for London with thoughts of becoming a writer. When his father died, Jack returned to claim his inheritance. He helped to turn the farm into a success but had a stormy relationship with younger brother Joe, who had stayed and worked on the farm through thick and thin and was now seeing his elder

brother return to run it. But Jack's literary ambitions never disappeared. He found success as a novelist with his book *Field of Tares* and moved to Rome to work on a film script of the story. He returned to Emmerdale in 1980.

Two years later, Jack married divorcée Pat Merrick, the childhood sweetheart he had jilted when they were teenagers. He had then headed for London and she married Tom Merrick and left Emmerdale. But Pat and Tom split up after several years, she returned to the village on a holiday with her aunt and fell for Jack again. She had two children, Sandie and Jackie, who was revealed to be Jack's son from the couple's earlier relationship, although he had not known she was pregnant when they parted.

After their marriage, Pat gave birth to another son, Robert, in 1986. But, during her pregnancy, romeo Jack had an affair with auctioneer Karen Moore. He stayed with Pat after she gave him an ultimatum, but tragedy struck when she was killed in a car accident five months after Robert's birth. Swerving to avoid a flock of sheep, her car left the road and she died.

When Emmerdale was considered as the site for a nuclear waste dump in 1987, Jack found a focus for his anger. He fought the proposal with a one-man campaign and even spent seven days in jail for contempt of court, but the battle was won and the village was spared the site.

Old flame Marian Wilks – daughter of Henry – who was now married to an Italian, Paolo Rossetti, and had a baby son, Niccolo, came to Britain with her family for a holiday and Jack had a brief fling with her. But she soon returned to Italy. A rover himself, Jack left Emmerdale again, only to return and find love with Sarah Connolly, who worked in the mobile library.

Their relationship developed and she moved in with him.

When Marian's husband, Paolo, was found dead in Italy and she was suspected of causing his death, Jack flew to see her. Sarah believed he still held a torch for Marian and thought her relationship with Jack was over, but he returned and told Sarah that his future was only with her.

In 1993, Jack and Sarah were forced to move out of the farmhouse because of subsidence. They bought Hawthorn Cottage from Bob Thornby and amalgamated the dairy herd with that of Geoff Thomas at a nearby farm.

On 30 December that year, when Emmerdale was the scene of a plane disaster, Jack was one of the heroes who helped in the rescue operation. Under Frank Tate's direction, he used his tractor, and pipes left by a construction company installing new drainage, to replace the destroyed bridge over the village's stream, allowing the emergency services through. The disaster left Jack's mother in a coma, her new husband, Leonard Kempinski dead and Joe's stepson, Mark Hughes, also dead, as well as fields laid to waste from the chemicals and spillages, and the livestock decimated.

Sarah negotiated a loan from Frank Tate to set up a farm shop and Jack agreed to manage the model farm that Frank was opening at Home Farm.

Jack had proposed to Sarah every year since their relationship began, but she always refused. After the birth of their daughter, Victoria Anne, the couple finally tied the knot on 19 May 1994. It was a shock when Victoria was diagnosed as having a hole in the heart and even more devastating when Sarah admitted to having an affair. Although she left Emmerdale, Jack persuaded her to return and they picked up the pieces.

But more family troubles were just around the corner when son Robert disappeared in March 1995. Police searched for the missing boy to no avail. He had, in fact, willingly gone off with nearby hermit Derek Simpson and enjoyed spending time with him in the hills. Simpson eventually persuaded Robert to return home.

Clive Hornby (b. Liverpool, 20 October 1944) trained as an accountant and worked as an accounts clerk for six months, before playing drums for The Dennisons pop group, who appeared in stage shows on the same bill as The Beatles in the sixties.

Deciding on acting as a career, Clive worked backstage at the Liverpool Playhouse, then trained at LAMDA in London. He worked in repertory theatre in Greenwich, Guildford, Northampton, Dundee, Salisbury and Newbury.

His stage plays include *Candida, Oh! What a Lovely War, The Threepenny Opera, Macbeth, The Homecoming, How the Other Half Loves, An Inspector Calls, Present Laughter, The Recruiting Officer, After the Fall, The Glass Menagerie, See How They Run, Kennedy's Children, The Bed Before Yesterday, The Philanthropist* and the West End production of Agatha Christie's *Murder at the Vicarage*.

Clive appeared in the films *No Longer Alone* and *Yanks*, narrated the radio series *The War Behind the Wire* and acted on television in *Get Some In, Space 1999, Life at Stake* and *Minder*, before taking over the role of Jack Sugden from Andrew Burt in *Emmerdale*, in 1980.

Four years later, divorcé Clive married his screen wife Helen Weir, who has a son, Daniel, from her first marriage. The couple had another son, Thomas, in 1986 and Helen subsequently left the serial. They live on Ilkley Moor, just 20 minutes' drive from the *Emmerdale* studios.

SARAH SUGDEN

Arriving in Emmerdale as a librarian in the mobile library, Sarah Connolly was soon dating widower Jack Sugden and moved in with him – but immediately sealed off the connecting door between the farm cottage they shared and the house's main accommodation, where his mother Annie ruled the roost.

Sarah also took on the role of mother to Jack's son, Robert. When she learned that her library job was being axed, Sarah was left with a dilemma. She was determined to lead an independent life, despite living with Jack, and did not want to become involved in farm work.

So she took a job behind the bar at The Woolpack but eventually came round to working on the farm. She saw the day-to-day running of Emmerdale as a challenge and proved she could work as hard as any man. But the work was difficult and Kate Sugden once found Sarah in tears behind the combine harvester. Kate suggested she slowed down and told her it was not possible to become a farmer overnight. Sarah found it hard to heed this advice, and Jack asked Annie to talk to her. Sarah admitted she loved farming and was anxious to prove herself.

When Sarah's skiing chum Gerry asked her to join him and a group of friends on a holiday to Portugal, Jack was annoyed but told her to do as she wished, refusing to discuss the matter. She later had an argument with Jack in The Woolpack. She had never intended to take up the holiday offer but was hurt that Jack had jumped to the conclusion that she would,

because she was totally committed to their relationship and to Robert. When Jack flew to Italy to see his former girlfriend Marian Wilks – daughter of Henry – who was being held by police there following the death of her husband Paolo, she refused to believe he was going just to help an old friend and thought he must still love Marian. But, on his return, Sarah realized that she was the only woman for Jack.

In November 1991, high drama visited Sarah when she was kidnapped by released murderer Jim Latimer, who had a grudge against Jack that dated back to his trial. He held Sarah in a disused building, but she remained cool and was

Frazer Hines (b.. Horsforth, West Yorkshire, 22 September 1944) was twice-married JOE SUGDEN from the serial's first episode until 1994. Frazer started acting as a child, appeared in the film *King in New York* with Charlie Chaplin and, on TV, acted Jan in *The Silver Sword* and Jamie in *Doctor Who*, as well as Roger Wade, a boyfriend of Lucille Hewitt, in *Coronation Street* in 1965.

Sally Knyvette, best known as Jenna in *Blake's 7*, acted KATE SUGDEN (formerly Hughes), Joe's second wife. She was in the serial for two years, from 1988, and later appeared in *The Bill*.

Helen Weir played PAT SUGDEN (formerly Merrick), Jack's first wife and mother of Robert. As a child, Helen – who is married to Clive Hornby, who played her *Emmerdale* screen husband, Jack – had appeared in an episode of the magazine soap *Compact*. She has since played a hospital matron in *Heartbeat*.

Madeleine Howard (b. London, 15 March 1951) was the first actress to play SARAH SUGDEN (née Connolly), from 1988 to 1994. She made her TV debut as model Tricia Pope in the fashion-house serial *Gems* and appeared in *Howards' Way*.

Sara Griffiths (b. Sheffield, South Yorkshire) was Nick Bates's one-time girlfriend CLARE SUTCLIFFE, who ran off with money he pocketed from a robbery at the village post office. Sara's other TV appearances include *Doctor Who, Gentlemen and Players* (as Liz), *Sisters, The Chief, Van Der Valk, Rich Tea & Sympathy, The Ruth Rendell Mysteries* and the BBC serial *Castles* (as Anita Castle).

eventually released unhurt. She not only looked like Latimer's earlier victim, Sharon Crossthwaite, but shared the same initials.

Moving into Hawthorn Cottage after the farmhouse at Emmerdale started to subside meant accepting a new home that was crying out for work to be done on it. She had a pleasant surprise when she returned from a shopping trip to Harrogate with Annie to find that Jack and Joe had completely refitted the kitchen.

When Jack and Sarah's daughter, Victoria Anne, was born in 1994, Jack's mother Annie was lying in a coma after being injured as a passenger in Joe's car as a result of the plane disaster over Emmerdale. Sarah and Jack's trip to the hospital with Victoria helped Annie to regain consciousness. Sarah and Jack wed shortly afterwards, on 19 May, with Annie out of hospital and among the wedding guests.

Tragedy struck when Victoria was rushed back to hospital and diagnosed as having a hole in the heart. The baby survived, but Sarah was away from the farm for a while as she stayed with Victoria in hospital. On her return, Sarah received a succession of phone calls from a man. When Jack confronted her, she admitted to having had an affair with someone she had met at the hospital library. Sarah left Emmerdale with baby Victoria, although her dramatic walk-out was really aimed at triggering a response, rather than ending her marriage. She got the response when Jack met her on neutral ground in York – Sarah even persuaded Jack to dispense with his grubby boiler suit and kitted out a guy in it at Frank Tate's Bonfire Night party.

Sarah and Jack's worst moment occurred when Jack suspected his wife was having an affair with her boss when she started working for a university professor who was writing a book. He followed her, left Robert alone in the car and returned to find him missing. Robert had willingly gone off with a hermit called Derek Simpson and was, in fact, under under no threat. But, as far as Sarah and Jack were concerned, he had been abducted. Then, the couple received phone calls demanding £5000 if they wanted to see him alive again. But the police traced the calls and found that the demands were being made by Sam Dingle, who did not have Robert but saw the Sugdens' misfortune as a way of making money. As the police search intensified, Simpson persuaded Robert to return to his parents.

☆ ☆ ☆

Alyson Spiro took over the role of Sarah Sugden when actress Madeleine Howard decided to leave in the summer of 1994. Alyson had previously acted in *Brookside*, making her debut in the Channel Four soap in June 1989 as a single-parent scientist, Alison Gregory, with a daughter called Hattie.

The character became Dr Michael Choi's girlfriend and moved in with him four months later, but left the Close in April 1990 when Michael accepted a post in America.

Alyson has since taken two roles in *The Bill* and appeared in *The Enigma Files*, *King's Royal*, *Fell Tiger*, *Sam Saturday*, *Casualty* and *Prime Suspect 3*, as well as the films *She'll Be Wearing Pink Pyjamas*, *The Amnesty Files*, *Northern Crescent* and *The Birth of The Beatles*, as Astrid, Stuart Sutcliffe's girlfriend.

On stage, she gained experience of the classics with the Oxford Stage Company and the Young Vic, taking roles in *King Lear*, *Romeo and Juliet* and *The Merchant of Venice*. Alyson also worked with the New Shakespeare Company at the Open Air Theatre, Regent's Park.

Alyson lives in London, is married and has three daughters, Ella and twins Cara and Georgia, who were born in 1994 shortly before Alyson joined *Emmerdale*.

CHRIS TATE

Son of Frank and then managing director of his haulage firm, Chris Tate arrived in Emmerdale when his father bought Home Farm. He soon developed a relationship with Kathy Merrick – still getting over the death of her husband Jackie – and moved in with her. Chris booked a surprise Seychelles holiday for himself and Kathy to take her mind off the first anniversary of Jackie's death. But, as time went by, Kathy began to feel that Chris was taking her for granted, as well as being selfish and immature.

When his father was planning to have an operation to reverse his vasectomy, Chris confronted him to ask whether he was really planning to have children with Kim. This irritated Frank, who believed it was a private matter between him and Kim. Kathy warned Chris that he risked splitting up the family if he did not accept the idea that his father and stepmother wanted to start a new family, but this did not stop Chris blaming Kim when Frank, anxious about his forthcoming operation, hit the bottle.

More happily, Chris wrote a song, 'Just This Side of Love', for Kathy to sing at a village concert in November 1990. He secretly recorded the performance and made it into a single, which Kathy first heard – to her surprise – on the Woolpack jukebox. Chris also gave her a surprise present, spraying one of the records gold, framing it and hanging it on their wall. Chris and Kathy married exactly a year later, on 5 November 1991.

But Chris's irresponsible nature resurfaced when he lost his motorcycle to Alan Turner in a poker game. Kathy was furious, but her anger subsided when she realized it was a result of his father's decision to take part in the day-to-day running of his haulage company again. Kathy confronted Frank, insisting that he left the running of the company to Chris, and Frank tried to persuade Alan Turner to hand back the motorcycle, but he would only do so for £4000. Frank handed over the money, but Chris resented his father's interference. Kathy did a lot to change Chris's 'Hooray Henry' manner and make him more thoughtful, but the marriage proved stormy and the couple began to drift apart.

After his father split up with his stepmother, following her affair with the Hon. Neil Kincaid, and began to hit the bottle, Chris found himself in effective control of Tate Haulage. Unknown to Kathy, he tried to gain control of the company by buying Kim's shares – mortgaging his home, Mill Cottage, to do so.

But Chris ended up walking out on his father's haulage company when Frank succeeded in getting his daughter Zoe's backing so that Chris could not out-vote him in shares. Leaving the power struggle at Tate Haulage, Chris had an unsuccessful spell as manager of his father's holiday village, before borrowing enough money from Frank to start his own haulage business with just one truck.

Tragedy befell Chris when he was paralyzed in the 1993 air disaster after being dug out of rubble at The Woolpack. Wife Kathy had already withdrawn all conjugal rights after finding out that Chris had mortgaged their cottage. The tragedy happened on the night that Kathy was planning to leave Chris for smoothie American Josh Lewis. Consumed with guilt, she stayed with Chris, who was confined to a wheelchair.

With the aid of a computer, Chris was able to look after the business side of sister Zoe's veterinary practice and resisted help from Frank and the sympathy of Kathy, which was all she could offer him. He found a more understanding lover in Rachel Hughes, stepdaughter of Joe Sugden. She managed to get Chris out of his wheelchair and into the swimming pool. The couple had an affair and scandalized the village when Rachel became pregnant with baby son Joseph, born on 8 June 1995.

☆ ☆ ☆

Peter Amory (b. 2 November 1962) trained at RADA, where he won the Tree Prize, then played the title role in *Fool* on a three-month tour of Norfolk and Suffolk sponsored by Norfolk County Council.

He set up his own company, One Off Productions, with Ken Campbell and performed *Psychosis Unclassified*. Peter has also appeared on stage in *Wait Until Dark* at The Mill, Sonning, and *Busman's Honeymoon* at the Lyric Theatre, Hammersmith.

On television, he has appeared in *Boon*, two series of *Running Wild*, *Casualty*, *Chelworth*, *Inheritance*, *Inspector Morse*, *Gentlemen and Players* and *The Chief*. Peter joined *Emmerdale* in 1989 and, five years later, married his screen stepmother, actress Claire King. The couple live in Harrogate, North Yorkshire. Peter has a son, Thomas, from a previous relationship, with long-term girlfriend Sarah.

FRANK TATE

Since buying Home Farm and its 1000 acres, self-made millionaire Frank Tate has become 'lord of the manor' in Emmerdale. Twice married, he helped his first wife Jean – who was suffering from cancer – to commit suicide by leaving out enough pills for her to take an overdose. Many of the locals in Emmerdale were shocked when Frank admitted publicly to this at the 1990 hunt ball after a former employee, George Starkey, tried to blackmail him.

Second wife Kim – whom he married in 1986 – is 23 years younger than Frank, who has two grown-up children, Chris and Zoe, from his first marriage. The couple moved into Home Farm with Chris and Zoe in 1989. Desperate to have children, Kim persuaded Frank to have an operation to reverse the vasectomy he had

already undergone. A shadow in their marriage was Frank's reliance on drink. At one stage, Kim cleared the house of all bottles of alcohol.

Another shadow was Frank's attraction to housekeeper Dolly Skilbeck. Joe Sugden, at the farm for a dinner party, saw him kissing her in the kitchen. Dolly did not allow a relationship to develop, but she covered up for his drinking bouts until Kim eventually found out.

Frank upset son Chris when, as chairman of Tate Haulage, he decided to go into the offices daily and usurp Chris's responsibilities as managing director. This came after Kim, noticing that Frank appeared to be at a loose end, suggested he take a holiday, but he put on a suit, picked up his briefcase and went to work. Chris threw a tantrum and walked out, but he later returned and shared an office with his father.

Frank achieved one of his dreams when he opened a holiday village in Emmerdale, employing Joe Sugden as manager. But money and power were not enough to keep hold of Kim when she fell for local aristocratic landowner the Hon. Neil Kincaid.

When he found out about their affair, Frank threw Kim out of the house and subsequently horse whipped Kincaid in front of the local hunt. After this episode, he turned back to drink. Although Kim's affair was short-lived, she and Frank were divorced.

He saw the chance to rekindle the flames with his old love Ruth Jameson, who came to the holiday village. But she realized he still hoped to reunite with Kim and beat a hasty retreat.

Redeeming himself, Frank was at the centre of Emmerdale's rescue operation after the plane crash over the village on 30 December 1993. On his way to visit Kim with a belated Christmas present, hoping to heal the wounds of their broken marriage, he saw fireballs in the sky and, with the help of Vic Windsor, struggled in vain to fight the blaze at Kim's new stables.

Frank also had the idea of replacing a destroyed bridge over the village's stream by using pipes left by the construction company carrying out new drainage. He supervised Jack Sugden in his tractor, lifting and placing pipes until they formed a bridge that allowed the emergency vehicles to get through.

The tragedy meant that Kim's stables and her livelihood were destroyed, but it brought Frank and Kim back together. The couple realized that they had much to be thankful for and put their difficult times behind them.

At Jack and Sarah Sugden's wedding, in May 1994, Frank caught the bride's bouquet and asked Kim to marry him, although she had second thoughts after Frank suffered a heart attack on the way home from his Model Farm Open Day in 1994 and ended up close to death in hospital. However, the couple wed for the second time in a lavish service at Ripon Cathedral, on 22 December 1994, threw a huge party for all the villagers and honeymooned in Hawaii.

Norman Bowler (b. Norman Clifford Bowler in London, 1 August 1932) was evacuated to Wiltshire during the Second World War and, on leaving school, worked briefly in his father's watchmaking business, before sailing the world for two years as a deckboy on an oil tanker.

Returning to Britain, he trained as an actor at the City Literary Institute and acted in rep. In the fifties, he became part of the Soho set of writers, artists, photographers and actors.

His most notable theatre performances have been in *The Caretaker* in New York, and *Death Trap* in New Zealand. Under contract to MGM, Norman acted in the films *Tom Thumb*, *Naval Patrol*, *Von Ryan's Express* and *Julius Caesar*.

On television, Norman has appeared in *Harpers West One*, *Deadline Midnight*, *The Ratcatchers*, *Letters from the Dead*, *The Avengers*, *Mogul*, *Park Ranger* (starring as David Martin) and *Jesus of Nazareth*, as well as playing Det. Chief Insp. Harry Hawkins in *Softly Softly* and *Softly Softly: Task Force* for 11 years from 1966, and newspaper editor Sam Benson, who had a fling with motel manager Nicola Freeman (Gabrielle Drake), in *Crossroads* during the eighties. He joined *Emmerdale* in 1989.

Norman lives in Clifton, Bristol, with third wife Diane, an acupuncturist and practitioner of alternative medicine, with whom he has a son, Simon. He also has three other children – Caroline and Joshua, by his first wife, and

Tamara, by his second wife. Both marriages were dissolved. Norman and Diane, who have been married for more than 20 years, 'adopted' two children in Nepal after being touched by news of famine in India.

The actor has always suffered from wanderlust, setting out alone with just a rucksack on treks to remote spots. He has travelled up the Amazon and camped in the Himalayas and on Mount Kilimanjaro. In his spare time, Norman enjoys walking – especially along the Pennine, Cleveland and Ebor ways – sailing, ceramics and tennis.

KATHY TATE

Daughter of Caroline and Malcolm, Kathy Bates arrived in Emmerdale to live with her mother after her parents' separation. Rural life was new to her and she abandoned her A levels to follow her mother into employment at N.Y. Estates to help make ends meet. The sight of battery hens became too much for Kathy, so she left to take a job at Emmerdale Farm, but found the work hard and unglamorous.

Divorced Joe Sugden immediately took a fancy to Kathy, but he had to vie for her affections with his nephew, Jackie Merrick. It was Jackie who won and, after a stormy relationship – which included her affair with N.Y. Estates management trainee Tony Marchant – the couple married in February 1988, with Kathy wearing Annie Sugden's Edwardian wedding dress after a burst water tank ruined her own. They honeymooned in Tunisia, then lived in the attic at Emmerdale Farm, before moving to their own house, no. 3 Demdyke Row, in December.

After a year of marriage, Kathy became pregnant. Tragically, she suffered a miscarriage after contracting Chiamydiapsittaci, a rare virus from a sheep that she was tending on the farm.

As well as occasionally helping behind the bar at The Woolpack, Kathy landed a job at Hotten abattoir but lasted only a week. Tragedy followed soon afterwards when Jackie accidentally shot himself dead while hunting a fox for a £10 bet, in August 1989.

New romance came with the arrival in Emmerdale of Frank Tate's son, Chris. Kathy moved in with him and put the past behind her. At a village concert in November 1990, Kathy sang a song called 'Just This Side of Love', written for her by Chris, who secretly recorded her performance and made a record that sold well locally.

The couple married on 5 November 1991, although Kathy had by then had a close relationship with curate Tony Charlton, whose quiet charms were in sharp contrast to Chris's arrogant, business-like ways.

Frank Tate bought Mill Cottage as a wedding present for the couple, but Kathy despaired of her husband's blundering DIY activities. She loved Chris but was sometimes appalled by his immature ways – such as the loss of his motorcycle to Alan Turner in a game of poker.

Kathy left Emmerdale to work at the Tates' Home Farm stables but, when Kate Sugden was imprisoned for killing Pcte Whiteley in a hit-and-run accident, the Sugdens were short staffed and Kathy considered resigning from her new job and returning to Emmerdale. Kim Tate persuaded her that it would be a backward step. But Kathy's initial attempts to rid Chris of his arrogance and make him more caring counted for little as the pair drifted apart.

In 1993, not willing to be a party to her boss's deception, she quit her job at the stables after discovering a hotel bill that revealed Kim's affair with Neil Kincaid. She became Chris's secretary at Tate Haulage but was determined to prove she was more than just a dogsbody.

Chris wondered whether his wife was having an affair when she kept taking time off, but all was revealed when a giant haulage truck reversed into a space outside the office with Kathy, who had just qualified for her HGV licence, at the wheel.

Subsequently taking a job helping Lynn Whiteley to run The Woolpack wine bar – against the wishes of Chris, Lynn's sworn enemy – she met suave American wine salesman Josh Lewis. Kathy planned to leave Chris for him, but guilt pangs made her stay after Chris was paralyzed in the plane disaster over the village at Christmas 1993.

As the rescue operation proceeded and Chris was dug out of the rubble at The Woolpack, Josh – ever the gentleman – broke into the Tates' house and recovered the goodbye letter that Kathy had left.

But Kathy came to regret her decision as she proved unable to give wheelchair-bound Chris the support he needed and he turned to young Rachel Hughes for comfort. They had an affair and Rachel became pregnant with his baby.

Kathy left Emmerdale but returned in March 1995 after a short break and moved back in with Chris, determined to get a fair divorce settlement. She accepted £120,000 and, at the same time, let young Dave Glover romance her and decided to open a tea shop in the village.

Malandra Burrows (b. Malandra Elizabeth Newman in Woolton, Liverpool, 4 November 1966) started dance classes at the age of two. She was chosen to present a posy to Margot Fonteyn two years later and the ballerina asked her, 'And do you want to be a dancer when you grow up?' Malandra replied, 'No! I want to be an actress, like you!'

As a child, Malandra learned to play the violin and sang with her brother and sister, with her father accompanying them on piano. At the age of six, she sang and danced regularly in the ITV children's talent show *Junior Showtime* and, three years later, was the youngest winner of *New Faces*.

Malandra then concentrated on her school work, gaining nine O levels, before training at the Mabel Fletcher Drama School, in Liverpool. While there, she acted in fringe-theatre productions of *Dracula* and *Frankenstein*, and had bit parts in *The Practice* and *Fell Tiger*, before landing two roles in *Brookside*, as Sue and, for three months, Pat Hancock's girlfriend Lisa.

On leaving drama school in 1985, Malandra successfully auditioned for *Emmerdale* and was stunned that her character was so like herself – her parents were divorced, her father was called Malcolm and her middle name was Elizabeth.

The actress, who has starred in the pantomimes *Snow White* and *Cinderella* since finding fame in *Emmerdale*, also made a record in 1990. The song, 'Just This Side of Love', which was featured in the serial, was a Top 20 hit in real life.

Malandra, who lives in Leeds, became engaged to children's television presenter Mark Granger in 1989, but they split up the following year just before their planned wedding. Away from *Emmerdale*, she writes a newspaper column for the *Halifax Courier, Middlesbrough Gazette* and *Grimsby Times*.

KIM TATE

Kim Barker is a working-class girl made good, a secretary who married her former boss, a millionaire landowner, and gained a stepson, Chris, and stepdaughter, Zoe. She is also an avid horse-rider who moved to Emmerdale when Frank bought Home Farm and runs its stables.

Desperate to have a baby, Kim believed it would not be possible because Frank had had a vasectomy. But housekeeper Dolly Skilbeck told her she had read a magazine article saying that reversal operations were possible. She persuaded Frank to go ahead with one, although this turned stepson Chris against her.

When Jock McDonald made an arson attack on the stables at Home Farm and fell unconscious in the flames, Joe Sugden rushed in to save him. Kim's pregnant mare, Copper, went missing and Joe helped to look for the horse.

Kim was amused to find out that Joe Sugden believed Dolly was having an affair with Frank, when in fact she had simply been covering up for his drinking bouts. Later, as Kim offered Joe a shoulder to cry on after the imprisonment of his wife Kate for killing Pete Whiteley in a hit-and-run accident, Joe misconstrued her friendship and tried to steal a kiss in the taproom at The Woolpack. Embarrassed, he left Emmerdale for a break, and Kim told his mother Annie that she understood that his actions were a result of his missing Kate.

Kim helped the Tate family business when it was going through hard times by breeding and selling thoroughbreds and helping in the office. She became pregnant but kept the news to herself and suffered a miscarriage after being thrown from a horse at the Hotten Show. The Hon. Neil Kincaid, a local millionaire land-owner, was on hand to help and the pair subsequently had an affair. Kim left Frank for the aristocrat but eventually realized she was mixing with people from out of her class and the couple split up. The stables that Kim subsequently opened were burned down as a result of the plane crash over Emmerdale, and the tragedy brought Kim and Frank back together.

Kim had a new chance to show her business acumen when she took over management of the game farm in 1994. At the same time, Kim and Frank were planning to remarry. The couple tied the knot again at Ripon Cathedral on 22 December 1994 and honeymooned in Hawaii.

Claire King (b. Harrogate, North Yorkshire, 10 January 1963), the daughter of an Irish father and Scottish mother, was a disc jockey in Leeds while still in her teens, trained at Harrogate College's Actors' Institute and has worked both as an actress and a singer. She toured Britain with a raunchy punk group called To Be Continued and lived for a while with Geoff Bird – known as Cobalt Stargazer and a member of the group Zodiac Mindwarp – as well as presenting *Shout*, an American TV pop show. She has her own record label, Visual Records.

As an actress, Claire appeared on stage in *The Pleasure Principle* at the New End Theatre, Hampstead, and on television she acted a punk and a hooker in *Watch with Mother*, a model in both *Hot Metal* and *Starting Out*, and a doctor's receptionist in *The Bill*. Her first screen kiss was with Mel Smith in *Smith and Jones*.

In films, she played a groupie in the rock movie *Hearts of Fire* (starring Bob Dylan and Rupert Everett), a yuppie in 'The Comic Strip Presents...' production *Eat the Rich* and a prostitute in *The Cold Light of Day*. She was also in pop promotional videos for Zodiac Mindwarp and Elvis Costello, in the latter clad in leathers astride a motorbike and doing an impression of Vanessa White, hostess of the American game show *Wheel of Fortune*.

Claire is adept at many accents and can sound like characters as diverse as Marilyn Monroe, Vera Duckworth and Julie Walters.

She has ridden since the age of seven and it was her ability as a horse-rider that helped Claire to clinch the role of Kim Tate in *Emmerdale* in 1989, when she moved from London back to her native Harrogate. While working on the serial she fell for actor Peter Amory, who plays her stepson Chris Tate, and the couple married on 2 July 1994. Claire is the proud owner of two racehorses, called Digger and... Kim Tate!

ZOE TATE

Arriving in Emmerdale when her father Frank and stepmother Kim bought Home Farm, Zoe Tate was about to graduate from veterinary school in Edinburgh before taking up a job with local vet Martin Bennett in Hotten.

She helped to stop illegal hare-coursing – catching Jock McDonald red-handed – and, with her training, was able to diagnose Seth Armstrong's illness when he was poisoned as a result of bacteria seeping into the water supply. In 1991, she went on an animal rights march, only to find the target was her employer's surgery in Hotten. Three months later, she left her job and Emmerdale, selling her MG sports car to Eric Pollard and travelling to New Zealand, where she became a flying vet.

Zoe returned to Emmerdale in 1993 and found another job in Hotten. She also renewed her friendship with Archie Brooks, but it was always platonic. When Michael Feldmann started seeing Rachel Hughes, Zoe was determined to replace her in his affections. She invited him out for a Chinese meal and he cancelled a date at The Woolpack with Rachel. When the couple returned to Home Farm, Zoe invited him to spend the night with her, but she made it clear the following day that she was not looking for a relationship and he returned to Rachel.

Zoe then finally slept with Archie but subsequently told him that their relationship was a sham and she knew that she could not fall for any man – she was a lesbian. She made several calls to the Leeds Gay Switchboard but hung up each time they answered. It was, surprisingly, father Frank who gave her the support she needed when she confessed her sexuality to him. Zoe's homosexual friend Richard also helped her to come to terms with her sexuality and arranged for her to attend a gay disco.

In April 1995, Zoe and her new lover, Emma Nightingale, bought a house together in the village and Zoe set up her own veterinary practice.

Leah Bracknell (b. London, 12 July 1964) was brought up in Oxford, before training at the Webber Douglas Academy of Dramatic Art. She then toured with the Eastern Actors' Studio as Joanna in *All Sewn Up* and the Pandemonium Theatre company as Maria in *Out of the Valley* and Katie in *Flying Visit*. She also appeared on stage as Marina in *Pericles* for the Oxford Players, and Mephistophiles in *Dr Faustus* for the Klaxon Theatre Company.

She acted in four episodes of the Children's Film & Television Foundation cinema serial

Albert Shepherd took the role of FRED TEAKER in *Emmerdale*. He had previously played the G.I. marrying Elizabeth Taylor in the film *Secret Ceremony*, with Mia Farrow acting their daughter and Joseph Losey directing, and was in *Crossroads* as postman Don Rogers.

Margaret Stallard (b. Birmingham, 30 April 1929) played GRACE TOLLY, before joining *Crossroads* as Mrs Babbitt.

Leonard Maguire (b. Manchester, 26 May 1924) played a tramp called TRASH and was later in *EastEnders*. He has acted on TV since 1949 and in the films *The Honorary Consul* and *A Dry White Season*.

Rachel Davies was SHIRLEY TURNER (née Foster), the former prostitute who married Alan Turner in 1994 and was shot dead in a post office raid shortly afterwards. Rachel was also in *Coronation Street* as post office canteen worker Donna Parker, who was romanced by Alf Roberts, and in *Crossroads* as Elaine Winters, John Latchford's secretary, as well as *Making Out* (as shop steward Pauline) and *Band of Gold* (as Joyce).

Angela Thorne (b. Karachi, Pakistan, 25 January 1939), best known for her impression of Margaret Thatcher, especially in *Anyone for Denis?* on stage and TV, played CHARLOTTE VERNEY, wife of Gerald Verney, who took over the estate on the death of his Uncle George but had to sell because of capital transfer duties, much to Charlotte's distress.

Dennis Blanch (b. Barnet, Hertfordshire, 4 February 1947) switched sides of the law after portraying Det. Con. Willis in *The XYY Man*, *Strangers* and *Bulman*. In *Emmerdale*, he played first DEREK WARNER, a friend of arch-villain Harry Mowlam, in 1985 and then released murderer JIM LATIMER, who kidnapped Sarah Connolly, in 1991.

Anna Cropper (b. Brierfield, Lancashire, 13 May 1938), first wife of *Coronation Street* star William Roache and mother of actor Linus Roache, played NAN WHEELER. In 1962, she was in the *Street* as Joan Akers, who kidnapped baby Christopher Hewitt. More recently, she has appeared in *The Jewel in the Crown* and *Castles* (as Margaret Castle).

The Chiffy Kids and on TV in *The Cannon and Ball Show* and *The Bill*. Leah has also appeared in commercials in Europe and the Middle East.

When she landed the role of Zoe Tate in *Emmerdale* in 1989, Leah went to a real-life vet for advice on how to make her character realistic. Under the vet's supervision, she was even allowed to give a cat an injection. The storyline of her character being a lesbian was a first in a British soap. Leah and her partner, director Lyall Watson, have a daughter, Lily, and live in Yorkshire and London.

ALAN TURNER

Originally Emmerdale's baddy, the bumptious Alan Turner has become a bit of a comic character in the village. He arrived as manager of N.Y. Estates, later became boss of the trout farm and added to that ownership of The Woolpack pub at the beginning of 1991, when he mellowed and became a more genial host.

Alan, estranged from wife Jill, came from the south of England and, on arriving in Emmerdale, found himself in dispute with the Sugden family over farming matters. Joe had been particularly bitter at his appointment at N.Y. Estates because he had been doing the job in a caretaker capacity and expected to land it himself.

The pompous Alan also had to face up to being told where to stick his clever ideas by Seth Armstrong, whom N.Y. Estates appointed gamekeeper in an effort to stem his poaching.

In 1984, Alan tried to patch up his relationship with wife Jill. That ended in divorce, although she was the one responsible for appointing Caroline Bates as his secretary. The following year, Alan narrowly beat Seth Armstrong to a seat in the parish council elections.

His relationship with Joe Sugden changed when, in 1987, the two of them bought Home Farm after N.Y. Estates pulled out of the village. Eventually, Alan sold his shares in Home Farm to businessman Denis Rigg.

Alan's appalling son Terence, who thought the world owed him a living, came to the village after being sent down from Oxford and had a steamy romance with Sandie Merrick.

Then, Alan moved into his secretary Caroline Bates's cottage and, with Seth Armstrong, the pair began a game farm. A romance developed between Alan and Caroline, and they were engaged, but the marriage did not take place.

Caroline left the village for Scarborough to look after her ailing mother but, after he bought The Woolpack, returned to demand compensation for the cottage, in which she had been sitting tenant. Alan had been able to buy it only because they had intended to live there together. Trying to avoid spending any money, Alan took Caroline out for a picnic and asked her to marry him, but she said she wanted a financial settlement, not a marriage proposal.

In 1988, Alan had been banned from driving for a year after failing a breathalyzer test, but he still won a seat on the district council the following year, beating Kate Sugden.

When Alan took over as owner of The Woolpack in 1991, Henry Wilks – who had previously run it with licensee Amos Brearly – stayed on and was soon driven round the bend with Alan's ideas to take the establishment upmarket. When, that March, the Ephraim Monk's brewery was unable to supply beer while new pipes were being fitted, Alan switched to the rival Skipdale Brewery. Seth Armstrong complained about the quality of the new ale and led a walkout, which persuaded Alan to switch back to Ephraim Monk's. Four months later, Alan established a restaurant in the old tap room and sought to attract custom with his gourmet cooking. Shortly afterwards, Henry died.

Having sought romance with most of his female assistants over the years – including Elizabeth Feldmann, who managed his trout farm – Alan found love with Shirley Foster, whom he first met at a drop-in centre, where she was serving meals to the homeless and down-and-outs in a soup kitchen. He found her to be a warm, caring person and a love developed between them, although Alan was shocked to learn that Shirley was a former prostitute.

It was just as much a surprise to the locals when Alan wed Shirley, on 10 February 1994, and the couple made their way to the register office in an open, horse-drawn carriage. Shirley helped Alan to refurbish The Woolpack in the wake of the Emmerdale air disaster and encouraged him to mellow and become more understanding.

Life was looking rosy for Alan, but his happiness was shortlived. Shirley was shot dead three months after the wedding, following a raid at the village post office in which she and postmistress Viv Windsor were taken hostage and Shirley intervened to save Viv's life.

The grief led Alan to turn to the whisky bottle and the pub was soon suffering. Dodgy Eric Pollard offered his help and even persuaded Alan to sign the pub over to him, but he was eventually discovered to be cooking the books. Then, in an effort to bring new life to the hostelry, Terry and Britt Woods were appointed managers to be the pub's public face.

Richard Thorp (b. Purley, Surrey, 2 January 1932) always wanted to be an actor but began his working life in his father's shoe business. He performed in amateur dramatics and, when his father sacked him for continual bad timekeeping, Richard turned professional, training at the Guildhall School of Music and Drama.

He first found national fame as heart-throb Dr John Rennie in *Emergency – Ward 10* for the whole of its seven-year run on TV and, in that role, is one of the exhibits in the Museum of the Moving Image, in Bradford. The series began in 1957 and, to research his role, Richard attended a real-life operation – rushing out halfway through when he thought he was going to faint.

Richard featured in the films *The Dam Busters*, *The Barretts of Wimpole Street* and *The Good Companions*, and on TV in *Oxbridge 2000*, *Honey Lane*, *Public Eye*, *Maupassant*, *A Family at War*, *The Cedar Tree*, *To the Manor Born* and *Strangers*, as well as the Benny Hill and Harry Worth shows. He was in the West End stage productions of *Murder at the Vicarage* and *Moving*, alongside Penelope Keith.

He joined *Emmerdale* in 1982, on his 50th birthday. When his character became landlord of The Woolpack almost ten years later, Richard was able to call on his experience of running a wine business during the early sixties, when acting jobs were infrequent. He could also ask advice from his brother Pete, who is a Master of Wine by profession.

Richard and third wife Noola – a freelance TV floor manager – have a daughter, Emma, born in 1986, and live in a 17th-century manor house in Calderdale, Yorkshire. Richard also has three

Teddy Turner was **BILL WHITELEY**, father of tragic Pete, in *Emmerdale*. He had previously played Chalkie Whiteley in *Coronation Street*. Teddy, who also appeared in *Never the Twain* and *All Creatures Great and Small*, died in 1992 at the age of 75.

Fionnuala Ellwood (b. Fionnuala Rachel Ellwood in Dublin, 3 July 1964) played **LYNN WHITELEY**. Fionnuala, who also appeared on TV in *Prime Suspect* as a forensic scientist called Marion, was in the pilot of *Families* as horse-riding, moody Amanda Thompson (a role eventually taken by Laura Girling). She left *Emmerdale* in 1994, when her character moved to Australia to start a new life with sheep shearer Sven.

Jim Millea (b. Leeds) followed his role as **PETE WHITELEY** by acting dodgy secondhand car dealer Mr Fairbanks in *Families* and Carl Armstrong, estranged husband of Tricia, in *Coronation Street* for two episodes. He also played village bigot Jim Clayton in an episode of *Heartbeat*.

Arthur Pentelow (b. Rochdale, Lancashire, 14 February 1924) was the pipe-smoking retired Bradford wool merchant **HENRY WILKS**, who settled in Emmerdale as Amos Brearly's business partner at The Woolpack after the death of his wife. Arthur had previously appeared in the soaps *Compact* (as Langley), *United!* (as the supporters' club chairman) and *Coronation Street* (first as Emily Bishop's driving instructor, Mr Hopwood, in 1965, then as park-keeper George Greenwood, an old friend of Hilda Ogden, in 1968). The actor was in *Emmerdale* from its first episode until his death, on 6 August 1991.

Gail Harrison, who played **MARIAN WILKS**, daughter of Henry, has subsequently acted in *Hi-de-Hi!*, *Only Fools and Horses...* and *Game, Set & Match*, but is best known for her role as Isobel in three series of *Brass*.

Debbie Arnold (b. Sunderland) had already played one of Mike Baldwin's girlfriends in *Coronation Street* before she turned up in *Emmerdale* as **DEBBIE WILSON**, Eric Pollard's fiancée. The character turned the tables on the dodgy dealer by running off with the £2000 he gave her to start an antiques business, to which he would divert goods from Hotten Market, where he was manager.

children from his previous marriages and a step-daughter, Sarah, and is a connoisseur of good food and wine. He also loves motorcycles and is the proud owner of a Harley-Davidson Electra Glide 1350 cc bike.

DONNA WINDSOR

Youngest of the Windsor family, Donna is the only one of Vic and Viv's three children that they had together – and country life was quick to claim a casualty in Donna when she moved to Emmerdale with her parents after spending her early years in the hustle and bustle of London.

In 1994, Donna was injured after Michael Feldmann gave her a ride on a tractor at Emmerdale Farm that then toppled over. Mother Viv threatened to sue the Sugdens and a depressed Joe Sugden was on the verge of shooting himself when Donna's father, Vic, encountered him in the stables. Vic immediately insisted that the law suit be dropped.

☆ ☆ ☆

Sophie Jeffery (b. 27 September 1984) was only nine when she joined *Emmerdale* but already had a string of TV credits, including the roles of Connie in *Armed and Dangerous*, an episode in the 'Michael Winner's True Crimes' series, Letty Garth in *Middlemarch* and a gang member in *If You See God Tell Him*. She has also appeared in *EastEnders*.

SCOTT WINDSOR

Although his father was thrilled with the move to Yorkshire from London, Scott Windsor was not so keen. He was angry to be leaving city life for a future in a sleepy Dales village. He found it difficult to fit in at school and was involved in fights with other boys. But he found some satisfaction in helping Michael Feldmann in his new job as gamekeeper Seth Armstrong's assistant.

It was no surprise to father Vic and mother Viv when Scott ran away to London on Bonfire Night 1993. He returned to friends on his old Thamesmead housing estate and stayed with his Aunt Gina. Vic tracked down Scott and, after taking his son on a trip down memory lane, managed to convince him to return to his new life in the Dales.

But Scott was then bullied by classmate Glen, who stole goods from the Windsors' shop and coerced Scott into joyriding in Vic's prized Zephyr, which ended up with him crashing it. Glen forced Scott to blame Michael Feldmann, who had already been caught on the wrong side of the law. But Scott and his father eventually visited Inspector Ramsey at Hotten police station to confess.

Toby Cockerell (b. London, 17 October 1976) trained at the Anna Scher Theatre School and had already appeared on television in *Streetwise* (as Lee), *House of Eliott* and *The Bill* before joining *Emmerdale* in 1993.

The young actor has played Falstaff's Page in *Henry IV* for the RSC, acted in a BBC radio play called *Not Just Anybody – Family* and appeared in a police training video about juvenile crime that is shown in schools.

Toby, who lives in London, has a dog called Cleo and lists motorcycles, skiing and snowboarding as his hobbies, recalls his most memorable moment in *Emmerdale* being the burning down of a barn that went terrible wrong, so had to be rebuilt rapidly and burned down again!

VIC WINDSOR

Shortly after Vic Windsor was made redundant from the Ford plant at Dagenham, Essex, his father died, leaving him and wife Viv a flat in the East End of London. They decided to sell the flat and use the proceeds, plus his redundancy money, to make a fresh start for themselves and their three children.

Socialist Vic – born in 1958 and raised in a staunch trade unionist family – had only known city life but yearned to live somewhere as picturesque as he remembered from childhood weekends in Epping Forest. A series of violent incidents on the estate where the family lived,

including one in which a child was fatally stabbed, spurred him on to look for a safer, healthier environment. The family believed they had found it in the Yorkshire Dales village of Emmerdale, to which they moved in 1993.

Younger daughter Donna is the only one of Vic and Viv's three children that they had together. Kelly was Vic's daughter from his first marriage, to a teenage sweetheart who tragically died from cancer. Scott is Viv's son by her first husband, Reg, who abandoned her.

Vic loves fifties rock 'n' roll music, such as that of Elvis Presley and Bill Haley, and his pride and joy was a lovingly preserved Ford Zephyr. On moving to Emmerdale, Vic showed himself to be a townie at heart. He immediately caused chaos by driving his car too fast past a horse, with the rider nearly being thrown off, and leaving gates open so that cows got out.

A walk on the moors led to another potential tragedy when Vic lost his footing on a grassy slope and fell into the river below, where the current dragged him into a clump of foliage. His leg was trapped and his head began sinking into the freezing water. Biff Fowler, who was walking nearby with Luke McAllister and their friend Danny, heard Vic's cries for help and waded into the icy water. Unable to free Vic's trapped legs, Biff told Danny to look after him while he ran for help to Jack and Joe Sugden, who took a saw to the scene of the accident. Joe managed to free Vic, and Luke returned with Scott, Donna and Kelly, who had gone off looking for help, but in the wrong direction. Vic had learned a lesson in country life.

Vic's prized Zephyr was smashed when son Scott was forced by school bully Glen to go joyriding in it, but he bought a Lotus Cortina Mk II in need of rebuilding. He also acquired a vintage motorcycle from the late Wally Eagleton's yard.

⭐ ⭐ ⭐

Alun Lewis (b. Streatham, South London), the brother of actor Hywel Bennett, began his career as a stage manager with Birmingham Rep. After a year, he won a place at RADA, where his contemporaries included Robert Lindsay. Alun later became known to TV viewers as Tracey's jailbird husband Daryl in five series of *Birds of a Feather*, before joining *Emmerdale* in 1993.

He had appeared in the serial four years earlier as Sandie Merrick's boyfriend Tony Barclay. The actor's other TV appearances include roles in *Beryl's Lot*, *Rising Damp* and *Minder*. He also scripted one episode of *Birds of a Feather* in which man-mad Dorien becomes a belly dancer.

Alun, wife Andrea and their children, Thomas and Sarah, left London for Yorkshire in 1990, finding a new home in Birkenshaw, near Bradford. Like his screen character, Alun saw it as a good place to raise a family. He also has a daughter, Amelia, from a previous relationship.

VIV WINDSOR

A canteen supervisor at a light engineering factory, Viv Windsor left her job when she became pregnant with son Scott but was then abandoned by her husband, Reg Dawson, and left to bring up the boy alone. Her own family disowned her and the rift has never been healed. Viv then met and married widower Vic – three years her junior – who had a daughter, Kelly. The couple subsequently had their own daughter, Donna, and Viv is often cast in the role of peacemaker between Vic and Scott.

Since moving to Emmerdale in 1993 to reopen the village post office and stores, Viv has been the backbone of the business. But she feared what might happen when her former husband, Reg, was released from jail. He had a violent streak, which during their marriage had often left her battered and bruised. So it was a surprise when he turned up at the post office bearing gifts and quoting the Bible, claiming to have seen the light while in prison. He refused to believe that Viv and Vic's marriage was blessed in the eyes of God and claimed that Vic was committing a mortal sin by living with her.

At first, Viv allowed him to be reunited with his son, Scott, but Reg's demands that she should resume her place as his wife spurred Vic into action. He told Reg that a parolee was not allowed on post office premises and the police had forbidden his presence there.

Reg left but returned in May 1994 as one of several armed raiders who burst into the post office. They bungled the robbery attempt and took Viv hostage, going on the run and grabbing newlywed Shirley Turner. Her husband Alan lay in hospital wounded after stopping a stray bullet during the shoot-out.

The raiders took their two hostages to a deserted Home Farm, where Shirley intervened when Reg – who had by then accidentally shot dead one of his accomplices, mistaking him for a policeman – was about to shoot Viv. Shirley was killed in the blast and Reg was killed by a police marksman storming the house.

Viv attended Reg's funeral to see for herself that he was finally out of her life. But his will left money to Viv and Scott only on condition that Viv and Vic were divorced: Scott stood to gain £30,000 on his coming of age. The couple decided to benefit from the will by divorcing and immediately remarrying.

☆ ☆ ☆

Deena Payne (b. Diane Margaret Payne in Orpington, Kent, 29 August 1954) trained in dance and drama at the Arts Educational School, before becoming a singer touring with such stars as Alan Price and B. A. Robertson. She also made albums with Eric Burdon, Alvin Lee, John Farnham, Alan Price and B. A. Robertson, and was in the musical *Big Sin City* and the original West End cast of *They're Playing Our Song*.

During her years in the music business, Deena appeared on TV in *Oh Boy!*, *Top of the Pops*, *Superpop*, *Hogmanay*, *Get It Together*, *Gas Street* and *Pebble Mill at One*. Her other television appearances include *Rock Follies '77*, *The Bill* and *Tales of Sherwood Forest*, and she was in the films *Valentino* and *Music Machine*.

The actress, who is divorced from percussionist Frank Ricotti – who wrote the music for writer Alan Plater's three *Beiderbecke* series – lives in Hillingdon, Middlesex, with musician Steve Grant and their son, William Anthony Payne-Grant, born in 1992. Deena enjoys cycling, sewing, cooking and reading.

BRITT WOODS

Having worked in Lanzarote for years and run a bar in Benidorm with her husband, Britt Woods was eminently qualified to keep order behind the bar at The Woolpack. Alan Turner took on Britt and husband Terry to give the pub a new look while he looked after the business side.

Britt knew that Terry drank too much and was partial to the occasional dodgy deal, but she generally treated him with kid gloves. A more serious attitude was needed when Alan Turner discovered Terry's bootleg whisky scheme. To keep herself and Terry in a job, Britt suggested that she take charge behind the bar as manageress. Alan agreed, happy to see Terry reduced to collecting glasses and looking after the cellar.

☆ ☆ ☆

Michelle Holmes (b. Corinne Michelle Cunliffe in Rochdale, Lancashire, 1 January 1967) attended Oldham Theatre Workshop as a teenager and, aged 16, met Granada Television casting directors for the first time. They gave her the part of receptionist Susan Turner in the medical series *The Practice* and she stayed in the role for two years. Then, offered the part of Adrian Boswell's girlfriend, Carmel, in *Bread*, Michelle turned it down to star in the raunchy film *Rita, Sue and Bob Too*, about two schoolgirls sexually involved with a married man.

After roles in the *Brookside* three-part spin-off *Damon & Debbie*, as a punk called Jenny, and the comedy series *Divided We Stand*, Michelle landed the part of barmaid Tina Fowler in *Coronation Street*. She spent a year in Britain's top soap but decided to leave to do other work, which included developing her singing career with the funk duo the Dunky Dobbers, which she formed with actress Sue Devaney, who had played Debbie Webster in *Coronation Street*.

After making another film, *Once Upon a Time*, and appearing on stage in a Jim Cartwright play, *Eight Miles High*, Michelle returned to TV as Annie in *Mr Wroe's Virgins*, as well as playing Maggie Coles in *Firm Friends* (alongside Billie Whitelaw and Madhur Jaffrey), Yvonne in two series of the sitcom *Goodnight Sweetheart* (alongside Nicholas Lyndhurst) and Marie in the comedy-drama series *Common as Muck*, written by actor William Ivory, who played her screen boyfriend, Eddie Ramsden, in *Coronation Street*.

She had already appeared briefly in *Emmerdale* as Archie Brooks's girlfriend Lindsay, in 1993, when she returned to the serial as Britt Woods two years later. Michelle, who is single, lives in Manchester and enjoys singing, dancing, water-skiing and travelling.

TERRY WOODS

Alan Turner took on Terry Woods and his wife, Britt, as managers at The Woolpack in 1995. They were brought in to attract a wider clientèle to the pub after Alan's financial problems. The couple had previously run a bar in Benidorm and saw this as a chance to pull a sleepy Dales pub into the last quarter of the 20th century. But Alan made it clear that, although they were the new faces at The Woolpack, he was still the boss and running the business.

Terry and Britt seemed head over heels in love, but former rugby league player Terry's secret was that he had a drink problem. But he caused drink problems for Seth Armstrong and Vic Windsor when he stopped buying their home-made Moonshine whisky, telling them that he was getting it cheaper. Certain that he would not be able to buy it for less, Seth and Vic knew it must be their own whisky that was being stolen and finding its way to the pub. A spot of surveillance proved them to be right.

Alan Turner threatened to sack Terry and Britt, but Britt saved the day by offering to become manageress with sole responsibility behind the bar. However, this began to put a strain on the couple's marriage when Terry found that his job had been reduced to that of general dogsbody.

☆ ☆ ☆

Billy Hartman (b. Edinburgh) trained at the Queen Margaret College Drama School, Edinburgh, and quickly notched up a string of stage musicals to his name, including *Elvis* (as the young Elvis), at the Astoria Theatre, *The Hired Man*, also at the Astoria, *Oliver!* (as Bill Sykes), at Sadler's Wells, and *Which Witch*, at the Piccadilly Theatre.

He brought his singing skills to the fore when he performed the theme song for the television series *Dear Heart*. That and his version of the Elvis Presley classic 'Return to Sender' were both released as singles. He made other records with the Random Band and appeared on the original-cast albums of *The Hired Man* and *Which Witch*.

Billy's TV appearances have included *Oh Boy!*, *Let's Rock*, *Dear Heart*, *Russ Abbot's Madhouse*, *Minder*, *C.A.T.S. Eyes*, *Boon*, *The Lenny Henry Show*, *Fairly Secret Army*, *Shadow on the Earth*, *Vote for Them*, *Trainer*, *Don Giovanni*, *The Marriage of Figaro*, *Taggart*, *Civvies*, *Inspector Morse*, *Head over Heels*, *A Touch of Frost*, *The Bill*, *Casualty*, *In Suspicious Circumstances*, *Heartbeat* and *99-1*. He often finds himself cast in the role of villain. The actor played Dougal in the film *Highlander* and also appeared on the big screen in *April Fool's Day* and *Doody's Dream*.

Billy, who is in demand as a storyteller on tapes – including James Boswell's *The Life of Samuel Johnson* and Robert Louis Stevenson's *Travels with My Donkey* – is married to make-up artist Karen Hartley and lives in London.

Back row: Davie Sneddon (Derek Lord), Chic Cherry (Andy Cameron), Eric Ross-Gifford (Richard Greenwood), Phineas North (William Tapley), Jockie McDonald (Jackie Farrell), PC Douglas Kirk (Graeme Robertson). Third row: Alun Morgan (Mike Hayward), Eddie Ramsay (Robin Cameron), Michael Ross (Gordon MacArthur), Sam Hagen (Briony McRoberts), Morag Stewart (Jeannie Fisher), Mr Murdoch (Robert Trotter). Second row: Isabel Morgan (Eileen McCallum), Sheila Ramsay (Lesley Fitz-Simons), Susan Ross (Jacqueline Gilbride), Effie McDonald (Mary Riggans), Joanna Ross-Gifford (Tamara Kennedy), Carol Wilson (Teri Lally), Mrs Mack (Gwyneth Guthrie), Mairi McNeil (Anne Myatt). Front row: Dominic Dunbar (Gary Hollywood), Trish McDonald (Natalie Robb), Tiffany Bowles (Rachel Ogilvy), Menna Morgan (Manon Jones), Sarah Gilchrist (Shonagh Price), Gary McDonald (Joseph McFadden).

High Road was created by Don Houghton for Scottish Television when ITV was looking for a daytime soap. It had to compete with Southern Television's live serial Together and HTV's Taff Acre to get its chance for a long run on the network. The programme's original title was The Glendhu Factor, but this was changed to Take the High Road before the first broadcast, on 19 February 1980.

Scottish Television was originally commissioned to produce 26 episodes of the serial – set in the fictional village of Glendarroch, on the banks of Loch Lomond – and successfully beat off its rivals to win the contract for another series the following year. From 1987, the programme was broadcast twice weekly, every week of the year. In Scotland, it enjoys evening screenings, whereas in the rest of Britain it is shown during the afternoon. In recent years, there has been an increasing number of outdoor scenes, showing off some of Scotland's most beautiful scenery.

In 1993, the new ITV Network Centre decided not to continue showing the serial throughout the whole of Britain, but Scottish Television decided that it would still make just one episode a week for transmission in Scotland. However, ITV companies individually decided they still wanted to show the programme to the extent that it is seen in all regions again except Yorkshire and Tyne Tees. The serial's title was shortened to High Road in 1994.

TIFFANY BOWLES

Self-assured, middle-class teenager Tiffany Bowles arrived in Glendarroch with her friend Menna Morgan – niece of Alun Morgan – and moved into Alun and Isabel's house, turning their life upside-down and causing problems between them.

She indulged in amateur psychology and tried to put the couple's problems right, once sitting between them, taking their hands, patting them and joining them. Not surprisingly, this riled both Alun and Isabel.

Tiffany was soon seen as a freeloader, but her confidence and need to be the centre of attention were later interpreted as signs of insecurity.

Although water-sports instructor Phineas North was going out with Trish McDonald, this did not stop him bedding Tiffany when he took her to his parents' local holiday cottage. The relationship lasted just three days and Fin was soon back in Trish's arms.

☆ ☆ ☆

Rachel Ogilvy (b. East Kilbride) was discovered by new *High Road* producer John G. Temple in a Glasgow stage play and joined the cast shortly afterwards, in 1994.

She also played a presenter called Roz in *How to Get On*, the pilot for a BBC radio comedy series starring popular children's presenter Johnny Ball.

Rachel appeared alongside Jimmy Logan and *High Road* actor Graeme Robertson in the pantomime *Dick Whittington*, at the Adam Smith Theatre, Kirkcaldy, over Christmas 1994.

CHIC CHERRY

Cheeky Jack-of-all-trades Chic Cherry arrived in Glendarroch in 1994 to do repair work at the Ardnacraig Hotel and was soon charming all the females of the district with his gift of the gab. He had left his wife Senga behind in Glasgow because she treated him badly and he could not stand her. He also had a son – wide-boy Jaffa – and a daughter.

Chic did teenager Trish McDonald a favour by introducing her to his friend Danny Rollo, who ran the sleazy Cat Club in Glasgow and hired her to sing on Saturday nights.

Suddenly, Chic disappeared in the middle of a job at the Ardnacraig Hotel after pulling the reception area apart – because he heard that his wife was on his trail. When this threat disappeared, he returned.

☆ ☆ ☆

Andy Cameron is one of Scotland's best-known entertainers and has found international success as a comedian. He has had his own television series on the BBC and Scottish Television, and for 15 years presented *Andy Cameron's Sunday Joint* on BBC Radio

---

Ken Watson (b. London) played **BRIAN BLAIR**, Isabel Morgan's first husband, who spent ten years in jail for murdering a waitress who blackmailed him. Ken had already been on TV in *The Barretts of Wimpole Street*, *The Brothers*, *Emergency – Ward 10* and *Crown Court*. He also played club owner Ralph Lancaster in *Coronation Street* and both Gus Brantford and Phil Fletcher in *Emmerdale*.

Leon Sinden (b. Leon Fuller Sinden in Ditchling, East Sussex, 20 July 1927), brother of actor Donald Sinden, played estate lawyer **GEORGE CARRADINE**. He also acted on TV in *Scoop*, *Rebecca*, *The Assassination Run* and *Taggart*.

Glyn Owen was **PAUL CASSELL**, the owner of an Edinburgh advertising agency who fell for Elizabeth Cunningham. Glyn had appeared on TV as Dr Paddy O'Mara in the 1957 serial *Calling Nurse Roberts* and its better known sequel, *Emergency – Ward 10*, government spymaster Richard Hurst in *The Rat Catchers* and Edward Hammond in *The Brothers*. He later played Jack Rolfe in *Howards' Way*.

Scotland. He performs his cabaret act around the country and starred in the Borderline Theatre Company's production of *The Guid Sodjer Schweik* at the Edinburgh Festival.

He released a video called *Andy Cameron – A Bit South of the Border* and presented a tape about Rangers, one of Glasgow's two major football clubs. Andy has received both the Television and Radio Personality of the Year awards from the Scottish Radio Industries and the *Daily Record* newspaper.

Andy is a keen golfer who plays regularly in pro-am tournaments to raise money for charity. His own Andy Cameron Pro-Am tournament, held annually, raises thousands of pounds for children's charities. For his charity work, especially for children's charities throughout Scotland, he was honoured by the Variety Club of Great Britain with a tribute dinner.

SARAH GILCHRIST

When their mother fell ill, 16-year-old Sarah Gilchrist and her brother Callum found foster parents in Eddie and Sheila Ramsay, the divorced couple who remarried in 1994. Sarah proved to be a real handful for the couple, but this streak of rebelliousness was a response to the situation, as Sarah tested how much she could get away with.

When the phone call came to say her mother had recovered, Sarah and Callum returned home. But Sarah had experienced a taste of life away from home and, when the chance of a work placement came up at the Big House, she grabbed it. After a brief flirtation with Stephen Ogilvy, she fell for Gary McDonald.

Shonagh Price (b. Aberfeldy, Perthshire) is the daughter of actress Anna Hepburn, who won a Fringe First for her one-woman show at the Edinburgh Festival. Her mother also played a

Edith MacArthur (b. Ardrossan, Ayrshire, 8 March 1926) played Lady Laird **ELIZABETH CUNNINGHAM** (née **Peddie**), whose marriage to Edinburgh lawyer Peter foundered as she concentrated on making the estate viable. Edith had already appeared on TV in *Dr Finlay's Casebook*, *Love Story* and *The Sandbaggers*, as well as acting Judith Sutherland in *Sutherland's Law*. Since leaving *High Road* in 1987, she has appeared in *French Fields* and the 'Screen Two' production *The Long Roads*.

guest at the Ardnacraig Hotel in *High Road* when there was a food-poisoning scare.

Shonagh herself took a foundation course in drama in Dundee, before training at the Royal Scottish Academy of Music and Drama, graduating in 1992. She was well into her twenties when she landed the role of Eddie and Sheila Ramsay's foster child. She had already acted on television in *Strathblair* and *The Negotiator*, and on stage as Mary in *The Prime of Miss Jean Brodie* at the Lyceum Theatre, Edinburgh, as well as appearing for the city's Theatre Workshop in *The Skelpin' Weal*, the Wildcat theatre company in a children's show called *The Nightingale*, and the Fifth Estate company in *The Burgher's Tale*.

SAM HAGEN

Glamorous businesswoman Sam Hagen is the bitch of Glendarroch. She is dynamic and has no time for others who do not have her get-up-and-go. Greg Ryder brought her in as a systems analyst to push his business into the 21st century. Determined to get on in the world, using any means, Sam had a romance with Davie Sneddon, who knew a lot about Greg and owned land that he wanted to buy. So she tried to pump Sneddon for information, which caused ructions in the village.

Later, she had an affair with Greg. Sneddon got his revenge by hiring a private detective, who found out that Sam had years earlier conducted an affair with Greg during which they plotted to get their hands on the wealth of an older man, Simon Green, who ran a hotel chain of which Greg was manager and Sam a receptionist. Sam married him and shared with Greg his money when he died. When Sneddon informed Fiona of this, her marriage to Greg crumbled and the couple left Glendarroch, although there were later reports that they had reunited in London.

Sneddon realized how Sam had used him, got very drunk and was later seen roaming around with his shotgun. At the same time, Sam disappeared. Three months later, she was back – with the news that she had sold Alt-na-Mara and bought Glendarroch from the young Lord Strathmorris, pre-empting the possible return of Greg and Fiona. Sam then took up with interior designer Peter Odell, an old friend from London with whom she had previously worked.

☆ ☆ ☆

Briony McRoberts (b. Welwyn Garden City, Hertfordshire, 10 February 1957) has performed in many theatres throughout Britain, in such productions as *Much Ado About Nothing*, *Hay Fever*, *The Browning Version*, *Peter Pan*, *And Then There Were None*, *The Curse of the Baskervilles*, *Betzi* and *Charley's Aunt*.

She was in the films *Captain Nemo and the Underwater City* and *The Pink Panther Strikes Again*, and on television in *Bachelor Father*, *Lucky Jim*, *Peter Pan*, *True Patriot*, *The Crezz*, *Butterflies*, *Sink or Swim*, *Strangers*, *Diamonds*, *The Professionals*, *Malice Aforethought*, *Don't Wait Up*, *Mr Palfrey of Westminster*, *Fellow Traveller* and, as Carol, in *EastEnders*.

Briony, who is married to actor David Robb, landed the role of superbitch Sam Hagen while visiting Glasgow and dropping in on a producer friend at Scottish Television. Jim McCann happened to say the company was looking for someone in *High Road* and she fitted the bill.

PC DOUGLAS KIRK

Glendarroch's police constable, Douglas Kirk used to jump into situations feet first but has settled down and now considers more carefully the consequences of his actions.

One of his early successes in the village was taming Emma Aitken, the tearaway teenager who was finding her way in the world and beginning to grow up. Eventually, the relationship fizzled out and Emma left for France with her friend Lynne McNeil.

In 1995, PC Kirk moved out of the village to be based in nearby Auchtarne, letting his cottage to Davie Sneddon and Judith Crombie.

☆ ☆ ☆

Graeme Robertson caught the acting bug at the age of five while watching the stage version

Charles Jamieson (b. Charles Reginald Wingate Jamieson in Rutherglen, Strathclyde, 12 March 1952) played RUARI GALBRAITH, financial adviser to Sorry Watson, who introduced him to Glendarroch, where he met and fell in love with Fiona Cunningham, who had his son, David, but refused to marry him. Charles has appeared on television in *Blake's 7*, *The Omega Factor*, *Goodnight and Godbless* and *The Brief*.

Vivien Heilbron, who played Catriona in the 1971 film version of *Kidnapped* alongside Michael Caine, was KAY GRANT, the original district nurse in *High Road*. The character was popular in the village and delivered baby Donald Lachlan, but left Glendarroch to become a matron in a Glasgow hospital. Vivien, who is married to *Doctor Finlay* star David Rintoul, also acted Det. Sgt. Louise Colbert in the seventies police series *Target*.

Popular Scottish comedian Jimmy Logan played MAJOR ROBERT GROVES, a cousin of Lady Laird Elizabeth Cunningham. He was a conman who claimed to be an army hero but had, in fact, been drummed out of his regiment. When he ran up a massive bill at Blair's Store, he paid it off by pawning one of Elizabeth's diamond brooches.

Frank Wylie, who played gossiping postman FERGUS JAMIESON, previously appeared in the West End and on Broadway in *Chips with Everything*, and worked with the National Theatre for six years under Laurence Olivier, played Satan in Roman Polanski's film version of *Macbeth* and was also on TV in *Who'll Take the Low Road?*, *Softly Softly*, *The Rivals of Sherlock Holmes*, *Churchill's People*, *The Lost Tribe*, *Tales of the Unexpected*, *Doctor Who*, *King's Royal*, *Brigadista* and *Holy City*. He acted in *High Road* from 1982 until his death on 16 April 1994.

John Stahl (b. Sauchie, Clackmannanshire) played TOM KERR, known to all as Inverdarroch, the name of his farm. He was unlucky in love, never plucking up the courage to ask widow Lily Taylor to wed him and ending up with a broken marriage to district nurse Claire Miller, who had an affair with Davie Sneddon. John had previously acted in the Scottish Television serial *Garnock Way*.

of the TV children's talent show *Junior Showtime* in Scarborough. His mother encouraged him to step up on stage and do impressions of Edward Heath and Harold Wilson.

But Graeme's teachers at school thought food management was a safer career and he started his working life in a supermarket. He hated it so much that, after a few months, he secured an apprenticeship on the buses and worked as a mechanic for five years.

Deciding to bite the bit and go into acting, Graeme went to drama school and, eight months after leaving, landed a role in *High Road* as a worker at the marina. Three years later, he was cast as PC Kirk. Graeme, a founder member of the Scottish company Kaleidoscope Theatre, lives in Ayrshire with his girlfriend, Rosemary.

Alec Monteath (b. Doune, Perthshire) played DOUGAL LACHLAN, the canny Ardvain crofter whose first wife, Amy, died in childbirth but who later found happiness with second wife Gladys Aitken. Alec had previously been an announcer and newsreader with Scottish Television and BBC Scotland, and acted on TV in *The Omega Factor*, *Bothwell*, *Doom Castle*, *Hess* and the serial *Garnock Way* (as a surgeon). He was in *High Road* from its first episode, in 1980, until he left 11 years later.

Ginni Barlow, who acted GLADYS LACHLAN (formerly Aitken) – Dougal's second wife, who had a tearaway teenage daughter, Emma – had previously played a social worker in *Crossroads*, a physiotherapist in *Emergency – Ward 10*, a postmistress in *Dr Finlay's Casebook*, a police inspector in *Coronation Street*, a nursing sister in *Tutti Frutti* and pub landlady Effie Murdoch for three-and-a-half years in Scottish Television's weekly serial *Garnock Way*.

Frederick Jaeger (b. Berlin, Germany, 9 May 1928) played MAX LANGEMANN, the German entrepreneur who bought the Glendarroch estate when the serial began, intending to turn it into a place for his rich friends to hunt, shoot and fish. When his company's finances took a turn for the worse, he abandoned his plan and left the village. Frederick appeared in the BBC TV soap *The Grove Family* in 1959 and, since his *High Road* role, has been in such series as *Shoestring*, *Yes Minister*, *Love Hurts* and *Keeping up Appearances*.

GRACE LACHLAN

Dougal Lachlan's long-suffering mother, Grace, watched over him as he continued the family tradition, crofting at Ardvain, as the Lachlans had done for more than 100 years. After the death of Dougal's first wife, Amy, Grace was his only companion. She had her hands full because, in many ways, he was still not grown up, but their frequent arguments often hid the deep affection they clearly felt for one another.

When Dougal married Gladys Aitken, Grace thought herself in the way and left for a while, moving from one place to another. When Grace discovered that her sister, Maeve, who had lived near Glasgow and not seen her for many years, had died in a home, Dougal found her wandering around at Queen Street railway station. He took her back to the croft, where she shared the cottage with Dougal and Gladys.

Eventually, after Dougal and Gladys had reunited following Gladys's affair with an artist, they left Glendarroch to live in Yorkshire. Grace then moved in with villager Jean McTaggart.

Marjorie Thomson (b. Glasgow) began her acting career in 1946 with the Glasgow Unity Theatre. She performed at the first Edinburgh Festival, in 1947, and worked at the Citizens' Theatre, Glasgow, and with many repertory companies. Marjorie appeared in the film *The Gorbals Story*, with Roddy McMillan and Russell Hunter, went to Perth Repertory in 1953 and has lived in the town ever since. In 1958 she took part in the Royal Variety Performance at the Alhambra Theatre, Glasgow.

She appeared, with Stanley Baxter and Jimmy Logan, in Scottish Television's first programme and has also been on TV in *Dr Finlay's Casebook*, *Sutherland's Law*, *Skin Deep* and Scottish Television's first serial, *High Living*. She has been in *High Road* since the first episode.

Divorced from *Callan* TV star Russell Hunter in 1970, Marjorie has two daughters, Anne and Lesley, and enjoys reading, doing crosswords and watching TV quiz shows.

EFFIE McDONALD

As a spinster, Effie Macinnes was always on the lookout for an eligible man. When a fanciable one came along, she went for him, but she constantly aspired to something and, when she got it, no longer wanted it. In her head, she was still

19, filled with romantic notions and likely to be caught reading a 'Mills and Boon' love story.

Effie's other preoccupation is gossip, something she frequently did about her employer, Fiona Cunningham, when she was housekeeper at Glendarroch House. She continued in the job when the Ross-Giffords took over the estate, but was sacked by Lady Margaret when she found out that Effie was also moonlighting for Fiona Cunningham at the Ardnacraig Hotel. She was then employed full-time in the Ardnacraig kitchens, even surviving Joanna and Eric Ross-Gifford's takeover of the hotel.

It was after Jock McDonald's wife, Sadie, was killed that she finally found the man who had been so elusive in her life. Although he left the village for a while, he eventually returned and fell in love with Effie. The couple married in the summer of 1995.

Mary Riggans (b. Glasgow) enjoys television and theatre work, but radio is her favourite medium. As well as acting in dozens of *Saturday Night Theatre* productions, she has read *Morning Story* many times and was thrilled when Joyce Grenfell wrote to her, 'If I could write in Scots and make up a good story, I'd get you to read it.'

Mary – who describes herself as 'forty-ish' – began acting on BBC radio at the age of ten, in Scottish 'Children's Hour' and made her TV debut at 16, in *A Nest of Singing Birds* by Robert Kemp. Since then, she has appeared in such programmes as *Dr Finlay's Casebook*, *Sunset Song*, *Just Your Luck*, *The Prime of Miss Jean Brodie*, *Maggie*, *First Among Equals* and the Bill Bryden play *The Ship*, and has presented many schools programmes. She continued working while studying for an MA at Glasgow University.

Mary has appeared on stage in Arthur Miller's *A View from the Bridge* and Ostrovsky's *A Family Affair*, as well as touring Scotland twice in the title role of the Wildcat theatre company production of *Salon Jeanette*. She and husband Malcolm have a grown-up daughter, Samantha, and live in Edinburgh.

GARY McDONALD

On moving into Glendarroch House, trouble-maker Gary McDonald immediately created a bad impression by whistling at Fiona Ryder, thinking she was a secretary rather than his father Jockie's boss.

He showed a more responsible side to his character when he landed a job painting Morag Stewart's croft. Then he met Alun Morgan's niece, Menna.

But he found true romance with Sarah Gilchrist at his 18th birthday party, in 1995. He had asked her to come but she refused unless she could bring bad boy Stephen Ogilvy, but she turned up on her own.

Joseph McFadden was born of Irish parents who moved to Scotland in their teens in an effort to find work. Joseph began his acting career at the age of 13 when he was cast in *Taggart* as a boy whose father was killed.

He made his pantomime debut as Aladdin, opposite *High Road* actress Gwyneth Guthrie, in Glasgow over Christmas 1993. Gary lives in Glasgow.

JOCKIE McDONALD

After years of visiting the village in the course of his work as a general handyman, Jockie McDonald moved his family from nearby Auchtarne to Glendarroch.

He once had his own business in Auchtarne, but when that collapsed he turned to finding jobs wherever he could, often working at Glendarroch House. That did not find favour with workshy Archie Menzies because Jockie's efforts showed up his own.

In 1990, Jockie took his family – wife Sadie, daughter Trish and son Gary – to live at Glendarroch House, in Archie's old quarters.

It was a shock when Sadie was killed in 1994. Jackie could not bear to live at Glendarroch House, so moved back to Auchtarne but returned when Sam Hagen bought the estate. He found comfort in the arms of spinster Effie Macinnes, who finally got her man, and the couple were married in the summer of 1995.

Jackie Farrell (b. Paisley) is a former army P.T. instructor who began in showbusiness as a singer, dancer and comedy-feed in variety. He has also done stunt work and his many stage appearances include a tour of *Run for Your Wife*, starring Jimmy Logan.

On TV, he played a crooked councillor in the Scottish Television serial *Garnock Way*, which featured other actors later to appear in *High Road*, including Eileen McCallum, Alec Monteath, Paul Kermack and Michael Elder.

Jackie and wife Patsy live in Clydebank and have three sons. He enjoys golf, D.I.Y. and playing the piano.

TRISH McDONALD

Soon after her arrival in Glendarroch, teenager Trish McDonald was getting involved in all sorts of schemes. When she heard Dougal Lachlan moaning that he had no money, Trish took him seriously and set up a Dougal Lachlan Fund, without telling anyone what the money was for. When the truth came out, she had to give back all the cash.

Trish, who had a crush on labourer Kenny Tosh, was clever at school and destined for academic success. But her career began working behind the bar at the Ardnacraig Hotel. Trish fell for

archaeologist Nick Stapleton, who was in the village for a dig with one of Joanna Ross-Gifford's friends, but she realized he only wanted-ed to bed her – and ditched him.

Then along came water-sports instructor Phineas North. Trish was attracted to him but horrified when she found him sitting in his Land Rover injecting himself with a syringe. Only later did she find out that Fin was diabetic and giving himself an insulin shot. She tried to apologize but it took him some time to forgive her.

Odd-job-man Chic Cherry introduced Trish – a keen singer – to his friend Danny Rollo, who ran the Cat Club in Glasgow. He gave her an audition and a regular Saturday-night singing spot. Trish also accepted Fin's offer of being her minder and stayed at his Glasgow flat on the night after her weekly performance. The teenager lost her virginity to Fin during one of her stays there, but their relationship was not to last.

☆ ☆ ☆

Natalie Robb (b. Bellshill, Glasgow, 3 December 1974) was only 15 when she joined *High Road* in 1990 but already an experienced all-round entertainer, having been an actress, singer, impressionist, dancer and model.

At primary school, Natalie's teachers encouraged her to develop her talents. She first appeared on stage at the Crawford Theatre, Glasgow, for the city's Mayfest event. Then, she was in the musicals *Grease* and *Oliver!* at Sheilds Youth Theatre, before joining Glasgow Youth Theatre and acting in *Big Al* and *The Wiz*, both at the Mitchell Theatre.

Natalie won the BBC's *Young Entertainer of the Year* competition in 1988 as an impressionist and later impersonated Bros on *Going Live!* and appeared on the children's talent show *But Can You Do It on TV?* At the age of ten, she was in *Dreams and Recollections*, a dramatized documentary about the life of Charles Rennie Macintosh, starring Tom Conti.

Natalie also acted in *Return Journey*, playing Susannah York's best friend, and took the starring role in *Facts of Life*, a National Film Theatre production starring Paul Young (who played minister Gerald Parker in *High Road*) that has been shown by the BBC.

She made her first record 'Girls, Girls, Girls' at the age of 13 – impersonating top female pop stars – and was soon showing her all-round skills on the cabaret circuit. In 1995, she released another single, 'Take Me to Paradise'.

Natalie has done voice-overs for radio and television programmes, including *Taggart*, in which she had to sound like a choir of children singing. She later acted in *Taggart*. Her talents also extend to modelling, which she has done or

---

Gillian McNeill (b. Monifieth, 25 September 1965) played crofter's daughter LYNNE McNEIL, who gave up her university studies to work at Home Farm and, later, the new marina. Gillian, who joined *High Road* in 1987 and left six years later, is married to actor Richard Greenwood, who plays Eric Ross-Gifford.

John Young (b. Edinburgh, 18 June 1916) was widower MR (IAN) McPHERSON, Glendarroch's much-loved minister. He was also on TV in *Garnock Way*, *Hess*, *The Camerons*, *The Omega Factor*, *Days of Hope*, *McKenzie*, *Hamlet*, *Brigidista*, *The Houseman's Tale* and *The Justice Game*, and in such films as *Monty Python and the Holy Grail*, *Life of Brian*, *Black Jack*, *Chariots of Fire* and *Time Bandits*. Actor son Paul played Mr Parker, John's rival minister for a while in *High Road*.

the catwalk and for such magazines as *Hi!*. In 1994, she abseiled down Glasgow's highest building, the Moathouse Hotel, in aid of the breakthrough Cancer Research Fund.

MRS (MARY) MACK

Glendarroch's resident busybody and gossip, Mrs Mack, feels she has an absolute right to interfere in everyone's lives and has no time for anyone else's viewpoint. The middle of three sisters, she was devoted to her husband, Hector, and never worked out why he spent so much time in the greenhouse, where he died. When her elder sister, Lizzie Fraser, gave up the job of housekeeper to Mr McPherson at the manse (vicarage), Mrs Mack arrived from Glasgow to take over the job.

She became fiercely protective towards the minister but also set herself up as Glendarroch's guardian of morals and dispenser of the gossip. She never minces her words and does not worry about hurting other people's feelings.

Mrs Mack was very much in favour of Mr McPherson retiring when he first suggested the idea, until she realized that her position as his housekeeper might be threatened. She tried to persuade villagers that her presence was essential to the moral fabric of the community. When Mr McPherson was given notice to leave the manse, Mrs Mack barricaded herself in and, thanks to Sheila Ramsay – then a reporter on the Auchtarne Herald – the story made the front pages of major Scottish newspapers. In the final analysis, the minister's return was more a result of the villagers' stand against fiery fundamentalist Mr Parker, who would have taken over.

Later, as caretaker of the village hall, Mrs Mack banned Carol McKay and Effie Macinnes from running a tea room there, then stole the idea and started one herself in the manse, throwing the minister out of his study to do so, and employed Carol as a waitress. Mrs Mack was forced to close her tea room when Michael Ross became the new minister and moved into the manse.

When her late husband's brother died, Mrs Mack was surprised to hear that she was due to inherit something, and was rather bemused on finding out that it was a statue. Then, she fainted at an auction as it fetched more than £20,000.

Gwyneth Guthrie (b. Ayr, 28 April 1936) wraps a shapeless pinny around herself, jams an Oxfam-shop hat on her head, lowers her voice to a rasp of disapproval and, with a pursing of her lips, appears to age ten years when she appears in front of the cameras for *High Road*.

The character of Mrs Mack is a far cry from Gwyneth, who took to the stage at the age of four. Eight years later, she made her professional debut, broadcasting from Glasgow with the legendary 'Auntie Kathleen' Garscadden in Scottish 'Children's Hour', on BBC radio. She had been taken along to the local radio station by her mother, who also phoned church groups and youth clubs, asking if they needed an act.

Gwyneth was getting regular work in 'Children's Hour' and various radio plays, but her father, manager of the Clydesdale Bank in Ayr, insisted that she should gain another skill in case an acting career did not work out. She enrolled at Skerry's Secretarial College, in Glasgow, and worked in an office for a while.

Intent on furthering her career as an actress, Gwyneth successfully auditioned for the Royal Scottish Academy of Music and Drama, where she won the James Bridie Silver Medal. Then she joined Perth Rep. and continued to work in radio, on which in recent years she has played Mary Queen of Scots and French singer Edith Piaf. To get the effect of Piaf's gin-and-tobacco voice, she smoked until her throat was ragged.

Gwyneth has given poetry readings at the Edinburgh Festival and appeared on stage in the Sam Tree farce *For Love or for Money*, alongside Jimmy Logan, during a 14-week tour of Scotland. She was on TV in *Sutherland's Law*, *Hill o' the Red Fox*, *Degree of Uncertainty*, *The Lost Tribe*, *The Reunion*, *The Prime of Miss Jean Brodie* and *Something's Got to Give*. Gwyneth also featured in the films *Privilege* and *Years Ahead*.

When auditioning for the role of Mrs Mack in *High Road* in 1982, Gwyneth expected to play a gentle housekeeper, like Barbara Mullen's character in *Dr Finlay's Casebook*, but the quirky characterization came to her immediately. She has also played Mrs Mack's glamorous sister, Florence Crossan, who made visits to the village until the character's death, in 1995.

Gwyneth, who works for various charities, is married to businessman John Borland and lives in a 16th-century farmhouse in Darvel, 330 m (1000 ft) up in the Ayrshire countryside: it is the highest dairy farm in Scotland. They have three married daughters, Karen, Debbie and Olwen (christened Susan). Gwyneth enjoys visiting churches and archaeological digs, especially in York, near the countryside cottage that she and John rent for annual holidays. In 1987, she collapsed under the strain of *High Road*'s busy six-days-a-week schedule. Three years later, she was rushed to hospital after a heart attack scare while rehearsing for her role as the Fairy Godmother in *Cinderella*, at the Pavilion Theatre, Glasgow, but was released after tests.

ALUN MORGAN

Arriving in Glendarroch as foreman on the golf-course development, Alun Morgan had to keep a close eye on labourers Tee Jay Wilson and Kenny Tosh. The workers soon had their own eyes on local women Carol McKay and Lynne McNeil, and Alun himself established a rapport with shopkeeper Isabel Blair.

He was a few years younger than Isabel, but they struck up a friendship, although she found it difficult at first to contemplate a serious relationship while still coming to terms with the breakdown of her marriage to Brian. When it came to a choice between moving to a new job in Leicester or staying in Glendarroch and being promoted to director of the golf course, Alun originally intended to go, but he realized his love for Isabel and moved in with her.

The couple went on holiday to Gibraltar and came back married. But tragedy followed when Alun was injured in a car crash and lost his memory. Not knowing who Isabel was, he moved into the Ardnacraig Hotel and took months to overcome his amnesia, helped greatly by Jennifer Goudie, a fortune-teller. Isabel mistakenly thought they were having an affair.

Once over his injuries and with his memory intact, Alun moved back in with Isabel and helped her to build up the shop as a business.

Mike Hayward (b. Wales) was one of the new characters introduced to *High Road* in 1990 to give the serial a broader appeal across Britain. He previously appeared in *Coronation Street* as the man who ran off with Ken Barlow's second wife, Janet, whom Ken divorced, before she returned to sleep on his sofa one night and committed suicide. Mike, who was also on TV as a councillor in the two-part thriller *The Real Eddy English*, is married to a social worker, has two children and lives in London.

ISABEL MORGAN

Glendarroch's homely shopkeeper and post mistress is a matriarchal figure in the village, but she has suffered more than her fair share of tragedy, losing a husband and son, and battling successfully against breast cancer.

Born and bred in Glendarroch, Isabel married childhood sweetheart Brian Blair. When his parents died, the couple inherited the general store and post office. Isabel and Brian had just one child, son Jimmy. Isabel blamed her husband when her second pregnancy had to be terminated by a hysterectomy. Feeling rejected, he had an affair with a waitress at the Auchtarne Arms who then blackmailed him by threatening to tell Isabel. Concerned about his wife's mental condition, and the effect such a revelation could have on her, Brian murdered the waitress. At his trial, he said nothing about the circumstances and served ten years of a life sentence.

When Brian was released on licence, Isabel found it difficult to cope with his depression and he was unable to find work in Glendarroch. When offered work in London at a drugs rehabilitation centre, he asked Isabel to go with him but she refused and the two drifted apart. Isabel's grief was compounded by the death of son Jimmy, after being beaten up by a gang of thugs trying to burgle the Glasgow chandler's shop where he had worked since leaving home.

Looking for a new purpose in life, Isabel ran for election as a local councillor. She stood against Robert Watt, who by employing dirty tricks narrowly won the campaign. He was later arrested for failing to declare his interests in business tendering for council contracts. Asked to stand at the resulting by-election, Isabel declined.

Then, she has had another, more traumatic fight, against breast cancer, and a course of radiotherapy helped her to beat the disease. More emotional scars followed with the news that Brian was planning to marry a 26-year-old woman. Then, Susan Duncan, with whom Jimmy had lodged while in Glasgow, revealed that he was the father of her baby boy, Jamie.

The arrival in Glendarroch of golf-course foreman Alun Morgan brought Isabel new romantic interest. At first, she was not ready to rush into another relationship, but gradually she began to think that Alun might be the right man. The confidante of so many villagers, known as a good listener, needed time to get over the troubles that had beset her own life. When he had a choice between leaving for another job in Leicester or becoming golf-course director, Alun decided to stay and move in with Isabel.

They married during a holiday in Gibraltar and life was looking up for both of them. But their happiness suffered a setback when Alun lost his memory in a car crash. It was months before it returned and, in the meantime, he stayed at the Ardnacraig Hotel. Once Alun was fully recovered, he helped Isabel to run the shop, but she was later to resent his interference. Alun was keen to develop the shop into a modern supermarket, with Isabel as manager but with no financial responsibility, so he approached Sam Hagen with a view to buying the business. When Isabel found out, she was furious.

☆ ☆ ☆

Eileen McCallum (b. Glasgow, 2 December 1936) is the daughter of Gordon McCallum, writer of the BBC radio 'Children's Hour' series *Down at the Mains*. He acted and sang on BBC Radio Scotland for many years, although was a teacher by profession and eventually became a headmaster.

Eileen began her professional career at the age of 12 in Scottish 'Children's Hour' with the legendary 'Auntie Kathleen' Garscadden, appearing alongside other future *High Road* actresses Gwyneth Guthrie and Mary Riggans. During her teens, Eileen made numerous radio broadcasts. After attending Hutcheson's Girls' Grammar School in Glasgow, she gained an MA at Glasgow University and trained at the Royal Scottish Academy of Music and Drama, where she won the gold medal in 1959.

Eileen appeared in one of the first TV productions made in Scotland, a play called *Who Fought Alone?*, in which her husband was portrayed by the late Frank Wylie, who later acted postman Fergus Jamieson in *High Road*. Eileen made an impact on screen in three Lewis Grassic Gibbon plays – *Smeddum*, *Grey Granite* and *Sunset Song* – and was in the Scottish Television serial *Garnock Way*, as Jean Ross, before being asked to play Isabel Blair in *High Road* when it began in 1980. She was the voice of Edwin Muir's wife in *The Vision of Edwin Muir*, a Channel Four film, and has also appeared in *Just Your Luck*, *Just Another Saturday*, *Sweet Nothings*, *Baa Baa Black Sheep*, *The Steamie*, *Taggart* and *Doctor Finlay*.

On stage, Eileen has worked exclusively for the Royal Lyceum Theatre, Edinburgh. She was a member of the original company formed there by Tom Fleming in 1965: others included Tom Conti and *Callan* star Russell Hunter. She rejoined the company when director Bill Bryden was there in the early seventies and took part in his play *Willie Rough* and productions of *Kidnapped*, *The Thrie Estatis* and *The Miser*. Later, she returned to play Sadie the tea lady in the company's production of playwright John Byrne's *The Slab Boys* at the Lyceum, followed by performances at His Majesty's Theatre, Aberdeen, and Eden Court Theatre, Inverness.

Eileen and husband Tom Fidelo, an Italian-American art dealer, have four children, Mark, Neal, Sarah and Tim, and live in a Victorian town house in Edinburgh. The couple met at drama school and went to his native America to marry in New York, where they lived for five years. Their first two children were born there, before the couple returned to Scotland. Tom left acting to turn his interest in paintings and antiques into a business. Eileen's hobbies include sewing, knitting and cycling. Eileen, who was made an MBE in 1992, has resisted the temptation to broaden her popularity so that she can stay in her beloved homeland.

> **Frederick Bartman, a regular as Simon Forrester in the legendary TV series *Emergency – Ward 10*, played KLAUS MEIER, the second German industrialist to buy the Glendarroch estate.**
>
> **Paul Kermack, who had already acted Jock Nesbit in the Scottish Television serial *Garnock Way*, played Big House handyman ARCHIE MENZIES until the actor's sudden death in March 1990.**

MENNA MORGAN

Alun Morgan's niece, Menna Morgan, was soon causing problems for her uncle and his new wife, Isabel, when she arrived in Glendarroch.

On a trip to Wales, Menna met Tiffany Bowles at a disco and brought her back to Glendarroch. Tiffany moved in with Alun and Isabel, and began making life difficult for them.

☆ ☆ ☆

Manon Jones (b. Cardiff) joined the HTV Workshop at the age of 14, appearing in the Welsh children's series *Emlyn's Moon* and *The*

> **Ross Davidson (b. Airdrie, 25 August 1949) is a former P.E. teacher who shot to fame in *EastEnders* as tragic Andy O'Brien, yuppie Debbie Wilkins's boyfriend, who died when he was hit by a lorry while trying to snatch a child from its path. Ross was subsequently on TV as a presenter of *DayTime Live*, *POB* and *Run the Gauntlet*, and acted Supt. Brand in a three-part *Taggart* story, before joining *High Road* as PETER ODELL, an interior designer working at the Big House. The actor had a five-year affair with Shirley Cheriton, who played his screen love Debbie in *EastEnders*.**
>
> **Norman Bird (b. Coalville, Leicestershire, 30 October 1924) played conman ROGER PRIMROSE, who tried to wangle free board and lodging at the Ardnacraig Hotel by faking an accident and claiming negligence on Fiona Cunningham's part. His other TV appearances include *Worzel Gummidge*, *Yes Minister*, *The Practice*, *After Henry*, *Second Thoughts* and the role of Roy in *Kinsey*. He has also acted in dozens of films, including *Whistle Down the Wind*, *The Virgin and the Gypsy*, *Please Sir!*, *Young Winston* and *Omen III:The Final Conflict*.**
>
> **Paul Young (b. Edinburgh, 3 July 1944) played Auchtarne's hellfire minister MR (GERALD) PARKER, who took over at Glendarroch Church for a while after Mr McPherson's retirement. Paul, married to broadcaster Sheila Duffy, has appeared in the films *Geordie*, *Chato's Land* and *Madame Sin*, and on TV as Ken Miller in the comedy series *No Job for a Lady*. He is the son of John Young, who acted Mr McPherson.**

Chestnut Soldier. On leaving school four years later she joined *High Road*.

A keen photographer, Manon lives with her parents in South Wales but stays in Glasgow while filming. Her mother is an actress and singer who has also appeared in the serial and her brother, Iwan, is a professional snooker player.

Manon's favourite television character is Alf Roberts of *Coronation Street*, played by Bryan Mosley. 'He always seems to have the most mundane lines, but he looks so natural and Bryan handles the part brilliantly,' says Manon.

MR (OBADIAH) MURDOCH

Scotland's biggest hypocrite, the tweed-coated, agree-with-everybody Obadiah Arthur Murdoch is a pillar of the Church and Mrs Mack's sparring partner. Although he supports her in trying to protect the moral fibre of the community, this does not always protect him from her vicious gossip. Despite his public moral stance and position as clerk of the kirk session, Mr Murdoch was a well known poacher. He used to breed dogs for export and he revels in gossip and slander.

For years, Mr Murdoch kept secret his first name, Obadiah, which embarrassed him. When Archie Menzies found it out from the kirk and opened a book, Donald Lachlan won a competition to guess the name.

Once, while poaching, Mr Murdoch accidentally shot Eddie Ramsay, on the run from the army and living rough in the woods. Eddie survived and Mr Murdoch narrowly avoided being charged by the police.

When Mrs Mack's sister, Florence Crossan, arrived in the village, Mr Murdoch was smitten and asked her to marry him. Misunderstanding, she thought he wanted Mrs Mack and Mr Murdoch beat a hasty retreat.

He gave up his dog-breeding business and left Glendarroch for Australia in 1989 but returned the following year, quickly resuming his 'professional' partnership with Mrs Mack. Although he left the village again, he returned to commiserate with Mrs Mack on the death of her sister, Florence, in 1995, before returning to work in the Church of Scotland bookshop in Edinburgh.

☆ ☆ ☆

Robert Trotter (b. Dumbarton) made his first stage appearance as a wolf cub in the Gang Show of 1939 at the town's Burgh Hall, then performed as a boy soprano at many music festivals. Soon, he was making radio broadcasts with the Glasgow Orpheus Choir.

After gaining an MA at Glasgow University and serving in the Royal Navy, Robert was an English teacher at the Bellahouston Academy in Glasgow for 11 years and a drama lecturer at Glasgow University for five years, before turning to full-time acting and directing.

He worked at various theatres and on tour, as well as appearing at the Edinburgh Festival on several occasions. He performed with the Scottish National Orchestra in playwright Tom Stoppard's *Every Good Boy Deserves Favour* in proms in Edinburgh and Glasgow.

Robert worked in radio as a member of the BBC repertory company from 1978 and, switching to television, has been in such programmes as *History is My Witness*, *The Haggard Falcon*, *The Omega Factor*, *Badger by Owl Light*, *City Sugar*, *The Fetch*, *John Ogilvy Saint and Martyr*, *Square Mile of Murder* and *The Scotched Earth Show*, with comedian Rikki Fulton, Bill Paterson and *High Road* actress Eileen McCallum. Robert lives in Glasgow.

Glasgow, Fin acted as her minder and let her stay in his flat in the city, where she lost her virginity to him.

But, when Trish gave him the brush-off, Fin had a fling with Tiffany Bowles, taking her to his parents' holiday cottage. But Trish came running back to him and they resumed their relationship, although Fin did not take it very seriously and the pair eventually parted.

William Tapley grew up in South Australia and finished his schooling in America, before moving to Britain. He graduated from RADA in July 1993. He had already appeared on television in the 'Screen One' production *A Breed of Heroes* and *Which Way to the War?* when he landed the role of Phineas North in *High Road*.

William, who plays soccer, abseils, paraglides and cycles, sings with the London-based group Joyride. His girlfriend, Ann, is a model who sometimes appears in *High Road* as an extra.

PHINEAS NORTH

Water-sports instructor Phineas North – known as Fin – walked into the Ardnacraig Hotel and immediately set female hearts aflutter, although he seemed oblivious to the fact.

Trish McDonald, who worked behind the hotel bar, fell for Fin, but she thought he was into drugs when she found him in his Land Rover injecting himself with a syringe. After explaining to Trish that the dose was insulin and he was a diabetic, Fin took a while to forgive her for jumping to conclusions. When Trish landed a Saturday-night job singing at the Cat Club, in

EDDIE RAMSAY

Son of no-good Fraser, Eddie Ramsay looked as if he would turn out like his father. Saving Sheila Lamont from the unwanted attentions of her former boyfriend, Frank Riddle, he slept with Sheila and she became pregnant.

Worse came when Eddie broke into Blair's Store, then stole the local Highland Games money from the organizing tent. Brian Blair and Sorry Watson tracked down the culprit but saw the chance for Eddie to break out of a cycle of crime. Sorry paid for what was stolen and took Eddie back to Shetland with him to find a job and earn money to repay the debt.

Returning to Glendarroch a reformed man, Eddie was heartbroken when Sheila gave away their baby for adoption at birth. But, guilty at depriving Sheila of going to university because of her pregnancy, he tried to compensate by entering the revived Glendarroch Hill Race to raise money for a lifeboat on the loch, with the aim of giving her the prize money. Although he failed to win, Sheila was so touched that she continued seeing him and, in 1985, the couple wed and lived in Jock Campbell's cottage. Eddie had previously lodged there and Jock had by now moved into an old people's home.

But the marriage foundered after Sheila had an affair with an Open University lecturer. Eddie discovered this and, because he was also being falsely accused of stealing Mrs Mack's purse from the village hall at the same time, decided there was no future for him in Glendarroch. He left and joined the army, although later returned

147

when he faced a court martial after striking a bullying sergeant. The situation was resolved when his C.O. tracked him down to say that the sergeant himself was to be court martialled and Eddie would be required to give evidence.

Working in computers for the army, Eddie tapped into the Adoption Society's records and found out the name and gender of the child whom Sheila had given away for adoption years earlier – a girl called Allison Miller. Then, the adoptive father contacted Eddie when looking for a bone-marrow donor, wanting to know whether Allison had any brothers or sisters. Eddie returned to Glendarroch and told Sheila the story. By then, she was living with boyfriend Paul Martin, but Eddie and Sheila visited Allison in hospital.

In Glendarroch, Eddie took up for a while with Susan Duncan – mother of the late Jimmy Blair's love child – but then rekindled the flames with Sheila. They remarried in 1994 and, on experiencing problems in having more children, decided to foster. Their first two children were Sarah and Callum Gilchrist, whose mother was ill. They stayed until she left hospital.

Then, in 1995, Eddie and Sheila took in 15-year-old problem child Dominic Dunbar, who had previously been fostered out to many couples. His last foster mother had died and he moved in with Eddie and Sheila, who had to deal with the fact that he sniffed glue.

Robin Cameron gained an MA arts degree from Glasgow University and has had two stints in *High Road*. His other television parts include Neil Grant in *Maggie*, John in *A Woman Calling*, the title role in *Orpheus*, D.C. McDonald in two episodes of *Minder* and Charles McLaren in *Strathblair*. He has also appeared on TV in *Let Yourself Go*, *A Jacobite Adventure* and *The Justice Game*.

As well as acting in commercials for Northern Irish Electricity Board, Landmark chemists, Simmers biscuits and the *Today* newspaper, Robin has appeared on stage in *Romeo and Juliet*, *The Crofting Act*, *Othello*, *Measure for Measure*, *The Wonder*, *The Lambs of God* and *Surprised by Love*.

SHEILA RAMSAY

The tightly knit community of Glendarroch was shocked when schoolgirl Sheila Lamont became pregnant by Eddie Ramsay – and even more upset when she moved in with him. Sheila's parents, Dan and Irene Lamont, had their hopes of her going to university after leaving

Auchtarne High School dashed. Eddie, who had slipped into a life of petty crime, had reformed his ways by the time he met Sheila, rescuing her from the unwanted attentions of Frank Riddle, her ex-boyfriend. Their relationship developed and she found she was carrying his baby. Her father was furious and her mother distressed.

In the circumstances, Sheila left for Glasgow shortly before the baby was due and had it there. She sent it immediately for adoption without her and Eddie even knowing whether it was a boy or a girl. He did not know what she had done until her return to the village and wanted her to marry him.

Only later, in 1985, did she agree to marriage and the couple lived in Jock Campbell's cottage. Eddie had been living there, and Jock moved into an old people's home. He insisted that Eddie have the cottage as long as he married Sheila.

Sheila, who wanted to complete her education, started an Open University course, went away on a summer school and had an affair with a lecturer. Eddie, still finding it difficult to come to terms with the fact that she had given away their baby, found out and walked out on her to join the army.

When Robert Forsyth, the local vet who provided the *Auchtarne Herald* with Glendarroch news stories, decided to retire, he offered Sheila the chance to take over his role as a 'stringer' for the paper. She accepted and later combined the job with working at Blair's Store.

When the *Herald* was bought by Mark Ritchie, Sheila was given a full-time job writing for the paper and running the office. Following the launch of a free rival, the paper later closed and Sheila became Fiona Ryder's secretary at

Glendarroch estate, where Greg expanded his business after marrying Fiona.

Sheila became a more high-powered career woman. She also found a new boyfriend, Paul Martin – Greg's manager at the new marina – who moved in with her. That relationship eventually ended and was followed by a broken engagement to Tom Kerr.

Sheila then fell back into the arms of her ex-husband, Eddie, who had found out that the baby Sheila had given away for adoption years earlier was a girl called Allison Miller, who was in need of a bone-marrow transplant.

This paved the way for the couple to remarry, in 1994, with Sheila wearing the same dress as she had nine years earlier, after Effie Macinnes spilled red wine on her new one.

Experiencing difficulties in having more children, Sheila and Eddie decided to foster, taking in first Sarah and Callum Gilchrist, then glue-sniffing Dominic Dunbar.

☆ ☆ ☆

Lesley Fitz-Simons (b. Glasgow, 23 September 1961) ignored the advice of her careers teachers not to go into acting and took up professionally what her father had enjoyed doing as an amateur.

On completing her schooling at Kilsyth Academy, she went to Jeanne Gourlay, who taught her how to use her voice and move. Since then, she has passed on her love of acting to youngsters from Milton of Campsie, the village in which she grew up.

Lesley appeared in the memorable television series *The Prime of Miss Jean Brodie*, playing one of the schoolgirls in the first episode. Her other TV work has included *Square Mile of Murder*, *House on the Hill*, *Skin Deep* and a guest appearance in *Funny You Should Say That*, in which she was challenged to keep a straight face in the 'Don't Make Me Laugh' spot.

She joined *High Road* in 1983 and has made a TV commercial for skin lotion that was screened in Pakistan, which meant having her hair dyed black and her skin darkened, as well as learning a few sentences of the language.

On stage, Lesley played the Good Fairy in *Mother Goose* at the Gaiety Theatre, Ayr, alongside Frank Carson and *High Road* actresses Mary Riggans and Teri Lally.

In 1989, Lesley married Peter McIntyre, sales director of a building company, in Glasgow Cathedral, although the couple have since divorced. Away from the studios, Lesley enjoys baking, reading, walking and driving in the countryside.

MICHAEL ROSS

When he arrived in the village, Michael Ross was assistant to the fire-and-brimstone minister Gerald Parker, of St Ninian's in Auchtarne, who started preaching in Glendarroch Church when Mr McPherson was planning to retire. Villagers rebelled, the plan to link the two parishes was abandoned, Mr Parker returned to Auchtarne and Mr McPherson continued as minister.

Michael later returned to farming and became estate manager at Letir-Falloch. However, when Mr McPherson finally retired, Michael returned to the cloth, moved into the manse and has become an important part of the community. Michael caused controversy when he married Susan Duncan, a single mother who was going out with divorcé Eddie Ramsay. They had their own child, daughter Belle, in 1994.

☆ ☆ ☆

Gordon MacArthur (b. Elgin, Morayshire, 7 November 1961) trained at the Guildhall School of Music and Drama. He has appeared on TV in *Boswell's London Journal* and *The Justice Game*. On stage, he has acted at the Young Vic and Theatre of Comedy, and the Edinburgh Festival, in which he appeared in Robert Louis Stevenson's *Treasure Island*.

Gordon was asked to play a driver in a *High Road* Hogmanay storyline after being spotted by Scottish Television acting in the Borders Festival, an event organized by Lord (David) Steel's wife, Judy. Weeks later, he was asked back to play the assistant minister in the serial.

When Gordon was written out as a result of screen wife Jacqueline Gilbride's pregnancy – which saw the character of Michael sent to Zimbabwe on an exchange with a minister there because it did not seem appropriate to have the minister's wife giving birth shortly after marrying him – his replacement in the storyline, Doctor Ben, was played by Troy Fairclough, brother of Leeds United soccer star Chris. Michael is single and enjoys listening to music, and playing golf and the piano.

SUSAN ROSS

When Jimmy Blair left Glendarroch for Glasgow, Susan Duncan and her husband Bill gave him lodgings. On the first anniversary of Jimmy's murder, an 'In Memoriam' notice appeared in a newspaper, signed simply 'S'. Sheila Ramsay traced it to Susan, who later visited Jimmy's mother, Isabel, with her baby, Jamie. Isabel thought the boy must be Jimmy's.

Susan denied it, but Isabel's belief was confirmed when medical tests proved that Susan's husband could not father a child. When Bill became physically abusive, Susan walked out on him and went to live in Glendarroch, where she became nanny to Fiona Ryder's son, David.

Susan fell for Sheila Ramsay's ex-husband, Eddie – who eventually remarried Sheila – and then caused more of a stir in Glendarroch by marrying the minister, Michael Ross. Theirs is a fiery relationship. Susan does not see herself simply as a minister's wife, looking after the W.I. and serving tea to various committees. In 1994, she gave birth to daughter Belle.

☆ ☆ ☆

Jacqueline Gilbride (b. Jacqueline Gilbrook in Glasgow) trained at the Welsh College of Music and Drama. Before joining *High Road*, she appeared on TV in *Quartet*, *The Dark Room*, *The Justice Game*, *Changing Steps* and *Brag*, as well as Flora Extra Light and road-safety commercials. She was on radio in *Level 3*, as a singer, and the BBC Radio 4 pilot *Effects*. Jacqueline is married with a daughter.

Michael Browning (b. Ongar, Essex, 15 May 1930), SIR JOHN ROSS-GIFFORD from 1987 to 1990, also played Fawcett in *Emmerdale*, Henry Carter in *Crossroads*, brewery boss George Newton in *Coronation Street* and Tom Fisher in *Trainer*.

Caroline Ashley (b. Caroline Smith in Coatbridge, 4 March 1958) played FIONA RYDER, daughter of the Lady Laird, Elizabeth Cunningham. Fiona had an illegitimate son, David, by businessman Ruari Galbraith, before marrying Greg Ryder. The marriage broke up and the couple left Glendarroch, although they were later rumoured to have reunited in London. In real life, Caroline married screen husband Alan Hunter in 1993, after leaving the serial, and subsequently gave birth to a baby boy.

Alan Hunter (b. Liverpool) played GREG RYDER, the English businessman who bought up land in Glendarroch to develop into a massive leisure park, with a golf course and marina. He also met and married Fiona Cunningham. Divorcé Alan, who had previously appeared on TV in *Crown Court*, *Strangers*, *The Spoils of War*, *Squadron*, *Bergerac*, *Minder*, *Dempsey and Makepeace*, *Truckers*, *Hannay*, *The Bill* and *Snakes and Ladders*, later wed screen wife Caroline Ashley.

ERIC ROSS-GIFFORD

The only child of English aristocrats Sir John and Lady Margaret Ross-Gifford, Eric was brought up with a silver spoon in his mouth and educated at public school and Oxford University. In Glendarroch, he began to learn the bitter realities of life without such pampering, changing from a wimp who was dominated by his mother into a husband and father running the Ardnacraig Hotel.

Eric's parents took over Glendarroch House after the death of the Lady Laird, Elizabeth Cunningham, and Eric's girlfriend, Joanna Simpson, moved in with them. They later married, much to Lady Margaret's disapproval.

Sir John decided to return to London and made Eric and Joanna managers of the estate. However, they did not have the experience to do a good job and Eric made the fundamental mistake of appointing Davie Sneddon as factor (steward) of Glendarroch. It was a blow to Eric and Joanna when Sir John died, leaving the estate to Fiona Cunningham. Although Fiona initially refused to accept it, she eventually did so and gave the couple a half-share in the Ardnacraig Hotel.

Trouble has never been far away from Eric. Wife Joanna became pregnant but was unaware whether he was the father, after having a one-night stand with businessman Ruari Galbraith. Eric also had an AIDS scare after using a drug-user's needle and was fined after pleading guilty to a drink-driving charge. Happier times came with the birth of Eric and Joanna's daughter, Lucy, in 1993.

☆ ☆ ☆

Richard Greenwood (b. Richard Peirse-Duncomb in Wales, 1969) moved around as a child because of his father's army career. He was at St Andrews University for a year before deciding that, because he was spending much of his time in amateur dramatics, he should take up acting professionally.

Richard, who changed his stage name to Greenwood, appeared on television in *The Campbells* and *The Houseman's Tale* before joining *High Road* in 1987. He has also been in *Taggart*. On stage, he was in a touring production of *Witches of Traquair*, written by Ettrick shepherd James Hogg, and performed at the Wolsey Theatre, Ipswich, and the Pitlochry Festival Theatre.

In 1990, Richard married *High Road* actress Gillian McNeill and they live in Glasgow. He enjoys fishing, golf, playing board games and doing crosswords.

Eric and Joanna Ross-Gifford have had much heartbreak during their stormy marriage.

JOANNA ROSS-GIFFORD

Eric Ross-Gifford's mother, Lady Margaret, disapproved of his choice of Joanna Simpson as his wife, feeling that he was marrying beneath himself. The couple had met at Oxford University and moved to Glendarroch House when Eric's parents bought it.

In 1988, during their first year of marriage, Joanna had a one-night stand with businessman Ruari Galbraith after dining with him at a remote hotel in an attempt to patch up the troubles between him and Fiona Cunningham, who had fathered his son David.

Joanna was horrified to discover afterwards that she herself was pregnant, although Eric was thrilled by the prospect of becoming a father and celebrated the news, unaware that the baby might not be his.

Eric's father, Sir John, knew of the fling and had already advised Joanna to say nothing to Eric for the sake of the couple's marriage.

Eventually, Joanna did confess what had happened and Eric was devastated. At first, he walked out, going to stay with his mother in London, but he returned and the couple made up. To Joanna's relief, she had a miscarriage and lost the baby.

After failing to run the Glendarroch estate successfully, Joanna and Eric took over the Ardnacraig Hotel. She quickly established herself as the driving force and he took a job at the marina to bring in extra money.

In 1993, the couple were elated at the birth of their daughter, Lucy, who was given the half-share in the Ardnacraig Hotel owned by Greg Ryder when he left Glendarroch. The hotel underwent a facelift in 1995, when odd-job man Chic Cherry began work there.

☆ ☆ ☆

Tamara Kennedy (b. Tamara Brooks in Edinburgh, 23 May 1962), the daughter of a Polish father, always hoped to be a teacher or an actress. At St Denis School, Edinburgh, whose old girls include Hannah Gordon and former *High Road* actress Muriel Romanes, Tamara was trained by drama teacher Jan Moffat. She won the gold medal at the London Academy of Music and Dramatic Art and became a member of the National Youth Theatre. She also gained an MA in English and drama at Glasgow University.

Tamara has performed in theatres all over Scotland, including two seasons at the world's smallest, the 35-seater Little Theatre on the Isle of Mull. She acted in *Private Lives* at the Royal Lyceum Theatre, Edinburgh, starred in Noël Coward's *Hay Fever* at Perth Repertory Theatre and played Kate in *The Taming of the Shrew* and Titania in *A Midsummer Night's Dream*. When she auditioned for *High Road* in 1987, it was only her second TV screen test.

Married to social worker Robin Barbour in 1989, Tamara wrote and illustrated a children's book, *Happy Hettie Meets the Condiment Queen*. Her great-great-grandfather, the chemist Sir William Henry Perkin, discovered the dye purple.

DAVIE SNEDDON

The 'J.R.' of Glendarroch, Davie Sneddon arrived as a nasty piece of work operating the neighbouring estate of Letir-Falloch for Harry Shaw – pop star Vincent – and was soon angering villagers. He left behind a wife and a son, Drew, who was a chip off the old block.

The factor (steward) showed his true colours when he 'pelleted' bulls for the Highland Show, making them look fatter at market. Inverdarroch was blamed and thrown out of the show. Eric Ross-Gifford made a monumental error in offering him the job of factor at Glendarroch. Sneddon got his own back on the estate workers there who had been responsible for his loss of face at Letir-Falloch by sacking them. One of them was water bailiff Bob Taylor.

But Sneddon went too far in trying to blackmail Lady Margaret Ross-Gifford after finding her in a compromising situation with old flame Harry Somers. He wanted security of tenure from her husband, but she was planning to leave Sir John anyway and told him of Sneddon's threat. Finding that Sneddon had also illegally kept his job at Letir-Falloch, Sir John sacked him and he returned to the neighbouring estate.

During his previous spell at Letir-Falloch, Sneddon had been romantically involved with divorcée Lorna Seton, the Lady Laird's secre-tary. He was not interested only in love but wanted her to feed him information on prices, costs and customers for peat-cutting from the Glendarroch estate.

Later, he had an affair with district nurse Claire Kerr, who had just married Tom Kerr. On finding out about the affair, in 1990, Tom confronted Sneddon with a shotgun. Eventually, Tom broke the gun and slowly poured a glass from the whiskey bottle that Sneddon had pushed towards him, before leaving without another word. The scandal drove Tom to a nervous breakdown and led to Claire leaving the village for America. Sneddon himself fled Glendarroch, where he no longer had a job, following the sale of Letir-Falloch by Harry Shaw to a mystery buyer, who it transpired was Greg Ryder, who bulldozed the land and turned it into a leisure centre and golf course.

Months later, Sneddon returned, full of remorse, but was soon back to his old ways, shocking villagers by taking over Inverdarroch, the farm owned by Tom Kerrh, who had by then left.

Sneddon's next conquest was Sam Hagen, by then running the Ryder Corporation. He was also made estate manager, with a financial interest, at Alt-na-Mara. When Sneddon found out that Sam was seeing Greg Ryder, he hired a private detective, who discovered that she had once married an older man, acquiring his wealth and sharing it with Greg, who had been her lover. Sneddon passed on this information to Greg's wife, Fiona, who divorced him.

Next in line for Sneddon's affections was Lynne McNeil, who had previously worked for him. She shocked him with the announcement that she was pregnant, but did not tell him when it proved to be a false alarm, allowing the wedding plans to proceed. However, on the big day, Lynne realized that she could not go through with the ceremony and left Sneddon standing at the altar, humiliated.

It was not long before Sneddon had ensnared another woman, Judith Crombie, housekeeper at Glendarroch House, first to Lord Strathmorris, then to its new owner, Sam Hagen. The couple were thrown together by a mutual dislike of Sam and moved into P.C. Douglas Kirk's cottage, living as man and wife, after he moved to Auchtarne. But that romance, like all the others, eventually ran its course.

Derek Lord (b. Belfast) played the most disliked character in *High Road*, and the actor was axed. However, the producers failed to appreciate that viewers always like to see a baddie in a soap, and there was such an outcry that Davie Sneddon was brought back.

The son of a joiner, Derek was taken to London at the age of six months when his father started a building firm there. The family returned to Ireland when he was six because of his mother's homesickness. His father sold the London company to a partner who become a millionaire.

Derek's boyhood hero was the Irish actor Colin Blakely, and he admired Peter O'Toole and Walter Matthau. However, he planned a career in journalism and was offered a job as a cub reporter on the *Belfast Evening Telegraph*. The week before he was due to start work, his parents split up and he left Belfast with his mother to live in England, ending up as a quality-control inspector in a Coventry factory.

His parents reunited after two years, but by this time he did not want to return to Belfast and become a journalist. Instead, Derek emigrated to Australia, taking advantage of the £10 assisted-passage scheme offered by the British government. He hated the people Down Under, finding them rude and arrogant, and was picked on because of his accent.

During five years there in the late sixties, he did menial jobs. At one stage, he was so broke that he slept on the beach on an island off Australia's west coast, near Perth, famous for its 60cm (2ft) tall rats. He awoke with half-a-dozen crawling over him and went back to the mainland, working his passage on a millionaire's yacht. During that trip, he saw a newspaper advertisement, 'Actors Wanted', and bluffed his way through an audition for a touring theatre company. His first job was as the vicar in *The Admirable Crichton*, in Perth. He also appeared in *King Lear*, at Woomera Rocket Range.

Returning to Britain, Derek made a dozen films – including *The Black Windmill*, starring Michael Caine, and *Cal*, opposite Helen Mirren – and the TV series *Billy*, featuring Kenneth Branagh. He was spotted by Scottish Television while appearing on stage at the Tron Theatre, Glasgow. With his brooding, dark Irish looks, he was the ideal Davie Sneddon. But he might never have been asked to audition but for clairvoyant Margaret O'Flaherty, who had advised him to take the lower paid of two jobs that he would be offered. So, when given the chance to earn £1200 to do three days' work on a BBC production, he turned it down to star at the Tron Theatre, for £100 a week, in *Burke and Hare*, a play about grave-robbers. In fact, the BBC job was rescheduled and he managed to do both.

Members of the *High Road* production team went to see the play because Derek's stage wife was played by the serial's village nurse. They saw Derek playing a murderous bastard and realized he was ideal for the role of Sneddon, which had been created but not yet cast.

When he joined *High Road* in 1984, Derek, actress wife Lana McDonnell and son Barry were living in Bray, a small village outside Dublin. Derek continued to fly to Glasgow for recording each week for five years, then moved the family to Scotland, to a home near Largs, on the Clyde coast. Shortly afterwards, he was axed from *High Road* as a result of his character's nastiness. However, Scottish Television admitted that it had misread research and Derek was brought back after a flood of complaints.

Actor Liam Neeson was best man at Derek's wedding, and the *High Road* actor's son Barry has already appeared in the film *My Left Foot*. Derek has more recently acted the lead role of Nicola Stedahl in the TV drama *The Yugoslave Hitman*, during a break from *High Road*.

MORAG STEWART

The daughter of Jamie Stewart, whose croft shared a border with Dougal Lachlan's, Morag found herself doing most of the work on it. He contracted Alzheimer's disease and she nursed him without telling other villagers, until he moved to a home in Auchtarne.

Running the croft alone was hard work, but her determination often made it more efficient than others run by men. She is often seen in workshirts and dungarees.

Morag has never had a serious romance, although there have been interested men. After Dougal's wife died in childbirth, various people tried to pair him off with Morag, but it was an on-off relationship. It would simply have been a marriage of convenience – there were never any great flames of passion.

The good-natured crofter Tom Kerr also showed an interest in Morag, his neighbour. She had a soft spot for him, but there was no lasting romance and she encouraged Claire Millar, the new district nurse, to marry him – and was their bridesmaid. Morag also made a play for local vet Colin Begg, but nothing came of it. She received no thanks for telling Tom Kerr about his wife Claire's affair with Davie Sneddon.

As running her farm became more difficult, Morag gave up crofting and turned it into a goat farm. Sneddon lodged with her before his move into P.C. Kirk's cottage with Judith Crombie.

☆ ☆ ☆

Jeannie Fisher (b. Glasgow, 18 February 1947) trained at the Royal Scottish Academy of Music and Drama, then was an understudy at the Royal Court Theatre, London. Her many stage performances include *The Double Dealer*, *The Three Musketeers*, *Slag*, the world premiere of *Yarsdale* at the 1985 Edinburgh Festival, a *Macbeth* tour of India, *Whose Life Is It Anyway? and Blithe Spirit*. Jeannie has acted in many radio plays and appeared on television in *Canterbury Tales*, *The Silver Sword*, *Adam Smith* and *Arthur of the Britons*. She is single, has flats in London and Edinburgh, and enjoys reading and going to the cinema and theatre.

DR (ALEXANDER) WALLACE

After passing his medical exams, Sandy (Alexander) Wallace joined his father as partner in the local doctors' practice. He has become an important part of the community, an old-fashioned country general practitioner who has time to see people and talk through their problems instead of immediately referring them to a hospital. When Fiona Cunningham came to him worried about her son David, he had no choice but to send him for tests, although initial worries that the boy had a brain tumour were eventually alleviated.

☆ ☆ ☆

Michael Elder (b. London, 30 April 1931) was born of Scottish parents and came from a medical family – his father and sister are both general practitioners. He trained at the Royal Academy of Dramatic Art and has since worked at the Byre Theatre, St Andrews, the Citizens' Theatre, Glasgow, the Gateway Theatre, Edinburgh, and the Pitlochry Festival Theatre, and with the Edinburgh Lyceum and Scottish theatre companies. He performed his one-man show, *Whalers*, at the 1986 Edinburgh Festival – winning a Fringe First award – and on tour.

Michael has appeared on TV in *Sam*, *Edward VII*, *Weir of Hermiston*, *Five Red Herrings*, *The Prime of Miss Jean Brodie* and the Scottish Television serial *Garnock Way*, in which he portrayed a policeman. As well as playing Dr Wallace in *High Road*, he has been a writer and script editor of the serial. His other writing work includes TV scripts for *The Walls of Jericho*, *King's Royal* and *Murder Not Proven*, more than 150 radio scripts and 25 novels.

Married to actress Sheila Donald, Michael has two grown-up sons, Simon and David.

CAROL WILSON

One of life's eternal drifters, Carol McKay attended Auchtarne High School, a year behind Sheila Ramsay, her close friend and confidante, whom she later helped through marital upsets. On leaving school, Carol began a succession of jobs, and at one time posed a threat to Isabel Blair's stores by starting her own mobile shop.

She was a waitress at the Ardnacraig Hotel until she was replaced by Emma Aitken. Taking pity on her, Isabel Blair offered her a job in the shop but dismissed her after she arranged a wild party there one night and money was stolen from the post office safe. It turned out to be a practical joke played by Emma Aitken, with whom Carol had never got on.

Her idea of opening a tearoom with Effie Macinnes in the village hall was scuppered by caretaker Mrs Mack, who would not allow it. Instead, the village busybody started her own tearoom in the manse (vicarage) and offered Carol a job as a waitress. When the tearoom was forced to close, Carol returned to Isabel Blair's shop.

Carol was always looking for romance and lamenting the lack of 'action' in Glendarroch, and her youthful antics often got her into trouble. Men have been another disaster area. Woodcutter Jim Hunter tried to murder her when she believed herself to be pregnant. Brian Blair, with whom Hunter was lodging, threatened to tell the police if he did not leave the district. He left, later to return and die in a fire that he himself had started at the Glendarroch woodshed in an attempt to get even with Brian, by this time operating the sawmill.

Relationships followed with Willie Gillespie – who eventually returned to Glasgow after deciding that country life was not for him – and Tee Jay Wilson, another Glaswegian who arrived to work as a labourer on Greg Ryder's golf-course development. Their stormy relationship looked as if it had run its course when his ex-girlfriend, Shona, arrived with a baby and claimed that Tee

Jay was the father, but it transpired that the baby belonged to someone for whom she was babysitting.

Carol had already moved into a cottage with Lynne McNeil. Later, they were joined by Emma Aitken, whom Carol had previously disliked, but she came to realize that the hotel waitress was, like herself, simply looking for a good time in Glendarroch. Emma moved out after Kenny Tosh started dating her and ditched Lynne in the process.

Carol eventually married Tee Jay, but tragedy followed when they had a baby daughter, Mary, who suffered a cot death.

In 1994, happiness came to the couple with the birth of a baby boy, Jordan. But it was a further blow to them when Tee Jay was jailed after striking a thief who had robbed the shop.

Teri Lally (b. Teresa Lally in Coatbridge, Lanarkshire, 21 April 1961) decided to become an actress during her last year at St Columba High School, so moved to Edinburgh to attend Queen Margaret College Drama School.

On leaving, she qualified for her Equity actors' union card by forming a song-and-sketches group with college friends, playing at hotels and pubs in Edinburgh. Teri then had a part in *Cinderella* at the Civic Theatre, Motherwell, was spotted by *High Road*'s producer and offered the role of schoolgirl Carol McKay in the serial.

Her other TV work includes appearances in *The Video Show*, *Cameron on Camera* – an Andy Cameron special – *Ready or Not*, a Scottish TV 'Preview' play, and a celebrity edition of *Wheel of Fortune*. She has also appeared in commercials for the Bank of Scotland and William Low's.

Teri has made two films, both set in Scotland. In *Restless Natives*, she played tour guide Margot, who was courted by one of two young motorcyclists who robbed coachloads of holidaymakers and gave away money to the needy, in the process becoming rivals to the Loch Ness monster as a tourist attraction. Joe Mullaney, the other thieving motorcyclist in the film, played Teri's on-screen boyfriend, Willie Gillespie, in *High Road*, before Ewen Emery took over the role. She also had a small part in *Comfort and Joy*, directed by Bill Forsyth.

On stage, Teri played a French lodger in the farce *Don't Tell the Wife*, featuring Jimmy Logan, and appeared in *Never a Dull Moment*, as well as starring in the pantomimes *Babes in the Wood*, *Mother Goose* (in which Frank Carson and *High Road* actresses Mary Riggans and Lesley Fitz-Simons also featured), *Dick Whittington*, *Merlin the Magnificent* and *Cinderella*.

The actress shared a flat above a grocer's shop in Inverleith, Edinburgh, with a nurse and two actresses before marrying building inspector Kenny Mackenzie, after a five-year romance. One of her fans composed a romantic ballad to be performed specially for the wedding. The couple have since divorced.

Teri is now married to Scott Ferguson, Scottish Television's editor of news, sport and current affairs and brother of comedian Craig Ferguson. Their daughter, Lucy, was born in December 1993. They live in Glasgow. Teri enjoys reading, home decorating and going to the cinema.

TEE JAY WILSON

Beefy Tee Jay Wilson arrived from Glasgow, where he had been a building worker, to be a labourer on the new golf-course development in Glendarroch, under foreman Alun Morgan. His fellow worker on the course, Kenny Tosh, was soon after Lynne McNeil, although they broke up when he fell for Emma Aitken.

Tee Jay chased Carol McKay and an on-off romance developed. It was put to the test by the pestering of Tee Jay's former girlfriend, Shona, who came to Glendarroch with a baby, telling Carol that Tee Jay was the father. It transpired that she was simply looking after someone else's baby. The romance with Carol was back on, the couple wed and had a baby daughter, Mary, but they were both distraught after she suffered a cot death.

In 1994, Carol became pregnant with son Jordan. She was left on her own during the pregnancy when Tee Jay was jailed for nine months after chasing a robber from Blair's Store, catching him near the church and attacking him. Isabel Morgan was ostracized by villagers for telling police that she saw Tee Jay punch the robber after she had told him to stop. He was convicted of aggravated assault, the same charge that had led to a conviction during his youth. Tee Jay came out of prison after six months for good behaviour.

Andrew Gillan (b. Glasgow, 7 February 1966) trained at the Scottish Academy of Music and Drama, which he left in 1989. He has acted on stage in *The Gorbals Story*, *Vodka and Daisies*, *Greedy Grant* and *Mother Goose*, on television in an episode of *Taggart*, and in a German cinema commercial for *The Phantom of the Opera*. Andrew joined *High Road* in 1990, is single and enjoys swimming, writing music and reading.

The original 1988 cast of Home and Away. *Standing: Martin Dibble (Craig Thomson), Ruth Stewart (Justine Clarke), Lance Smart (Peter Vroom), Floss McPhee (Sheila Kennelly), Neville McPhee (Frank Lloyd), Carly Morris (Sharyn Hodgson), Donald Fisher (Norman Coburn), Frank Morgan (Alex Papps), Celia Stewart (Fiona Spence), Alf Stewart (Ray Meagher), Ailsa Hogan (Judy Nunn). Seated: Steven Matheson (Adam Willits), Tom Fletcher (Roger Oakley), Pippa Fletcher (Vanessa Downing), Sally Keating (Kate Ritchie), Bobby Simpson (Nicolle Dickson), Lynn Davenport (Helena Bozich).*

Home and Away was launched by the Australian 7 Network to compete against *Neighbours*, which it had previously screened but axed, only to see the rival 10 Network revive the programme and make it a success. Based around Tom and Pippa Fletcher, who moved to the small coastal town of Summer Bay, where they bought a caravan park and became foster parents to a string of waifs and strays, *Home and Away* was created by executive producer Alan Bateman after he visited a small town in southern New South Wales where a plan to house foster children in a new home there was dividing the community. Bevan Lee, a former actor who had been a writer and storyline editor on *Sons and Daughters* for its first three years, was brought in as series script editor and began fleshing out the story, which was to feature large numbers of children and young people, many of whom had experienced mental or physical abuse.

The one-hour pilot episode was well received when it was broadcast in Australia in January 1988, resulting in the serial being given the go-ahead. Within six months, it was one of Australia's top programmes. When ITV bought *Home and Away* as a rival to *Neighbours* – screened by the BBC – British viewers first saw the new soap on 11 February 1989, although viewers in the London and Yorkshire regions saw that pilot episode a day later, and it was soon drawing large audiences. One of the serial's biggest attractions is its frequent outdoor shots, often on the white-sand beaches that are a part of Australian life and culture for so many who live there. But it is the programme's ability to present stories about and for young people that has made it a success on both sides of the world.

DONNA BISHOP

Principled but with a heart of gold, Donna Bishop is an enthusiastic young guidance counsellor. The youngest in a large family, she enjoyed performing in school musicals during her childhood and was the last to leave home. At 18, she faced the choice of marrying fiancé Rob Storey and settling down or continuing her education by moving to the city. She opted to further her career, gaining a Bachelor of Psychology degree and becoming a school counsellor. For two years, she worked at a school in the city, dealing with sexual and emotional abuse cases, before returning home to work at Summer Bay High School.

She was glad to move back to her family but apprehensive about meeting Rob again because they had parted on bad terms. Fortunately, there were no ill feelings. That could not be said when a former boyfriend, Andrew Warren, turned up as the school's new maths teacher. They had lived together in the city, but Donna left when he started beating her up.

Nicola Quilter studied for a year at the Victorian College of the Arts and another at the Actors Centre, in Sydney. She then played the lead role of Tessa in the film *Driven Mad* and acted Louise in the Australian soap *Chances*, Shirley in *Boys from the Bush* – seen in Britain – Louise in *Skirts* and Sally in *Under the Skin*, as well as appearing in *Police Rescue* and playing a character called Kelly in *Home and Away*. She later returned to the serial as Donna Bishop.

On stage, Nicola has appeared in *Aberration*, *Funeral Games*, *At the Foot of the Mountain* (which she wrote and performed with the Big Bird Theatre Company), *Dracula Baby*, *Reidy River*, *The One's Out of Town*, a tour of *Hair*, *Three Winters Green* and *The Crucible*.

SELINA COOK

Born and brought up in Summer Bay, Selina Cook comes from an unloving family and consequently craves affection. Her family's lack of money frequently put her in awkward social situations. She was already part of the smoothies set in the Diner and spending nights out at the Surf Club when she tried to seduce teacher Luke Cunningham at Summer Bay High's debutante ball. But he made it clear he did not want her attentions and the incident earned Selina a reputation as a slut.

She later cleaned up her act and proved to be a tart with a heart. It was a shock to Selina when she fell for Jack Wilson, another wild child, after years of chasing anything in trousers. When Jack invited her over to the Rosses' house for dinner, she jumped at the chance. She had a common bond with him – he also had grown up without love. When the couple went to the debutante ball, Donald Fisher caught them kissing in the car park.

Selina was not so pleased when she found that Jack was also seeing 16-year-old Sonia Johnson, who had already had a fling with Tug O'Neale and was out for a good time. Selina was so angry that she hit Jack.

Then, when Jack three-timed her and Sonia with Angel Brooks's sister, Frankie, the girls teamed up to teach him a lesson, luring him into a caravan, locking it and stealing his clothes.

Selina found a new home when Irene Roberts decided to foster her, although the teenager was unsure what she was letting herself in for when Irene enrolled her in a school that specialized in teaching tearaways good manners.

Selina turned her attentions to newcomer Curtis

Toni Pearen, ex-girlfriend of former *Home and Away* star Mat Stevenson, played rookie teacher BETH ARMSTRONG, who gave private lessons to dyslexic Tug O'Neale after his car accident. Toni previously played teenager Toni Windsor in *E Street*. She was also in the films *All Men Are Liars*, as the lead singer in an all-girl rock group, and has had a string of hit singles in Australia, and released an album, *Intimate*.

Cornelia Frances (b. Liverpool, 7 April 1941) has a reputation for playing baddies in Australian soaps. She was Sister Grace Scott in *The Young Doctors* and Barbara Hamilton in *Sons and Daughters*, before joining *Home and Away* as former judge MORAG BELLINGHAM, who was the mother of Bobby Simpson and gave her away for adoption.

Cathy Godbold acted tragic MEG BOWMAN, who moved to Summer Bay with her mother to spend her last days there before dying of leukaemia in 1992. Cathy, who had played Jeremy Sims's rebellious younger sister, Nicki Taylor, in the Australian soap *Chances* for a year, subsequently starred as Uri in the short-lived comedy series *The Newlyweds* alongside former *Neighbours* actress Annie Jones, and guest-starred in the sitcom *Hey Dad*.

Mat Stevenson (b. Melbourne, Australia, 15 April 1969) appeared in *Neighbours* as Skinner, arch-enemy of Nick Page, with whom he competed for Sharon Davies's affections, before joining *Home and Away* as ADAM CAMERON.

Emily Symons (b. 10 August 1969) played dizzy blonde MARILYN CHAMBERS, who fell for Lance Smart but was eventually swept off her feet by farmer Phil Bryant and left Summer Bay to get married. Emily was previously in *Richmond Hill*, as spoiled brat art school student Anne Costello. She has also presented the Australian TV show *Video Smash Hits*. On leaving *Home and Away*, Emily married English artist Nick Lipscombe and moved to London, although she returned to *Home and Away* in 1995.

John Adam was saxophone-playing teacher LUKE CUNNINGHAM, although he previously appeared in the serial as DAVE PORTER, an army pal of teacher Grant Mitchell. He had also acted in *E Street* and *A Country Practice*.

Australian rock star JOHN FARNHAM played himself paying a surprise visit to Sally Fletcher after she won tickets to one of his concerts but contracted chickenpox and was unable to go.

Richard Norton (b. 17 December 1970) portrayed Ryan McLachlan in *Neighbours* before joining *Home and Away* as SIMON FITZGERALD, who pretended to be the father of Sophie Simpson's baby. The real father, David Croft, was killed after being run over by a car driven by Karen Dean. Richard later moved to Britain to present the children's TV show *Parallel 9*, although he was later replaced by ex-*Neighbours* star Lucinda Cowden.

Vanessa Downing originally acted PIPPA FLETCHER (who became Pippa Ross after actress Debra Lawrance took over the role), although Carol Willesee had first been cast as Pippa but left shortly before the serial went into production. Vanessa had previously appeared on TV in *The Restless Years*, *Sons and Daughters* and the TV movies *Double Sculls* and *Melba*. She was also in the films *The Disappearance of Azaria Chamberlain*, *The Boy Who Had Everything* and *The Everlasting Secret Family*.

Reed, but he decided to stay with his 'sister', Shannon, and Damian Roberts also turned her down. She did not have much more luck when she landed a job at the Diner, throwing it into total chaos because she was unable to add up. When she fell for Irene Roberts's nephew, Nelson, the romance was short-lived – he left town with his mother Wendy after a few weeks.

Tempany Deckert (b. Melbourne, 2 March 1978) joined a local theatre group at the age of 11, found an agent and landed her first professional role as a young girl asking awkward questions in a sex-education video. She subsequently appeared in an episode of *RFDS*, had a couple of walk-on roles in *Neighbours* and worked on corporate and educational videos, before being offered the role of Selina Cook in *Home and Away*. She deferred her Higher School Certificate exam to do so.

Tempany, who had been studying Japanese for the previous three years, enjoys shopping and, on moving from Melbourne to Sydney to work on the soap, particularly looked forward to exploring all the shops there. Shortly after joining *Home and Away*, Tempany started dating a production assistant on the serial, although the relationship did not last.

DONALD FISHER

Self-righteous headmaster Donald Fisher seemed to be the bitter enemy of pupil Bobby Simpson – until he discovered he was her father. Bobby had been born to High Court judge Morag Bellingham after Fisher had a relationship with her, then the girl was brought up by no-good Al Simpson, before being fostered by Tom and Pippa Fletcher.

There had been ill-feeling between Fisher and the Fletchers from the day that the family moved to Summer Bay. Fisher, then deputy head of Summer Bay High School, was generally disliked in the community, although felt that he had done much for it. Deep down, the moral crusader was hurt. To an extent, the principles he taught were decent, but he failed to see that he was too narrow-minded to be accepted.

He had a supporter in church-going Celia Stewart, but others, including former girlfriend Ailsa Stewart, tried to make him more tolerant towards others. He believed that his position at the school made it impossible for him to condone the behaviour of certain people.

His standing in the community was threatened when his former wife, Barbara, arrived at the school as a relief teacher. The resulting friction was compounded when son Alan came to stay. He had dropped out of school to pursue his love of surfing but was persuaded to return to the classroom. First, he flouted his father's authority in front of other pupils, then he began seeing Bobby Simpson.

Fisher's attitude towards his son changed when he found out that Alan had a serious brain disease. Alan tried to use it to destroy his father's reputation, but Bobby intervened to stop him. The relationship between father and son continued to improve and Fisher backed Alan when he decided to turn professional as a surfer. Tragically, Alan died suddenly from his terminal illness.

Fisher had disapproved of his son seeing Bobby Simpson, but his attitude towards her changed when he discovered that she was his illegitimate daughter. After the initial shock to both Fisher and Bobby, the two forged a new relationship and she moved into his house. Later, he took in foster child Viv Newton, who had run away from her father, a fire-and-brimstone preacher who beat her.

His career was threatened when Al Simpson, Bobby's original foster father, arrived in Summer Bay and revealed another of Fisher's dark secrets. The headmaster believed he had killed Matt Wilson's brother Shane in a shooting accident but had never confessed. Simpson blackmailed him, but the real story eventually came out – it was Simpson who pulled the trigger. Bobby, relishing in the experience of finding the love of her real father, was instrumental in seeking the truth, risking her own life when she was held hostage by Simpson.

Fisher was grief-stricken when Bobby died in a boating accident. By then, she had married Greg Marshall and had a stepson, Sam. Fisher took the boy in, although Sam later went to live with Michael and Pippa Ross.

Fisher's own estranged daughter, Rebecca, arrived on his doorstep in 1994 after realizing she was not cut out to be the concert pianist he had always hoped she would be. He felt she was wasting the chance of a lifetime.

Rebecca soon had her eye on saxophone-playing teacher Luke Cunningham, which annoyed her father. But, after initially being flattered, Luke began to find her obsession with him embarrassing and ditched her. She packed her bags and returned to the city. This led to Fisher blaming Luke for robbing him of another daughter. Luke left Summer Bay shortly afterwards to look after his retarded brother, Bill, when his mother went into hospital.

Norman Coburn (b. Sydney, 6 March 1937) started acting at the age of 14, working in radio and theatre in Sydney. He toured Australia for two years with the newly formed Elizabethan Theatre Trust in the mid-fifties.

With limited opportunities for actors in Australia at that time, Norman moved to Britain and worked in repertory theatre across the country. He also appeared on television in various plays and such programmes as *Monitor*, the BBC soap opera *Compact*, *No Hiding Place*, *Dixon of Dock Green*, *The Professionals* and *Coronation Street*.

Norman, by this time married and with a family, returned to Australia in 1981, missing the sunshine and hoping for work after his experience in Britain. He has acted in productions for the Griffin Theatre Company, the Ensemble Theatre, the Genesian Theatre, the Northern Territory Theatre Company and the Phillip Street Theatre, playing the title role in *Macbeth* and Polonius in *Hamlet*.

On TV, he has appeared in *Step in the Right Direction*, *Coral Island*, *The Young Doctors*, *A Country Practice*, *1915*, *Peach's Gold*, *Waterloo Station*, *Special Squad*, *Possession*, *Rafferty's Rules*, *Losing*, *Land of Hope* and *Five Mile Creek*. He was in the films *Circle of Deception*, *Oscar Wilde* and *Valiant Soldier*.

When he took the role of Donald Fisher in *Home and Away*, Norman became aware that he was slightly over-acting for the cameras, as if he were still in theatre. After seeing his performances in early episodes, he began to adapt for television, and his character has become one of the programme's mainstays.

Norman, who is divorced from his British wife, singer-dancer Tina Scott, has a son, Troyt, and daughter, Nana, an actress who started her

Roger Oakley (b. Auckland, New Zealand, 21 August 1943) was TOM FLETCHER, husband of Pippa and one of the mainstays of the serial, from episode one. He had previously appeared in many programmes, including *The Sullivans* (as Major Barrington), *Skyways*, *Cop Shop*, *The Young Doctors*, *Sons and Daughters*, *Carson's Law* and *A Country Practice*. Tom had a heart attack and died when Roger decided that *Home and Away*'s schedule was too gruelling.

Peter Bensley, who as teacher **ANDREW FOLEY** was engaged to Carly Morris for a while, was previously Matt Delaney in *Prisoner: Cell Block H* and Dr Marshall in *The Young Doctors*, and later acted in *The New Adventures of Black Beauty*.

Gavin Harrison (b. Gavin George Harrison on 29 December 1970) played bad boy **MAURICE 'REVHEAD' GIBSON**, leading Karen Dean astray, before joining *A Country Practice* as mild-mannered Hugo Strezelecki.

Dannii Minogue (b. Melbourne, 20 October 1971) was tearaway EMMA JACKSON, who went out with Adam Cameron. Dannii, sister of former *Neighbours* star Kylie Minogue, was already a well known model and had a non-speaking role in *The Sullivans*, as well as playing Penny Seymour in the Australian soap *All the Way*. She left *Home and Away* to launch a career in pop music, releasing a single, 'Love and Kisses', and an LP. In 1993, she married former *Home and Away* star Julian McMahon.

Kelly Dingwall was BRIAN ('DODGE') KNIGHT, a street kid from the age of 11 who led Steven Matheson into bad ways. Kelly had previously acted both Robert McNicol and Wayne Bailey in *A Country Practice*, and appeared in *E Street*.

Julian McMahon (b. Julian Dana William McMahon on 27 July 1968), son of former Australian Prime Minister Sir William McMahon, played **BEN LUCINI**, the former soldier who married Carly Morris. He then toured in the UK stage musical of *Home and Away*, before acting alongside Elliott Gould in the film *Exchange Lifeguards* and joining the American soap *Another World* as handyman Ian Rain. He married Dannii Minogue in 1993.

career in TV commercials at the age of ten and joined the *Home and Away* cast as bitchy Vicki Baxter, a rebellious pupil at Summer Bay High School who caused problems for her real-life father's character and foster child Viv Newton, as well as for teacher Grant Mitchell.

SALLY FLETCHER

After her parents died in a boating accident when she was just three years old, Sally Keating went to live with her grandmother. However, Mrs Keating was diagnosed as having Alzheimer's disease two years later and, as her condition worsened, Sally often took time off school to look after her.

When a teacher reported this to the local welfare department, Sally was put in a home, where she retreated into a fantasy world, creating an imaginary friend called Milko. He was the one person who could not be taken away from her.

Sally soon became friends with Lynn Davenport, an unwanted child who had persistently run away from home and was then sleeping in the same dormitory as her. When Lynn was found a foster home, she refused to go without Sally, so Tom and Pippa Fletcher agreed to take them both in.

Insecure and expecting to be taken away at any time, Sally began to feel happier after Tom and Pippa became her legal guardians. She became a favourite with many people in Summer Bay, and Lance Smart was a special friend. It was a shock to the whole Fletcher family when Tom died of a heart attack. Pippa subsequently married divorcé Michael Ross.

Sally fell in with the wrong crowd at school when Craig and other older boys dared her to do crazy things – such as stealing underwear from washing lines – if she wanted to join their gang. She even cast aside her best friend, Gloria. Later, as she gained an interest in boys, Sally had a crush on Damian Roberts.

When Tom and Pippa started rowing and their marriage began to crumble, Sally ran away under the strain of it all. But she returned and the family were eventually reunited.

☆ ☆ ☆

Kate Ritchie, daughter of a Sydney policeman, started dancing at the age of three and has competed in many eisteddfod competitions. She began appearing in TV commercials at five and played Molly, the child lead, in the Australian miniseries *Cyclone Tracy*, before being chosen to play Sally Keating in *Home and Away*. Kate appeared in the stage productions *Annie*, *The*

Sound of Music, *Carousel* and *Say It with Music* for the Campbelltown Theatre Group between 1985 and 1987, and wrote and produced her own school play, *The Magic Rose*. She continued her dance training in ballet, tap and jazz.

When her *Home and Away* character kept speaking to an imaginary friend, Kate simply thought of speaking to her sister Rebekah. Her real-life family keeps her feet on the ground.

ANGEL PARRISH

Arriving in Summer Bay when rock group Frenté were playing there in 1993, teenage runaway Angel Brooks claimed to be their tour manager, sold Shane Parrish illegal tickets for the concert – and immediately became the target of his affections, even though he lost $50.

After several years of living on the streets, braided beauty Angel decided to settle in Summer Bay. She confessed to Damian Roberts that she might have been responsible for starting a fire at her old school. Donald Fisher found her a place to shelter and she was later fostered by Pippa and Michael Ross.

Angel and Shane were soon going out together and, when they both contracted measles at the same time, they hoped it would give them a chance to stay at home together. But they found themselves too ill to do anything except sleep!

Everyone in Summer Bay was shocked to discover that Angel had given birth to a baby at the age of 14. The boy, Dylan, was given up for adoption, her mother rejected her and Angel turned to a life on the streets. Now, she wanted

Sharyn Hodgson (b. Sydney, 25 August 1968) was tragic CARLY LUCINI, taken in by the Fletchers after she suffered a fractured skull at the hands of her violent father. Worse came when Carly left, headed for the city and was raped while hitch-hiking. She had a string of broken relationships but finally found happiness with Ben Lucini. Sharyn played Leanne in *A Country Practice*, before joining *Home and Away*, in which she also acted Carly's twin sister, SAMANTHA MORRIS, in a handful of episodes.

Nicolle Dickson (b. Sydney, 1 January 1969) played rebellious BOBBY MARSHALL (previously Simpson), illegitimate daughter of Donald Fisher and Morag Bellingham. Bobby's marriage to Frank Morgan failed and she subsequently wed Greg Marshall. Bobby died in a boating accident in 1993. Nicolle earned a reported £120,000 a year in *Home and Away*. After leaving, Nicolle took a business course in Sydney and guest-starred as a tough teenager with learning difficulties in the Australian soap *G.P.* In 1995, she returned to *Home and Away* to play scenes in which Ailsa Stewart hallucinates and sees Bobby standing in her kitchen.

Lisa Lackey (b. Sydney, Australia, 2 March 1971) played ROXY MILLER, long-lost elder sister of Blake Dean. In Summer Bay, she fell for handyman Rob Storey but split up with him after beating breast cancer. Before joining *Home and Away*, Lisa worked as a model. After leaving in 1994, she appeared in an Australian drama series called *Spellbinder*.

Craig McLachlan (b. 1 September 1965) left his role as Henry Ramsay in *Neighbours* and had a haircut to play unorthodox teacher GRANT MITCHELL in *Home and Away*. Craig, who had previously appeared in *The Young Doctors* and *Sons and Daughters* and is divorced from first wife Karen, later married former *Neighbours* star Rachel Friend, although they have since split up. He left *Home and Away* to further his pop music career, recording such hit singles as 'Hey Mona' with his group Check 1-2. He also appeared in the miniseries *Heroes II – The Return* and the police series BUGS (as surveillance expert Ed), and starred in the West End production of *Grease*.

to find Dylan and, once Shane got over the bombshell, he helped her to search for the boy.

They found Dylan living with his grandmother. To her grandmother's dismay, Angel was determined to tell him that she was his mother. Unfortunately for Angel, he refused to believe it. When Angel arranged a weekend visit to Summer Bay for Dylan, she spoiled him, although he did not endear himself to Donald Fisher when he spilled red cordial over his treasured photographs of his dead daughter, Bobby. He hit the roof and told Angel she was not fit to be a mother.

Angel's relationship with Shane was all but over after all his pranks and run-ins with Jack

---

Alex Papps was FRANK MORGAN, who left girlfriend Ruth Stewart when she became pregnant by someone else and married Bobby Simpson, only to leave her and go to New York with Ruth. When the relationship went sour, he returned to Summer Bay, hoping to woo Bobby back, but she was by then involved with Greg Marshall. Alex had previously appeared in *The Henderson Kids* as Vinnie and in *Prisoner: Cell Block H*, and became infamous as Greg Davis, who burned down Charlene's caravan in *Neighbours*. After leaving *Home and Away*, he appeared in *The Flying Doctors* as Nick Cardaci, a country boy working on a cattle station.

Judy McBurney (b. Sydney, Australia, 19 May 1948), who acted Pixie Mason in *Prisoner: Cell Block H* and Tania Livingstone in *A Country Practice*, as well as appearing in *It Stands to Reason* – the Australian version of *Till Death Us Do Part* – was seen in *Home and Away* as AUDREY ORCHARD, running a dating agency that Donald Fisher phoned after being set up by Shane Parrish. He thought he was contacting a cleaner.

Bruce Roberts (b. Bruce Andrew Roberts on 4 October 1968) played college dropout-turned-policeman NICK PARRISH, whose brother Shane later arrived in Summer Bay. Nick himself had a rocky romance with Lucinda Croft, whom he lost to romeo Ryan. Bruce left *Home and Away* in 1994 to move to Britain and live with gymnast and Sky Television sports presenter Suzanne Dando, with whom he had starred in the pantomime *Sleeping Beauty* the previous Christmas. Bruce himself has also presented sports on Sky.

Wilson. But she was not impressed when he took a job as a refuse collector in an attempt to cast himself as a real man, not a silly schoolboy. She let Tug O'Neale take her to Roxy Miller's fundraising debutante ball in 1994, although she admitted that she still loved Shane and was soon back in his arms.

Shortly afterwards, on a romantic picnic, Shane proposed and the couple planned their 1995 wedding. It was in starting a bank account together that Angel stumbled on some old family papers and decided to search for her younger sister, Frankie. Angel tracked her down and brought her back to Summer Bay, but the sisters were soon squabbling. They played in the same side in a school netball match, but neither would pass the ball to the other and they almost came to blows, costing their team the game.

Fiancé Shane had problems of his own when his father died and he was reunited with his mother, Ros, who disapproved of Angel. But the sight of him playing with Angel's son made her change her mind. Angel had a brush with death when she was left paralysed from the waist down after running out in front of Alf Stewart's vehicle. She was confined to a wheelchair, but the wedding went ahead.

☆ ☆ ☆

Melissa George (b. Melissa Suzanne George in Perth, Western Australia, 6 August 1976) took up rollerskating at the age of seven and won the bronze medal at the National Rollerskating Championships in 1989 and 1990. She also represented Australia at the Junior Pacific Rollerskating Championships in 1991 and won a silver medal for Outstanding Figure Skating Performance.

After appearing in many fashion parades and television commercials, Melissa won the Directions West Model Award for her age group and was named Western Australia's Teenage Photographic Model of the Year.

Switching to acting, she moved to Sydney in January 1993 to join *Home and Away* in the role of Angel Brooks. The following year, she won a Logie Award for Most Popular New Talent and the People's Choice Award for Favourite TV Drama Star (Female). The latter was presented to the actress by her own idol, Kylie Minogue. She also posed naked for an arty Australian magazine called *Black & White*.

Melissa, who enjoys shopping, rollerblading, dancing and going to the cinema and theatre, is single and lives in Sydney. During her first year in *Home and Away*, she split up with her model boyfriend Chris Roe. Shortly afterwards, Melissa learned that her mother had multiple sclerosis.

SHANE PARRISH

After hitching a lift to Summer Bay with Alf Stewart, Shane Parrish went to live with brother Nick, the local policeman, at Donald Fisher's house. As the youngest child, he had been spoilt by his parents and encountered trouble with the police. He soon put people's backs up, attended Summer Bay High School and became best friends with Damian Roberts.

Pippa and Michael Ross were worried that he was a bad influence on Damian, a concern that proved to be justified when he poured paint into Donald Fisher's golf club bag and burgled the surf club kiosk.

Shane stumbled across Lucinda Croft and her ex-fiancé, Ryan, kissing while she was engaged to his brother Nick. But he did not tell Nick, hoping to spare his brother's feelings, and sought revenge on Ryan, harassing him, stealing his prized car and generally trying to run him out of town.

He put Nick's career on the line many times. When complaints were made to the police, Nick tried to get to the bottom of them. Ryan accused him of sticking up for his brother and not investigating complaints. Shane went to court falsely accused of receiving stolen goods and, because of his previous offences, was sent to a centre for young offenders, but escaped. But he was released and granted a pardon after Tug O'Neale confessed. Shane refused to return to school, moved to the city and signed on the dole.

Without money, he started begging in the streets but was spotted by Michael Ross, who dragged him home. Nick then asked Michael to give Shane a job at the boat shed. Michael agreed,

but Shane refused to take the work. Nick kicked him out in the hope of persuading Shane to make something of his life or go back to school.

Shane became close to Sarah Taylor when they were rehearsing for a musical and Tug ruined the performance on the night by punching him for kissing Sarah on stage. That ended Tug's relationship with her, but Shane was by then dating Angel Brooks.

Shane was annoyed that Angel went into business with Damian, producing T-shirts. Feeling left out, he found a friend in Kevin, a talented artist who had been persuaded to move to Summer Bay by Roxy Miller and was soon selling aboriginal art to tourists.

More trouble followed when Shane took Angel to a ballet and, on their way home, the pair were mugged. As a result, Shane felt a bit of a wimp and took up boxing, to Angel's disgust. Instead, he decided on karate but needed the money for lessons. To get it, he took up bowling, hoping to take the prize money in a tournament at the local bowling club.

In the meantime, he tackled an intruder in Fisher's house, where Angel was also living. He recognized him as the mugger and beat him up. Recalling her own life as a street kid, Angel begged compassion for the intruder, which incensed Shane. He came round and, after winning the bowls tournament, donated the prize money to the Youth Refuge.

It was a shock when Shane learned that Angel had a three-year-old son, Dylan, given away for adoption at birth when she was only 14. At first, Shane felt betrayed and could not understand how she could have slept with someone else, but he eventually began to understand her predicament and helped to search for the boy.

During the trip, the couple spent a night together in a motel room, but Angel was stunned to find that Dylan would not accept her as his mother when she tracked him down and told him the truth. Eventually, she brought Dylan back to Summer Bay for a weekend visit and Shane was cast in the role of doting father.

But Shane and Angel's relationship was soon on the rocks and he tried to impress her by taking a job as a refuse collector, thinking that it would prove to her that he was a real man, not a silly schoolboy. Shane was heartbroken when Tug O'Neale took Angel to Roxy Miller's fundraising debutante ball in 1994, although Angel admitted that she still loved him. They were soon back together, Shane proposed and the couple planned their wedding.

Shortly after becoming engaged to Angel, Shane heard the news that his father had died. He was always at loggerheads with his father and had not seen him since moving to Summer Bay three years earlier. He announced that he would not be going to the funeral, but Angel realized that he was refusing to accept the fact that his father had died before they could make their peace. He was persuaded to go to the funeral, where he met his estranged mother, Ros, who said she wanted to reunite the family. Although Shane initially resisted this display of motherly love, he broke down at the graveside and Ros comforted him.

Ros initially disapproved of Shane marrying Angel, but she saw him playing with Dylan and began to change her mind. She also admitted that she had let Shane down during his childhood and he, in turn, confessed that he had not made life easy for his parents.

When Alf Stewart accidentally ran over Angel, critically injuring her, Shane was in no mood for his apologies. But all turned out well as Shane and Angel wed in 1995, bringing some much needed happiness to Summer Bay.

☆ ☆ ☆

Dieter Brummer (b. Dieter Kirk Brummer in Sydney, Australia, 5 May 1976), who is half-German, began acting classes at the age of ten with the Sydney Talent Company, where other students included Les Hill, later a star of *Home and Away* himself. After getting work in com-mercials for products such as McDonald's and Cadbury's chocolate, he landed the role of Shane Parrish in *Home and Away*, at the age of 15. He made his debut in April 1992. The role of Shane, stealing cars, causing trouble and generally being a baddie, made Dieter one of Australia's most popular teen stars. He has also presented *The Great Outdoors*, *People's Choice Awards* and *Perth Telethon* on television.

Dieter, who enjoys motor racing, bike racing, and playing squash, the clarinet and saxophone, is single and lives in Sydney.

CURTIS REED

A bookworm and computer whiz-kid, Curtis Reed is a bit of a loner who enjoys nothing more than sitting by himself, listening to his favourite grunge music bands, such as Nirvana, and thrash music. His adoptive mother, Elizabeth Reed, was killed in a car crash, so he and his adoptive sister, Shannon, went to live with foster parents. The secret they shared was that they had fallen in love.

He had always longed to live by the water, so moving to Summer Bay was his dream come true. Despite setting himself apart from others, he soon earned respect from his peers as the schoolboy who can dispense good advice.

☆ ☆ ☆

Shane Ammann (b. Shane Allen Ammann in Switzerland, 8 October 1979) grew up in Nigeria, Hong Kong and Australia as his father's business interests meant the family moved around the world.

He first appeared in TV commercials at the age of eight and quickly notched up screen acting credits. Shane starred as Greg in *Butterfly Island* and played Andrew in *Paradise Beach* as well as guest-starring in *Skippy* and *Time Trax* and appearing in the films *The Flood* and *The Renegade*. When he landed the role of Curtis Reed in *Home and Away*, making his first appearance in September 1994, Shane and his mother moved to Sydney, while his father and sister remained on the Gold Coast.

SHANNON REED

Shannon was fostered at the age of 12 by Elizabeth Reed, who later adopted her. Tragedy struck when Elizabeth died in a car accident, so she and Curtis – also adopted by Elizabeth – had to find foster parents. Passionate about environmental matters, Shannon and Curtis took

---

Gwen Plumb (b. Sydney) was Summer Bay gossip MRS PETERS in the pilot episode of *Home and Away* but, while waiting to hear whether the programme would become a serial, agreed to appear in the short-lived serial *Richmond Hill* as Mum Foote, who took in wayward children. Gwen previously played Ada Simmonds in *The Young Doctors*, for its entire run of almost seven years, and farmer's wife Mrs Forbes in *Neighbours*. She returned to *Home and Away* briefly in 1995 as ELIZABETH. In 1974, the Queen honoured her charity work with a British Empire Medal.

Matt Doran (b. Australia, 30 March 1976) was in the ill-fated soap *E Street* and the TV movie *Pirates' Island* before joining *Home and Away* as DAMIAN ROBERTS, son of Irene and brother of Finlay.

Tina Thomsen (b. 17 November 1975) played FINLAY ROBERTS, who fled to Summer Bay to escape her violent mother. Fin came close to death when she went scuba-diving with boyfriend Blake and became trapped in a wreck.

---

part in many Clean-Up Australia events and set up their own recycling system when living with Elizabeth.

Shannon is intelligent and takes care of finances for herself and Curtis, and sees a career in finance or economics as a possibility.

She thrives on standing up for the rights of herself and others, and was class representative on the student council at her previous school. But her outspokenness often lands her in trouble. Shannon is also a sports enthusiast who loves team sports, which provide her with a challenge.

When looking for new foster parents, Shannon and Curtis – by then boyfriend and girlfriend – lied to the authorities that they were blood-related brother and sister so that they would not be separated. The lie was helped by the fact that details of their adoption were lost in the files of bureaucracy.

☆ ☆ ☆

Isla Fisher (b. Isla Lang Fisher in Muscat-O-Man, Saudi Arabia, 3 February 1976) was born of Scottish parents living in the Middle East because of her father's job as a banker. The family moved around to Cebu, Brunei, Iran, Cambridge and Australia, settling in Perth.

By the age of 11, Isla had an agent, although her parents did not encourage her to go into acting. After TV commercials, Isla starred in the children's miniseries *Bay City* and, at the age of 17, moved to the Gold Coast, to take the role of feisty Robyn in *Paradise Beach*. When the series ended, she moved to Sydney, auditioned for *Home and Away* and first appeared as Shannon Reed in September 1994.

IRENE ROBERTS

Mother of Finlay and Damian, Irene Roberts's husband left her when the chldren were small. She became an alcoholic and beat the children, relying on Fin to cook and look after her brother. Not surprisingly, her children fled to Summer Bay and moved in with Michael and Pippa Ross.

She followed them there in an effort to get them both back. There was a tussle at the top of the stairs and Fin and Damian thought they had killed her, but the 'body' had disappeared when they returned. She was in hospital with concussion.

Michael and Pippa subsequently fostered Finlay, who was keen to resume her education and do her Higher School Certificate.

When Fin fell for Blake, went scuba diving with him and almost died when she became trapped in a wreck, Irene rushed back to Summer Bay, worried, and subsequently turned over a new leaf. She landed a job at the Diner.

Irene's desire to help Alf Stewart when the Summer Bay Bowling Club's annual general meeting had to be postponed through lack of support led to chaos. She offered to join to boost numbers and, on the green, the strict club manager Barry threw Nick Parrish and Luke Cunningham off for not wearing whites. This incensed Irene, who picked Barry up on a technicality. A fracas followed in which Irene threw Barry in the memorial rose garden.

Irene turned doting mother when Fin took exams to determine whether she would go to university. On leaving the exam hall, Fin realized she had made a crucial mistake in one paper and felt that she could not go on. But Irene tried to persuade her to go back and Fin was delighted when she learned that her grades were good enough to get her into university. However, the university then told her that she needed higher grades to get the course of her choice. Heartbroken, she looked to carve out another career for herself.

Nathan, Irene's elder son, arrived in Summer Bay after being let out of jail. He was soon in trouble again, bedding Sarah Taylor and stealing school fees, with the result that he was sent to a detention centre.

Irene then bought the Beach House for herself, Fin and Damian, hoping to bring the family together in one home. But Fin, who had been living with the Rosses, left for teacher-training college in the city, leaving behind her problems of drug dependency and boyfriend Hayden Ross's gambling addiction.

When Irene advised Tug O'Neale to buy a lottery ticket and he won, she believed she had psychic powers and started playing Gypsy Rose, advising Summer Bay residents on what to do.

In an attempt to make up for her lost daughter, Irene fostered Selina Cook and resolved not to make the same mistakes that she made with her own children. She started by enrolling the teenager into a deportment school, which specialised in teaching tearaways good manners.

☆ ☆ ☆

Lynne McGranger (b. 1953) trained at the Riverina College of Advanced Education, gaining a teaching diploma for primary education. She later studied at the Q Theatre and had ten years' ballet training.

She then spent a further seven years with the Q Theatre, acting in such productions as *How the Other Half Loves*, *Paradise Regained*, *Happy End*, *Twelfth Night* and *As You Like It*, and three years with the Murray River Performing Group.

As well as performing in cabaret at the Funny Business Theatre Company, Lynne wrote her own musical, *Dags in Full Flight*, and performed with the Melbourne Workers Theatre at the Melbourne Comedy Festival.

On television, she played Janet in *The Flying Doctors* and Dot in *Skirts*, as well as appearing in *Unit 64* and the film *Seven Deadly Sins*. Lynne took over the role of Irene Roberts in *Home and Away* from Jacqui Phillips in 1992, when the character was brought back into the storyline.

MICHAEL ROSS

Pippa Fletcher was devastated by the death of her husband, Tom, with whom she had become a foster parent in Summer Bay. But she found new love with divorcé Michael Ross, who had a son, Hayden, from his first marriage.

Michael and Pippa wed in January 1992, despite the disapproval of Hayden and Pippa's youngest foster child, Sally Fletcher. Suddenly, Michael found himself responsible for Sally, Bobby Simpson and Sophie Simpson, as well as stepson Christopher.

Shortly after the wedding, Hayden left Summer Bay to live with his mother, and runaway Finlay Roberts moved in with Michael and Pippa.

Michael was delighted when Pippa gave birth to baby son Dale, although there was bad news when the company that owned Michael's boat shed went bankrupt. Far worse was to come with son Dale's cot death.

His other son, Hayden, returned shortly afterwards, intent on making a good impression. But

Michael realized that his newly found interest in horses stretched only as far as the money he could make out of them.

Hayden tried to persuade Michael to lend him $30,000 so that he could set up a surf shop and his father took out a mortgage on the caravan park, against Pippa's wishes. But it was soon revealed that Hayden needed the money to pay off his gambling debts and he did not get the cash. More trouble came with the arrival of foster son Jack Wilson in the Ross household. He got into scrapes with Shane Parrish and was eventually suspended from school for setting off the fire alarm.

Then, cash problems at the boat shed put financial pressures on the Ross household. Although Pippa considered taking a cleaning job to help out, Michael insisted that he would sort out the mess, although it was only Alf Stewart's offer of money that eventually saved the day.

Michael and Pippa began to drift apart and the friction between them intensified. When Pippa agreed to give Sally money to go away to summer camp, Michael flipped, saying that money in the Ross household was too tight.

When Pippa arranged a family dinner for their wedding anniversary in 1994, Michael failed to turn up, saying there was too much work to do at the boat shed. Pippa left for her mother's to allow Michael time to sort his feelings out.

Pippa returned, but the relationship did not improve and Michael moved out of the house and into his boat shed. He returned for Christmas lunch, but Pippa ordered him out and, with the strain showing on the whole family, Sally ran away. She eventually returned and Michael and Pippa took their first steps toward reconciliation by taking marriage guidance counselling.

☆ ☆ ☆

Dennis Coard (b. Australia) worked as an Australia Telecom engineer, before training at the Victorian College of the Arts. His many stage appearances include seasons with the Melbourne Theatre Company, in such productions as *The Cherry Orchard*, *The Recruiting Officer*, *Our Country's Good*, *Dreams in an Empty City*, *Macbeth*, *Heart for the Future*, *See How They Run*, and with the State Theatre Company of Southern Australia in *Marat/Sade*, *The Comedy of Errors* and *Our Country's Good*.

On television he played Palmer in *The Flying Doctors* and appeared in *Mission Impossible*, as well as the films *Return Home*, *Blowing Hot and Cold* and *Jigsaw*, before joining *Home and Away* in 1990.

A divorcé, he fell for his screen wife, Debra Lawrance, and the couple subsequently married, with Debra giving birth to a daughter, Grace. The couple are both involved in work for charities, including the Society for Aid for Children Inoperable in Mauritius, which sponsors sick children whose families cannot afford to send them overseas for life-saving operations.

PIPPA ROSS

Calm, self-confident and giving, Pippa Fletcher proved herself to be a model foster mother over the years, coping with conniving Carly, simpering Steven, dangerous Dodge and many other youngsters. She had found a worthwhile purpose in life, but her happiness took a jolt when husband Tom suddenly died.

It had been love at first sight when teenager Pippa met Tom, a friend of her brother, but he treated her like a sister. Years later, after he returned from the Vietnam War, they met again, fell in love and married.

They proved to be the perfect couple, blissfully happy. But one thing was missing. For medical reasons, the couple were unable to have children of their own. Tom, who came from a broken home and was fostered from the age of two, had the idea of taking in foster children.

Clearly, he wanted to give a good home to youngsters who found themselves in the same position as he had.

Pippa had to decide whether she really wanted to give up her job to do so. Putting Tom's happiness first, she opted to become a foster parent, and their first child was Frank Morgan. Soon,

Tom and Pippa's 'family' consisted of Frank Morgan, Carly Morris, Steven Matheson, Lynn Davenport and Sally Keating.

When Tom lost his job, with the resulting financial loss, there was the risk that the welfare department would take the children away. So Tom and Pippa moved to the small coastal town of Summer Bay and bought a rundown caravan park, which they turned into a business.

Most of the community accepted them, but some were wary of having a bunch of delinquents in their midst. One of the protesters was the local school's then deputy headmaster Donald Fisher, arch-enemy of young tearaway Bobby Simpson, whom the Fletchers then fostered. Eventually, he discovered that Bobby was his illegitimate daughter, they became close, and she went to live with him.

The Fletcher family was complete when Pippa found that she was pregnant with son Christopher. One low point in the marriage, however, was when Tom mistakenly thought Pippa was having an affair with Zac, who arrived in Summer Bay to catch a shark that had been spotted there. He was on the verge of leaving her when he realized his mistake.

This came as he was adjusting to a normal life again after suffering a heart attack. It was a crushing blow to Pippa when Tom died of a another attack at the wheel of his car a year later.

But new love came into Pippa's life with the arrival in Summer Bay of divorcé Michael Ross, who took over the boat shed. They married in 1992 and even had a baby son, Dale, although Pippa experienced high blood pressure throughout her pregnancy. There was a further tragedy for Pippa when Dale suffered a cot death.

In the wake of their loss, the Ross clan began experiencing financial difficulties at the boat shed, so Pippa tried to get a cleaning job. But Michael put his foot down and said she was not to, feeling that he should be responsible for bringing in the family's money. Alf Stewart stepped in to help with Michael's cash problems.

It seemed that Michael could do no right when he commented that he liked women with a bit of meat on them. Believing this meant she needed to lose some weight, Pippa started a strict exercise regime, but her aim to make cycling part of it did not go according to plan when she fell off her bike in front of Jack Wilson and Shane Parrish. But this did not deter Pippa and the diet continued.

When she did plan something special to eat – a dinner on their wedding anniversary in 1994 –

Michael failed to turn up, pleading that there was too much work at the boat shed. Pippa decided to leave him to sort out his feelings and went to visit her mother. The couple were later reunited after accepting that they needed marriage guidance counselling.

☆ ☆ ☆

Debra Lawrance took over the pivotal role of Pippa when Vanessa Downing decided to leave *Home and Away*, following the departure of her screen husband Roger Oakley.

Debra has gained extensive experience in television, films and theatre since graduating from NIDA in 1977. Her dozens of television appearances included roles in the hit serials *Cop Shop*, *The Sullivans*, *Skyways*, *Prisoner: Cell Block H* (first in a guest role, then as regular character Daphne), *Holiday Island*, *Carson's Law*, *A Country Practice* and *Sons and Daughters*.

Debra's other television parts included Maggie Kelly in *The Last Outlaw*, Nurse Conrad in *I Can Jump Puddles*, Barbara in *The Keepers*, Pat in two series of *Fast Lane,* and Jenny Lawler in

---

Rebekah Elmaloglou (b. 23 January 1974) played SOPHIE SIMPSON, daughter of Al Simpson, the bad guy who raised Bobby before he went to jail. Sophie gave birth to daughter Tammy in 1992 after her romance with David Croft, who tragically died in a car crash before the birth. After leaving *Home and Away*, Rebekah guest-starred in *A Country Practice*, which was axed shortly afterwards, and played superbitch Sophie in *Paradise Beach*, which suffered the same fate.

Fiona Spence (b. Kent, 1948) played bicycle-riding CELIA STEWART, who ran the grocery store with her brother Alf, which put her in the perfect position to hear and pass on the Summer Bay gossip. Fiona was already well known to audiences worldwide as prison officer Vera Bennett in *Prisoner: Cell Block H*, nicknamed 'Vinegar Tits'.

Justine Clarke played bitchy RUTH STEWART, known as 'Roo', who was pregnant at the age of 16 and gave the baby up for adoption. Justine appeared in TV commercials from the age of seven and was a semi-regular in *A Country Practice* before joining *Home and Away* when it began. When she left, Justine became a star of a new Australian soap opera, *Family and Friends*, and appeared in the wartime drama *Come in Spinner*.

How the World Really Runs. She was also in the films *Before the Night Is Out*, *Flute Man*, *Silver City*, *Two Brothers Running* and *Evil Angels.*

Her screen marriage to actor Dennis Coard was followed by romance off screen with the couple's real-life wedding and the birth of a baby daughter, Grace. The on-screen storyline of baby Dale dying led to Debra and Dennis becoming involved in charity work for Barnardo's and Foster Care Week in Australia.

AILSA STEWART

Warm-hearted and generous to a fault, Ailsa Hogan believes in giving everyone a fair chance, especially if people are down on their luck. She moved to Summer Bay to take over the grocery store and the locals were quick to accept her as one of the community.

Alf Stewart was immediately taken with her and romance blossomed. However, his daughter, Ruth, did everything possible to split the couple up. It looked as if she had triumphed when she found out Ailsa's dark secret.

Her father, a bully and a drunkard, constantly beat her mother and, one day when he came home and set about her, Ailsa killed him. As a result, she was sent to prison. Ruth confronted Ailsa in front of the guests at her engagement party. It was a bombshell for Alf, and the locals shunned her. However, love survived and the couple married quietly in a register office before springing the news on their friends.

Ruth seized another chance to drive the couple apart when they were on opposing sides over the Macklins' plans to build a leisure complex in Summer Bay. After a violent quarrel, Ailsa left Alf but later returned and the couple re-affirmed their marriage vows.

The relationship with her stepdaughter improved when Ailsa was supportive over Ruth's pregnancy. Ruth later left Summer Bay with her former love Frank Morgan, after his marriage to Bobby Simpson broke up.

Ailsa became joint owner of the Diner, with Bobby Simpson, and it turned out to be a successful business venture. However, at the age of 42, she became pregnant and suffered postnatal depression, to the point where she almost suffocated baby Duncan with a pillow. Fortunately, she recovered with the help of family and friends.

Ailsa was the only one who saw through Alf's wicked sister, Morag Bellingham, when she returned to Summer Bay after the death of her illegitimate daughter, Bobby Marshall (formerly Simpson). Fighting for custody of Bobby's stepson, Sam, Morag insisted she had turned over a new leaf and was fit to take him in.

But Ailsa found out that Morag had planned to take Sam away to a private school long before headmaster Donald Fisher had made the suggestion. As a result, Sam stayed in Summer Bay, first with Fisher – Bobby's real father – and then with Michael and Pippa Ross.

☆ ☆ ☆

Judy Nunn (b. Perth, Western Australia) is the daughter of teacher-turned-actress Nancy Nunn, who was pregnant with her while starring in the radio serial *Heritage Hall* in the fifties. Nancy also directed radio plays, and it seemed natural to Judy that she should enter showbusiness.

She made her professional debut at the Perth Playhouse when she was 12 years old, moved to Sydney at the age of 19 and to Britain three years later, hoping to further her acting career at a time when there were limited opportunities in Australia.

Judy worked in London's West End, appearing on stage with John Gregson and Julia Lockwood in *Goodbye Charlie*, Jessie Matthews in *The Hollow*, and Wilfred Pickles in *Gaslight*, and acted in repertory seasons in Crewe, Worthing and Bournemouth, and in fringe theatre productions.

She was also in BBC radio plays and on British television, in the series *The Befrienders* and episodes of *The Onedin Line* and *Z-Cars*.

Judy returned to Australia in 1973, after six years away. Her many stage appearances since then include *Blithe Spirit*, *The Winter's Tale*, *The Taming of the Shrew*, *The Norman Conquests* and *Travesties*.

She has been in the films *Hostage*, *The Box* and *Song of Norway*, and on television in *The Box* (as bitchy Vicki Stafford for more than three years), the short-lived *Skyways*, *Mother and Son*, *Prisoner: Cell Block H*, *A Country Practice*, *Sons and Daughters* (as Irene Fisher), *Bit Part*, *Yes What* and *Holiday Island*, as well as the TV movie *The Newman Shame*. She also presented a television documentary *The Land We Love*.

Judy, who joined *Home and Away* when it started, has also written theatre, radio, film and TV scripts – including those for *Neighbours* and *Possession* – as well as children's books and a novel called *The Glitter Game*, set behind the scenes of a television soap opera.

She and husband Bruce Venables, a former Hong Kong and Australian policeman who became an actor in 1986, have also written books together.

The couple married in the same week that Judy filmed her screen character Ailsa Hogan's wedding to Alf Stewart. Bruce also appeared in the first episode of *Home and Away* as a police officer, speaking the serial's first words. In a car chase with a young Frank Morgan, he shouted, 'Frankie… Frankie… Frankie… Whatever will your mother say?'

ALF STEWART

Known as a good-natured rogue, Alf Stewart is one of Summer Bay's most successful and respected businessmen. By the age of 30, he owned the liquor store, boat hire service, caravan park and a yacht brokerage.

Married to a local girl, his world fell apart when, in 1985, his wife drowned and he was left to bring up teenage daughter Ruth. He eventually sold his house to Tom and Pippa Fletcher because the memories became too painful. With it, he sold the caravan park, which he had let go and was in a state of disrepair.

Life seemed pointless to Alf until Ailsa Hogan arrived in Summer Bay to take over the grocery store. Warm-hearted and generous, she was welcomed by the community, especially Alf, whose grocery needs suddenly rocketed.

Romance developed, but Ruth tried to end the relationship, doing everything she could to split up the couple. She found out that Ailsa had killed her bullying father and served a jail sentence, then confronted her before guests at the couple's engagement party. It was a shock to everyone, none more so than Alf, but he and Ailsa weathered the storm.

After their wedding, Ruth found another opportunity to break the two up. She took advantage of Alf and Ailsa being on opposite sides over businessman Gordon Macklin's plan to build a leisure complex in Summer Bay. Alf was strongly in favour of the idea, but Ailsa disagreed and, after a terrible quarrel, she walked out on him. But she returned and they reaffirmed their marriage vows.

Alf ran the grocery store with prim and proper sister Celia, and Ailsa owned the Diner, with Bobby Simpson (later Marshall). Alf and Celia had to buy new premises after the original ones were burned down by Brian 'Dodge' Knight, who stayed with the Fletchers for a while, until the police caught up with him and revealed his criminal past. Celia later left Summer Bay and Alf employed a string of assistants, including dizzy Marilyn Chambers. Alf and Ailsa also looked after Emma Jackson and Blake and Karen Dean for a while.

There was friction in the Stewart household when Alf let his sister, Morag Bellingham, stay after the death of Bobby Marshall, her illegitimate child. Alf tried to persuade Ailsa that wicked Morag had turned over a new leaf, but his wife was not convinced and she saw through Morag and her plans to get custody of Bobby's stepson, Sam.

Another stray who ended up in the Stewarts' house was Sarah Taylor, whom Alf almost threw out after finding her making love to Nathan Roberts – Damian and Finlay's elder brother – on the back seat of a car. The couple split up shortly afterwards and Nathan continued his life of crime, stealing school fees and being sent to a detention centre.

Alf himself almost split up two other young lovers when, in 1995, he ran over Angel Brooks, who rushed out in front of his vehicle. The accident left Angel paralysed below the waist. She survived, but her fiancé, Shane Parrish, took a while to forgive Alf.

Ray Meagher played rugby football professionally before turning to acting and becoming a veteran performer in television, films and theatre, an actor whose face is familiar to the Australian public but whose name might be hard to recall.

The hundreds of roles he has played include a horse thief, a back-slapping bore, a cynical newspaper editor and a tough policeman. Jumping from one part to another, he has rarely been out of work.

Ray's dozens of television appearances include *Matlock*, *Number 96*, *Pig in a Poke*, *The Restless Years*, *Prisoner: Cell Block H* (twice, including three months as nasty Vietnam veteran Geoff Butler, husband of an inmate), *Cop Shop*, *Skyways*, *Holiday Island*, *Kingswood Country* twice, *A Country Practice* twice, *Rafferty's Rules*, *Willing & Abel*, and the mini-series *The Great Bookie Robbery*, *The Shiralee*, *True Believers* and *Spit MacPhee*. Ray's many films include *Newsfront*, *Breaker Morant* (as Sgt. Major Drummond), *Hoodwink*, *Runaway Island*, *Mail Order Bride* and *Blue Lightning*. He is married to theatrical agent Lee Leslie.

ROB STOREY

A 'bloke's bloke', Rob Storey was born and brought up in Summer Bay with a passion for the outdoors. A Jack-of-all-trades, who can do anything from cleaning pools to fixing TV aerials and wallpapering – and working as a surf lifesaver at weekends – he is laid back, partial to a can of Victoria bitter and hates white wine.

Dependable, Rob always sticks up for his friends and will help out anyone in need, although he loves the occasional practical joke. He also has a reputation in Summer Bay as being a bit of a ladies' man.

Roxy Miller caught his eye, but she decided he was a bit too rough and ready. She also declined his knight-in-shining-armour offer to fix a blown tyre on the school netball team's bus, which was travelling to a match. But Roxy realized how unreasonable she had been and later apologized. The two fell into each other's arms and were subsequently unable to keep their hands off each other.

Their world appeared to be falling apart when, during a shower together, Rob noticed a lump on Roxy's breast. It turned out to be a tumour and Roxy had to undergo surgery. She recovered but, despite Rob's support throughout the ordeal, she realized she did not love him and left Summer Bay for good.

Matthew Lilley graduated from the acting school NIDA in 1992 after gaining experience in classical and modern plays, from *Twelfth Night* and *As You Like It* to *Stags and Hens*. He immediately found stage work in *Romeo and Juliet*, as Romeo, performed at Bondi Pavilion by The Renaissance Players, *Fire in the Sky*, *Macbeth* and the David Williamson play *Money and Friends*, as Justin.

The actor made his TV debut as Constable Palazzi in the Australian school soap *Heartbreak High*, before joining *Home and Away* in 1994. He has also been in training videos for McDonald's and the Australian Navy.

JACK WILSON

Jack Wilson was just eight when his father walked out on the family, leaving his mother to bring him and his brothers and sisters up alone. When she found a new boyfriend, life went further downhill for Jack.

At first, Jack took a liking to the new man in his mother's life because he took him out and treated him like a son. But, once he married his mother, everything changed and Jack felt bitter and betrayed.

Eventually, as his mother's health deteriorated, the couple decided to foster out one of the children. That was Jack, and he blamed his stepfather for 'getting rid' of him.

When he moved in with Michael and Pippa Ross as their foster son, aged 15, this bitterness spilled over in his relationship with Michael. He believed that all men must be like his stepfather.

Jack sees himself as a bit of a ladies' man and was soon fighting with Shane Parrish and Tug O'Neale, as well as with Michael. This caused friction in the Ross household.

More trouble came when Jack set off the fire alarm at school because he had not done his homework. But Shane Parrish saw what he had done and blackmailed him into being his dogsbody. Headmaster Donald Fisher was determined to catch the culprit and Jack, equally determined to end Shane's hold over him, confessed and was suspended.

On his return, he was horrified to find that Fisher had charged Shane with looking after him. But Jack had the last laugh in a truth-or-dare game that ended with Shane being pasted with custard pies.

Romance came with the arrival of Selina Cook and Jack borrowed $90 from Damian Roberts to buy her some shoes for the debutante ball. In an attempt to repay the money, Jack offered to install a private telephone line in Damian's room – for $90! As he tampered with the wires, taking the line off Michael and Pippa's, he cut off one of Michael's phone calls and Pippa heard him making an intimate call to Selina. Then, Donald Fisher caught Jack and Selina kissing in the car park at the ball.

But the course of true love did not run smooth and Selina found out that Jack had been seeing another woman, Sonia Johnson. Her first reaction was to hit him. That did not stop him going after Angel Brooks's sister, Frankie, when she arrived in Summer Bay. After several close calls, Jack was caught with Frankie by Sonia. The three-timing teenager was taught a lesson when all three girls got together and plotted their revenge. Frankie lured him into a caravan for what he thought would be a night of passion, but the trio promptly stole his clothes and locked him in.

Jack was caught out again when Sally Fletcher tricked him into buying 'gravity-defying' boots to make him appear taller. She then cut the bottom of the legs off his trousers to make him look as if he had grown!

Daniel Amalm (b. Daniel Edvard Amalm in Brisbane, Australia, 16 February 1979) is the son of a Swedish father and Maltese mother. His unusual surname is pronounced Or-malm.

He showed an early aptitude for music, learning the guitar, studying with the Queensland Conservatorium of Music, and was runner-up in the ninth Australian Classical Guitar Competition. He also performed as a soloist with the Queensland Youth Orchestra.

Daniel was a regular busker in the Queen Street Mall, where he was spotted by the manager of jazz great George Benson. He was invited to meet George, who was so impressed with Daniel's talent that he made a donation towards the classical guitar that Daniel was saving his busking money to buy.

Branching out into modelling, he won two local competitions, before landing an audition for the role of Jack Wilson in *Home and Away* at the age of 14. A Japanese student staying with his family was asked along and Daniel's father suggested that they audition his son, too.

Now living in Sydney, Daniel enjoys rollerblading and going to the cinema and gym in his spare time.

Standing: Amanda Woodward (Heather Locklear), Jake Hanson (Grant Show), Matt Fielding (Doug Savant) and Michael Mancini (Thomas Calabro). Sitting: Billy Campbell (Andrew Shue), Alison Parker (Courtney Thorne-Smith), Sydney Andrews (Laura Leighton), Jo Reynolds (Daphne Zuniga) and Jane Mancini (Josie Bissett).

Melrose Place, launched in America in 1992 by top producer Aaron Spelling, is the steamy, twentysomething soap intended to be an adult-style *Beverly Hills 90210* and an early episode provided a link with that series by featuring a guest appearance by Luke Perry. *Melrose Place* is set in a trendy Los Angeles apartment block and began by following the lives of eight friends. After a lukewarm start, former *Dynasty* superbitch Heather Locklear was brought in to spice things up as maneater Amanda Woodward and rising film star Daphne Zuniga arrived as photographer Jo Reynolds towards the end of the first series. The ratings soared and, in 1994, the soap topped the American viewing figures. In Britain, it became Sky One's most popular programme.

The programme became even more steamy and was popular with a young adult audience. It also provided a spin-off, *Models Inc.*, in 1994 after former *Dallas* actress Linda Gray made a guest appearance in *Melrose Place* as Heather Locklear's estranged mother, now running a Los Angeles model agency. Another superbitch to arrive was Laura Leighton as Sydney Andrews, Jane Mancini's sister from hell. But it was the return of Marcia Cross as Dr Kimberly Shaw that provided *Melrose Place* with its biggest ratings grabber, when she injured Michael Mancini in a hit-and-run accident disguised as his ex-wife Jane, a whodunit that continued into the third series.

SYDNEY ANDREWS

Trouble-making superbitch Sydney Andrews, sister of Jane Mancini, was a frequent visitor to Melrose Place before moving into the trendy apartment block and getting a waitressing job at Shooters. First on her hit list was Jane's ex-husband Michael. His girlfriend Kimberly arrived home to find the two in bed.

Michael won Kimberly back, but the couple were badly injured in a car accident and he was heartbroken to hear that Kimberly had died after being moved to a Cleveland hospital by her parents. Sydney told Michael she loved him, but he sent her packing, saying she had been the cause of the whole situation.

At a party, Sydney met hostess Lauren Etheridge. Short of money to pay the rent, Sydney joined her group of call girls and was soon raking in the money, as well as taking cocaine from Lauren. When Sydney told Lauren she wanted to come off the game, she was approached by a potential client who agreed to pay her $2000, only to handcuff and arrest her for prostitution after she accepted the money. Michael bailed her out and the charges against Sydney were dismissed after she testified that she was lured into the business by Lauren and threatened.

Sydney was on hand to help when Michael – still on painkillers following his car crash with Kimberly – took an overdose. After hearing him hallucinating and mumbling about Matt Fielding changing the blood-test report, Sydney blackmailed Michael into letting her move in with, then marry, him.

Sydney took over Lauren Etheridge's call-girl business when Lauren was jailed. Then, Kimberly's return (her parents had lied about her death) led Michael to tell her that he was divorcing her, and Amanda allowed Sydney to rent her old apartment. Shortly afterwards, she also lost the call-girl business, when Lauren was released from prison. Desperate for money, she became a topless dancer at the Body Stocking Club, under the name 'Jungle Jane'. But she was horrified one evening to see Billy, Matt, Jake and Michael in the audience and ran off stage, after which the manager fired her.

Falling into prostitution on her own account, Sydney was beaten up by more experienced rivals on Hollywood Boulevard. She then went along with Kimberly in her attempt to murder Michael for all he had done to them. When Kimberly badly injured Michael in a hit-and-run incident, wearing a blonde wig and driving Jane's car, Jane was arrested and, pleading her innocence, suggested that Sydney had good reason to commit the crime. Kimberly also implicated Sydney by offering her an alibi but telling the police a different story and planting the blonde wig in Sydney's apartment. Sydney was arrested, ruled unfit for bail and admitted to Hidden Hills Sanitarium – and released on parole only when she agreed to sign a confession of guilt. When Jane's new boyfriend, Chris Marchette, made obscene phone calls to Sydney and attempted to rape her, Jane refused to believe her. Jake Hanson realized what Chris was up to and supported Sydney, offering her a room in his apartment. and becoming her lover.

Laura Leighton made her first television appearances in commercials, including one for Pizza Hut. A chance visit to casting director Eric Dawson, an old friend, led her into the role of Sydney in *Melrose Place* when the producers were searching for an actress to play Jane Mancini's sister-from-hell. After joining *Melrose*, she started dating co-star Grant Show.

BILLY CAMPBELL

Lovable wimp Billy Campbell was a cab driver, but his ambitions to write led him into glossy magazines as a fact checker, then writer. He had an on-off relationship with flat-mate Alison, not helped by her going off to Seattle with environmentalist Keith Gray, then supervixen Amanda Woodward making a play for Billy.

After a fling with Amanda, he eventually elbowed her out and decided to make a go of it with Alison, although she paid for taking Billy from Amanda, who as her boss made her life hell at work. Billy realized that Alison had been through a lot of heartbreak over the years and was willing to do anything for her, although he was jealous that she seemed more interested in spending time with computer expert Steve McMillan. Mistakenly believing that Alison had slept with Steve, Billy jumped straight back into Amanda's bed, but Billy and Alison made up.

As his writing career on *Escapade* magazine went from strength to strength, Billy was given the opportunity to become a junior editor in New York. He took the job and tried to maintain a long-distance relationship with Alison.

On her first visit, she found Billy arriving back at his apartment with an Oriental model called Andrea and left immediately, but she returned and gave Billy a chance to explain. After another argument, in which Alison refused to move to New York, the couple decided to split up.

But Billy gave up his job and returned to Los Angeles with a marriage proposal. There was no happy ending, though. Alison walked out on Billy just before the wedding ceremony after realizing that her terrible nightmares of the pre-

173

plays his on-screen girlfriend – lives in Los Angeles. His brother worked for Bill Clinton's presidential campaign.

MATT FIELDING

Although gay social worker Matt Fielding provided a shoulder for many of his peers to cry on, he had difficulty finding love himself. He also had problems after wedding illegal immigrant Katya to stop her being deported. Katya and her daughter, Nikki, lived with Matt, but he went through the ordeal of being questioned by the immigration authorities. When Katya's favourite uncle in Russia fell ill, she flew out to visit him while Matt looked after Nikki.

He found a boyfriend in naval officer Jeffrey, who was trying to keep the fact that he was gay secret. Matt persuaded him to tell his commander the truth, but Jeffrey had doubts about doing this – and was transferred to the East Coast.

A new man came into Matt's life when Rob arrived to be best man at Billy Campbell and Alison Parker's abortive wedding.

☆ ☆ ☆

Doug Savant comes from southern California and studied at UCLA (University College of Los Angeles), before acting in Los Angeles regional theatres. He is best known on TV as the young Mack MacKenzie in flashback in the *Dallas* spin-off *Knots Landing* but also guest-starred in *Cagney & Lacey*, *China Beach* and the pilot of *In the Heat of the Night*.

He starred in the TV movies *Aftermath* and *Bonnie & Clyde: The True Story*, and appeared in the feature films *Masquerade* (as Officer Mike McGill, opposite Rob Lowe and Meg Tilly), *Hanoi Hilton*, *Trick or Treat*, *Paint It Black*, *Red Surf* and *Shaking the Tree*. Married with two children, Doug lives in Los Angeles.

vious months had been a reminder of her childhood, when her father abused her. Billy tracked Alison down at her sister Meredith's apartment in San Francisco and found out the truth.

With another marriage ceremony planned, Billy had a change of job. He was fired by *Escapade* magazine and Amanda hired him at D&D Advertising. He and Alison argued there and Billy decided their relationship was over and accepted Amanda's offer of another apartment.

It annoyed Alison when Billy started dating Elizabeth Wyatt, his assistant at D&D Advertising. Elizabeth was also working for Alison, who had her fired when she felt she was finding time to do Billy's work but not hers. Billy then fell for Susan, Alison's new flatmate, who was put under pressure by Alison not to see him. This led to Susan moving in with Billy.

Andrew Shue (b. Wilmington, Delaware, 20 February 1967) graduated in history from Dartmouth College, where his football coach – former Aberdeen player Bobby Clark – persuaded him to move to Scotland and play professionally for Queen's Park in the Scottish League. He then moved on to the Bulawayo Highlanders in Zimbabwe and while there also taught maths and worked on a documentary about his experiences in Africa.

Returning to New York City, he trained as an actor and appeared in the films *Cocktail*, *Adventures in Babysitting* and *The Karate Kid* – all of which his sister, actress Elizabeth Shue, was in – before his James Dean good looks secured the role Billy in *Melrose Place*. He stepped into it when unknown actor Stephen Fanning was dropped after a week's rehearsals. Andrew, who for a while had an off-screen romance with Courtney Thorne-Smith – who

JAKE HANSON

Hunky mechanic and biker Jake Hanson is one of life's drifters, never sure what he wants. When he arrived in Melrose Place, he was unemployed. Ashamed of not finishing his studies at high school, Jake asked Alison Parker to help him to prepare for exams he was now taking – but not to tell anyone. This led to rumours that they were having a romance.

After a fling with starlet Sandy Louise Harling, he started dating photographer Jo Reynolds, but Amanda Woodward stepped in to claim his affections. Jake did not help the new relationship by accusing Amanda's father, Palmer, of cooking the books at the garage where he worked as a mechanic. It ended when Jake co-operated with FBI agents to prove the guilt of her father in his fraudulent business dealings. Amanda evicted Jake from his apartment, but he kicked the door down and moved all his belongings back in. Amanda made up with him only after her father confessed his crimes to her.

But Amanda two-timed Jake with her mother's boyfriend, Chas Russell, and he went back to Jo, saying he had always loved her. She cooled the relationship and he found himself footloose – and unwilling to respond to Amanda's apologies and advances.

Relaxing on his boat, Jake rescued a beautiful blonde called Brittany Maddocks from the water after she had been involved in a violent argument with her husband. She caused trouble for him when he took fugitive Palmer Woodward to Mexico on his boat. Brittany, who had been conniving with Amanda's father, shot Palmer while at sea and escaped in a powerboat as she detonated explosives in Jake's boat. He survived only by jumping overboard.

Jake decided to visit Vince Conners, the father he had never seen, after being born as the result of a one-night stand. Vince, who was married, allowed him into his house on condition that he pretended to be the son of one of his college friends and leave after dinner. But Vince's wife, Erica, insisted he stay the night and Vince admitted he had thought of Jake many times over the years and wanted to keep in touch.

When Jake received a large reward for helping the FBI in the Palmer Woodward case, he bought Shooters. He also saw Sydney – Jane Mancini's poison sister – in a new light when no-one believed her claims that Jane's new boyfriend, Chris Marchette, had made obscene phone calls and tried to rape Sydney. He heard Chris threatening her and began to think she was not insane, as others painted her. Sydney moved in with Jake and they became lovers.

Grant Show (b. Detroit) grew up in northern California and was a keen wrestler at high school, where he was a leading member of the drama club. He then did a variety of jobs, before deciding that acting was for him.

Grant is best known on American TV as Officer Rick Hyde in three series of the daytime soap *Ryan's Hope*, after which he travelled to London to train at the London Academy of Music and Dramatic Art. Returning to America, he acted in the Broadway production of *The Boys of Winter* and starred in *On the Waterfront* at the Cleveland Playhouse.

On television, he appeared in the series *True Blue*, the miniseries *Lucky* and *Chances*, the TV movie *Fatal Crossing* and many pilots for series that never materialized. He was out of work for a year and a half before landing the role of Jake Hanson, who appeared in two episodes of *Beverly Hills 90210* as Luke Perry's mentor, who taught him everything from surfing to motorcycling, and romanced Kelly (actress Jennie Garth). The character then switched to *Melrose Place* and during the first few episodes was trying to keep the relationship going.

Grant lives in Los Angeles and enjoys riding his Harley-Davidson motorcycle.

JANE MANCINI

Fashion designer Jane Mancini divorced her doctor husband Michael after he had an affair with his work colleague Kimberly. Then her own sister Sydney stepped in to tempt Michael into bed. When she confronted Sydney, her sister claimed that Michael had raped her, but Jane was not deceived.

Jane started seeing Robert, although he was shocked when she offered to take care of Michael in her apartment after he was badly injured in a car crash. Michael succeeded in getting Jane back by setting up a sex trap for Robert. With Sydney's help, he hired a call girl called 'Diane' to lure him into bed, videotaped the evidence and delivered it to Jane, who promptly ditched Robert. But Jane dropped Michael when Sydney subsequently told her what he had done.

She opened her own design studio, Mancini Designs, with money left to her in her grandmother's will, but Michael achieved a half-share by claiming that they were still married and he was entitled to half of the business.

Chris Marchette – a client for a chain of stores – told Jane his firm would invest in a new factory for her to design a whole line of clothes exclusively for its stores. As her business partner, Michael blocked the deal but Jane found comfort in Chris's arms. Chris showed another side to his character when he made obscene phone calls to Sydney and tried to rape her, although Jane did not believe her sister's claims. She was also unaware that Chris was a gambler who was on a high when he won, but sank into gloom and despondency when he lost.

> **William R. Moses** (b. Los Angeles, USA, 11 November 1959), who had previously appeared as Cole Gioberti in *Falcon Crest*, played Alison Parker's boyfriend KEITH GRAY, who stalked her after they split up.

MELROSE PLACE

Totally besotted, Jane ran off to Las Vegas with Chris to get married. Michael chased after them, with Kimberly in tow, and caused chaos at the wedding by shouting the claims that Chris had tried to rape Sydney. As the couple ran off, Michael and Kimberly married there instead.

☆ ☆ ☆

Josie Bissett (b. Seattle, Washington) started her career as a model and actress in America and Japan, appearing in dozens of TV commercials. She played Cara in two series of *The Hogan Family*, has guest-starred in many TV series, including *P.S. I Luv U*, *Parker Lewis Can't Lose*, *Quantum Leap* and *Doogie Howser, M.D.*, and starred in the TV movies *Danielle Steel's Secrets* and *Posing*. She was in the films *The Doors*, *Book of Love* and *Mikey*. Josie lives in Los Angeles with actor husband Rob Estes.

MICHAEL MANCINI

Doctor Michael Mancini, original manager of the apartment block, had the responsibility of being a newlywed while paying off a student loan. But his hectic workload did not stop him dallying with nurses, then sealing the fate of his marriage by falling for fellow doctor Kimberly Shaw. His wife, Jane, divorced him.

Although he allowed Jane's scheming younger sister Sydney to seduce him, Michael won back Kimberly and asked her to marry him. As he handed her the engagement ring on a drive home, the car skidded and turned over, leaving Michael injured and Kimberly in a coma. Her parents had her moved to a hospital in Cleveland and Michael later heard that she had died.

Michael then put paid to Jane's new relationship with Robert by setting him up with a call girl and videotaping their sex session. Jane took Michael back but ditched him when Sydney told her what he had done. When Sydney found out that Matt had changed Michael's blood-test results, she blackmailed Michael into marrying her. Just as he was about to be fired at the hospital, Michael blackmailed his boss, Dr Stanley

Linda Gray (b. Santa Monica, California, 12 September 1942), who played Sue Ellen in *Dallas* – twice married to J.R. Ewing – was HILLARY MICHAELS, mother of Amanda Woodward, before spinning off into her own series, *Models Inc.*, as the boss of a modelling agency.

Cassidy Rae played novice model SARAH OWENS in several episodes of *Melrose Place* before switching to the spin-off series *Models Inc.*

Levin into announcing him as the hospital's new chief resident doctor, after finding out that he was seeing a prostitute.

Then, Michael was shocked by the return of Kimberly, who said her parents tried to stop her seeing him again by telling the hospital that she had died. Michael told Sydney he was divorcing her, but he did not realize that Kimberly had come to exact her revenge. She removed a sticker saying that a patient of his should not be given penicillin and he was demoted.

Kimberly's plans turned to murder. First, she poisoned his beer, but Jane revived Michael on finding him unconscious. Then, wearing a blonde wig and driving Jane's VW Rabbit, Kimberly ran him over, although he survived.

When Jane and her new boyfriend, Chris Marchette, ran off to Las Vegas to wed, Michael was concerned that Chris would gain a share in Mancini Designs, in which he had a half-share. With Kimberly in tow, he succeeded in stopping the wedding by shouting out Sydney's claims that Chris had tried to rape her. Michael and Kimberly got married themselves.

☆ ☆ ☆

Thomas Calabro (b. Brooklyn, New York) was a regular in the cast of the American series *Dream Street* and has also appeared in the miniseries *Vendetta* and the TV movies *Out of the Darkness* and *Columbo: No Time to Die*, as well as guest-starring in *Law and Order*.

A keen stage actor, Thomas is a member of New York's Actor's Studio and Circle Rep. Lab. He has performed off-Broadway in the production *Wild Blue*, portraying seven different characters in a showcase of eight plays. He has acted in regional productions of *Sweet Basil*, at the Cincinnati Playhouse in the Park, and *Open Admissions*, at the Long Wharf Theatre, Connecticut, and directed a production of *Orphans* at homeless and rehabilitation shelters in New York City. He lives in Los Angeles.

ALISON PARKER

Sweet-natured, bright-eyed Midwest girl Alison Parker rose from receptionist to advertising executive at D&D Advertising and ended up fighting her boss, Amanda Woodward, in both the boardroom and the bedroom. This was something she had to learn after a conservative upbringing, during which her parents instilled her with a set of basic morals.

Alison shared a flat with Billy Campbell, with whom she had an on-off relationship, but fell for radical environmentalist Keith Gray. This made Billy jealous, but he was quick to offer Alison a shoulder to cry on when they split up.

Billy then had a fling with Amanda, but he ditched her to return to Alison, which made work life difficult for her. Just as worrying was when Alison became victim of a crazy stalker, who turned out to be her former lover Keith.

Billy grew jealous of Alison's friendship with computer expert Steve McMillan, who had started going out with Jo. When Steve tried to bed her, she felt it was too soon to dive headlong into another relationship. But Billy believed Alison had slept with Steve and, feeling betrayed, jumped straight into bed with Amanda again. Billy and Alison eventually made up at a Christmas party.

Amanda got her own back on Alison by taking away the Microcomp account from her on the pretext of her 'unprofessional' relationship with Steve. But Alison complained to their boss, Bruce Teller, who put her back on the account.

When Billy took a junior editor's job in New York, Alison was not willing to travel with him but tried to conduct a long-distance romance 5000 km (3000 miles) apart. This did not work and the couple split up, but Billy gave up his job, returned to Los Angeles, presented Alison with a gold ring and proposed on bended knee. However, Alison jilted him on their wedding day, saying she still loved him but could not get married. This followed the realization that her recurring nightmares of the previous months had been a reminder of her childhood, when her father molested her.

Although Billy and Alison made up, they squabbled when Billy was hired by Amanda at D&D Advertising. After Alison suggested that Escapade – a client of D&D – needed a totally new campaign to stop it looking like a dozen other magazines, Billy told her their relationship was over. Alison was riled to see her new flat-mate, Susan, leave to move in with Billy. Then, in a drunken state while driving alone, Alison collided with a cyclist and failed a breathalyzer test. Further trouble came when Amanda was fired from her job as art director of D&D Advertising and Alison was promoted, only to see Amanda return as president. Billy, in his new role as vice president, was ordered to sack Alison. Down and all but out, Alison tackled her alcoholism at a clinic.

Courtney Thorne-Smith landed a role in the film *Lucas* at the age of 17. Her other feature films include *Summer Release*, *Summer School*, *Revenge of the Nerds II* and *Side Out*. She also acted on TV in *First Flight*, *Fast Times at Ridgemont High*, *Infidelity*, *Day by Day*, *Anything But Love* and *LA Law*, before joining *Melrose Place*. She had an off-screen romance with fellow *Melrose Place* star Andrew Shue.

JO REYNOLDS

Single-minded divorcée Jo Reynolds is a fashion photographer who puts her career before romance and, when it comes to upholding principles, she is at the front of the queue. But, when Jo arrived as a new tenant in Melrose Place, she proved to be a bit of a mystery woman. She soon became attached to mechanic Jake Hanson but lost him to Amanda Woodward. Jo then started dating Amanda's new work colleague, computer executive Steve McMillan, but he stopped seeing her after saying he believed she still loved Jake and he would not play second fiddle.

She had no more luck with her next boyfriend, Reed Carter, a former childhood friend whom she met again at a high-school reunion. He had just been in prison for two years, convicted of narcotics smuggling, but claimed to have been framed.

When Jo found packets of brick cocaine on his boat, Reed took her hostage. She tried to kill him by grabbing a speargun that was on board and firing an arrow into him. This failed to immobilize him, so she took his shotgun and killed him. Jo was arrested for murder, but the charge was dropped when the judge accepted that she had acted in self-defence.

It was a shock when Jo's doctor informed her that she was pregnant – Reed was the father. She almost miscarried when she fell down some stairs in a tussle with model Sarah Owens's violent boyfriend on a photoshoot.

Jake returned to Jo when he found out Amanda was having an affair with her mother's

Mad at the Moon and *Chameleon*. Daphne's introduction to *Melrose Place* during the first series, as well as that of Heather Locklear, led to the programme becoming a huge success. Daphne also appeared as Jo Reynolds in the 1994 pilot episode of the spin-off series *Models Inc.*, as a guest at a party to celebrate the modelling agency's tenth anniversary.

KIMBERLY SHAW

Doctor Kimberly Shaw was the woman who broke up Michael and Jane Mancini's marriage, although her relationship with fellow doctor Michael was threatened when Jane's sister, Sydney, appeared on the scene and seduced Michael. He won Kimberly back and asked her to marry him. But, as they drove home, he tried to pass her the engagement ring, dropped it and the car skidded and turned over, leaving Michael injured and Kimberly in a coma.

Kimberly's mother moved her to a hospital in Cleveland, telling Michael never to see her daughter again. Shortly afterwards, Michael heard of her death. So it was a shock when she reappeared months later at his beach house, saying her parents had tried to end their romance by telling the hospital that she had died.

Now, she was back to reclaim him and he would have to get rid of Sydney, whom he had married. Michael told Sydney he was divorcing her. He did not know that Kimberly was wearing a red wig to hide a long, deep, ugly scar across her skull and she was seeking revenge. At the hospital, she took a sticker off a patient's chart saying that no penicillin should be administred – leading to Michael's demotion – and then planned Michael's murder.

First, she tried to poison his beer, but Jane found him unconscious and revived him. Then, she ran him over in Jane's VW Rabbit. As a result, Jane was arrested and Kimberly implicated Sydney by offering her an alibi but telling the police she was elsewhere at the time. Kimberly also planted the blonde wig she had used – to look like Jane – in Sydney's dresser drawer.

But Kimberly continued to deceive Michael and, when they chased to Las Vegas to stop the planned wedding between Jane Mancini and Chris Marchette, the couple decided to get married themselves in the wedding chapel there.

boyfriend, Chas Russell, but he then cooled the relationship. Another shock came with the attempt by Reed's parents, Dennis and Marilyn Carter, to gain custody of the unborn child. When Jo gave birth to a baby boy, Austin, she plotted with Dr Kimberly Shaw to enter in the medical records that the baby was stillborn so that the Carters could not claim it. But Kimberly – desperate to have a child – tried to take the baby for her own, before Jo faced another drama when her nanny tried to steal Austin.

☆ ☆ ☆

Daphne Zuniga (b. Berkeley, California, 1963) was a rising Hollywood actress when she was brought in to pep up *Melrose Place*. She made her film debut in the 1981 picture *The Dorm That Dripped Blood* and followed it with *The Initiation*. Then, she acted in *Vision Quest*, alongside Matthew Modine (retitled *Crazy for You* for release in some countries and on video because of Madonna's appearance singing her hit song of that title). It brought Daphne to the attention of director Rob Reiner, who cast her opposite John Cusack as college students on a cross-country trip from New England to Los Angeles in his teen comedy *The Sure Thing*.

Daphne subsequently starred in the disastrous *Modern Girls*, the Mel Brooks spoof *Spaceballs*, *Last Rites* (in which her character seduced a priest played by Tom Berenger), *Gross Anatomy* (with Matthew Modine again), *Staying Together* (also titled *A Boy's Life*), *The Fly II*,

☆ ☆ ☆

Marcia Cross studied acting at the Juilliard School and guest-starred in such series as *It's Garry Shandling* (as the star's girlfriend), *Cheers*, *Quantum Leap* and *Murder, She Wrote* before joining *Melrose Place*. Her other TV appearances have included *The Last Days of*

English-born Phillip Lewis, who took over as lead singer of American heavy-metal group LA Guns when Axl Rose left to form Guns N' Roses, played a ROCK STAR spotted by Jake Hanson buying art from his ex-girlfriend.

Frank and Jesse James, *Almost Grown* and *Pros and Cons*, and Marcia has acted in the films *Bad Influence* and *Storm of Sorrow*. On stage the actress has played Sylvia in *Two Gentlemen of Verona* and Viola in *Twelfth Night*, both at the Old Globe, San Diego, and understudied the part of Sophie in the Broadway production *Artist Descending a Staircase*. Her other theatre appearances include *La Ronde*, *Emerald City*, *The Merchant of Venice* and *My Daddy's Serious American Gift*.

AMANDA WOODWARD

Owner of the apartment block, Amanda Woodward is the superbitch who plays God with the residents' lives and has made a play for most of the men. She's also art director of D&D Advertising, the agency where Alison Parker worked as an advertising executive.

She split up Alison and her boyfriend Billy – but only temporarily – before getting her hooks into hunky mechanic Jake Hanson. That relationship ended when Jake – who worked in her father Palmer's garage – gave FBI agents evidence to prove that Palmer was a crook. She slept with Billy again after he mistakenly believed Alison had slept with Steve McMillan, but Alison and Billy were reunited. Amanda made up with Jake after her father confessed to being guilty of the charges.

She continued her campaign against Alison by taking the Microcomp account away from her, but Alison complained to their boss, Bruce Teller, and he put her back on it. Bruce later carpeted Amanda for sacking Sarah Owens, a model from the Models Inc. agency, from a photoshoot and declaring that no models were

to be hired from that agency in future. Bruce forced her to apologize to the boss of Models Inc., not realizing that she was Amanda's mother, Hillary Michaels, who had deserted Amanda and her father years earlier.

Hillary persuaded her to hire her younger boyfriend, Chas Russell, as junior account executive. Amanda seduced Chas but fired him after Jake found out. Amanda was stunned when Chas filed a sexual harassment law suit against D&D Advertising, claiming he had rejected her continual advances. But he lost the case.

It seemed a blow when Amanda was sacked from D&D Advertising, with Alison taking over her job. But a consortium of doctors then bought a controlling interest in D&D and Amanda was appointed president. She made Billy vice president and told him that his first executive assignment was to fire Alison.

Heather Locklear (b. Los Angeles, USA, 25 September 1961) dropped out of UCLA (University College of Los Angeles), where she was studying for a psychology degree. Before leaving, she came to the attention of a casting director after modelling for a sportswear catalogue and appeared in several TV commercials. On leaving, she attended acting classes.

The blue-eyed blonde appeared in the TV movies *City Killer* and *Jury Duty*, and worked as a model, before landing a part in the motorcycle-cop series *CHiPS* and then the roles of goody-goody trainee policewoman Stacy Sheridan in *T. J. Hooker*, alongside William Shatner, and superbitch Sammy Jo Carrington in the glossy soap *Dynasty* – making both series at the same time. She beat 400 other actresses to the role of Sammy Jo, the wife of Blake Carrington's son Steven. Heather also appeared in the miniseries *Dynasty: The Reunion* in 1991.

She made guest appearances in *The Love Boat* and *The Fall Guy* – starring Lee Majors – and, more recently, was in the unsuccessful American sitcom *Going Places*, the TV movies *Rich Man, Single Women* and *Her Wicked Ways*, as well as the films *Firestarter* and *The Big Slice*.

Dynasty and *T. J. Hooker* producer Aaron Spelling originally asked Heather to join *Melrose Place* for just four episodes of the first series, but her character was such a hit that she was asked to stay on. The love triangle between Amanda, Billy and Alison helped to turn the programme into a ratings success.

Divorced from Motley Crüe drummer Tommy Lee in 1994, Heather – reported to have had £6000 bust implants – wed Bon Jovi guitarist Richie Sambora in a ceremony at the American Cathedral on Avenue Georges V, Paris, in December 1994.

Annalise Hartman (Kimberley Davies), Cody Willis (Peta Brady), Sam Kratz (Richard Grieve) and Danni Stark (Eliza Szonert) are four of the lively younger residents of Erinsborough who are featured in Neighbours.

Neighbours' success in Britain, Australia and other countries represents a complete turnaround from its early days. First broadcast by the 7 Network in Australia on 18 March 1985, the new serial failed to capture the public imagination and was axed before the end of its first year. But Grundy Television, which produces *Neighbours*, persuaded the rival 10 Network to take the programme. With changes that included the arrival of Jason Donovan as Scott Robinson and Kylie Minogue as Charlene Mitchell, the serial became a massive hit. In Britain, BBC1 first screened *Neighbours* on 27 October 1986, broadcasting each episode twice a day, five days a week. The combined daily audience figures – split almost equally between each screening – meant that *Neighbours* was soon challenging *Coronation Street* and *EastEnders* at the top of the TV ratings.

Set in Ramsay Street, in the fictional Melbourne suburb of Erinsborough, *Neighbours* was created by Reg Watson – first producer of the British serial *Crossroads*, who returned to his homeland of Australia in 1973 to create such hit soaps as *The Young Doctors*, *Sons and Daughters* and *Prisoner: Cell Block H* – and it has a particular appeal to young people. Its storylines centred around the Robinson, Ramsay and Clarke families, although the only surviving member of the original cast is Anne Haddy, who plays the late Jim Robinson's mother-in-law, Helen Daniels. The Willis and Alessi families then took over the spotlight, before the Starks and Kennedys arrived. *Neighbours* is recorded at television studios in Melbourne, with outside shots in Pin Oak Court, Vermont.

RICK ALESSI

Second-generation Italian immigrant Benito Alessi and his Australian wife Cathy hoped for great things from their younger son, Rick. Realizing that his brother, Marco, was simply one of life's drifters, they hoped that Rick would turn out to be the academic one and sent him to a private school. But Rick did not live up to their expectations, rebelled at school and was always the one behind practical jokes. Eventually, he was expelled and turned up on Marco's doorstep in Ramsay Street. Rick's parents later moved into no. 22 after Paul Robinson and their niece, Christina Alessi, married and left Erinsborough.

At the local high school, Rick carried on where he had left off during his previous 'studies'. But he started to behave better when he realized that the school's principal, Dorothy Burke, lived across the street from him.

After falling for classmate Debbie Martin, Rick won a trip to London to see Michael Jackson in concert. Neither Rick's nor Debbie's parents would have let them go, but a plan was devised whereby Debbie's grandmother, Helen, would tell her parents that she was taking Debbie on a trip to the Outback on a painting holiday and Marco would tell his parents that he was looking after Rick in Europe.

When Marco and the lovebirds arrived in London, he soon disappeared – taking the opportunity to escape from loan sharks and Helen developed an ear infection, which confined her to bed. This left Rick and Debbie to their own devices in London. But, when they met a leukaemia victim called Terry, the couple let him have their tickets for the concert. This act of charity was reported by a TV programme that interviewed Rick and Debbie. The news reached Australia and there was hell to pay when their parents found out. But nothing could stop the pair's romance blossoming, although the announcement by Benito and Cathy that they were moving to Sydney in 1994 worried Debbie enough to let Rick make love to her while they were babysitting Hope Gottlieb.

Rick stayed on in Erinsborough by arranging a grant for children studying away from home and lived in a room at Lassiter's in exchange for working in the kitchens there. But Debbie fell for Lassiter's chef Harvey Johnson and moved in with Lou Carpenter at no. 24 Ramsay Street.

Tragedy followed when Rick bought a flash car and accepted a challenge from Lenny and Briggs. Cody Willis joined Rick as his passenger in the car with Briggs, Danni and Lenny in the other car. As Rick and Cody rounded a bend, they were horrified to see their opponents' car wrapped round a tree, leaving Danni injured and Briggs dead. Rick had to pay back the cost of the smashed car from the car yard, but his mother agreed to pay off the debt if he moved in with the Carpenters.

Later, Rick fell for his Japanese-language teacher, Sally Pritchard, three years his senior. When he left school to become a trainee at the Waterhole, he signed a long-term contract with Lassiter's, wangled an advance on his salary, bought a ring and proposed. But Sally turned him down and left Erinsborough.

Devastated, Rick started playing the field and no female in Ramsay Street was safe from his advances. When Rick overcame his fear of

> Twins Gillian and Gayle Blakeney (b. Brisbane, Australia, 23 March 1966) were CAROLINE and CHRISTINA ALESSI. Since leaving the serial, the twins have recorded pop records and appeared on British television in such programmes as *Take Your Pick*, alongside Des O'Connor.
>
> Experienced soap actress Elspeth Ballantyne, sister of producer Jane Ballantyne, joined *Neighbours* as CATHY ALESSI. She had already made her name on television as Lori Grey in *Bellbird* and Meg Morris in *Prisoner: Cell Block H*.
>
> Felice Arena (b. Victoria, Australia) acted MARCO ALESSI, who disappeared in London when loan sharks were chasing him. Felice himself moved to Britain to star in the musicals *Hair* and *Godspell*.

heights by going through with a parachute jump, student Cody Willis admitted a crush on him after noticing that his parachute trainer Cassie seemed interested.

☆ ☆ ☆

Dan Falzon (b. 24 November 1974) was still at school when he joined *Neighbours* in 1993. He had been in the state hockey team for the previous five years and also enjoys cricket, soccer, swimming and tennis.

At the time he was filming romantic scenes in the serial where his character proposed to his former teacher, in real life he was splitting up with his girlfriend, university student Donna Gluyas, who – like his screen love – was three years older than him. The couple had met two years before at the Australian holiday spot Surfer's Paradise and Dan blamed the long hours working on *Neighbours* for the break-up of their romance. Dan lives in Melbourne with his Italian family.

Ian Smith (b. Melbourne, Australia) played fuddy-duddy HAROLD BISHOP. Ian has also been a writer, scripting some episodes of *Prisoner: Cell Block H* – in which he starred as Ted Douglas and of which he was associate producer – and then *Neighbours*, before playing Harold.

Anne Charleston (b. Melbourne, Australia) was no-nonsense MADGE BISHOP (née Ramsay, previously Mitchell). Anne previously acted on TV in *Cop Shop*, *The Sullivans*, *Skyways* and *Prisoner: Cell Block H* (in three roles: Mum's daughter, a policewoman and Mrs Keen, mother of Rebecca Keen). After leaving *Neighbours*, she moved to Ireland, from where her great-grandmother was deported.

James Condon (b. Fremantle, Western Australia, 27 September 1923) played conman DOUGLAS BLAKE, who cheated widow Helen Daniels – actress Anne Haddy, to whom the actor is married in real life – out of money. James was also in the soaps *The Young Doctors*, *Sons and Daughters* and *Prisoner: Cell Block H*.

Maggie Dence, who played prim and bossy teacher DOROTHY BURKE, was previously best known for the role of Rose Sullivan in *The Sullivans*. Her other soaps include *Kingswood Country*, *Skyways*, *A Country Practice* (three times), *Prisoner: Cell Block H* (as Bev Baker), *The Flying Doctors* and *Rafferty's Rules*.

LOU CARPENTER

Growing up in Queensland, Lou Carpenter was the childhood sweetheart of Madge Ramsay, but she ditched him and wed Fred Mitchell. When he heard that the couple had divorced, Lou travelled to Erinsborough to win her back. He showed her that his secondhand car business had made him a wealthy man, but Madge opted to wed Harold Bishop instead.

Lou's younger sister, Brenda Riley, later rented no. 24 Ramsay Street from Madge and Harold while they were on a trip round Australia. Lou's estranged son, Guy – by ex-wife Kathy – turned up and managed the coffee shop with Brenda. Lou arrived in town and set about making his peace with Guy. Much harder was coping with Madge's return following Harold's death on their trip. His presence encouraged Madge to share her grief with her family in Brisbane.

Lou was determined to win the woman he had once lost and, on Madge's return in 1992, he proposed to her. She politely turned him down and decided to leave Erinsborough, with Lou taking over no. 24.

Having by now lost most of his wealth, Lou opened a new secondhand car business, Carpenter's Cars. But the recession forced him to sell half the business to Benito Alessi, who agreed to be a silent partner. But he was far from silent after losing his job at Lassiter's, started selling cars himself and caused friction.

Resolving to be young again, Lou started dressing like a teenager and made a play for sexy Annalise Hartman, who humoured him because she was interested in an older man's money. She even went along with his wedding plans until her mother arrived and told Lou that she was only 17, when he thought she was 21. His own daughter, Lauren, came to Ramsay Street and had an affair with Brad Willis, who was engaged to – and later married – Beth Brennan.

It was finally Lou's turn for romance when wealthy Cheryl Stark fell for him. But he ran scared when she wangled a date with him, gatecrashed his cards night and rented the house next door. Then, she started buying up his used cars one by one just so that she could talk to him. When she proposed, he turned her down.

Lou panicked when Cheryl – who had two teenage children, Brett and Danni – moved into no. 22 Ramsay Street. But a few disastrous dates with Wendy Slater proved to Lou that Cheryl was more his type, although Cheryl was not sure about entering a relationship now that her children were back. But Lou won her over and Cheryl moved her family into his house.

Cheryl then became pregnant and came to terms with the fact that she would be an older mother. After overhearing her say that marriage was every woman's dream, Lou proposed again – over the public address system at the Waterhole.

☆ ☆ ☆

Tom Oliver (b. Fareham, Hampshire) wanted to be a jockey while growing up in Britain, but he was soon too tall and heavy. Instead, he joined the Merchant Navy and, on his third trip to Australia, jumped ship and settled there.

After three years of working as a ranch hand on a massive cattle station, he started acting. He has since appeared on television in *Prisoner: Cell Block H* (as Ken Pearce, the reformed criminal who took a shine to Bea Smith) and in the film *ABBA The Movie*, as a bouncer. He first played Lou Carpenter in *Neighbours* briefly in 1989 and was asked back four years later, when the character became a regular.

Tom, who is married to an American called Jan, had previously worked with *Neighbours* actress Anne Charleston – who played Madge Bishop, to whom his character proposed – in a sixties TV play called *The Shifting Heart*, in which he also proposed to her. Away from the studios, Tom enjoys horse-riding and gardening.

HELEN DANIELS

The Robinson family called Helen Daniels 'The Rock of Gibraltar', going to her for wisdom and kindly advice. The voice of reason, she is often the mediator in neighbourhood disputes, although she is reluctant to interfere in other people's lives. Mother-in-law of Jim Robinson, Helen was widowed in the early seventies, with the death of husband Bill, who she later found had conducted an affair with her sister Laura. A few years later, Helen moved in with Jim and his four children and her granddaughter Lucy when her daughter Anne died in childbirth.

Although Helen is a budding artist and an avid reader with an interest in politics and world affairs, looking after the family became her pre-occupation when she took over the running of the Robinson household.

It was Helen who intervened and gave wise advice when grandson Scott Robinson's marriage to Charlene was on the rocks. Then, when orphan Nick Page's grandmother died, leaving him homeless and lonely, Helen took him.

The keen artist's trusting nature was taken advantage of when she met conman Douglas Blake at her first public exhibition. He was a charmer who promised to marry her and made her part with her savings under the guise of buy-

Elaine Smith played stripper DAPHNE CLARKE (née Lawrence), whom Des Clarke married. But Daphne died in a car crash, leaving Des to bring up their son, Jamie. Elaine had previously acted Helen Gray in *A Country Practice* and later played Dr Sissy Wetherall in the *Flying Doctors* sequel *RFDS* and starred in the series *The Paper Man*. She also played opposite David Soul in the musical *Blood Brothers* on stage in New Zealand.

Paul Keane (b. Sydney), who played lovable bank manager and coffee-shop manager DES CLARKE, worked as an electrician and a storeman on leaving school. He switched to acting and appeared on TV in *Sons and Daughters*, before joining *Neighbours*. He also played the drums and performed in a group called Suitably Rough with fellow *Neighbours* stars Alan Dale, Elaine Smith and Peter O'Brien, as well as in Craig McLachlan's group Next Door. After leaving the serial, he fought drug addiction and played in a pub band.

Veteran actress **Myra de Groot** (b. Britain) left Britain for America in 1958, starred in the sixties comedy series *Bewitched* there and moved on to New Zealand, before settling in Australia. She played EILEEN CLARKE, Des's interfering mother, until her death from cancer in April 1988.

Rachel Friend played BRONWYN DAVIES, Henry Ramsay's girlfriend, until she decided to leave shortly after her screen lover Craig McLachlan. The romance spun off into real life and the pair married in 1993, although they split up the following year. Rachel now works as a television journalist in Australia on *The Midday Show*.

Brian Blain (b. Queensland, 1935) had already acted Gordon Hamilton in *Sons and Daughters* when he appeared in *Neighbours* as Helen Daniels's bigamist husband MICHAEL DANIELS.

Ally Fowler (b. Alexandra Fowler), who previously appeared in *The Young Doctors* and played Angela Hamilton in *Sons and Daughters*, arrived in Ramsay Street as ZOE DAVIS. She subsequently acted in *The Flying Doctors* and the drama *Frankie's House*.

ing property. Even worse was the time when Helen was left $150,000 in the will of Jim's mother, Bess. It was discovered that the currency was Hong Kong dollars, worth only about $20,000 in Australia. Then, she received a blackmail demand for $20,000, with threats to the safety of her family. The blackmailer was Bob Landers, father of Todd and Katie, and he was arrested by the police. Despite this, the Robinsons put up his bail and allowed him to stay for a few days to be with his children.

But Helen's worst moment was when she had a stroke and went into a coma. She was in hospital for weeks, and the residents of Ramsay Street set up a rota so that someone would always be at her bedside to talk to her, in the hope of bringing her out of the coma. It worked and was a mark of the high regard in which Helen is held by both family and friends.

Romance came back into her life with the arrival in Erinsborough of debonair Michael Daniels, her late husband's cousin. The couple married, but heartbreak followed when Helen found out that he was a bigamist.

She was helping other people with their problems again when she read letters that revealed that Jim was not Julie Martin's father. Helen told Julie, who believed her mother must have had an affair but, in searching for her natural father, she found out that she had been born after her mother was raped.

New love came into Helen's life with the return to Erinsborough of Len Mangel, former husband of busybody Mrs Mangel. He made her feel good but was eventually rumbled by Helen's step-grandson, Michael Martin, who found out that he was still living with his previous girlfriend, Gwen, and wanted Helen only for her widow's pension.

☆ ☆ ☆

Anne Haddy (b. Quorn, South Australia, 5 October 1927) became obsessed with acting while in her teens. As an only child, she invented characters, dressed up and produced plays with other children.

While at Adelaide High School, art teacher Keith Michell – now a famous actor – applied Anne's make-up in a play, *Androcles and the Lion*. After leaving school, Anne acted in radio plays and schools broadcasts while working by day in Adelaide University's book room.

She left for Britain at the age of 23, hoping to find acting work, but ended up working for Kellogg's as a secretary. She met and married her first husband, Max Dimmitt, before returning to Australia, where they had two children, Jane and Tony.

Anne was in demand in the theatre and radio, and also presented *Play School* on television. In addition, she has appeared on TV in *Skippy the Bush Kangaroo*, *Prisoner: Cell Block H* (as Alice Hemmings, Doreen Burns's estranged mother), *Skyways* (as Toni Lee), *Cop Shop* (as Louise Francis), *Sons and Daughters* (as housekeeper Rosie Andrews), *The Young Doctors* and *The Flying Doctors*. She was in the films *Hostile Witness* (with Ray Milland), *A Town Like Alice* and *Newsfront*.

The actress has had a string of personal tragedies. In 1971, while rehearsing the stage play *National Health* in Sydney, she fell and broke her wrist. Because the play was set in the ward of a London hospital, there were nurses on hand to give advice to the cast.

Eight years later, Anne collapsed from a heart attack and had to have bypass surgery. Shortly afterwards, she fell and broke a hip. Then, Anne discovered she had cancer of the stomach, but it was diagnosed early and the growth was removed. In 1983, she was back in hospital, having one of her four heart bypasses unclogged.

Anne and her second husband, actor James Condon – who played scheming Douglas Blake

---

Simone Robertson (b. Sydney, Australia, 28 May 1975) was PHOEBE GOTTLIEB (née Bright), who became pregnant at 17 by her boyfriend who died, was then held hostage by a crazed gunman and eventually married Stephen Gottlieb. Simone had previously acted in the film *Father*, where she met actor boyfriend Benjamin Mitchell, who later played lawyer Cameron Hudson in *Neighbours*.

Lochie Daddo (b. Christopher Lachlan Daddo) was STEPHEN GOTTLIEB, who married Phoebe Bright and was confined to a wheelchair after being injured in an explosion at the Waterhole. Lochie, brother of *Models Inc.* star Cameron Daddo, later played a gay man called Patrick in *G.P.* and an ex-jailbird called Angel in *Paradise Beach*, as well as reporting for the Australian travel programme *Getaway*, seen in Britain on Sky Travel.

Annie Jones (b. Annika Jasko in Adelaide) appeared in *The Henderson Kids* and, for four months, in *Sons and Daughters* before acting JANE HARRIS in *Neighbours*. She subsequently played hairdresser Paris in *Chances* and starred in the miniseries *Jackaroo*, the 13-part *Embassy* and the sitcom *The Newlyweds*.

in *Neighbours* – live in Melbourne. The actress has eight grandchildren.

MARK GOTTLIEB

When Lassiter's chef Harvey Johnson left his job, Mark Gottlieb arrived as his replacement – and things were soon getting steamy in the kitchen. Elder brother of Stephen Gottlieb, Mark came to Erinsborough and landed the job – after travelling the world for several years – by putting on a phony French accent and calling himself Marcel. He was soon rumbled, but no-one complained.

Gaby Willis and Annalise Hartman both fought for Mark's affections and, for a while, he enjoyed playing one off against the other. Eventually, he settled for Annalise.

When wheelchair-bound Paralympics fundraiser Katerina Torelli arrived in Erinsborough and had a crush on him, he cancelled a date so that he could talk over plans with Katerina, and Annalise became jealous. Katerina told her that Mark had been having an affair with her. It took a lot of persuading for him to convince Annalise that it was a pack of lies. Mark and Annalise were reunited after a romantic break in Paris and set a date for their wedding. But Mark put paid to a happy ending by jilting Annalise and deciding to become a priest.

☆ ☆ ☆

Bruce Samazan (b. Madagascar) worked as a model before gaining fame as police constable Max Simmons in the Australian soap *E Street*, which was short-lived but managed to win him a Silver Logie award for his performance. When the serial was axed, he joined *Neighbours*. He also presented the country and western music show *Stampede*, travelling 1600 km (1000 miles) to Brisbane from the *Neighbours* studios in Melbourne every week to record it. In an attempt to become a pop star, Bruce released a rap single in Australia called 'One of a Kind', but it failed to make the charts.

Bruce met girlfriend Romy Meerkin when she visited the *E Street* set as part of a project for her university degree. He asked her out to dinner and the two have since been inseparable.

ANNALISE HARTMAN

Sex siren Annalise Hartman gained a reputation for chasing anything in trousers after growing up without a father. Her mother, Fiona, walked out on him, although she told her daughter at the time that he had died. Fiona was Jim Robinson's last romantic conquest before his death. She intended to get her hands on his money and, when he suffered a fatal heart attack, she went off to Jim's stockbroker to cash in his shares and returned to the house with Rosemary Daniels to 'discover' Jim's body.

Following in her scheming mother's ways, Annalise made a play for 50-year-old second-hand car salesman Lou Carpenter in an attempt to get his money. But he dumped Annalise when her mother arrived and told him she was only 17, when he had thought she was 21.

Annalise also defrauded Lassiter's by checking in as a guest and not paying her bill, although she was forced to pay off the debt by working as a chambermaid. Then, she worked in the Waterhole and the coffee shop, flirting outrageously with customers. She had romances with Russell Butler and Lassiter's chef Harvey Johnson, before falling in a big way for Harvey's replacement there, Mark Gottlieb – taking him from under the nose of her arch-rival, Gaby Willis, in 1994.

By then, Annalise had surprised everyone by landing a job as P.A. for a business executive in a city firm. Then came the news that her mother had been killed and she had a brother she never knew existed, Luke Foster, who claimed to have been put up for adoption by her mother several months before Annalise's birth. Luke arrived in Erinsborough, but Mark warned Annalise that he was just a gold-digger and eventually discovered that Luke was not her brother at all, just a conman.

Working at the Waterhole again, Annalise was stalked by a customer who took a fancy to her

NEIGHBOURS

from a small country town, hoping the city would offer more excitement.

Politically aware, Libby aligns herself with her grandfather's Communist beliefs, which have brought arguments with father Karl. She is also a feminist but hoped for a relationship with a boy, having had her heart broken by a previous boyfriend in the country.

☆ ☆ ☆

Kym Valentine trained in jazz and ballet for 13 years and had appeared on TV in many commercials, as well as *Candid Camera*, *Swap Shop*, the documentary *Adult Illiteracy*, the educational programme *Save Nugget End* and the sitcom *My Two Wives* before joining *Neighbours* in 1994.

Away from the studios, Kym enjoys water-skiing, bushwalking, volleyball, rollerskating, swimming, ice-skating and aerobics.

and held captive in the cellar after closing time, until Mark came to the rescue and freed her.

Annalise and Mark's romance survived an attempt by disabled Paralympics fundraiser Katerina Torelli to woo him and he joined Annalise on a trip to London when her poems were published and the couple subsequently had a romantic break in Paris. Returning to Australia, they set a date for their wedding, but Mark stood Annalise up at the altar.

☆ ☆ ☆

Kimberley Davies is one of four children who helped their parents to run a farm in rural Victoria. Her goals were 'to travel, work as a model and an actress'. At the age of 11, she won a Fellowship of Australian Writers award and, six years later, abandoned a law degree to become a model after being spotted by a talent scout. She worked alongside such catwalk beauties as Claudia Schiffer and Elle MacPherson.

Before joining *Neighbours*, Kimberley had a well publicized romance with Scott Michaelson – who played Brad Willis in the serial – although they had split up by the time they started working together. In 1994, Kimberley started dating model and medical student Jason Harvey, with whom she had previously worked on modelling assignments.

LIBBY KENNEDY

The middle of Karl and Susan Kennedy's three children, Elizabeth arrived in Erinsborough as a sophisticated, intelligent 16-year-old who liked to look different from other teenagers. She also had a bad temper and a tendency towards melodrama, and was pleased when her family moved

MALCOLM KENNEDY

Bright, confident and lively teenager Malcolm is eldest of the Kennedy children. He mixes easily with people of all ages and gets on particularly well with his father, unlike sister Libby. Malcolm is also adept at playing the 'big brother' and other children know that to criticize any of the Kennedy clan is inviting trouble.

Malcolm's great passions are sport and astronomy, which means he takes a great interest in Black Holes, the Hubble Space Telescope and anything else that extends his knowledge of the universe and how it works.

☆ ☆ ☆

Benji McNair (b. Benjamin McNair) attended Mona Vale Film & TV School and a National Institute of Dramatic Art summer school before joining the Australian Theatre for Young People.

He had already guest-starred on TV as Morgan in *G.P.* and Alan in two episodes of *Home and Away* by the time he joined *Neighbours* in 1994. He also appeared in various commercials and training films.

SUSAN KENNEDY

Born into a family of teachers, practical, no-nonsense Susan Kennedy met husband Karl during her first year at university and the couple were married after her graduation. Susan went into teaching but was unable to work full-time after the birth of her first son, Malcolm. Less than a year later, daughter Libby was born and the family moved to the country. By the time Susan and Karl's third child, Billy, was born, Karl was working as the local doctor and Susan was doing only occasional stints of casual teaching. One of the reasons for moving to Erinsborough was to do more teaching work.

Jackie Woodburne took a three-year part-time drama course at the National Theatre, Melbourne, under the direction of Joan Harris. She also did a ten-week course in clowning skills and subsequently worked as a clown at community functions. Jackie then performed with the theatre group Skids, providing musical entertainment in schools and at festivals.

This led to appearances in such children's television programmes as *Words Fail Me*, before Jackie landed roles in *Skyways*, *Cop Shop* (as Gina Rossi), *The Young Doctors* (for nine months), *A Country Practice* (three times), *Carson's Law*, *Prisoner: Cell Block H*, *The Flying Doctors* and the American TV movie *The Flood*. She joined *Neighbours* in 1994.

SAM KRATZ

Biker Sam Kratz, who had worked as a builder's labourer, a plumber, car mechanic, farmhand, on fishing trawlers and in a circus, roared into Ramsay Street clad in leather and soon set female hearts a-flutter. Although he is a nice guy, trouble follows him wherever he goes.

He found a job looking after the Stark children while Cheryl recovered from an accident in hospital. Danni caught Sam putting video recorders and other items in Lou Carpenter's garage and used this information to blackmail him into accompanying her to the debutante ball.

But Sam was soon chasing man-eating Annalise Hartman, and the two shared a passionate kiss, but she returned to boyfriend Mark Gottlieb.

☆ ☆ ☆

Richard Grieve grew up in Hong Kong, London and Kuala Lumpur, before returning to Melbourne in his teens to complete his education. He studied in dance and drama at the Victoria College and NIDA, before appearing on television as Shane in the soap *E Street* and Charles in the comedy *The Newlyweds*. He joined *Neighbours* as Sam Kratz in 1994, quickly becoming its latest heart-throb.

The actor also spent seven months on a stage tour of *How to Succeed in Business Without Really Trying* and enjoys horse-riding – he started at the age of four and later learned dressage and polo – skiing and playing the violin.

Maxine Klibingaitis (b. Maxine Koren Klibingaitis in Ballarat, Victoria, Australia, 17 May 1964) was Bobbie Mitchell, one of the younger inmates in *Prisoner: Cell Block H*, before taking the role of TERRI INGLIS in *Neighbours*.

Kristian Schmid (b. Australia, 28 November 1974) played TODD LANDERS, nephew of Beverly Marshall. Todd and sister Kate ran away from their bullying father. When Kristian left the serial, he moved to Britain and starred on TV in *The Tomorrow People* and presented the Saturday-morning show *Going Live!*

British actor **Derek Nimmo** (b. Liverpool, 19 September 1932), most famous for playing clergymen in *All Gas and Gaiters*, *Oh Brother!* and *Oh Father!*, took the role of Rosemary Daniels's noble friend LORD LEDGERWOOD on Madge and Harold Bishop's visit to Britain.

John Morris had already played an undertaker in *Sons and Daughters* and Dr Phillip Matheson in *Home and Away* when he took the role of Doug Willis's gay boss ANDREW MACKENZIE, on whom Debbie Martin had a crush.

Mark Little toured in cabaret as an alternative comedian before playing JOE MANGEL, who had a son, Toby, by first wife Noleen before marrying Kerry Bishop, who already had a daughter, Sky. On TV Mark had previously appeared in *Skyways*, *Cop Shop*, *The Sullivans*, *Carson's Law*, *Rafferty's Rules*, *The Flying Doctors* and *The Dunera Boys*. He has since become a presenter of *The Big Breakfast* on TV in Britain and appeared in the pilot *No Worries*.

Veteran actress **Vivean Gray** (b. Britain) played interfering gossip MRS (NELLIE) MANGEL until she found public recognition too much to cope with. She had already appeared in *The Sullivans* as the awful Mrs Jessup and inmate Edna Pearson in *Prisoner: Cell Block H*.

Julie Mullins (b. 27 February 1965) took over the role of gossiping, interfering JULIE MARTIN (née Robinson) in 1992, previously played by Vikki Blanche, who left five years earlier and then acted Paula Patterson in *The Flying Doctors*. Julie Martin met an untimely death.

DEBBIE MARTIN

Daughter of widowed bank manager Philip Martin, Debbie found herself with a new mother when he married Julie Robinson – and the two females got on like a house on fire.

But Debbie was soon getting into trouble when the family moved to Ramsay Street. She fell for classmate Rick Alessi and the couple went on a trip to London after winning tickets to a Michael Jackson concert. Their parents would not have allowed this, but a plot by Debbie's grandmother, Helen Daniels, and Rick's brother, Marco, covered for them – until they gave the tickets away to a leukaemia victim and were interviewed for a TV show, an interview that was also screened in Australia and seen by the lovebirds' parents. They had to weather the storm when they arrived back in Erinsborough, but Rick ditched Debbie when she went out with Lassiter's chef Harvey Johnson.

Then, Rick spotted her with no-good Darren Stark in a stolen car and chased them. She begged him not to tell anyone about the incident.

Craig Slater tried to woo Debbie by organizing a 17th-birthday party for her and was furious when she refused to be his girlfriend. Debbie threw him out of the house, with the result that he cried uncontrollably. Craig had a nervous breakdown, caused by problems he was having with his father at home. Julie helped Rick and Debbie campaign to set up a helpline for teenagers at Erinsborough High School and Craig was eventually reconciled with his father.

Debbie herself had a crush on Andrew MacKenzie, Doug Willis's boss at Lassiter's, not realizing he was gay. She became obsessed with him and asked him to the debutante ball, only to be turned down flat.

Coming to terms with that rejection, the pressures of schoolwork and the rocky state of her parents' marriage, Debbie started bingeing on food, then making herself sick. Friends found secret hordes of food under her bed and the reality that she might have bulimia nervosa came home to her family when she collapsed at a practice session for the debutante ball and was rushed to hospital.

Debbie was then admitted to a clinic and Helen Daniels's daughter, Rosemary, offered her kindly advice before returning to America.

Marnie Reece-Wilmore (b. Sydney) moved to the town of Orange at the age of 12, but her family disliked it so much that they moved back to Sydney. Like her *Neighbours* character, Marnie always hated school and often made herself sick to avoid going. As well as taking an interest in drama at school, she took radio presenting courses in her spare time.

Getting into acting was a dream come true for her and, shortly after joining *Neighbours*, Marnie fell for a cameraman on the programme. The couple subsequently moved into a house in Melbourne together and have a terrier called Zack.

MICHAEL MARTIN

Son of widower Philip Martin, Michael was not as pleased as his father when Julie Robinson came into the family's lives. He resented her and, when his father married Julie and they had a daughter, Hannah, he made his stepmother's life hell.

His plan to drive Julie out of Ramsay Street almost ended in tragedy when he drugged her so badly that she lost consciousness and nearly drowned in the spa.

Michael himself was once a drug-pusher, but he tried to ensure justice when Darren Stark pulled a gun on a petrol station attendant, attempting to stop him but getting injured in the crossfire. He turned up on the doorstep back at home in pain and Julie slammed the door in his face, thinking it was another of his ruses. Philip arrived home to find his son collapsed in agony on the doorstep.

His home life seemed to be going downhill and stepsister Hannah accused him of always hurting people. Michael said he wanted to leave home, but sister Debbie thought that all he needed was a girlfriend and introduced him to Cody Willis – although this did not please Cody's mother, Pam, who thought that Michael was totally the wrong sort for her daughter.

His relationship with his father began to go downhill, to the point where he upset Philip by asking Doug Willis to partner him in a father-son cricket match.

But, after his secret dates with Cody, Michael started seeing Danni Stark and was caught in bed with her by Lou Carpenter. He was also with her outside a nightclub when she had a diabetic fit. Such was the pressure from their parents to split up that the couple eventually ran away.

☆ ☆ ☆

Troy Beckwith was working as a dry-cleaning apprentice when he landed the role of Michael Martin in *Neighbours* – and continued working in the job at weekends! He previously appeared in the serial as school bully Darren Wood, who fought with Todd Landers and Cody Willis. In 1994, he promoted Australian Safe Sex Week.

PHILIP MARTIN

Bank manager Philip Martin was having an affair with employee Julie Robinson when he and his wife, Loretta, were involved in a car crash that killed her and left him paralyzed. Wheelchair-bound, he found it impossible to look after his two children, so bank teller Julie stepped in to care for the whole family. This led to marriage and another child, daughter Hannah. Philip began walking again and, after losing his job, the family moved to Julie's home town of Erinsborough. Philip's daughter, Debbie, treated Julie like a sister, but son Michael resented her.

When Julie found out that she had been born as the result of a rape, she was too disgusted with herself to tell Philip and demanded a divorce. The couple split up but were reunited at Helen Daniels's surprise birthday party. When the Martins' house was put up for sale, they were forced to move. Julie's grandmother, Helen Daniels, lived across the road, so it was convenient for them to move in with her.

After working as a school caretaker in Erinsborough, Philip became head of the hotel chain Lassiter's but then decided to run his own business by buying the newsagent's from Wendy Slater, leaving Gaby Willis in charge of Lassiter's. But this did not please Julie, who saw it as a downturn in Philip's career pattern and did not relish the thought of serving in a shop for the rest of her life.

Philip's relationship with son Michael was getting increasingly rocky and he was jealous that Michael was turning to Doug Willis for friendship and advice. In an attempt to mend fences, Philip arranged a day out at the zoo, but Doug and his daughter Cody tagged along, Michael and Cody fell out and Philip and Doug ended up sniping at each other all day.

Philip's relations with Julie went downhill again, but it was an unexpected tragedy when she died for real at a murder party.

☆ ☆ ☆

Ian Rawlings (b. South Australia) first appeared on television as a model in the game show *Wheel of Fortune*, but he was best known for his role as evil Wayne Hamilton in *Sons and Daughters* before joining another soap, *The Power, The Passion*, when it was launched.

When that serial was axed after just eight months, Ian earned money by becoming a sales-

Lucinda Cowden (b. Ballarat, Victoria, Australia, 24 April 1965) appeared on TV in *Prisoner: Cell Block H* (as Mandy Wright) and *The Power, The Passion*, before joining *Neighbours* as MELANIE PEARSON. Lucinda has since presented the British children's show *Parallel 9*.

Nadine Garner had already appeared in *The Henderson Kids* when she turned up in *Neighbours* as runaway RACHEL. She subsequently acted in *Boys from the Bush* and the British TV series *Class Act*.

Beth Buchanan, who played Madge Bishop's 16-year-old niece, GEMMA RAMSAY, appeared five times in *A Country Practice* and acted in *The Flying Doctors, G.P.* and, later, *Paradise Beach*.

Peter O'Brien (b. Murray Bridge, Australia, 25 March 1960) played SHANE RAMSAY, before starring as Dr Sam Patterson in *The Flying Doctors* and acting in the British series *The Gift, The Trials of Oz, Taggart* and *Crime Story*. In Australia, he had previously appeared on TV in *Carson's Law, Prisoner: Cell Block H* and *The Henderson Kids*.

Kylie Minogue (b. Melbourne, Australia, 28 May 1968) started acting as a child and appeared in *Skyways, The Henderson Kids* and *The Sullivans* before joining *Neighbours* as CHARLENE ROBINSON (previously Mitchell). She left the serial after finding success as a pop singer, with such singles as 'Locomotion' and 'I Should Be So Lucky', and starred in the film *The Delinquents*.

Fiona Corke (b. Melbourne, Australia, 24 September 1961) played GAIL ROBINSON (née Lewis), second wife of Paul. Fiona has also acted on TV in *Secrets* and *The Man from Snowy River*.

Alan Dale (b. Dunedin, New Zealand, 6 May 1947), a former disc jockey who played reliable and understanding widower JIM ROBINSON, previously acted in 72 episodes of the New Zealand TV series *Radio Waves*. Moving to Australia in 1979, he was offered the role of Dr John Forrest in *The Young Doctors*. He joined *Neighbours* after negotiations to cast actor Robin Harrison in the role of Jim broke down. He has since appeared on TV as a villain in *Time Tracks*.

Melissa Bell was the third actress to play LUCY ROBINSON, after Kylie Flinker (b. Melbourne, 20 April 1974) and Sascha Close. Melissa appeared as nurse Emily Harris in *Paradise Beach*, both Janine and Bonnie in *E Street*, and a radio announcer's neglected daughter, Rachel, in *G.P.*

Ashley Paske (b. Wollongong, 17 July 1970) appeared as Adam Campbell in four episodes of *A Country Practice*, before becoming a regular in *Richmond Hill*, as Marty Bryant, the policeman's son who had been in a juvenile detention centre after being caught joyriding. Aged 19, he joined *Neighbours* as heart-throb MATT ROBINSON, Jim Robinson's nephew and illegitimate son of Hilary.

Stefan Dennis (b. Melbourne, Australia, 30 October 1958) played PAUL ROBINSON, victim of two disastrous marriages, who ran the Lassiter's complex. Before joining *Neighbours*, he appeared on TV in *The Sullivans*, *Cop File*, *The Flying Doctors*, *Prisoner: Cell Block H* (as a juvenile runaway who shared a kiss with Doreen Burns), *Carson's Law*, *The Young Doctors* and *The Henderson Kids*. He originally auditioned for the role of Shane Ramsay before getting the part of Paul. Stefan released his first single, 'Don't It Make You Feel Good', and followed it up with 'This Love Affair'.

Darius Perkins was the original SCOTT ROBINSON, before Jason Donovan (b. 1 June 1968) took over the role. Jason made his TV debut aged 11 in *I Can Jump Puddles* and followed it by playing Kylie Minogue's brother in *Skyways*, then appeared with her in *The Henderson Kids* and later, of course, *Neighbours*. He left to concentrate on his pop career and acted in the miniseries *Heroes*. Darius Perkins, who had previously appeared briefly in *Prisoner: Cell Block H*, later played Gary Samuels in *Home and Away* and featured in *The Flying Doctors*.

Josephine Mitchell, who appeared in eight episodes of *The Young Doctors*, played Jo Loveday in *A Country Practice*, Penny O'Brien in *E Street* and a policewoman called Jane – who had a fling with teacher Grant Mitchell – in *Home and Away*, acted disabled Paralympics fundraiser KATERINA TORELLI, who had a crush on Mark Gottlieb, in *Neighbours*.

man at a freight shipping firm, before taking the part of nice guy Philip Martin in *Neighbours*. Ian is married and lives in Melbourne. He is a partner in a Sydney beauty salon called Chatterleys and enjoys playing squash, jogging and cycling.

BRETT STARK

Expelled from private school along with his sister Danni, teenager Brett Stark returned to his mother, Cheryl, who had moved into Ramsay Street. Trouble loomed when wild child Sassy became totally infatuated with him, to the disgust of her boyfriend, Stonefish. But Brett managed to persuade Debbie Martin to accept him as her escort for the 1994 school debutante ball.

Brett Blewitt (b. 17 November 1976) studied drama at the Keane Kids Studios for three years before joining the Australian series *My Two Wives* as Jack. He subsequently appeared as Jeff in the soap *G.P.* and played a small role in *Home and Away* before taking the part of Brett Stark in *Neighbours* in 1993.

CHERYL STARK

When the Lims moved out of no. 22 Ramsay Street, wealthy Cheryl Stark – who had to bring up four children after the death of her second husband, a railway worker – moved in with her son, Darren, who had just been released from a detention centre. With experience as a barmaid and having just won $1.3 million on the lottery, she also bought the Waterhole pub. Her arrival next door unnerved Lou Carpenter, because she had romantic notions about him. Cheryl even started buying up his used cars one by one so that he could not avoid her. She proposed, but he turned her down.

Lou, who had always carried a torch for Madge Bishop, accepted that his ideal woman had gone and, in an attempt to ward off Cheryl's advances, began seeing Wendy Slater, but their dates proved a disaster. By the time he was prepared to succumb to Cheryl's romantic overtures, her other children, Brett and Danni, had returned to the fold from boarding school and she had reservations about starting a relationship. In the end, she not only gave in, but moved into Lou's house with Darren and Danni. There was also another Stark child – daughter Janine, who left home to join the navy.

As the relationship with Lou proceeded apace, Cheryl found she was pregnant and began to worry about giving birth at her age, especially after Pam Willis warned her that there could be grave medical implications for older women. But she decided against going for an amniocentesis test, which would determine whether the baby had Down's syndrome.

When Lou decided it was time to propose again, he asked Cheryl to marry him over the public address system at the Waterhole and she accepted. Cheryl, by this time, had relinquished the Waterhole and become a major shareholder in Lassiter's, saving many jobs in the process. Her presence made Philip Martin decide to leave his job as manager there and buy a newsagent's.

Happiness came to Cheryl and Lou with the birth of a baby girl after a difficult pregnancy for Cheryl. She experienced water retention, high blood pressure and blurred vision and, during a family argument, suffered a seizure. As a result, she gave birth to daughter Louise after an emergency caesarean.

Caroline Gillmer trained at the Ensemble Theatre and, after appearing on stage in the musical *Godspell*, won acclaim throughout Australia for her role in *Guys and Dolls*. She has also acted in many productions with the Melbourne Theatre Company, from Shakespeare to farce and new Australian plays. She was co-producer, writer, director and star of Two Australia's productions of *Gershwin* and *The Twenties and All That Jazz*, also singing on the original cast albums. Her other stage musicals include *Side by Side by Sondheim, Nine, Only Heaven Knows* and *Simply Irresistible*.

On television, Caroline acted in *The Sullivans, Prisoner: Cell Block H, Starting Out, Carson's*

Law, A Country Practice, Cyclone Tracy, The Magistrate, Brides of Christ (as Sister Philomena), *Seven Deadly Sins* (as Greed) and *The Flood*, before joining *Neighbours*.

She was also in the films *Fighting Back, High Country, An Indecent Obsession, A Cry in the Dark* (as Amy Whittaker, alongside Meryl Streep and Sam Neill in the real-life story of Lindy Chamberlain, accused of murdering her baby), *Passover Feast* and *Antonio's Angel*.

DANNI STARK

Cheryl Stark's teenage children, Brett and Danni, arrived on her doorstep at her new home in Ramsay Street after being expelled from school. Trouble was bound to follow their arrival.

Danni got off to a bad start with fellow teenager Debbie Martin, but the pair made up their differences when they were locked in a department store overnight and ran riot in the toy department.

A diabetic, Danni was persuaded to attend a diabetes education programme for teenagers. She was not keen on going but became more enthusiastic when she met a fellow-diabetic called Martin, but he was only interested in friendship.

Involved in more trouble, Danni was injured and a schoolmate called Briggs killed when they challenged Rick Alessi and Cody Willis to a car race against Rick's flash new motor. The car driven by Briggs ended up wrapped around a tree.

Then, after her mother had moved the family into Lou Carpenter's house and the couple planned marriage, Lou found Danni in bed with Michael Martin. The couple were encouraged by their mothers to cool their relationship, but Danni continued seeing Michael and kept partying until she collapsed in a diabetic fit outside a nightclub. Thinking she was drunk, the police arrested her, and her mother was quick to condemn Michael for getting Danni into trouble. In a last-ditch attempt to stay together, Danni and Michael ran away.

Eliza Szonert (b. 29 January 1974) played the title role in *Cinderella* with Oxford Children's Amateur Theatre Group for five months in 1992, before training with St Martin's Theatre Company and on a Swinburne University 'Showbiz' course the following year, after which she joined *Neighbours* as Danni Stark.

As well as snow- and water-skiing, basketball, swimming, tennis and rollerblading, the actress

Scott Michaelson (b. Melbourne, Australia, 12 September 1968), who worked as a stockbroker and a builder's labourer at one time, played scruffy BRAD WILLIS, son of Doug and Pam, who married Beth Brennan in 1994. But he had also appeared in the serial during its first two years as an extra and an angry customer at the coffee shop. After leaving, he made a guest appearance in *Paradise Beach*.

Terence Donovan, father of actor-singer Jason, followed his *Home and Away* role as nasty Al Simpson, who brought up Bobby Simpson, with that of builder DOUG WILLIS in *Neighbours*. Terence's long career includes appearances in such TV programmes as *No Hiding Place*, *Danger Man*, *The Champions*, *Man in a Suitcase* and *The Prisoner* in Britain, and *Cop Shop* (as Det. Sgt. Vic Cameron), *A Country Practice*, *Prisoner: Cell Block H*, *Sons and Daughters*, *G.P.* and *The Flying Doctors* (as Jim Cardaci, father of Nick Cardaci, played by former *Home and Away* star Alex Papps) in Australia, as well as the films *Oliver!*, *Breaker Morant* and *The Man from Snowy River*.

Rachel Blakely (b. Borneo, 28 July 1968) played GABY WILLIS, who had a son, Zac, by flying instructor Jack Flynn, and left Erinsborough to run a new branch of Lassiter's in Darwin. Real-life husband Peter Craig once played one of Daphne Lawrence's boyfriends in *Neighbours*.

Sue Jones (b. Wales) was PAM WILLIS, mother of the Willis clan, until she and husband Doug moved to Darwin to be near daughter Gaby and grandson Zac. Sue had previously appeared on TV in *Matlock*, *The Box*, *The Sullivans*, *Cop Shop*, *Skyways*, *The Flying Doctors* and *Boys from the Bush*. Since leaving *Neighbours*, she has appeared in the Australian sitcom *The Newlyweds*.

Guy Pearce (b. Britain) played teacher MIKE YOUNG, then joined *Home and Away* as David Croft, who fathered Sophie Simpson's baby daughter, Tammy, before dying in a car crash. Guy also played a rancher in *The Man from Snowy River* on TV and, in the cinema, Errol Flynn in *My Forgotten Man* and outrageous transvestite Felicia in *The Adventures of Priscilla Queen of the Desert*.

enjoys travelling and has gone as far afield as Germany, Austria, Italy, Poland and America.

CODY WILLIS

When her parents, Doug and Pam, moved into no. 28 Ramsay Street, Cody Willis was a pupil at Erinsborough High in the same class as Todd Landers. She was a bright and happy child, but also shy and insecure. Cody always knew how to get what she wanted. Although she had been dating Josh Anderson, she really wanted Todd, but Melissa Jarrett was dating him. That did not stop her and the two became inseparable.

When her parents tried to cool the romance, Cody and Todd ran away. But Cody went down with 'flu after sleeping rough in a barn and Todd was forced to take her home. Although it meant splitting up with Todd, Cody left Erinsborough when offered a scholarship to study in America.

She was back two years later to find a welcome from a legion of male admirers, including Rick Alessi and Michael Martin, but she rejected both of their advances at first – and even bet her friends she would remain boy free for the rest of the year. Eventually, headstrong Cody confessed to her friend Debbie Martin that she had had her heart broken in America and was scared of getting hurt a second time.

The truth was revealed when American Drew Grover arrived on Cody's doorstep in 1994. They had to admit that they had married while Cody was in America so that he could transfer a family inheritance into her name to avoid paying tax. Although it was a business arrangement, she fell head over heels in love with Drew and was devastated when she discovered that he was having an affair with her best friend.

Cody thought that Drew was coming to pick up the pieces of their marriage and was heartbroken again when he announced that he was there merely to discuss a divorce. Cody was then left without her family when her parents moved to Darwin, but she stayed on in Erinsborough with Marlene Kratz to finish her exams.

Peta Brady took over the role of Cody Willis from Amelia Frid, who had played it since 1990 but left when her character went to America. Peta joined the cast at the age of 22, after taking a three-year degree in performing arts.

The actress met her boyfriend, actor Danny Symmonds, in high school and they are still together, despite both doing different work in different places over the years.